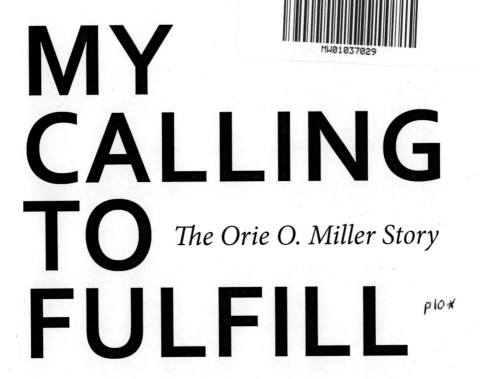

MY CALLING TO FULFILL

The Orie O. Miller Story

p10*

"Orie Miller's tireless and inspiring leadership form the cornerstone of Mennonite Central Committee's ongoing ministry in the name of Christ. We trust he would view today's MCC as a worthy legacy of his vision and wisdom."
— J Ron Byler and Donald Peters, executive directors, MCC U.S. and MCC Canada

"I found this engaging biography a fascinating page turner. In a world where loyalties to jobs, churches, and spouses seem shallow and ephemeral, it was refreshing to learn of Miller's deep and abiding loyalty to the Mennonite church. I'm glad his hoped-for pulpit became a 'plane' that has carried North American Mennonites around the world."
— Jewel Showalter, writer and international resource person

"Frequently criticized and frequently praised, Orie O. Miller combined the worlds of business and church mission. For anyone interested in Mennonite history, or in biographies of people who have made a difference, this compelling story is a must-read."
— Merrill F. Raber, retired psychotherapist and consultant

"John Sharp is one of the preeminent storytellers among Mennonites today. He has drawn upon personal interviews, extensive reading of Orie Miller's correspondence, and multiple primary and secondary sources. The result is an engaging set of stories, put into the social and political context of the times, about one of the most important Mennonite leaders of the twentieth century."
—James Juhnke, professor emeritus of history, Bethel College

"*My Calling To Fulfill* chronicles the life of one of the most influential Mennonite church leaders of all time. Orie O. Miller's global vision was anchored in a deep commitment to the church and a vibrant faith in Jesus Christ."
—Edgar Stoesz, former Mennonite Central Committee associate executive secretary

"This look into the life of an iconic twentieth-century American Mennonite leader is must reading. It unites deep personal calling, church loyalty, business acumen, administrative initiative, and an instinctive, prophetic sense of what organizational forms the Mennonite heritage could take in the twentieth century."
—John L. Ruth, author, *The Earth Is the Lord's*

"As a leader in multiple Mennonite causes, Orie Miller wore the plain coat prescribed by his church but with the necktie appropriate to his business approach. This excellent biography offers much wisdom about integrating our discipleship and vocation in service to the church and the world."
—Peter H. Rempel, former Mennonite Central Committee staff

MY CALLING TO FULFILL

The Orie O. Miller Story

BY JOHN E. SHARP

Herald Press

Harrisonburg, Virginia
Kitchener, Ontario

**Mennonite
Central
Committee**

Library of Congress Cataloging-in-Publication Data
Sharp, John E., 1951-
  My calling to fulfill : the Orie O. Miller story / John E. Sharp.
      pages cm
  Includes bibliographical references and index.
  ISBN 978-0-8361-9933-8 (pbk. : alk. paper) 1. Miller, Orie O., 1892-1977. 2.
Mennonites--Pennsylvania--Akron--Biography. I. Title.
  BX8143.M54S53 2015
  289.7092--dc23
  [B]
                                        2014045981

MY CALLING TO FULFILL
© 2015 by Herald Press, Harrisonburg, Virginia 22802
    Released simultaneously in Canada by Herald Press,
    Kitchener, Ontario N2G 3R1. All rights reserved.
Library of Congress Control Number: 2014045981
International Standard Book Number: 978-0-8361-9933-8
Printed in the United States of America
Cover and interior design by Reuben Graham
Cover photo by Burton Buller

Photos and illustrations used in this book are used by permission, and their sources
are given with each caption.

Unless otherwise indicated, all Bible quotations are from the *The Holy Bible, King James
Version*.

To order or request information, please call 1-800-245-7894 or visit www.heraldpress.com.

19 18 17 16 15   10 9 8 7 6 5 4 3 2 1

Contents

Foreword

One of the major architects of North American Mennonite Church life in the twentieth century was Orie O. Miller. Miller was born on an Indiana farm in 1892. Most of his adult life he lived in Akron, Pennsylvania, the hometown of his wife, Elta Wolf Miller. From this base he managed a shoe manufacturing company and administered the increasingly worldwide program of Mennonite Central Committee.

Although a successful business executive, Orie Miller had a primary passion of ministering "in the name of Christ," to quote words used for almost one hundred years to describe one of the organizations he helped found, Mennonite Central Committee. This ministry was rooted in local congregations—Forks Mennonite near Middlebury, Indiana, and Ephrata Mennonite in Ephrata, Pennsylvania. As a Goshen College student he heard the call to service in international relief and reconstruction. After experience in post–World War I Beirut and Constantinople, he was one of the first North American Mennonites to enter Russia and the Ukraine as a relief worker in 1920.

With this experience he quickly joined the administrative body of Mennonite Central Committee, the major involvement of his life for the next thirty-five years. As a business leader and church administrator he also accepted responsibilities to the executive committees of two mission boards, Goshen College, Mennonite World Conference, and a variety of other church institutions. In retirement he continued to work on the boards of Mennonite Economic Development Agency (MEDA), Schowalter Foundation, Mennonite Christian Leadership Foundation (MCLF), and a number of local involvements.

A number of people were persuaded that the twenty-first-century Mennonite community ought to have a fresh and more comprehensive understanding of Orie Miller's contribution to church life and ministry. The organizations that he influenced, as well as others, provided funding for the project. Most of the funding came from Mennonite Central Committee (MCC). Other organizations that supported the project include Eastern Mennonite Missions (EMM) and Everence / Mennonite Foundation (formerly Mennonite Mutual Aid). Much of the initiative for this project came from the Anabaptist Center for Religion and Society (ACRS) at Eastern Mennonite University. This group also provided significant financial support.

We are grateful to John Sharp, a longtime writer, pastor, historian, and teacher of history for providing this new, comprehensive biography. He spent much of the past three years immersed in the Orie Miller papers, organization records, and in interviewing the diminishing number of individuals who worked with or remember this remarkable church leader. We commend this engaging narrative, which is both relevant and inspiring.

> *—Editorial Committee*
> *Robert S. Kreider, North Newton, Kansas*
> *John A. Lapp (chair), Goshen, Indiana*
> *Calvin Redekop, Harrisonburg, Virginia*
> *E. Morris Sider, Grantham, Pennsylvania*

Author's Preface

Orie O. Miller's passing was announced during the annual meeting of the Mennonite Board of Education at the Four Horsemen Hotel in Chicago, January 11, 1977—the day after his death.

"Who is Orie Miller?" I murmured. I was a recent college graduate and the staff minute-taker. Paul Bender, first and longtime Mennonite Board of Education staff member, leaned over and kindly filled me in. The board crafted a tribute to send to the family, which I dutifully recorded. Chair Charles Gautsche offered a prayer of thanksgiving for Miller's enormous contributions to Mennonites, Brethren in Christ, and Christians around the world. I remembered then that I had perused Paul Erb's 1969 biography of the outstanding administrator and churchman. Later, I recalled that I had even typed notes from my reading on my portable Corona typewriter.

More than thirty years later, I was invited to write a new biography of Orie Miller. In my first meeting with the editorial committee in Akron, Pennsylvania, I told the story of my embarrassing admission of ignorance years ago. John A. Lapp, Cal Redekop, and E. Morris Sider smiled. Lapp said, "Well, now you can answer that question for yourself and for others who may not know about Orie Miller."

For his colleagues and protégés, Orie is unforgettable. Many describe him in superlative terms as "the greatest man I ever knew" (Edgar Stoesz) and as "the most remarkable Mennonite of his generation, perhaps of our century" (Robert Kreider). But Orie Miller is relatively unknown to those under sixty. I have come to think of this group—those in leadership roles as well as those in the pew, those within the Mennonite and Brethren in Christ household of faith and those beyond—as my primary audience.

The title of this book, *My Calling to Fulfill*, captures Orie's lifelong passion. He responded eagerly, obediently, and repeatedly to the call of the church to help fulfill its mission to serve humanity. He found honor in the church's call, which he believed to be God's primary means of calling disciples and healing the nations. Orie was a servant, ready and willing to go where called. He became a leader, persistent and tireless in calling others to service.

Miller's gift was administration—seeing a need, designing a solution, clarifying its purposes, rallying the church's support, and calling hundreds to fulfill the mission. Multiple times he circled the globe, seeing a world often troubled—broken by war, poverty, and disease. He recognized it as a world that God loved, and for whom Jesus lived, taught, healed, and died. To serve God's people everywhere, Orie applied inventive solutions to a myriad of ministries.

Robert S. Kreider's characterization written in 1969 still sparkles today: "He has seen more of the world than Marco Polo. He has opened more mission fields than David Livingston. He has been as innovative in the world of church ministries as Thomas Edison was in the world of technology."[1]

Orie Miller's service had many expressions: education, missions, peacemaking, postwar reconstruction, refugee resettlement, mental health, economic development, finances, and business. He believed these were all signs of God's reign. As Orie often said, God is at work "reconciling the world to himself" and "making all things new."

For twenty-three years, Miller simultaneously served as chief executive of both Mennonite Central Committee and Eastern Mennonite Missions—all without salary. Under his leadership, both agencies expanded their work dramatically. For much of his life, he was a member and officer of a host of Mennonite boards and committees—as many as twenty-five at a time. Beyond the Mennonite world, he also served on the boards of several ecumenical ministries. In his lifetime, he served on more than sixty boards, commissions, and committees. He seemed exceptionally suited to his times, but he would have been outstanding in any era. His college classmates rightly observed that he characteristically "made more opportunities" than were offered him.

Orie's church was the "old" Mennonite Church (MC) of Swiss-South German origin, an heir of Anabaptism. Orie's church, influenced by the

Swiss "Schleitheim Brotherly Union" of 1527, carefully maintained its identity as a "separated" people against the dangers of assimilation. Bishops, ministers, and deacons—as leaders of congregations, conferences, and the denomination—were vigilant guardians of the boundaries that preserved the church from the "world."

Orie lived comfortably in the two worlds of business and church. Daily, he signaled his dual roles by wearing a necktie (the attire of business) under a plain coat (the mark of obedience to the church). He earned a living by selling shoes wholesale to stores throughout the East and Midwest and, with the advent of air travel, to the West Coast. As a partner in the company, he shared corporate profits. He drew generously from his personal wealth to support a wide variety of causes and people in need. As one who bridged these worlds, he had a passion for involving entrepreneurs and business leaders in mission projects.

He provided well for his family financially, but like others of Orie's generation, fulfilling the call to the church and its institutions overshadowed his role as husband and father. Elta raised the children and endured her role as the supportive spouse.

While Orie remained loyal to the Mennonite Church, he served more widely in inter-Mennonite and ecumenical ministries. At a time when his peers were cautious about interacting with other Mennonite groups, Orie saw strength in cooperation. Brethren in Christ, Mennonite Brethren (MB) and General Conference (GC) Mennonites were his people too. He consulted with Canadian Mennonites, assisted in relief and resettlement efforts, invited Canadians to participate fully in MCC and its governance, and established MCC offices north of the forty-ninth parallel. While Orie's passion was global, he lived his adult life in Akron, Pennsylvania. The primary context for his work and for this biography is the United States.

Miller, along with missionaries and mission leaders, helped lead Mennonites from rural isolation to global engagement. Historian James C. Juhnke has rightly observed that the Mennonite Church's "semi-episcopal church polity tended to produce leaders more influential and dominant than did the GC and the MB branches."[2] Orie Miller and Harold Bender were agents of change during the cultural shifts and the theological debates of the first half of the twentieth century. The challenges confronting Mennonites and Brethren in Christ were many: regional and historical differences; the modernist-fundamentalist debate; militarism; two world

wars; wartime suffering of churches in Russia, Europe, China; urban-
ization; institutionalization of church ministries; growing ethnic diversity; and the enormous growth of churches in the Global South. All of
these forces caused the church to reexamine its core beliefs and long-held
practices.

The church needed leaders to help bridge historical, regional, and
global differences; to help it understand new worldviews; and to mediate
the inevitable differences. How would the church negotiate such transitions without fragmenting or compromising its core convictions? Who
could lead the church safely through such transitions? Who could link
Mennonites to other Christians in worldwide missions and service? Who
could lead a people preoccupied with local concerns to embrace a global
vision? For such a time, Orie O. Miller was uniquely gifted. Among
Mennonites in the twentieth century, perhaps no one was more influential
in shaping the life of his people than Miller.

While he may have been the most remarkable Mennonite of his generation, I believe Orie Miller's story can inspire yet another generation of
people to faithful and imaginative service to the church and the world.

Acknowledgments

A biography such as this requires more than a lone author to fulfill its objectives. Many people have assisted me in a variety of ways, and to them I acknowledge my indebtedness and gratitude.

A special thanks to Mennonite Central Committee (MCC), which blessed the project and provided most of the funding for it. Thank you to former executive director of the binational MCC, Arli Klassen, and J Ron Byler, executive director of MCC U.S. (who now leads the organization with his counterpart, Donald Peters, executive director of MCC Canada), for appointing the project committee and approving the financing.

There are many others to thank. All are listed according to the roles they held when I was working on the project. For their assistance, I wish to acknowledge the staff at the Mennonite Church USA Archives in Goshen, Indiana, at the time of my research. I'm grateful to them for access to crucial collections, including the Mennonite Central Committee collection that was formerly housed there and the Orie O. Miller Personal Collection of eighty boxes: Colleen MacFarland, archivist; Natasha Sawatsky-Kingsley, assistant archivist; Madison Sayre, archives associate; Rich Preheim, director; and Andrea Golden, office manager. I also thank Victoria Waters, Carol Miller, John D. Roth, and Joe Springer of the Mennonite Historical Library in Goshen, Indiana—especially for their flexibility and hospitality after normal working hours. I thank John D. Thiesen, archives director, and James Lynch, assistant archivist, at the Mennonite Library and Archives in North Newton, Kansas, for access to the P. C. Hiebert Collection. I am indebted to Alf Redekopp, archivist at the Mennonite Heritage Centre Archives in Winnipeg, Manitoba; and to Peter H. Rempel, executive director of Mennonite Central Committee Manitoba. At the Lancaster Mennonite

Historical Society in Lancaster, Pennsylvania, I have been ably assisted by
Steven L. Ness, librarian and archivist; Rolando L. Santiago, director; and
Carolyn C. Wenger, archivist and museum curator. Thank you to Joel D.
Alderfer, collections manager, and to Forrest L. Moyer, project archivist,
at the Mennonite Heritage Center in Harleysville, Pennsylvania.

At Eastern Mennonite Missions in Salunga, Pennsylvania, I am grateful to Norman Shenk, longtime treasure of EMM, who provided an in-
sider's view of the Miller Hess shoe company, EMM, and of Orie himself;
Galen Hershey, facilities manager; Annie Kauffman, for making available
electronic copies of the *Missionary Messenger*; Jewell Showalter, for assistance and encouragement; and Richard Showalter, former president, for
access to mission board records in Salunga.

I thank the seventy-five or more persons who knew Orie and who
added depth and breadth to my understanding of Orie Miller during recorded interviews (see A Note about Sources for complete list). Thanks
also to Elizabeth Raid, who provided manuscript excerpts of her Howard
Raid biography; Goshen College students Daniel Penner and Susanna
Stoltzfus, who shared research papers; John Eicher, graduate student at
the University of Iowa, for sharing unselfishly copies of his research files
from Fernheim and Menno Colonies, Paraguay. Thanks also to James C.
Juhnke, Theron F. Schlabach, and Leonard Gross for their sage counsel
and to Juhnke for research notes; to Ron Kennel of Goshen, Indiana,
for research assistance; and to Larry Zook, president, Landis Homes in
Lititz, Pennsylvania. The residents of Landis Homes are a treasure trove
of memory.

I am indebted to archivist Gundolf Niebuhr for access to the Fernheim
Colony Archives in Filadelfia; anthropologist Wilmar Stahl, also of
Filadelfia, for graciously providing transportation and translation; to
Fernheim Colony for generous hospitality; and to Peter Duerksen for his
financial contribution to this project. I am also grateful to Wilmer Martin
of TourMagination for accommodating my travel to Paraguay; and especially to Edgar Stoesz, tour leader, who also arranged and translated interviews in the Mennonite colonies of Paraguay and shared his considerable
personal knowledge of his friend and mentor, Orie Miller.

To those who were generous with hospitality, I thank you: John and
Virginia Spicher and Tom and Ruby Sawin in Harrisonburg, Virginia;
Mahlon and Dorothy Miller, Nora Miller, Darrell and Karen Sommers,

Vi and Crist Miller of Goshen, Indiana; Mary Mae and Norm Klassen of Phoenix, Arizona; Mike, Mary, Sam, and Julia Zehr of Landisville, Pennsylvania; Deb and J. W. Sprunger of Lancaster, Pennsylvania; and Lin and Darlis Sharp of Belleville, Pennsylvania. Thanks also to Cliff Brubaker and staff at Amigo Centre in Sturgis, Michigan, for lodging and meals during a week of writing.

Thanks also to MCC personnel including Frank Peachey, for access to MCC records, photos (with assistance from Brenda Burkholder), and library; Tina Mast Burnett and Mary Lou Matteson for hospitality; and Anne M. Good, Laura Wagner, and Kenneth Langeman, of MCC financial services. To Everence and Larry Miller, president, for funding and interest in the project.

The project committee and I gratefully acknowledge the funding and strong support of Cal Redekop, Ray Gingerich, Catherine R. Mumaw, and others of the Anabaptist Center for Religion and Society (ACRS); the assistance of Nate Yoder, Eastern Mennonite University archivist; and Randy Schweitzer, chair of the Shenandoah Valley Chapter of MEDA. We are grateful to Hesston College and to Sandee (Goering) Zerger, vice president of academics, for support, benefits, and the continued use of a college office during a leave.

I appreciate the warm cooperation of the Miller family: John W. and Louise Miller, Ed Miller, Larry Beach, Tina Bechtel, Eunice Litwiller Miller, Jean Carper Miller, and other family members who answered my endless stream of questions.

I am especially grateful to Beth Hershberger of Hesston, Kansas, who actually loved the exacting nature of interview transcription; Natasha Sawatsky-Kingsley of Goshen, Indiana, who gave me exceptional, efficient, and cheerful service as research assistant; and to Bill Zuercher, for his eagle eye, red pen, and generous gift of time in proofreading the manuscript multiple times.

I give special thanks for my community of scholars: John A. Lapp of Goshen, Indiana; Cal Redekop of Harrisonburg, Virginia; E. Morris Sider of Grantham, Pennsylvania; and Robert S. Kreider of North Newton, Kansas. Lapp (chair), Redekop, and Sider represented a larger project committee, which included Laura Schmidt Roberts of Fresno, California; José Ortiz of Goshen, Indiana; and Peter H. Rempel of Winnipeg, Manitoba. They were responsible to find a writer, support and counsel the writer, raise necessary funds, and shepherd the project through to publication. Kreider was drawn into the project for his wealth of knowledge, wisdom, broad experience, and his personal relationship with the subject of this biography.

This group had much to offer, having been actors in much of the narrative I was creating. They were as gracious as they were perceptive. They commented on content, context, style, tone, and balance of each chapter. They mused about the larger themes and asked probing questions. While there was still time for rewrites and revision, they provided chapter-by-chapter critique. I, of course, had complete freedom to modify their counsel, and I alone am responsible for any errors, lapses, and deficiencies in the text.

When the first draft was completed, we all sat around the dining room table of my Hesston home. We talked about photos, publishers, titles, and more. We discussed the many themes that emerged in the narrative. We marveled at the relevance of those themes to today's world—Mennonite and beyond. Our twelve hours together ended with gratitude and thanksgiving. It was a holy moment.

I am profoundly grateful for my community of scholars, who enlarged my world, enriched my journey, and enhanced the narrative. I hope readers will also be inspired to such reflection.

I also acknowledge the capable assistance of Maureen Epp, editor, who improved the manuscript immeasurably by eliminating redundancies, pointing out inconsistencies, noting lapses in content, and improving the flow of ideas and text. Her work has made this book a much better product.

And thanks to Herald Press editors Valerie Weaver-Zercher and Amy Gingerich, who provided counsel and shepherded this book to its final form. I thank publisher Russ Eanes for his enthusiastic support of the project.

And finally, I'm grateful to our daughter Laura Sharp, who shares our living space, and to Michele Miller Sharp, my wife, who unfailingly and wholeheartedly supported me at every turn. Every writer should have such support!

—*John E. Sharp, Hesston, Kansas*

Timeline

1892 July 7	Orie Otis Miller born to Daniel D. (1864–1955) and Jeanette Hostetler (1870–1938) Miller, Middlebury, Indiana
1906	converted, baptized, and becomes member at Forks Mennonite Church
1908–12	superintendent, Forks Mennonite Church Sunday school
1910–12	teacher at country schools, north of Middlebury and Nihart
1910	starts part-time studies at School of Business, Goshen College
1912–15	student, Goshen College
1912	transfers membership to College Mennonite Church
1913–15	principal/instructor, School of Business, Goshen College
1913–15	licensed minister, Barker Street Mission, Michigan
1915	graduates from Goshen College
1915 Aug. 26	marries Elta Wolf at Orie's and Elta's Akron home
1915	salesperson and director, Miller Hess shoe company
1916 Sept. 23	Lois Wolf Miller born (marries Ronald O. Beach Sept. 6, 1937; dies March 28, 1987)
1916–39	sales director, Miller Hess shoe company
1917–	director, Miller Hess shoe company

1919 Jan. 4	volunteers at Mennonite Relief Commission for War Sufferers (MRCWS) meeting for relief work in Middle East
1919 Jan. 25	leaves New York by ship to work with Near East Relief (NER) in Beirut
1920 July 27	Mennonite Central Committee (MCC) "crystallizes" at Prairie Street Mennonite Church, Elkhart, Indiana
1920 Sept. 1	leaves New York by ship with Arthur Slagel and Clayton Kratz, first MCC mission to Russia
1920–21	director, MCC Relief Unit in Constantinople and South Russia
1921–35	assistant to Levi Mumaw, executive secretary, MCC
1921–37	chair, Young People's Problems Committee
1921–66	member, Mennonite Board of Education (MBE)
1922–55	financial agent and member, MBE executive committee
1922 Jan. 9	receives medal in New York from NER for meritorious and humanitarian service
1922 March 18	Albert Wolf Miller born (marries Esther Lehman June 5, 1943; dies Jan. 28, 1996)
1923	secretary, Goshen College administrative committee to reorganize college
1924–26	executive committee, Mennonite Colonization Board
1924–77	member, MCC
1924–26	chair, Goshen College alumni fundraising committee
1924–32	founding editor, *Missionary Messenger*, Eastern Mennonite Missions
1924 Feb. 16	Daniel Wolf Miller born (marries Eunice Litwiller; dies Feb. 23, 1993)
1925–35	vice president, EMM (appointed Aug. 5)
1925–53	secretary, Peace Problems Committee (PPC), Mennonite Church

1926 Dec. 22	John Wolf Miller born (marries Louise Heatwole; lives in Kitchener, Ontario)
1928–63	executive committee, MCC
1930 Aug. 8	Robert Wolf Miller born (marries Jean Carper 1951; dies June 17, 1996)
1932–44	Goshen College Alumni Association board of directors
1932–49	Inter-Board Committee, Mennonite Church General Conference
1932–56	member, Mennonite Relief Committee (later renamed the MRSC)
1932–33	associate editor, *Missionary Messenger*, EMM
1933 Dec.	explores Africa with Elam Stauffer for EMM mission field
1933–35	chair, Goshen College Administrative Committee
1935–63	Continuation Committee, Conference of Historic Peace Churches
1935–58	executive secretary-treasurer, MCC
1935–58	secretary, EMM
1935–38	auditing committee, Mennonite Publication Board
1936	attends Mennonite World Conference, Elspeet, the Netherlands
1937–39	vice chair, Commission for Christian Education
1937–39	secretary, Young People's Institute, Commission for Christian Education
1937	appointed to Hesston College Local Board
1939–54	treasurer, Miller Hess shoe company
1939	chair, Goshen College Administrative Committee
1939 March 31	Albert N. Wolf dies (born 1868)
1939–49	member, Industrial Relations Committee
1939–49	secretary, Inter-Board Committee
1939–54	secretary-treasurer, Miller Hess shoe company
1940–52	vice chair, National Service Board for Religious Objectors (NSBRO)

1940–60	board of directors, New York Theological Seminary
1944–52	vice president, Mennonite Camp Association
1944–58	treasurer, Peace Section, MCC
1945–54	board of directors, Cooperative Assistance and Relief Everywhere (CARE)
1945–62	president, Mennonite Mutual Aid, Inc. (MMA), director until 1965
1946	helps launch Church World Service, cooperative ministry of thirty-seven denominations
1948	named Goshen College alumnus of the year
1948	chair, Hesston College Administrative Committee
1948	organizes Mennonite World Conference (MWC) Assembly, Goshen, Indiana, and North Newton, Kansas
1949–63	member, General Council, Mennonite Church
1950 Jan.	delegation to Tanganyika with Amos Horst, Lancaster Conference bishop
1952	attends MWC, Basel, Switzerland
1952	attends International Missionary Council, Willengen, Germany
1952–65	director, Mennonite Mental Health Services, MCC
1952–67	member, Israel Evangelism Committee
1952–53	chair, NSBRO
1953–77	Mennonite Economic Development Associates (MEDA)
1953–63	treasurer, Peace Problems Committee
1954–69	president, Schowalter Foundation (founded 1954)
1954–62	president, Miller Hess shoe company
1954–56	member, Budget and Finance Committee, Mennonite Church
1954–58	president, Mennonite Auto Aid, a subsidiary of MMA
1947–58	president, Menno Travel Service

Age 60 (handwritten note next to 1952)

1955–65	member, Investment Committee, MBE
1952–65	founder and board member, Mennonite Foundation, a subsidiary of MMA
1956–58	Committee on Coordination, Mennonite Church
1957	appointed to African Committee of the Division of Foreign Missions
1957	attends MWC, Karlsruhe, Germany
1958 Jan. 10	retires as executive secretary-treasurer, MCC, appointed associate executive secretary
1958 Feb. 14	Elta Wolf Miller dies of cancer-induced peritonitis, Graduate Hospital, Philadelphia, Pennsylvania
Feb. 18	Elta's funeral, Ephrata Mennonite Church
1958 March 11	retires as secretary of EMM, appointed associate secretary
1958 May 15	calls meeting to organize Council of Mission Board Secretaries (COMBS), to coordinate programs of MCC and mission agencies
1958–67	president, Mennonite Indemnity, Inc., reinsurance corporation for Menn. Aid societies
1960–	director and officer, Miller Hess and four corporate affiliates
1960	leads in organizing Congo Protestant Relief Agency (CPRA)
1960–66	chair of board, American Leprosy Mission (member from 1950)
1960 Jan. 9	marries Elta Myers Sensenig
1961 Dec. 13	convenes the first meeting, Landis Homes planning committee
1962–	chair of board, Miller, Hess & Company
1963–	Joint Coordinating Committee, Mennonite seminaries
1963–67	president, Goodville Mutual Casualty Company, Goodville, Pennsylvania
1964 Feb.	Landis Homes opens, capacity 29 residents

1964–	chair, Finance and Admissions Committees, Landis Homes
1965–77	executive secretary emeritus, MCC
1966–68	assistant chair, American Leprosy Mission board of directors
1966–77	honorary member, MBE
1967–	executive and finance committees, Menno Housing
1967	attends MWC, Amsterdam
1968, March 25	dinner celebrating 44 years of service with EMM
1969 March	hospitalization due to light stroke during MEDA trip around the world
1972	moves into Landis Homes with Elta, cottage #32
1975 March	moves from cottage to infirmary, Landis Homes
1977 Jan. 10	dies, 6:45 p.m., at Landis Retirement Home, Lititz, Pennsylvania
1977 Jan. 15	memorial service, Ephrata Mennonite Church

handwritten margin note: At EMC he spoke slowly I saw him up close in Science Center Aud. down front. I was on faculty 1968–72 age = 80

handwritten margin note: age 85

Chapter 1
On Cloverdale Farm: 1892–1912

"Our fathers gave both Harold Bender and me a home and church life advantage."

On a wintry night in about 1912, Daniel D. Miller drove his horse and carriage from his home on Cloverdale Farm near Middlebury, Indiana, to Goshen College some fifteen miles away. Daniel, or D. D., was bundled up against the snow, still falling after a midwestern blizzard the day before. A trim man at five feet six inches and 125 pounds, he was also intense, determined, and on a mission. D. D. was a widely traveled evangelist, bishop of numerous Amish Mennonite (AM) congregations, and an officer on various Mennonite Church boards. But tonight he was worried about his oldest son, Orie.

Orie was a Goshen College student, but not an ordinary one. He was also the principal and teacher of Goshen's academy-level Commercial School of Business. He was a serious student and a sober teacher—too much so for some of his students. Neat and trim, at five feet ten he was four inches taller than his father. A country boy, sometimes sarcastic and inclined to criticism, he lacked the genteel manners of his later years.

Orie was surprised to see his snow-covered father appear on campus. D. D. had a book in hand, one that Orie had given him to read on Sunday. The Monday snowstorm had given D. D. all day to read the book. Father and son were close, each having high regard for the other. Typically, they shared a common mind, but not when it came to this book. *Sixty Years with the Bible: A Record of Experience* by William Newton Clarke had pushed Orie to think new thoughts about the Bible: its origin, composition, and interpretation.

The "warmly evangelical" Clarke (1841–1912) was the premier American liberal theologian of the time. *Sixty Years* describes Clarke's journey that began with a literal interpretation of an infallible and inerrant Bible, which he learned from his father. By the end of his journey Clarke had come to see the Bible as "a divine gift and a perpetual inspiration, but not as an infallible standard."[1] Historical and higher criticism had led him to a richer understanding of Scripture, not as an object of study but as "an expression of principles" and thus "a means of study."[2]

Orie hoped the book could enlighten his father. D. D., on the other hand, believed that the book was dangerous and would take his son too far afield from an Amish Mennonite reading of the Bible. Why was this book in the library of a Mennonite college? The school's critics, D. D. among them, believed that such books were symptomatic of the school's growing modernism, a charge that would later lead to its temporary closing. Father and son talked long into the night without resolving their differences.

As Orie watched his father leave the campus and disappear into the wintry night, he was suddenly moved by his father's extraordinary effort and concern. Even so, "I still felt that he needed the help more than I did," Orie remembered nearly fifty years later.[3] Orie's son John W. Miller believes this book was formative for Orie, "open[ing] him to the world of the Bible in a pragmatic sense," rather than an ideological sense, which is how fundamentalists viewed the Bible."[4]

Despite their occasional differences, Orie and his father maintained a close relationship until D. D.'s death in 1955. They both, each in his generation, had a profound effect on the church they loved.

TWO AMISH FAMILIES

Orie's parents, Daniel D. (1864–1955) and Nettie (Jeanette) Hostetler (1870–1938) Miller, were fifth- and sixth-generation descendants, respectively, of Swiss Amish immigrants. Their ancestors were among the five hundred Amish who emigrated between 1707 and 1774 from Switzerland, France, and Germany. Both families settled in the Northkill

Amish community of Berks County, Pennsylvania, the earliest Amish settlement in the New World.

In 1757, during the French and Indian War (1754–63), Anna Hochstetler and two children were killed by a band of Lenni Lenape Indians and French scouts, while Jacob and two boys were taken captive. The older son, John, Nettie's ancestor, who lived on his own property, witnessed the attack from a distance. He and his wife, Catherine Hertzler, were among the families who left the Northkill settlement to relocate in Somerset County, Pennsylvania.

Future generations of Miller and Hochstetler families became part of a larger westward migration of Americans in the nineteenth century. The first Amish arrived in northern Indiana in 1841, only three years after Chief Shipshewana and his Potawatomie people had been deported. These Native Americans were forced to travel the infamous sixty-one-day "Potawatomie Trail of Death" to their exile in the Western Territory (Kansas). The aging Chief Shipshewana, however, returned to his homeland where he died in 1841 just as the Amish were arriving.[5] Today over a million tourists annually visit the tiny town of Shipshewana, named for the Potawatomie chief, not to remember his people but to see the Amish who still live there.

In 1856, the Daniel P. (for Pennsylvania) and Anna (Hershberger) Miller family moved from the Conemaugh settlement of Somerset and Cambria Counties, Pennsylvania, to Newberry Township in LaGrange County, Indiana, where D. D. was born in 1864. Also in 1864, Moses J. and Elizabeth (Mast) Hostetler from Somerset County via Holmes County, Ohio, arrived in LaGrange County and settled on a farm near the small town of Emma. Here in 1870, Nettie (Jeanette) was born to Samuel J. and Catherine (Mehl) Hostetler.[6]

The Hostetlers (now using the anglicized form) were content to remain on their Emma farm. But wanderlust and the promise of economic opportunities persuaded the Millers to pack covered wagons and move roughly six hundred miles west to Hickory County, Missouri, in 1870 when D. D. was four. However, Missouri's promise remained unfulfilled and prosperity a dream. The family lived in a small, rough cabin where D. D. and a brother made their sleeping "nest" under the kitchen table each night. In wintertime, snow often sifted into the cabin and onto the comforters under which they slept.

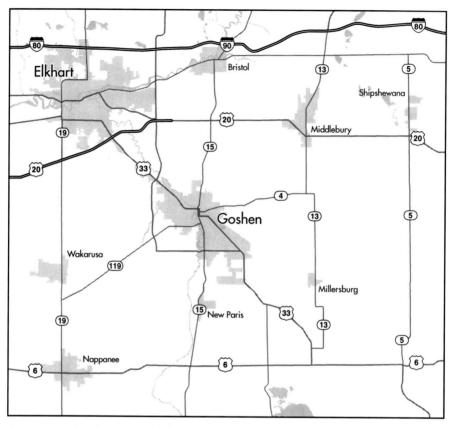

Area map: Forks, Cloverdale, Middlebury, Goshen, and Elkhart, Indiana. Reuben Graham.

Farming conditions were catastrophic. Hail, torrential rains, drought, hot winds, chinch bugs, and grasshoppers destroyed crops two years in a row. Mother Anna struggled to feed the family of eight, supplementing their daily diet of cornbread and water with mush and milk and, occasionally, wild game. According to family memory, had not Grandfather Joseph been an excellent shot, they might have starved. After four years of Missouri living, some of the Millers gave up and started back to LaGrange County, with fifty dollars supplied by Indiana friends. It took four weeks of walking, riding, herding cattle, and sleeping by the roadside to get back to Indiana.[7] For eight-year-old D. D. Miller, the years of Missouri deprivation and the long journey home were unforgettable—experiences he later recalled for his children and grandchildren.[8]

Perhaps it is no surprise, given the hardscrabble experience in Missouri, that farming never occupied D. D.'s best efforts. Early in life, he determined to be a schoolteacher. Despite his parents' reluctance and his grandmother's persistent fear that education would destroy his faith, he pursued his goal. One of his teachers provided an alternative model. D. (Daniel) J. Johns was also an Amish Mennonite minister, proving that education and faith were not incompatible. After finishing country school, D. D. prepared for teaching by attending the LaGrange Normal School. At sixteen, he passed the requisite examinations and began teaching in country schools, continuing for twenty terms—four at Garden City, Missouri, and sixteen at a variety of Indiana schools. While teaching at the Emma school, beginning in 1888, D. D. lived in the home of one of his students, Nettie (Jeanette) Hostetler. A year later, on May 26, 1889, they married and made their home with the Hostetlers.

A CLARION CALL TO ACTIVISM

D. D. had been "soundly converted" at the Sycamore Grove congregation in Garden City, Missouri. After his return to Indiana, he was active in the Forks Amish Mennonite Church in Newberry Township, six miles from Middlebury. (Amish Mennonites had emerged as a progressive wing of the Amish after 1850.) In 1890, a year after his marriage, D. D. was ordained as deacon at the Forks church. Two more ordinations followed: as minister in 1891 and as bishop in 1906.

Forks Mennonite Church, 1949 meetinghouse. Ernest E. Miller, *Daniel D. Miller: A Biographical Sketch.*

With his ordinations came a passion for evangelism, which took D. D. to Amish Mennonite and Mennonite congregations across the country. His itinerant ministry took him away from home, sometimes for as long as six weeks at a time and for as much as six months a year—a life Nettie and the children learned to accept. Not so father-in-law Samuel J. Hostetler. He objected not only to D. D.'s frequent absences from home but also to his revivalist preaching, a departure from the Amish tradition of a communal discipleship-based faith. Hostetler offered the home farm as leverage to keep his son-in-law at home, but to no avail. D. D. had a mind of his own and a calling to follow.[9]

In addition to his congregational responsibilities as a bishop and his itinerant ministry as an evangelist, D. D. became an institution builder and manager. He was not a visionary, but his judicious business sense, strong administrative skills, and levelheaded counsel made him a valuable member of boards and committees that directed the church's education, mission, and service ministries.[10]

In 1890, there were 41,541 Anabaptist heirs—Amish, Mennonites, Brethren in Christ, and Hutterites—in the United States. The largest group among them was the "old" Mennonite Church (MC), numbering 17,078. In the decade between 1916 and 1927, Amish Mennonite adherents who had left the Old Order Amish joined MC conferences, and by 1926 the MC population in the United States was 34,039.[11]

In the spirit of the times, Mennonites and Amish Mennonites held a large gathering in northern Indiana in 1892, the year Orie was born. This was the first of three annual Sunday school conferences where leaders rallied a new generation to "aggressive" and "progressive" programs of mission, charity, and service. To facilitate such ministries, MC and AM leaders enlarged the work of the Mennonite Evangelizing Board (1892); founded Elkhart Institute (1895), forerunner of Goshen College; and formed a binational denominational body, the Mennonite General Conference (1897). Though they had been in North America two hundred years, MC and AM congregations had organized only in regional conferences until now. The building of Mennonite institutions continued: the Mennonite Board of Education (MBE, 1905), Mennonite Board of Missions and Charities (MBMC, 1906), and Mennonite Publication Board (1908) were all established by the time Orie was sixteen years old.

Some thirty years ahead of the Mennonite Church, in 1860, a few South German congregations in the Midwest had linked with a Pennsylvania congregation to organize a general conference to facilitate missions, publication, and higher education. The General Conference (GC) of Mennonites, as it was named, was enlarged by Dutch-Prussian-Russian (and Swiss) immigrants who arrived in the 1870s, bringing a wealth of experience in building and managing such institutions in Europe.

Also among the 1870s immigrants were members of the more evangelical Mennonite Brethren (MB) Church, founded in 1860 as a renewal movement in Russia. At a time when MC membership was still skeptical of mission work, both GC and MB churches in the 1880s sent "foreign" missionaries to Native American groups in Indian Territory (Oklahoma). Both denominations soon established institutions to organize and promote higher education, relief, immigration, deaconess ministries, hospitals, charitable homes, missions, and publications. Most notably for the GC Mennonites was the founding of Bethel College in North Newton, Kansas (1887), and for MB adherents the establishment of Tabor College in Hillsboro, Kansas (1908).

John F. Funk, pioneer publisher and leader within the Mennonite Church, issued a clarion call to activism through his *Herald of Truth* and *Herold der Wahrheit*. He drew a new generation of awakened or "quickened" leaders to Elkhart, where his publishing enterprise was located, making the city a center of the new activism, a Mennonite expression of the Progressive Era.[12] Funk, together with other church elders, built the stage on which Orie Miller would perform. They established the modern church institutions that he would multiply and manage with uncommon talent, efficiency, and discipline. Orie Miller later reflected that the work of their fathers had given him and Harold Bender, Goshen College dean and author of the seminal book *The Anabaptist Vision*, both a "home and church life advantage."[13]

Orie recalled his father's enthusiasm about his "contacts" in Elkhart, though occasionally he was also discouraged, even depressed, by church troubles. When returning from preaching at a mission or board meeting, D. D.'s experiences became the topic of family conversations. Church institutions and leaders became household names. Traveling missionaries and church leaders often dined and slept at Cloverdale Farm, the Miller family home. Occasionally, boards or committees gathered there to do their work. Orie long carried the vivid memory of a meeting where a churchwide music committee designed the *Church and Sunday School Hymnal*, published in 1902.[14]

THE SHAPING OF A FIRSTBORN

Orie (Ora) Otis was born on July 7, 1892, three years after D. D. and Nettie were married. Orie's name was chosen to honor D. D.'s friend, colleague, and former schoolteacher D. J. Johns, who was also the bishop who ordained D. D. as deacon, minister, and later as bishop. In the five years before Orie was born, D. J.'s wife, Nancy (Yoder) Johns, bore two sons, one named Ora,[15] and the other Otis,[16] and the Millers called their firstborn after these two. It was a name Orie never liked—typically, he signed letters as "O. O. Miller." Having begun the alliterative naming pattern, matching his own, D. D. (or was it Nettie?) continued the form, perhaps with a chuckle, in naming the rest of their sons: E. E. (Ernest Edgar), T. T. (Trueman Titus), W. W. (William Wilbur), and S. S. (Samuel Silas). The six daughters happily escaped the pattern and were named more conventionally: Ida Mae, Clara Olivia, Kathryn Pearl, Bertha Elizabeth, Alice Grace, and Mabel Ann.

In 1899, D. D. and Nettie purchased the 280-acre Cloverdale Farm along the Little Elkhart River on the eastern edge of Elkhart County. It was three miles southeast of Middlebury and sixteen miles east of Elkhart, close enough to feel the currents of Mennonite activism in the thriving city. Here on what they considered the home farm, the last six of eleven children were born. D. D. liked saying that he was the father of "five and a half dozen children."[17]

Orie fit the profile of a firstborn—conscientious, responsible, and respectful, rarely in need of correction. As an elder brother, he played the role of peacemaker and mediator in sibling disputes. With his mother, he planned and assigned work to his siblings. His management skills blossomed early. One Sunday morning at Forks church, Orie and Ernest—ages four and three—were sitting on the front bench of the "amen corner," a section of benches to the side of the pulpit. Having been given a banana, Orie carefully managed its consumption: small bites for Ernest and larger bites for himself. He was, after all, a year older.[18] Throughout Orie's boyhood and adolescence, his siblings believed him to be always good and

D. D. and Nettie Miller family, ca. 1910 (*back row, from left*: Wilbur, Ida, Ernest, Orie, Trueman, Clara; *front row*: Kathryn, D. D. with Samuel, Alice, Nettie with Mable, Bertha). John W. Miller.

always obedient. Younger brother Wilbur was shocked to discover some years later that the conscientious Orie had once skipped school to attend the LaGrange County fair.[19] It was a double transgression; fair attendance for the Miller children was always off-limits.

Though the farm was not D. D.'s passion, it was a good place to raise a family. With discipline, thrift, and hard work the Millers became moderately successful, eventually holding title to three farms. Until they reached the age of twenty-one, the Miller children turned over to their parents the wages earned from other jobs. This Orie did until after his second year at Goshen College. With the children's help, D. D. and Nettie paid down the farm mortgage faster and all gained a sense of ownership in the farm. The older children shared in the decision making as well as the work. Farmwork and family life were structured and disciplined. Nothing was haphazard on Cloverdale Farm.[20]

Church and board work occupied the uppermost place in D. D.'s life. For him, the call to serve the church trumped all else, including family— a pattern that Orie later replicated. Only once, when daughters Clara and Ida had life-threatening cases of pneumonia, did D. D. interrupt his preaching appointments to return home. Increasingly, D. D. delegated

farmwork and responsibilities to Orie, who stepped ably into the role
of surrogate father and in turn delegated the work to his siblings. He
began carrying such responsibilities as early as age ten and did it so well
that younger brother Samuel thought he had two fathers—Orie at home
and D. D. "on the train."[21] Neither D. D. nor Orie was good at working
with his hands, so when something needed fixing on the farm, they called
on Uncle Ed Hostetler, because, they said, he had "better tools."[22] Later,
when married and asked by his wife, Elta, why he did not help around the
house, Orie said he had no "everyday clothes." He believed his talents lay
elsewhere, and to do himself what he could assign to others was a waste
of his time and energy.

Thrift was the order of the day in the Miller household. Orie learned
early about careful stewardship of money. D. D. and Nettie had started
married life with "two cows, a bed, a table, and chairs," but with careful management, they gradually improved farming operations and were
able to live more comfortably. Nettie was self-disciplined, frugal, and generous, with an eye for beauty and design. She knew how to turn extra
garden produce, dried fruit, eggs, and baked goods into "pin money" to
furnish the house and to buy extras for the children. One summer Nettie
and the children spent countless hours in the marshes picking huckleber-
ries to sell in order to buy Orie a new buggy. The black four-wheeled
buggy featured red wheels and axles.[23] Since neither white horses nor red
buggies were common, Orie must have cut a striking figure with his white
trotter, Pearl, hitched to the two-toned buggy. As their income increased,
D. D. and Nettie were often the first in the community to innovate by
installing plumbing, electricity, and buying the latest farm implements.
Nettie's fine taste kept lawn, garden, and flower beds tidy and farm buildings painted.[24]

D. D. was progressive in farming methods, but he could be inflexible in
his application of church discipline. When Indiana-Michigan Conference
regulations in the 1920s called for bonnets, Nettie said she would make
them for her girls, but D. D. would have to make them wear them—
and he did. The required bonnet was large, black, and cloth-covered, tied
with ribbon under the chin. While they were functional, more important to church leaders was that wearing a bonnet—unlike stylish hats—
marked a woman's spirit of cooperation and demonstrated her loyalty
to the Mennonite Church. Nettie was not the only one to question the

bonnet requirement. A woman at College Mennonite Church in Goshen told D. D., her bishop, that she had read the Bible cover to cover but "saw nothing about bonnets."[25] When conference leaders in 1923–24 required ministers to sign their compliance with new, stricter rules of order, D. D. held the line—even when the five disciplined and ousted ministers included his son Wilbur, at that time pastor at the Forks church. Nettie, caught between husband and son, wept Sunday after Sunday at Forks church after Wilbur was expelled.[26] During the same time, four congregations left the conference to affiliate with the freer GC Mennonite Central District Conference. When a group of members splintered from the First Mennonite Church in Middlebury to form a new congregation, Forest Oaks, they left with bitter memories of Bishop D. D.'s rigidity.[27] His colleague Sanford C. Yoder described him as "fearless in the face of opposition" and "severely honest in all his duties."[28]

While he was known to be uncompromising, D. D. was, in his younger years, a popular preacher. He was bilingual, able to preach in both English and German. Where repetition of stock phrases and uninspiring delivery were the norm, D. D. set a new tone with his expository preaching, succinct texts, quotation of Scripture, colorful illustrations, and frequent bursts of song during the sermon. "Oh for a Closer Walk with God" was his favorite hymn. He often asked the members of his congregation to memorize and quote his preaching texts. These informalities invited people in the pew to be more than spectators and had the added benefit of waking dozing farmers.

Son Ernest remembered two kinds of sermons: hastily constructed last-minute sermons and thoughtfully prepared ones. For last-minute sermons, D. D. drew ideas from the *Pulpit Magazine* and in delivering them walked the pulpit a great deal as though attempting to "whip himself up." The second type of sermon—reflective, calm, and personal—was worked out in his mind while cultivating corn or milking cows.[29] Long years later, Forks church members remembered appreciatively D. D.'s habit of greeting people at the door as they arrived.[30]

Orie absorbed D. D.'s affection for the church. His father's service and the exposure to significant church leaders and activities prepared Orie for a "momentous" event during the Christmas holidays of 1905. The preaching of Daniel Kauffman at Forks church moved him to stand to signal his readiness to identify with Christ and the church. Kauffman

(1865–1944) was then at an early stage of his long ministry as the most influential MC leader of D. D. Miller's generation; Orie was thirteen and the first of his peers to respond to Kauffman's invitation. In a nearby stream on April 1, 1906, bishop D. J. Johns baptized Orie, along with a large group of peers. This moment of conversion and the baptism that followed marked the beginning of Orie's lifelong loyalty to the church and his unusually productive service to both the church and the world.[31] Though Orie later referred to this as his conversion, it was not so much a crisis experience as it was marking a transition from childhood faith to owned faith, a lifelong identification with the church and a commitment to serve Christ.

STUDENT AND TEACHER

Second only to the call of the church, Nettie and D. D. valued and promoted education. There was an abundance of books and magazines for all

Orie as teacher at the Nihart Country School, 1910–11. John W. Miller.

ages in the home. D. D. and Nettie paid for the education of the children until they were prepared to teach. As important as farmwork was, it was never an excuse to miss school. A souvenir card for the East Brick School of Middlebury Township for 1902–3 shows Orie as a seventh-grader, one of seven. In one list, he appears as "Orus O." and another on the same card names him "Orio O."

Newton Nussbaum was the teacher for all thirty-two pupils. Three were Orie's siblings: Ida in second grade, Trueman in third, and Ernest in grade five. All eleven of the children attended high school and normal school, and most went to college. Orie led the way. After attending country schools, he took four years of high school in

Middlebury, one of only two from the Forks congregation to attend high school at the time. Daily he drove Pearl and his black-and-red buggy the three miles from Cloverdale Farm to town and back.[32]

Orie finished high school in 1910. That fall he was back in the classroom—as a part-time college student and as a teacher of country schools. He taught for one year in a school north of Middlebury and a second year at the Nihart School in York Township, between Middlebury and Goshen. Both were one-room schools with eight grades, requiring the teacher to prepare for twenty-six to thirty class periods per week. The Nihart School souvenir card for 1911–12 lists thirty students, with such names as Berkey, Artley, Nussbaum, Lockridge, and Nihart. On the cover is a photo of Orie, hair neatly combed to the right in a small wave, his oval face and narrow lips resembling his mother's. Dressed in a double-breasted wool suit and narrow necktie, he appears to be a no-nonsense teacher.[33]

While Orie was teaching in country schools, he continued to study at Goshen College and in 1912 he graduated from the Goshen College School of Business. During the spring semester of that year, Orie received a phone call that had far-reaching effects.

Chapter 2
Finding Life's Work: 1912–1915

"I may turn out to be of use somewhere in this old world with you helping me. Won't we try hard, Elta, dearest, to be of some use to society?"

As Orie was about to graduate from Goshen's School of Business, he received an important phone call from Noah Ebersole Byers, president of Goshen College. Byers, scholarly and sophisticated, had served as president of Elkhart Institute from 1898 to 1903, and then of its successor, Goshen College, since 1903. Now he was recruiting a teaching principal for Goshen's School of Business, the program of study that Orie was just completing. Would Orie be willing to fill that role beginning in September? Byers had first cleared this with D. D., Orie's father, who was also a member of the Mennonite Board of Education, the governing body of the college. Orie accepted the assignment with his father's encouragement and blessing.[1]

As soon as the spring term ended, Orie enrolled in the MacCormac Business College on East Madison Street in downtown Chicago to take advanced courses, in order to better prepare for his teaching role. He had only the summer to do so.[2]

Having begun his studies at Goshen in 1910, Orie already felt at home on campus. His first association, however, dated from 1903, when his father took ten-year-old Orie to a wheat field on the south side of Goshen. It seemed to be a field like any other, until Orie learned that it was to

Goshen College, depicted on 1915 postcard produced by Indiana News Company, Indianapolis. *GAMEO*.

become the campus that would replace Elkhart Institute.[3] Now he was on that campus in a dual role. As a student, Orie was taking classes toward a bachelor of arts degree in English; in his faculty post, he was replacing his former teacher, Frank S. Ebersole, who had resigned after five years of service.[4]

The School of Business aimed to equip its graduates to join the workforce and earn an income, or to put it more colorfully, as did the 1915 yearbook, the *Maple Leaf*, to solve the "bread and butter" problem. The school claimed that its curriculum was "as good as is given in any business college."[5] Orie was the principal and taught bookkeeping, commercial law, commercial arithmetic, and penmanship. His smooth, legible handwriting style was surely a result of his penmanship training and teaching. John Weaver, his assistant, taught shorthand and typing.[6]

In addition to his multiple roles as both faculty member and student at Goshen College, Orie took on numerous other roles. In the 1913–14 academic year, he chaired the Young Men's Christian Association (YMCA), served on one of its subcommittees (the Committee on Day Student Problems), and remained on the YMCA cabinet the next year. At least twice, Orie attended the annual ecumenical YMCA conferences at Winona Lake, Indiana, and Lake Geneva, Wisconsin. The Winona Lake

Goshen School of Business faculty and students, 1915; Orie is seated in the middle of the front row. Goshen College *Maple Leaf.*

campground was the home of Billy Sunday, a famous National League baseball player and the most prominent revivalist preacher in America in Orie's time. Such speakers captivated and inspired their audiences to engage in Christian service. These interdenominational gatherings were an early influence on Orie's later comfort with ecumenical relationships.

Having transferred his membership from the Forks church to Goshen's College Mennonite Church in 1912, Orie was active in the congregation as well as on campus. He served as a leader of the Young People's Bible Meeting, a local chapter of a larger Mennonite movement for youth. The meetings were designed to promote biblical literacy, develop Christian character, promote mission work, and increase loyalty to the Mennonite Church.[7] Many young people gave their first public speech as a devotional or topical address at these meetings. It was good preparation for future church workers. Occasionally, Orie participated in programs of the Christian Workers' Band, intended to give students hands-on experience in Christian witness. During the 1915 spring term, he helped plan and

Goshen College Glee Club, 1915. Orie is in the second row, second from left. Goshen College *Maple Leaf.*

lead Workers' Band activities but was often too busy to attend the meetings. Although Orie never developed into a strong speaker, from early life he thought preaching would be his calling. He traveled with a gospel team in 1912, and during his last two years at Goshen College, Orie preached regularly at the Barker Street Mennonite Church, just across the Michigan border.[8]

Orie also participated in on-campus literary society debates as well as in intercollegiate debate competitions. He sang in the college glee club, a men's musical ensemble with a versatile repertoire of songs suitable for social, cultural, or religious settings. He said later that he was no singer and had never served as a chorister, but he could harmonize in four-part singing. David Sauder, a member of the Ephrata Mennonite Church in Pennsylvania, which Orie later joined, reports that Orie could carry a tenor line quite well.[9]

ELTA WOLF

In the spring of 1913, Orie began courting Susan Elta Wolf. The relationship started with a double date. Orie and a friend had asked two women for an evening out, but they had not decided how they would pair up. As the two men waited for their dates to descend the stairs from their third-floor rooms in Kulp Hall, Orie solved the problem by claiming as his date

the one who came down last. Though
his plans were rarely so haphazard,
his choice was in character; he did not
need to be the main man nor did his
date need to be the foremost woman.
The second woman down the steps that
spring night was Elta Wolf, the woman
he would marry in 1915.[10] She was
also the major factor in determining his
"life work," as he often put it.

Susan Elta Wolf at Goshen College,
1914. Goshen College *Maple Leaf*.

Elta was the only child of A. N.
(Albert Netzley) and Anna (Hess) Wolf
of Akron, Pennsylvania. A. N., of
Church of the Brethren heritage, joined
the Mennonite Church soon after he married Anna Hess in 1888.[11] In
1901, Wolf was among the founding partners of the Miller Hess shoe factory in Akron, which became a major employer in the region and would
provide a generous income for Orie and Elta. Other partners included A.
N.'s brother Samuel, a Church of the Brethren minister, and his brother-
in-law Simon P. Hess. Anna's other siblings, several of whom were prominent in founding both the city of Hesston and Hesston College, lived
in Kansas.[12]

Elta Wolf carried an air of eastern reserve and refinement. Some thought
her aloof, but she was actually shy; in a 1914 *Maple Leaf* photo she has
a bashful, tentative look. The yearbook editors chose the final lines of
William Wordsworth's "She Was a Phantom of Delight" to describe her:
"A perfect maiden nobly planned / To warn, to comfort and to command /
And yet a spirit still and bright / With something of angelic light."[13] If not
a perfect maiden, the well-born Elta became Orie's main comforter, "commanded" well their home, and enabled his lifelong service to the church.

As the only child of the Wolf family, Elta enjoyed a privileged upbring-
ing, with hired "girls" to help with household work and money enough to
supply wants as well as needs. She and her parents maintained an intimate
relationship throughout life, but one sees it most clearly in their correspondence while Elta was a student a Goshen College. Anna often greeted
her as "My darling Elta," finding the separation difficult and longing to
have her daughter home again: "Oh, Elta, you don't know how I love you.

Sometimes I think it can't be possible that it will be five weeks until I can see you. Six months is too long to separate a love as strong [as] ours."[14]

Anna filled her letters with advice. She reminded Elta to be sociable and was concerned that her daughter not be thoughtless and rude. Anna wondered if Elta's ideals for a man were too high. She was glad Elta was no longer seeing "Lloyd," because he was not good company for her and did not "think of religion." Still, she chided Elta for insulting him by neglecting to answer his letters in a timely fashion. And about "Mr. Yoder," why had Elta turned him down? Anna offered her view of the ideal man: "A young man with good morals, a Christian, good common sense, a kind heart, and even tempered"—an apt description of Orie! "You will never meet anyone that is faultless." Anna was happy with Elta's A in German, her first in that course. Of course, a mother must warn a daughter about potential dangers: I "do not know which is worse; at the theatre your spiritual body is in danger and on a boat [on the Elkhart River], your physical [body is at risk]."[15]

Anna's letters also included news about the shoe business. In March 1913, floods in the Midwest were interfering with Papa's shoe sales, and since the bookkeeper at Miller Hess had quit,[16] A. N. had much more work. It would be so helpful if Elta could keep the company books, "but there are so many other things that you should learn." Anna could not do all the housework, but she was reluctant to hire someone when she would eventually have Elta's help. That raised the question of Elta's future: "We think you'd better say good-bye to Goshen in June. It is now high time that you set your heart on other things":[17] managing a home, sewing, cooking, and baking. Elta was ambivalent. When she began her college course work, she had determined to finish it and return home with a degree, but she was ever sensitive to the wishes of her parents.

Elta went home to Akron that June and never returned to Goshen as a student. Her welcoming

Goshen College couples, ca. 1914. Orie and Elta are pictured on the far left. MC USA Archives–Goshen.

party at the Akron train station included her parents, two friends, and her "little namesake." Carrie (Reitz) and Nathan Myers, family friends and caretakers of one of the Wolf farms, had named their daughter for Elta Wolf. In a twist of history, little Elta eventually became Orie's second wife. "Poor little girl!" Elta wrote to Orie. She was so unhappy to see a big Elta arrive on the train instead of a small one; little Elta ignored big Elta and kept looking for the expected playmate.[18]

For the next two years, Orie and Elta carried on weekly correspondence. His first letter greeted her as "Dear Friend Elta" and closed with "Your loving friend Orie Otis." In time, Orie would sign off as "Yours as ever with best love."

A BUSY SUMMER

One catches a glimpse of Orie's full schedule when later in June he found himself at home on Cloverdale Farm with a case of the mumps. It required a great deal of effort to find substitutes to teach his business courses, his Bible class, and his Sunday school class; to chair the devotional committee; to lead the Young People's Bible Meeting; and to fill in as "master" of the men's dorm. His brother Ernest agreed to attend faculty meetings in Orie's place and do his janitorial work in the dorm. After this litany, Orie said he had had no clue that "running a school" required so much effort! There was no one who could do Orie's twenty-hour student load, of course. That he had to do himself.

Orie knew he needed to develop more patience, and his case of the mumps was helping. He was confined to a room where only his parents and his sister Ida interrupted his solitude. During his convalescence, Orie developed a routine. His days began at six with "Morning Watch," or Bible reading and prayer, then breakfast. He did coursework until ten, read the newspapers until noon, and more coursework until two. Midafternoon, his mother, Nettie, came to his room for several hours of conversation. After supper, Orie read for pleasure until eight. He read Emerson, Kipling, and Tennyson as well as a volume on the psychology of religion and a few popular novels. He finished his day with "good long talks with Papa."[19]

In July he marked a passage of time—his twenty-first birthday. "Say Elta, by the time you get this I'll be a man. Then I'll have the right to vote, make contracts for myself, pay taxes, make and spend my own money and do all that becomes a man." He had up until this time given all his earnings to his father, continuing a multigenerational pattern. He recognized that Elta also was coming of age and would soon become a real woman "(ha!)." He closed on a characteristically serious note: "Well here's hoping we both make good and never betray the trust & confidence our parents have in us."[20]

By mid-July, after a two-week absence, Orie returned to Goshen College in time to observe a historic transition. Even as the school was celebrating its tenth anniversary, president Noah E. Byers and dean C. Henry Smith resigned. Under their able leadership, Goshen College had become a place of vigorous intellectual inquiry and broad cultural expression, which students found exhilarating. Its rising academic standards had gained the respect of graduate schools, but not that of an ambivalent Mennonite constituency. Indiana-Michigan Conference leaders and other critics in the East were increasingly suspicious of the school's intellectual achievements and cultural life, fearing these demonstrated a lack of spiritual vitality and commitment to the church.

To counter the "modernist" drift, influential leaders began imposing restrictive standards that required teachers and administrators to identify more closely with the church, purge the school of liberal theology, and adopt plain dress as an expression of loyalty to the Mennonite Church. For women, this meant a black bonnet, black stockings, and a cape dress; for men, a plain, black suit coat without lapels and buttoned up to the collar. Conformity, uniformity, and obedience to the church replaced intellectual freedom, cultural expression, and ecumenism. President Byers resigned to become dean at Bluffton (Ohio) College, a GC Mennonite school with more intellectual and cultural freedom. Dean C. Henry Smith and professor Boyd Smucker followed Byers to Bluffton.

When the Mennonite Board of Education met to reorganize the college on July 10, 1913, Orie was present. He reported to Elta that the board had appointed J. E. (John Ellsworth) Hartzler as president and business manager, and Paul E. Whitmer, professor of Bible and English, as dean. Hartzler, who had been dean of the Bible School, was a gifted orator and a popular evangelist. The board hoped he would be able to win the support of the school's critics.

Orie believed that the MBE recognized the serious nature of the current crisis and so gave the faculty more academic freedom. President Byers, in his low-key and "very impressive" farewell address to the board, said that the latitude of the board's concessions surprised him. Among the reasons for his resignation was the board's halfhearted support of Goshen, leading him to think he himself may have been the cause. To survive and flourish, the school needed the kind of solid support

Orie the teacher (*left*), with colleague. Goshen College *Maple Leaf.*

from the board that Byers had observed other church boards giving to programs of missions and publication.[21]

INDECISION

Orie felt pulled in both directions. He had begun his postsecondary education under the Byers administration, and Byers had hired him to teach. The professors and administrators were his friends and mentors. Yet Orie was also the son of D. D. Miller, a member of the MBE and of the executive committee of the Indiana-Michigan Conference, both calling the college to greater accountability to the church. While Orie became a lifelong advocate for Goshen College, his greater loyalty was to the church. The college, as all institutions, was to be a servant of the church.

In the midst of the Byers-Hartzler transition, Orie continued his busy summer school schedule of work and a bit of play. He organized a men's weekly prayer meeting, which he hoped would stir the spiritual consciousness of the men, who were less interested in "religious matters" than the women were. And no one, it seems, had initiated any social events during the weeks of his absence, so Orie proposed and planned one; the "boys" invited the "girls" to the men's dorm, where they "worked stunts" and served ice cream.

Overhearing Orie's lament to a colleague that the summer term was dead in comparison to the spring term, the summer-term women began "nagging" Orie about his opinion that they were "such a dead bunch." A few days later, a group of women appeared at breakfast wearing black dresses as a sign of mourning. They paraded into the chapel and sat conspicuously in the front row where Orie, the man in charge, could not possibly miss them. But he could ignore them, which he did. He could see no humor in the adolescent funeral caper. To Elta, he griped, "The whole affair nearly made me tired that they should make such a fuss" over a minor comment.[22]

At the annual summer YMCA conference at Winona Lake, Indiana, Orie was one of fifty Mennonites among the thousands inspired by dynamic speakers. British evangelists Rodney "Gipsy" Smith and G. Campbell Morgan were among the featured preachers. Orie thought enough of the famous preachers to buy a photograph of the two posing together. William Jennings Bryan, United States secretary of state under Woodrow Wilson and three-time presidential candidate, was to be on the program, but political duties kept him in Washington, DC. From Winona Lake, Orie gave Elta the results of his summer student efforts: an A in geography, psychology, and trigonometry, and a B+ in geology. Not so bad, he thought, for having missed five weeks of the term, two because of the mumps and three for the overlapping of terms that had left him little time for studying.

At home in Akron, Elta maintained a busier than usual schedule, cooking, keeping house, and caring for her mother, who was in bed with rheumatism. She was also contemplating the differences between Goshen Mennonites and Lancaster Mennonites, who were more culturally conservative. Her year at Goshen had given her a point of comparison for rethinking the traditional customs of her Ephrata Mennonite congregation and the Lancaster Mennonite Conference to which it belonged. "I think one can be a Christian and not wear a [large, black] bonnet, but as for the [white muslin] Prayer Head Covering . . . I want to wear it and would feel guilty if I didn't."[23] Eastern Pennsylvania clothing traditions would continue to be a topic of conversation for Orie and Elta.

AN AKRON CHRISTMAS

Orie spent the 1913 Christmas holidays with Elta in Akron. It was his second visit, having met her parents earlier in the fall. During this festive week, Orie proposed to Elta and they agreed to marry in September 1915, some twenty months down the road. Elta's father, A. N. Wolf, and his partners offered Orie a place in Miller Hess, so his vocational plans seemed to be settled. They needed his skills and experience as a bookkeeper, and A. N. wanted an apprentice who would eventually take his place as wholesale shoe salesman. The Wolfs also planned to buy and remodel a house across Main Street for Elta and Orie.

Orie enjoyed the holidays despite his embarrassment for having blown certain things out of proportion, such as objecting to Elta's wish to miss church so they could spend more time together. Thankful for what Elta and her parents were offering, Orie was relieved that his vocation was now settled and that his business training and teaching had prepared him well for his new role. He would not need to "step into the dark" when his college days ended in the spring of 1915. He told the Wolfs that he was eager to become a Pennsylvanian.[24]

But Orie's certainty was short-lived; not everyone at Goshen College shared his happiness. Colleagues would be left behind, and for some it would be inconvenient. His assistant, Mrs. Weaver, was upset because she wanted to finish her college education, and Orie's leaving would make that impossible.[25] More significantly, president J. E. Hartzler wanted Orie to stay at Goshen to manage the business office and continue teaching business courses. Now Orie was confused. Despite his recent promise to be in Akron by September of 1915, he now felt "almost morally obliged" to accept the president's offer. He asked Elta to discuss with her parents a possible delay in his coming to Akron. They could still get married in September but live in Goshen temporarily, maybe for as long as a full academic year. "Elta, tell me exactly how your parents feel about it." The Wolfs were not pleased. Orie consulted his own father, but the question remained unresolved.[26]

SUMMER 1914

By June 1914, summer school was in full swing. Orie was taking German and algebra and teaching his usual business courses. He reported to Elta the beginning of a construction project: teams of horses and graders were excavating for a new science hall, the school's third building, which would not be finished until 1916. As in the previous year, Orie was responsible for all student religious activities. He asked Elta to pray for wisdom to make the right decision about his vocation and their future.

Orie also worked to refine his manners, to be more polite, more cultured, less sarcastic, and less "slammy." In a candid moment, the more polished Elta had pointed out these deficiencies in Orie. She now regretted it, saying that he was "kind and honest and that's really what culture is."[27] By the end of July, Orie could report that he hadn't slammed anyone all summer. He hoped that he was approaching Elta's ideal for him. He was sure that he was now more polite and that he was remembering to improve his posture by walking straight with shoulders back and head held up. Plaintively he added, "Elta, give me credit at least for trying."[28]

In addition to his school routine, Orie took on various preaching assignments. His regular pulpit, assigned by the college and the conference, was the Barker Street Mennonite Church, a congregation of about forty members just across the Indiana line in Michigan. Each Sunday he rose at four in the morning, took the trolley to Elkhart and boarded the train to Vistula, Indiana. A member of the congregation picked him up in a buggy, sometimes a car, and took him home for breakfast. After the service came dinner in someone's home, a two-hour nap, then back to the church to conduct the evening service. Then he returned to Goshen by way of buggy, train, and interurban trolley. This grueling routine foreshadowed his lifelong commitment to the church that called on him again and again. He rarely refused an assignment.

One Sunday in mid-June, Orie told Elta, his preaching had not gone well. The first twenty minutes were fine, but then some disturbance in the audience upset him. Added to that, the last part of his sermon had not been well-organized, so it "fell flat." On his return home, he got drenched from walking several blocks between stations in Elkhart in a pouring rain. By the time he arrived on campus he was one very wet student preacher.

In Akron, Elta had happily begun to drive her father's new "machine," his first, and looked forward to getting a driver's license. But A. N., her driving instructor, had lately decided that it was too dangerous for Elta, citing his near accident and daily newspaper reports of other mishaps. Elta was so disappointed she cried, even while acknowledging that her father's decision was "sensible." Elta also reported to Orie a change in the family routine. For the first time the Wolfs were having daily family worship, a result of Elta's exposure to the spiritual climate at Goshen College, which emphasized practices of personal piety.[30]

While Elta kept busy learning the domestic skills she would need for her new home, she also maintained a busy social life. She regularly attended Young People's Bible Meetings, sometimes at Ephrata and sometimes at other Mennonite churches. Often she went with her parents or relatives to revival meetings, Sunday school conferences, and other special church events. Elta's many friends frequently dropped in unannounced at the Wolf house on the corner of Main and Eleventh Streets for casual visits, as did neighbors and relatives. She and her friends also planned more formal dinners and socials. She was sure Orie would have enjoyed the party she hosted for Goshen College students who lived in the Lancaster area.

In late June, Orie wrote to Elta about Goshen's major summer event, the choral society's presentation of Handel's cantata *Saul* on the campus lawn. Alvin J. Miller, president of the society, was the director; Orie, "your humble servant," was vice president; and Amos E. Kreider was treasurer.[31]

The day before the letter was written, an event halfway around the globe triggered events that would profoundly affect the future for Orie and other Goshen students such as Alvin J. Miller—and would alter the course of human history. On June 28, 1914, Serbian nationalists assassinated archduke Franz Joseph Ferdinand, heir to the Austrian throne, sparking World War I. The catastrophic misery caused by the war would call Orie to Syria, and then to South Russia to help heal the wounds of war.

On the evening of August 6, the fifty members of the cast of *Saul* and their faculty sponsors posed for a photo on the lawn. Women were dressed in white robes with long sashes around the waist. Sashes also crowned their long, flowing hair. The men wore dark robes and dark sashes. Most were barefoot, some wore sandals, and some as soldiers held spears. Orie, sober faced as usual, stood robed and barefooted behind the Witch of Endor and her two assistants.[32]

The performance that followed the next night seemed to delight the audience. Orie was more critical; he thought some singers did not know all the choruses and the sopranos were a bit flat sometimes. A repeat performance a week later again saw a good crowd in attendance. Many people who lived on nearby streets enjoyed the cantata from the front steps of their homes. No one at Goshen or in the community had ever put on such a major production. The local newspaper enthusiastically proclaimed it "one of the greatest musical successes ever given in Goshen by a local organization." Susan Fisher Miller points to the cantata performance and photo as an iconic expression of Goshen's first ten years of free-flowing immersion in the arts. The next ten years would not be so free.[33]

PERPLEXING CHOICES

The fall semester found Orie as busy as ever, taking and teaching courses. But on a Saturday in September, he took a break for his first lesson in "running an auto." The car was D. D.'s; Ernest drove it to the college to pick up Orie and gave him his first lesson. Orie drove most of the fifteen miles to Cloverdale Farm with Ernest as tutor, teaching his older brother how to steer, start, and stop the car. The next day, D. D. and Nettie drove Orie to Barker Street church for his preaching duties.

Once again Orie worried about his future vocation. What had been so gloriously clear last Christmas had quickly become murky. By mid-September, his resolve returned. Innumerable conversations, particularly with his father, led Orie back to his original commitment to Akron and the shoe company.[34] Elta and the Wolfs were, of course, relieved. Elta was sympathetic to Orie's sadness about moving so far away from his parents and promised to build a close relationship with them by writing frequent letters and visiting when possible.

With this, Orie's imagination once again turned to life in Pennsylvania. Cultural differences between the more relaxed Midwest and the more traditional and regulated Lancaster Mennonite Conference frequently appeared in his and Elta's correspondence. Orie assured Elta that he understood that she would conform to the plain dress standards of her church, including cape dresses—designed with an extra layer of fabric to obscure breasts, worn out of a concern for modesty. "I don't believe you will be any prettier than you were before, but I like you better for doing it," Orie wrote, seeing Elta's conformity as evidence of her desire to cooperate with the church and thus serve as a good example to others. Nevertheless, he was glad that she did not believe the cape to be essential to Christianity. If that were the case, his mother would be among the lost! He admitted that it would seem odd at first to adopt the more conservative eastern standards, but he would try to adapt. A long conversation with Indiana bishop Jacob K. Bixler had convinced Orie that in order to be effective in Lancaster County, one should be "at once conservative in doctrine and progressive in method."[35] This became Orie's modus operandi and it served him well.

By early 1915, Orie was revisiting his decision to go to Akron. The Goshen College offer was still on the table and Nettie was hoping Orie would stay in Indiana. Elta, meanwhile, made it quite clear that she did not want to live in Goshen; if that's where Orie wanted to be, he would have to live alone. Another conversation with D. D. put Orie back on track for Akron. He told Elta that she could thank his father "for urging me to leave here and go to Akron next fall. He seems to see God's hand in it more than I do I guess. Not that his urging was necessary but it makes me feel surer that I'm doing right if he is so confident of it."[36] Clearly, it *was* necessary!

Furthermore, Goshen College had hired his brother Ernest as business manager, as Orie had recommended, thus reducing the pressure on Orie to stay. "That settles it. I couldn't stay here now even if I wanted to," he assured Elta. "So don't worry any more my dear about J. E. [Hartzler] persuading me to stay," he wrote, apologizing repeatedly for having caused Elta and her parents such concern.[37] Both Elta and Orie were again confident about their future—even as they continued to reassure each other. Elta told Orie that A. N. Wolf had announced Orie's coming to Miller Hess employees and they had greeted the news with enthusiasm.

In February, when word of Orie's new resolve to go to Akron had been made public, J. S. (Jonas) Hartzler, the college's business manager, pulled him aside to warn him about what he could expect from Lancaster Conference leaders. Most had no love for what they viewed as the liberalism of Goshen College. Leaders such as John H. Mosemann Sr., Noah Mack, and Benjamin Weaver would not trust a Goshen graduate no matter what he said or did, so Orie had better be prepared. In Indiana, Hartzler assured Orie that he was on good footing. The next day he attended Forks church, where the Sunday school superintendent asked him to speak, and then one of the ministers persuaded Orie to preach the sermon. Orie was surprised and unprepared; he had not even brought a Bible. No layman had ever preached the Sunday morning sermon at Forks; Orie was the first. On the spot, he recalled a sermon given elsewhere based on Hebrews 12:1 and preached to an attentive audience.[38]

And then another opportunity presented itself, shaking his resolve to live in Akron. The Maple Grove congregation in nearby Topeka needed a pastor. If Orie were to be ordained for ministry there, he could also attend seminary in Chicago. Since Orie had always sensed a calling to ministry, how could he say no? And how could he say no to God, if indeed God was calling him to pastoral ministry? His parents and his Goshen College mentors encouraged him to stay in Indiana. Losing no time, Orie began studying Greek.[39]

This turn of events caused anxiety in Akron. Had Orie not already accepted a job with Miller Hess? Elta dreaded telling her parents of the new development, but finally,

> I told my parents all about it last evening and it surely came as a thunderbolt out of a clear sky. Orie dear I wish you would manage to come [to Akron] some Sunday. I never saw my father so worked up about anything before. He scarcely slept two hours last evening and is not himself at all today. I can scarcely tell you how he feels about it and I think you and he must see each other. I think what hurts him so much is that these plans should be made so quickly, when he had so fully trusted and counted on the ones we discussed so much [at] Christmas.[40]

In a few days, however, the Topeka plan fell apart. Orie's friend Amos Kreider had spoken to the Topeka deacons before they knew of Orie's interest. Kreider had at first turned down the Topeka pulpit, expecting to be ordained at the College Mennonite Church. When the bishops failed to act, Kreider offered to serve the Topeka congregation after all. Oddly, those who had encouraged Orie to consider the Topeka ministry apparently had not consulted the congregation.

Though his father said there were other pastoral assignments available in the conference and Orie could live on a farm that D. D. wanted to buy, Orie again set his sights on Akron. As a sign of his renewed resolve, he asked his future father-in-law for the address of a trade journal that he could order; he was ready to begin learning the shoe business.[41]

SIGHTS SET ON AKRON AGAIN

In March, A. N. Wolf graciously reaffirmed his desire to have Orie work for the company. The public nature of their family plan had compounded Wolf's distress. The entire Akron community knew he had purchased a house on Main Street for Orie and Elta. At that very moment, carpenters and plumbers were at work remodeling the house. A. N. assured Orie he would not hold Orie's vacillation against him. Wolf acknowledged Orie's desire to serve God and the church and assured him that God could use Orie in Lancaster just as well as any other place. In fact, the Ephrata church needed his gifts. "I am very sure if the Lord does not want you to be in the shoe business or to live in Lanc[aster] Co[unty], he will find you here and put you in the right place."[42]

Orie was alternately "happy as can be" and "feeling blue." He was not sure why he got depressed when he had so many blessings: Elta, parents, money, education, friends, faith, a good job, sound health, and much more. He recalled how Elta could always cheer him when she was on campus. "I need you so these days," he wrote. He wondered again whether he would be able to "work in alright" in the Lancaster Conference. He acknowledged how the unexpected unnerved him and left him feeling incompetent. Still, he was hopeful: "I may turn out to be of use somewhere in this old world with you helping me. Won't we try hard, Elta, dearest, to be of some use to society?"[43]

Orie and Elta continued to discuss Orie's role in Pennsylvania. He was learning about the shoe industry and advertising by reading the trade journal he had subscribed to. At the same time, his Old Testament class stirred his interest in seminary. "At times yet an almost irresistible longing seizes me to go on to school and directly into church work, but that only for a short time. In all my saner moments my plans that are made seem much more satisfactory to me."[44]

A visit to Akron from George Bender, Mennonite mission leader from Elkhart, underscored the expectations that Indiana church leadership had for Orie's future and reawakened Elta's uncertainty. Bender was afraid that Orie would hide in a shoe shop and do no religious work. During a sleepless night, Elta reviewed their plans. Should she have stayed at Goshen, where it would be easier for Orie to serve the church? It is only natural, she reasoned, that a college graduate would want to continue his education. "What hurts me," she told Orie, "is the thought that some people think you are simply coming down here and wasting your life in a shoe shop." She did not want to ruin Orie's dreams and ambitions. She would rather live on an Indiana farm with a happy husband than to live in Pennsylvania with one who was unhappy.[45]

It was now Orie's turn to reassure Elta that they had made the right decision. Orie outlined the possibilities ahead. Perhaps his adjustment to Pennsylvania would not be so hard. He looked forward to learning to know people in her world and was sure that he could find his place in the Ephrata congregation and Lancaster Conference. Living in Indiana would not be easy for Elta. She had not been raised on a farm or even in the country, and besides, her leaving Akron would devastate her parents.

Settling in Akron was the most sensible thing to do, Orie reasoned. He wanted to make Elta happy and did not want to take the Wolfs' only daughter from them. Indiana was not perfect. The church was more progressive, but not everyone was happy about that. Some were resisting change and frustrated its progress—which is "pretty hard on my Christianity." Maybe their marriage would serve a greater purpose, Orie mused. Perhaps they could live down some of the prejudice the East has for the West. Orie ended his letter with a prophetic benediction: "May we two in our union create a closer union between Eastern and Western Mennonitism."[46]

Throughout the spring, Elta kept Orie posted on Akron life and the carpenters' progress on their house. Orie said it gave him a funny feeling to think about the house they were to share, but he was quite sure he would like it with Elta living in it. He was optimistic about contributing his talents and energy to the Ephrata church. "I look forward to the day, when I shall have my life work question settled." [47] Finding his "life work" would continue to be a recurring theme for ten more years.

FROM INDIANA FARM TO PENNSYLVANIA CITY

In June 1915, Orie received his bachelor's degree in English from Goshen College. In addition to his English concentration, he had taken a wide variety of liberal arts courses such as history, astronomy, physiology, and German. His grades were evenly divided between As and Bs.

When school ended, Orie went to Cloverdale Farm to work for his father. D. D.'s offer to buy a 210-acre farm just a mile from Cloverdale for Orie was still open, and Orie was somehow convinced he could "make a pretty good farmer yet."[48] Farming looked especially appealing in 1915, since the crop yields were good. When farmers have money, Orie observed, they will spend more on shoes and tobacco, and that was good since the Wolf farms in Akron grew tobacco and Miller Hess produced shoes. Orie idealized farm life even as he worked harder than ever before. He joked that he might become more interested in his future father-in-law's fields on the side of the hill than in the shoe factory. "Oh, I get all kinds of notions in my head. What I need to do is get at something definite once, then I'll like it."[49]

The Lancaster mistrust of
Goshen College continued to be
a topic in Orie's and Elta's correspondence that summer. Elta reported that bishop Noah Mack
had from the Ephrata pulpit proclaimed Goshen College a haven
of false doctrine, denying that the
Bible was divinely inspired. As a
result, Elta was having a hard time
treating him with respect. She was
encouraged, however, that not all
Lancaster ministers were as narrow as Mack. She was certain that
she and Orie could be a positive
influence "by living right here,
and by our lives show them that
the people of Goshen College have
Christianity too."[50]

Orie at Goshen College, 1915. Goshen
College *Maple Leaf*.

One can hardly overestimate the influence of Goshen College on Orie.
There he formed a network of friends and colleagues, mentors and teachers—relationships he would continue to nurture to the end of his life.
There he met Elta, with whom he would share life for forty-three years.
Goshen gave him a broad liberal arts education with a concentration in
classical literature and an introduction to systematic theology and biblical studies. From his faculty post, he observed the church at work.
Theological wrangling and partisan politics among church leaders that
could have caused Orie to become cynical, as it did some of his peers,
instilled in him instead a sense that the church and its institutions were
worthy of his loyalty and service. Whether east or west, at its best or its
worst, the church was still the body of Christ.

On July 7, his twenty-third birthday, Orie was reflective. His first
twenty-three years had prepared him for the next twenty-three, which he
expected to be his most productive years. He was beginning to make the
mental transition. His Indiana era was over and his life in Pennsylvania
was about to begin.

Orie's move from an Indiana farm to a small Pennsylvania city represented a shift from a generations-long, intimate relationship with the land. Farming for Mennonites and Amish was more than a way to make a living. As Royden Loewen and Steven M. Nolt observe, "Faith and soil, values and land, memories and nature, were all inter-related." Farming was a way of life that nurtured a sense of place that in turn shaped identity as a people rooted in the soil. They understood that they were stewards of the land, responsible to maintain its productivity beyond themselves for future generations. Their stewardship was more than inherited knowledge and common sense; it was also an act of faith.[51]

Orie and his brothers—who also left the farm for other vocations—were the vanguard of a larger post-Depression migration from rural to urban areas. Before Orie's death in 1977, a third of all American and Canadian Mennonite farm families would be living in towns and cities with populations of 2,500 or more. It remained for Orie's sisters to continue "an Anabaptist approach to land" shaped by the legacy of *Gelassenheit* (humility) and gratitude.[52] Clara (and Art Augsburger) and Alice (and Chauncey Oesch) farmed Cloverdale and Brookside, to which Orie and Elta's children would return for idyllic, cherished summer vacations.

Chapter 3
Borough on a Hill: 1915–1919

*"I feel we are not giving of our means
and selves enough for the Master."*

Akron is aptly named a "high place," *akros* in Greek. The high place is 520 feet above sea level and drops 200 feet on its northwest slope to the Cocalico Creek. In 1830, the hamlet on the crest was called New Berlin, an echo of the first Caucasian settlers' homeland. Midway between the summit and the creek was another small hamlet known as Akron. In 1863, when the Columbia & Reading Railroad built a depot in Akron, the smattering of houses on top of the hill gave up its name to identify with the all-important railroad stop. Railroads and depots often determined the economic viability of a community. Akron's organizational evolution transformed it from a village to a borough in 1895. The borough's population at the time of its founding was 606, scattered over two hundred acres.[1]

Akron is located in the heart of Pennsylvania's Lancaster County, which contains some of the nation's richest soil and has been famous since 1839 as the tobacco capital of the state.[2] In the last decades of the nineteenth century, Akron had more than fifty cigar makers. Three hundred of its six hundred residents were engaged in the manufacture of cigars. Anyone with a knife, board, and a chair could shop around for the best-paying producer. Every available space was used to roll cigars: spare rooms in homes, shops, and warehouses.[3]

Akron was not alone. In 1887, nearly a thousand cigar factories in Lancaster County produced two billion cigars. In the twenty-first century, Lancastrians complain of tourist traffic; late in the nineteenth century, hundreds of tobacco wagons clogged the streets of Lancaster on their way to the city's one hundred warehouses.[4] Pennsylvania's tobacco production peaked in 1918 with forty-nine thousand acres cultivated.[5]

While midwestern Mennonites looked askance at Lancaster's tobacco production and use, tobacco farmers had tradition on their side. There was a time when some Mennonite meetinghouses featured spittoons near the pulpit for ministers who chewed, and it was not uncommon to see men smoking cigars before and after services. Then there was the economic benefit. Tobacco was a lucrative cash crop. Its labor-intensive production provided year-round work for large families, and it seemed to complement an earthy, plain lifestyle. It appeared to easterners that those who developed a conscience against tobacco were compromising long-cherished principles of separation, simplicity, and sobriety.

A story from the colorful life of Illinois minister C. F. (Clayton Freed) Derstine shows the values at play. When Derstine was being considered for the office of bishop, an Illinois farmer, concerned about Derstine's piano, a symbol of conformity to the world and a threat to congregational singing, voiced his objection to bishop Ezra Yordy. The bishop suggested they call on Derstine. After discussion and prayer, the farmer said to Derstine, "You get that piano out of the house and I'll listen to you as bishop. Otherwise I won't." As always, Derstine had a quick return: "You throw your cigars away and I'll listen to you." The cigar-smoking critic gave up and went home.[6]

Among Akron's cigar producers were Elta's father, A. N. (Albert Netzley) Wolf, and his brother S. N. (Samuel Netzley). Grandson John W. Miller remembers A. N. smoking cigars, chewing tobacco, and using a spittoon, which was a fixture in the house.[7] At the turn of the century, the enterprising Wolf brothers shifted to a new commodity, the production of shoes. It was a profitable move. By the time Orie Miller arrived in 1915, Miller Hess was producing 1,200 pairs of shoes a day.[8]

AKRON IN 1915

When Orie arrived in Akron, there were no paved streets, and horses still dominated the traffic, but not for long. As shoe production had replaced

South Ninth Street, Akron, looking northward, before 1907. H. M. Adams, *Lancaster County Postcards: Windows to Our Past.*

cigar making for the Wolfs and their partners, so cars were now beginning to replace horses and carriages on the streets of Akron. The borough was then developing public utilities. A water company had been formed in 1910–11; gas utilities were still a year in the future; and electricity was two years in coming. Visible from a long distance was the one-hundred-foot "standpipe" storage tank, the result of the 1910–11 waterworks. The stamped iron plate on the upright tank identifies A. N. Wolf as a borough council member. The opening of the Akron National Bank in 1912 testified to the borough's growing prosperity.[9]

Forming the perimeter of Akron's square were the bank, a hotel, a restaurant, an apartment house, one of two grocery stores, and a post office. Here Elta often waited expectantly for Orie's Indiana letters, delivered to the depot by train, then carried up the hill to the post office. The two grocery stores were social centers where news and gossip flowed freely. The hotel served food and drink, and until Prohibition, beer. A bus dropped off bundles of the *Reading Eagle* at the hotel, where delivery boys picked them up and tossed them onto porches. Students walked to the two-story brick school on West Main Street, where five teachers and a principal taught eleven grades. Students who wanted a fourth year of high school went to nearby Ephrata.[10]

By 1915, Akron's population had grown to 720.[11] The borough was a relatively homogeneous "Pennsylvania Dutch" Protestant community without Jews, African Americans, and only a few Roman Catholics. Its

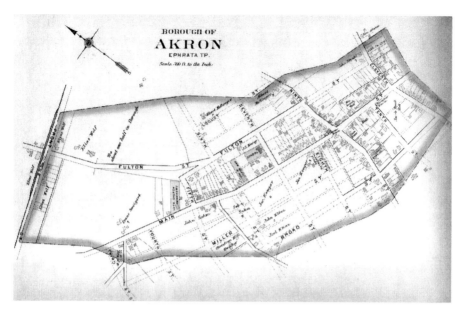

Borough of Akron, 1890. Akron Seventy-Fifth Anniversary.

churches were Lutheran, Evangelical Congregational, and Church of the Brethren. As for political preferences, Akron was solidly Republican. An old-timer claimed that he could count Democrats, a "rare and suspect breed," on one hand.[12]

MARRIED LIFE

Orie and Elta were married on August 26, 1915, in their newly refurbished home on Main Street. (Church weddings were a later development.) D. D. Miller, just back from representing Mennonite peace concerns in the nation's capital, performed the ceremony. He, Orie's mother, Nettie, and brother Ernest represented the Indiana Millers. The local paper reported that "an elegant dinner" followed the ceremony in the Wolf home across the street.[13]

The newlyweds' home was a two-story frame house with shutters and an open porch wrapped around its southwest corner—the corner that pointed toward the Wolf house. It was a few yards east on the opposite side of the street from Elta's childhood home. The large Wolf home stood on Akron's highest plateau, on the southeast corner of Main and Eleventh Streets. The newlyweds' front door faced southward toward the Wolfs' backyard.

In their summer correspondence before their marriage, Orie and Elta had discussed the furnishings for their house. "Elta, just so the library doesn't get too nice for me to make myself comfortable and enjoy myself in. That's to be my den you know. That furniture for those two upstairs rooms will surely be nice." And then there was the electric washing machine that Elta's father bought and installed. Since it would be so much easier for his wife, Anna, he had decided that she should take her weekly laundry to Elta's house. Nor did he neglect recreation; he planned to build a tennis court in the backyard. It seems A. N. Wolf spared no expense for his only daughter. "I believe your parents like us pretty much to get all those things for us," Orie commented. "But I guess it's you especially they are doing it for. But anyway I am glad I am getting you so I can share those things with you."

Orie's business training had not prepared him for domestic expenditures. After an earlier shopping excursion with his mother and sister Ida to buy home furnishings in Goshen, he had exclaimed to Elta, "My! Such stuff costs money, doesn't it?" He was beginning to understand just how good he and Elta had it. "Believe me you and I would have to skimp along some if we had not such good kind hearted parents that provide things for us." It was "more than many people have after years of hard work."

They would not use material goods selfishly. "It will mean more efficient service on our part to the people we touch, a more useful life than would be possible if we had to worry about these things. I am glad and happy about it all but I often pray that these things may not spoil us." Their shared compassion for the poor, a hallmark of his future service, was already evident. "I hope we can feel a greater sympathy for needy ones about us and that we might never want all these things for their own sake as you said in your letter today."[14]

An early photo of Orie, Elta, and the Wolfs visiting on the Miller porch shows A. N. Wolf pointing playfully, perhaps for the benefit of the photographer, toward Orie perched on the porch railing. Both men are dressed in identical white shirts and black bowties, Lancaster Conference style. Elta and Anna are wearing light-colored plain dresses. Anna too has a playful look directed toward A. N., while Elta looks down as though she is not a part of the conversation.

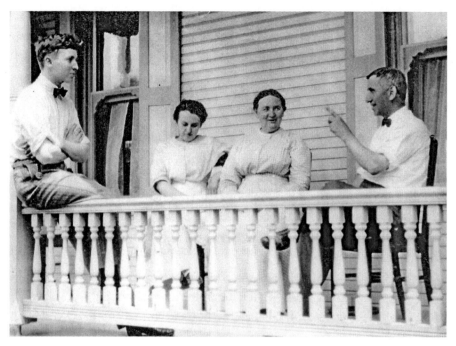

A Sunday afternoon conversation on the Millers' front porch, 1915, between (from left) Orie, Elta, Anna, and A. N. Wolf. John W. Miller.

MILLER, HESS & COMPANY

Orie Miller walked four blocks to his new job at the Miller Hess shoe factory, on the southeast corner of Main and Seventh Streets. The company had been in operation for fifteen years. Though named for two of its founders, Orie found it convenient; the coincidental convergence of names led many outside of Akron to conclude that the "Miller" was for *Orie* Miller. At least one colleague believed that Orie was not overly concerned about correcting the assumption.

Miller Hess was organized on April 17, 1901, to manufacture shoes and boots.[15] Founding partners were Peter B. Miller, Albert N. Wolf, and Simon P. Hess of Akron;[16] and Frank J. Conlin of Camden, New Jersey. In December, three additional partners joined the venture: Charles M. Conlin,[17] Samuel N. Wolf, and Wayne E. Brubaker.[18]

The company was incorporated on Valentine's Day, 1911, as Miller, Hess & Company, Inc., capitalized at $100,000.[19] S. N. Wolf was president, Wayne Brubaker was vice president, and A. N. Wolf was secretary-treasurer. In 1914, a new addition was built that extended the factory eastward along Main Street at a cost of $6,587. New machines and more

Founders of Miller, Hess & Company. Edward L. Miller.

Employees of Miller, Hess, ca. 1910. Akron Seventy-Fifth Anniversary.

employees increased daily production from five hundred to twelve hundred shoes. Less than a year after Orie joined the company, he, Clarence Hess, and Charles D. Wolf purchased some of the Conlin shares. Hess, a son of Simon P., supervised production and purchasing, while Orie Miller and A. N. Wolf handled sales and the business office.

S. N. Wolf had been selling hand-rolled cigars in upstate New York. When shoe production started, he added shoes to his sales inventory.[20] A. N. joined his brother on the road selling shoes and then became sales director. Once Orie arrived in Akron, he quickly learned the shoe market and after one year, at age twenty-four, replaced his father-in-law as sales director. The same year, 1916, Orie purchased shares in the company, making him a company director, though he was never involved in the production of shoes.

"I feel that I am growing into the business and continue to like it," Orie reported to his former Goshen College classmates in 1916. "I am kept very busy, but have most of my evenings for reading."[21] Since Lester Hostetler has mastered theology, Orie quipped in another letter, Lester would soon graduate, but for himself there was no graduation on the horizon. Even so, Orie assured his friends that he was not stagnating in Akron. There was no industry more interesting to study than the shoe industry, especially during the uncertainties of the current war. Costs of materials were rising at an unprecedented rate, changing so rapidly that "cost sheets must be revised daily to be worth anything." Perhaps justifying his vocational choice, Orie assured his classmates that he liked what he was doing, "even if the thing that interests me most is trodden upon by you."[22]

Orie and others of his generation exemplified the midcentury transformation of Mennonites from a land-based economy to one of cash, credit, wages, and entrepreneurship. Mennonites were ambivalent about money and capitalism. While ministers warned about the dangers of "mammon" and "filthy lucre," bankruptcy carried great stigma, and it was often the successful farmers and business people who were called into church leadership. As the competition for land and the cost of land increased, more Mennonites became entrepreneurs. The Wolf brothers' shoe enterprise was one of the earliest among Mennonites, and soon other entrepreneurial efforts followed: large-scale farming, construction companies, car and implement dealerships, meat processing plants, production of farm equipment, recreational vehicles, furniture, and more.[23] The reluctance to talk about money matters in the church lasted well into the 1980s, when stewardship advisor John H. Rudy's bold claim of "I like money!" in church papers was still striking.

When Orie was considering a career in shoe sales, he wondered whether it was an honorable calling. Some of his peers believed it was not and chided him for turning away from potential church leadership roles to hide out in a shoe shop and make money. Orie's use of his wealth for the benefit of the church enhanced his reputation and made his counsel especially valued in managing money-strapped church institutions.

A BIRTH AND EPHRATA MENNONITE CHURCH

Also in 1916, the Miller household expanded to three. On September 23, Elta gave birth to Lois Wolf Miller, the first of five children and their only daughter. On Miller Hess letterhead, Orie announced Lois's arrival to his former Goshen College classmates: "Little Lois is here, and expects to make her home with us for some time. She has several qualifications . . . that may make her a credit to the class. She has an excellent voice, which with a little training may make her famous. She has already shown signs of having a strong will, and a mind of her own."[24] Of course, A. N. and Anna Wolf were delighted grandparents.

Orie with Lois on the front porch of their Akron home, 1917. MC USA Archives–Goshen.

Orie had meanwhile joined Elta's church in Ephrata, and with deferential respect for its leaders entered into the congregation's life. Ephrata Mennonite Church was among the earliest city congregations in a denomination made up of farmers, rural people, and country churches. The congregation was organized in 1901, with ninety-six charter members who had come from the Groffdale and Hammer Creek districts. When the members met to consider a meetinghouse, they selected A. N. Wolf as secretary of the building committee. In July, the builders broke ground, and in December the congregation dedicated its meetinghouse on West Fulton Street.[25] In 1911, by the unanimous vote of its 140 members and the consent of Lancaster Conference bishops, the church became an autonomous congregation.[26] But when Orie arrived in 1915, the congregation had no resident minister.

Orie took membership in the congregation seriously. He was teaching an occasional Sunday school class and speaking on a variety of topics at Young People's Bible Meetings. He attended revival meetings and Sunday school conferences. With Mahlon and Noah Zimmerman, Orie reopened a Sunday school at Indiantown, some thirty miles from Akron. With Elta, he attended social events where he learned to know her friends, who also became his friends. The two developed a special group of lifelong friends they referred to as "the bunch." Members included Ellen Landis; Dora and Wayne Aungst; Willis and Emma Baer; Clayton and Martha Yake; local business leaders and spouses Jack and Ada Leed and Ross and Anna (Neuhauser) Witmer; and the Millers.

Characteristically, Orie embraced the congregation and took on responsibilities offered him. In his later work, Orie helped the congregation to think beyond its four walls by serving as a link to the wider church and the world. Ray Horst, who grew up in the congregation, recalled that Ephrata church had more students who attended Goshen College than any other Lancaster Conference congregation. Orie became influential without throwing his weight around. "He had tremendously creative ideas and . . . he knew how to put wheels under his ideas so things would happen."

The Millers frequently invited guests to their home for Sunday dinner. Nellie Miller (Mann), on her way to Constantinople in 1921, reported to her fiancé after dining at Orie and Elta's table that it was "a very pretty home" and "almost everything in it is about the best." Elta's "hired girl, one who for many years had worked for her mother," helped prepare the meal. If this evening was any indication, Nellie believed the Millers "must have a great deal of company."[27]

Though Elta was a woman of means, Ruth Brunk Horst described her as a "humble, giving person." Ray Horst called her "the poorest rich woman I ever knew," meaning she was frugal but generous.[28] Horst and

Ephrata Mennonite Church. John E. Sharp.

the other young men in the congregation looked forward to seeing Orie's annual purchase of a new Packard, which they called a "glorious chariot." Orie's purchases could hardly be considered an act of humility, but Horst did not view it as pretentious. Orie and Elta's generosity to the congregation seemed to mute any criticism regarding the Packard. Furthermore, Orie set an example of servanthood during the church ritual of footwashing, which followed communion, by always washing feet with Arthur, an individual who was "very limited physically and mentally."[29]

Horst recalls that the only critical attitudes toward Orie came from the shoe factory; employees grumbled that instead of giving so much money away to the church and to world missions, Orie could have increased their wages.

A PERPLEXING ORDINATION

While Orie soon won the confidence of his congregation, it would seem that the odds of serving in the Lancaster Conference were stacked against him. In 1914, the Board of Bishops ruled against the wearing of long neckties for men in favor of the traditional black bowties. Long ties signaled the erosion of a carefully guarded identity as a plain and separated people, whereas bowties symbolized respect for tradition. A second action followed a "vigorous protest" against the modernism of Goshen College. The board ruled that it would approve no Goshen College student or faculty member for any appointments to serve in the conference.[30] Orie had been both a student and faculty member at Goshen, and, as he had in the Midwest, wore a business suit and long necktie.

Despite such odds, Orie gradually won the favor of Lancaster Conference leaders—so much so that when in 1918 the Ephrata congregation was ready to choose a resident minister, Orie was one of six nominees. The congregation recognized his interest in Christian service, and conference leaders appreciated his cooperative and respectful spirit. Orie was, as John L. Ruth, author of the seminal Lancaster Conference history put it, a "surprising" blend "of personal initiative and submission to authority."[31]

Others in the "class" of candidates with Orie were Amos Horst, George Geigley, Henry Graybill, Harry Hess, and Mahlon Zimmerman—congregational leaders and teachers. The selection of ministers was no mere vote, nor was it a popularity contest; the final choice was made by lot. Ideal candidates did not seek ministerial office but submitted obediently and meekly when called. It was not a matter of possessing special gifts but of leading exemplary lives, showing dedication to congregational life, and exhibiting attitudes of appropriate humility.

Officiating ministers interviewed each candidate to discern his readiness to serve, respect for conference leaders, and obedience to the *Ordnung*, the covenant of established order. When the day came—in this case, Saturday, July 20, 1918—members gathered in hushed tones with great expectation. In the drawing of the lot, commonly used by MC and Old Order congregations, they would see God at work directly and visibly. Stories abounded of previous ordinations, often memorable and sometimes miraculous. In the days leading up to an ordination, such stories were told and retold.

After final prayers for God's leading, the nominees filed in to sit on a front bench facing a table with identical hymnals or Bibles, one for each candidate. Only one contained the "lot," a slip of paper, typically inscribed with Proverbs 16:33: "The lot is cast into the lap, but the whole disposing thereof is of the Lord" (KJV). On the opposite side, sometimes a note was scrawled, such as "Today you have been called to Christian ministry in this congregation."

Orie had little doubt that the lot would fall to him. Though he later said he never had much confidence in the lot, he was cooperative, believing he would be called as his father had been called to pastoral ministry or evangelism. He had nearly scuttled plans to move to Akron for a pastoral assignment in northern Indiana. He and Elta had often talked about whether it would be possible for him as a midwesterner and a Goshen College graduate to serve in a Lancaster Conference congregation. That possibility was now before him. After a sermon on the qualifications of a minister and the duties of a congregation, the great moment was at hand. With the drawing of the lot, one man's life, and that of his family, would be forever changed.

Orie, the oldest of the candidates—two weeks past his twenty-sixth birthday—was at the head of the row and the first to select his book. He reached for the first book, hesitated, then reached over it to pick up the second book. Amos Horst, seated next to Orie, took the first book. When each candidate had drawn a book, the presiding bishop took the book from each one in turn. When he opened Orie's book there was no lot. Instead, the lot was found in Amos Horst's book—the one Orie had passed over. As Orie looked on, Horst knelt on the floor while the bishop laid hands on him in the sacred ritual of ordination.

Orie was perplexed and confused. Why had the outer call not confirmed the inner call? What did this mean for his life work? One can imagine the conversations that day with Elta and her parents, and the troubled sleep that followed. Orie later remembered this as the most difficult moment of his life. With the benefit of hindsight, ordination as minister would have greatly restricted Orie's future worldwide ministry. There would be another call.

TRUE PATRIOTISM HAS NO NATIONAL BOUNDARIES

When World War I war broke out in Europe, *Gospel Herald* editor Daniel Kauffman, whose preaching at Forks church had converted Orie as a teenager, was quick to denounce the war. Genuine patriotism is not nationalism, but rather "a loyalty which seeks the glory of God and the good of fellowmen" in every country. "True patriotism," he declared, "has no national boundaries."[32]

When the delegates of the MC General Conference gathered at Archbold, Ohio, on August 18–20, 1915, they reaffirmed long-held

convictions against participating in warfare. No one claiming to be
Christian, they said, "should engage in carnal warfare under any circumstances, nor for any cause." As in all times, one should pray for government leaders, but rather than heeding the government's order to destroy
its enemies, Christians should answer Jesus' call to love enemies. The assembly authorized letters of concern to U.S. president Woodrow Wilson
and Canadian prime minister Robert Borden.[33]

The Mennonite commitment to nonviolence was challenged when the
United States entered the war. On August 20, 1917, a somber general assembly convened in a tent pitched next to the Yellow Creek Meetinghouse
west of Goshen. The United States had declared war on Germany on
April 6, Congress passed the Selective Draft Law on May 18, and the first
Americans were called to military duty on June 5. It was the first draft
since the Civil War. The assembly delegates passed a resolution resolving to "meekly but faithfully stand true to the principles of the Gospel,"
even if it should lead to suffering. "Surely," the statement read, "no one
who really understands our position will accuse us of either disloyalty or
cowardice." Young men who were drafted should "meekly inform" the
commanding officers "that under no circumstances can they consent to
service, either combatant or non-combatant under the military." If necessary, they should submit "to any penalty the government may see fit to in-
flict." The assembly sent three representatives to convey their sentiments
directly to secretary of war Newton Baker: D. D. Miller, Aaron Loucks,
and S. G. (Samuel Grant) Shetler.[34]

As a participant in the first "total war" in human history, the United
States mobilized civilians and retooled factories to produce material resources to support the war effort overseas. Highly publicized Liberty
Bond drives with quotas assigned to townships and counties pressured
Mennonites and others who were conscientiously opposed to the war. In
this atmosphere of hyper-nationalism, those who refused to fight were
considered un-American, especially if they spoke German, and those who
did not buy Treasury bonds were exposed in the local newspapers as
slackers. Overnight, Mennonites found themselves at odds with neighbors
and business associates. President Woodrow Wilson accused "hyphenated
Americans" of disloyalty and treachery. In one of his final speeches, he
said, "Any man who carries a hyphen about with him carries a dagger
that he is ready to plunge into the vitals of this Republic whenever he gets

ready." Such a person is "an enemy of the Republic."[35] Mennonites, of course, had no such sinister intentions, but they were still "hyphenated" German-American Mennonites.

While in Nashville, Tennessee, on a sales trip, Orie wrote to Elta from the Hotel Hermitage that he had visited Mennonite conscientious objectors (COs) at Camp Taylor. He saw his brother Trueman and Goshen College friends Ernest Stahley and Floyd Yoder. Though he was a bit too far south to sell the Miller Hess line of shoes, he liked the time it gave him to think. "I tell you Elta this is a wonderful [terrible] world and a wonderful [terrible] time we are living in." He was seeing signs of "war, war, war all along the way" with "soldiers on every hand." He reported a good visit with an officer from a camp in Georgia, which prompted him to exclaim to Elta, "If we people don't make some sacrifice for the ideals we stand for commensurate with what many, many make for democracy, we will be the losers spiritually and they gainers." It prompted him to consider "how little sacrifice I have made so far, the kind of sacrifice that is felt I mean." His reading that day from the book of Philippians also stirred him: "I feel we are not giving of our means and selves enough for the Master."[36] Orie's growing conviction about sacrifice and service would lead him to relief work and to promote peace, service, and missions around the globe.

A MENNONITE COMPROMISE

As in many other communities, the Mennonites in Lancaster County felt the pressure to purchase the "voluntary" Liberty Bonds. Their refusal to participate hampered the success of the bond drives and frustrated officials in their competition with other municipalities to prove that they were "100 percent patriotic." In Akron, a local Jewish farmer who served on the bond quota committee "was after everybody."

Lancaster followed the lead of Fulton County, Ohio, Mennonites, who had worked out a compromise with W. L. Crooks of Cleveland, Ohio, a Federal Reserve Bank official. Mennonites could make loans to their local banks according to an assigned quota. Conscientious objector loans would earn less interest than Liberty Bonds would, but the money was to be designated for nonmilitary purposes. Mennonites would not be funding the war directly, but their loans counted toward the quotas of Liberty Bond drives. Crooks reasoned that his plan put Mennonite money on the same basis as their grain; what happened to the grain after it was sold was no longer their responsibility.[37]

When bishop Eli Frey from Fulton County presented the design to the Lancaster bishop board on July 18, 1918, the board adopted the Crooks plan.[38] Orie, meanwhile, arranged for the purchase of civilian bonds from a Quaker trust company in Philadelphia, and at his Akron bank purchased a thousand-dollar certificate, telling the banker, "You can do with it what you wish, but I can't buy war bonds."[39] After World War II, Lancaster Mennonites discontinued this practice. They recognized that the nearly five million dollars they had invested in civilian bonds were, in the end, no different from war bonds.[40]

THE WORLD AT WAR

The slaughter of twenty million people between 1914 and 1918 in World War I shattered most notions of progress, the belief that the human spirit was evolving into ever-higher levels of knowledge, wisdom, and morality. On the contrary, the war demonstrated that twentieth-century Europeans could be as brutal as the most barbaric of their ancestors. Rarely had there been so little to gain and so much to lose. Never had there been such a war of attrition as that on the Western Front—stretching from the Swiss border to the English Channel—where five thousand, sometimes fifty thousand lives a day were sacrificed to gain ten or twenty yards.

Of all the war's consequences, foremost for those who survived was disillusionment. As D. H. Lawrence wrote, "All the great words . . . were canceled out for that generation." He knew that "the great words and beliefs of the time before 1914 could never be restored."[41] For Orie Miller and those of his generation who refused to fight the war, Menno Simons's noble words and core convictions lived on: clothing the naked, feeding the hungry, comforting the sorrowful, sheltering the destitute, serving those who harm you, and binding up the wounded.[42]

Enacting those convictions of service was the focus of the Mennonite Relief Commission for War Sufferers (MRCWS) when it met at the East Chestnut Street Meetinghouse in Lancaster City on January 4, 1919. The commission had been organized in December 1917 as a response to the U.S. declaration of war and the draft earlier that year. Mennonites were moved to compassion when they became aware of the distress of the war's victims. Without prompting, money began flowing into the treasury of the Mennonite Board of Missions and Charities in Elkhart, Indiana. In turn, the board appointed the commission to manage the contributed funds.

The Relief Commission had originally planned to meet in Elida, Ohio, in December 1918 during a General Missionary Conference, all of which was cancelled because of the "Spanish influenza," which killed more Americans than the war itself.[43] Since John H. Mellinger, representing Lancaster Conference, was an active member of the commission, and since Lancaster Mennonites were a major source of funding, the commission was meeting in their territory. D. D. Miller, a member of the commission, invited Orie to attend.

Orie looked on as the commission acted to support reconstruction work in France under the American Friends Service Committee (AFSC) and relief efforts in Turkey and Syria organized by the American Committee for Relief in the Near East. But the members of the commission would do more than that; they would also send volunteers to these places of need. Who would be willing to go to the lands of the Bible, where the suffering was so great?

Orie was deeply moved by what he was hearing. Had the lack of ordination at Ephrata six months earlier spared him for such a ministry as this? Aaron Loucks, chair of the Relief Commission, mentioned Orie as the type of volunteer they were looking for.[44]

When Orie heard his name, his heart skipped a beat. As the discussion continued, Orie's sense of call deepened. When he looked toward his father across the room, D. D. was looking directly at him. As their eyes met, each knew the thoughts of the other. In a flash of clarity, Orie responded to his father's silent nudge and volunteered to go to the Middle East!

A heavy sense of reality followed. What about Elta, Lois, his work, and A. N. Wolf? Lois Wolf Miller was sixteen months old. What kind of a man leaves his family and his job for a foreign land he has never seen to serve people he has never met?

How would he break the news to Elta and her parents? With D. D.'s support, Orie did just that. A sense of disbelief followed Orie's announcement. Elta's shock was tempered by her sense of Orie's call and their many conversations about Christian service. As she would do many more times, she acquiesced and tried to make his call hers too. To his father-in-law, A. N. Wolf, Orie's abandonment was senseless and irresponsible.

Chapter 4
Sacrifice for a Noble Cause: 1919–1920

*"During the world's reconstruction period
we can conscientiously help, and act positively,
showing the world the sincerity and consistency
of our [Christian] profession."*

On January 25, 1919, only twenty-one days after Orie volunteered at the Lancaster meeting of the Mennonite Relief Commission for War Sufferers, Elta, A. N. Wolf, and Elta's friend Martha Martin stood on Pier 62 in New York Harbor and watched the USS *Pensacola* disappear over the Atlantic horizon. Orie was on his way to Beirut, Syria (now Lebanon), along with eight other Mennonite volunteers who were serving at the call of the commission. It would be fifteen months before he returned home. No one could know that this was the first of more than sixty transatlantic crossings for Orie.[1]

World War I had ended in November 1918, though the Treaty of Versailles would not be signed until June 28, 1919. While the Allies claimed victory and Germany admitted defeated, there could be no real winners in a war that claimed twenty million lives. Those who marched off to war were initially thrilled with thoughts of gallantry and adventure. Those who lived to return home did so battered and disillusioned.

The United States, with about three hundred thousand casualties, emerged from the war in a position of strength. Exports of weapons and war matériel to Britain pulled the country out of a serious economic recession. In contrast to European nations in ruin, the American economy was the strongest in the world, and its international political prominence had no equal.

Mennonites, having profited from war production, donated a portion of their profits to relief organizations. The Relief Commission, looking for fields of service, found two organizations prepared to receive funds and send volunteers to war-torn regions: the American Friends Service Committee and the Near East Relief (NER). Mennonites were drawn to the Middle East because it was the land of the Bible: the home of the patriarchs; the promised land of refuge for the Hebrews delivered from Egyptian bondage; the land where Jesus walked; Jerusalem, the city of Pentecost; and Antioch, where the followers of Jesus were first called "Christians." By the time Orie and his colleagues were settled in Beirut, Syria, Mennonites had contributed about $463,000 to the Mennonite Relief Commission. Orie was among the thirty-one volunteers assigned to the Middle East. Fifty others served in France under the Friends (Quakers). Still others served in Austria, Germany, and Eastern Europe.[2]

The needs in the Middle East were enormous, a result of the Ottoman Empire's ethnic cleansing policy toward its Armenian and Christian citizens. During the war, between 1915 and 1918, the empire systematically killed more than one million and left a million more orphaned and destitute, scattered across the Middle East. Alarmed by the atrocities, Henry Morgenthau, U.S. ambassador to the Ottoman Empire, urged Americans to action in 1915. In a matter of days, a group of distinguished New Yorkers—civic, business, and religious leaders—founded the agency that came to be known as Near East Relief.[3] By the time the Mennonite relief workers arrived in Beirut, the NER had raised $33,387,439.80—including nearly half a million dollars from Mennonites.[4]

The Mennonites aboard the *Pensacola* were among the hundreds of volunteers who went to the Middle East to relieve the suffering of Armenians. Seven of the nine were young men like Orie: C. L. (Chris) Graber from Wayland, Iowa; Silas Hertzler from Newport News, Virginia; Ezra Deter from Morrison, Illinois; David Zimmerman from Ephrata, Pennsylvania; and the Stoltzfus brothers, Frank and William, from Lima, Ohio. Of the seven, only Orie was married. In addition, Aaron Loucks, Relief Commission chair, and his assistant, William A. Derstine, were on a special assignment to find a field of service for Mennonite

The first nine Mennonite relief workers, Near East Relief, 1919. Orie Miller is standing in the center, fourth from left. MCC.

volunteers. The Mennonites would serve under the NER or the Red Cross, but would be safely isolated as a self-contained unit. The nine Mennonites on the *Pensacola* were among the forty-two relief workers on board. Passengers and crew numbered 150.

The *Pensacola* was one thousand miles from New York in late January when Elta penned her first letter to Orie, thought he would not see it until mid-March. Orie's surprise announcement on January 6 had caught Elta and the Wolfs off guard, but they had three weeks before his departure to adjust to the new reality. By the time they parted at Pier 62, Elta was a willing partner in Orie's mission. There had never been a question about whether Orie and Elta would give their lives in service; it was a matter of when and where. Elta wrote of their "perfect understanding" of the mission—"trusting, loving, and believing in each other as we do, makes this separation much easier for me. . . . We both felt it your duty to go and now we want to bear it bravely, although it will be hard at times."[5]

A. N. Wolf had a harder time coming to terms with Orie's decision. It complicated his work at the shoe factory, but he had little choice. He could do it for a while, until Orie's wanderlust wore off and he returned to his senses. Meanwhile, A. N. was looking after Elta. He paid her expenses to travel to New York City to see Orie off. At home, the Wolfs often ate at Elta's house, since Anna, the maid, helped care for Lois and made meals. Elta's chickens were laying well, and the sale of eggs was almost enough to pay for groceries. In the community, Orie's mission was attracting a lot of attention. "People are very sympathetic and kind," Elta wrote. "After church on Sunday night quite a few people talked so nice to me."

Elta reported in a February letter that Orie's brother Ernest was also bound for Beirut. Among the nine in the second wave of Mennonite volunteers were Ernest; Jesse Smucker of Smithville, Ohio; Paul V. Snyder of Plainview, Texas; and Leon Myers of Lancaster, Pennsylvania.[6] Elta, meanwhile, wondered whether she should train as a nurse. It would prepare her for a mission assignment, but she was reluctant to leave Lois.[7]

On board the *Pensacola*, Orie began his diary, recording his observations about his traveling companions and the crew, about what he was reading in preparation for service in the Middle East, and a continued certainty of his call to go there. As he would do regularly for the next fifteen months, Orie enclosed a copy of his daily diary in letters to Elta, family, and friends. When it had made its rounds, Elta sent the diary to Vernon Smucker, Mennonite Publishing House (MPH) editor at Scottdale, Pennsylvania, for publication in the *Christian Monitor*, other Mennonite church papers, and the *Sugar Creek Budget* in Ohio for Amish readers.

The mountains of Crete gave Orie his first-ever view of snowcapped mountains on the evening of February 18. Then the voyagers were treated to a spectacular Mediterranean sunset. Even though Orie was colorblind, he thought it the most beautiful sight he had ever seen. Soon they could see Mount Lebanon and the contrasting lower hills of Judea. That night those who were to be posted temporarily in Beirut received their first two months' allowances. Tomorrow they would see Beirut. With the destination so near, the Mennonite workers were "mightily concerned" about what they would encounter. Not yet the confident Orie of later years, he wrote, "We tremble to think of all that may be involved in the decisions that we as a group of inexperienced young men may make during the next few weeks."

CONDITIONS IN BEIRUT

On February 19, after twenty-six days on the Atlantic, the *Pensacola* dropped anchor in the port of Beirut. Until the five tons of relief supplies were unloaded, the volunteers had time to explore the city. Orie made note of camel caravans; emaciated children barely dressed, some crying of hunger; soldiers in uniform from many nations; and some well-dressed Syrians. Orie had never imagined he would see "such a mixed up motly" collection of people in a single city. And, of course, now the foreign North American Mennonites were added to the mix.

The volunteers were directed to the Red Cross headquarters where they learned that the NER and the Red Cross were partners in the relief efforts. At the Red Cross office they met Red Cross major James Nichol, chief of Syrian relief operations. Nichol had been an ordained educator under the Presbyterian Board of Foreign Missions in Tripoli, Syria. Until the war interrupted his work, he was superintendent over more than one hundred schools in the region.[8] Orie would quickly come to admire the major and learn from him how to organize and delegate work. The Mennonites agreed that evening that all except Loucks and Derstine would work temporarily with the Red Cross in Beirut. The two older emissaries would go on to Constantinople to arrange a permanent Mennonite field of service. The others, meanwhile, had chosen Orie and Silas Hertzler to be the channels of communication between the volunteers and the Red Cross.

The first task assigned to the Mennonite "boys" was to assemble Reo trucks and Ford and Chevrolet cars as they were lifted from the ship to the dock. "I am no mechanic," said Orie, "so I just did what I was told to do." Orie, who had as a youth on Cloverdale Farm learned the art of delegation, was

Orie in Near East Relief uniform, 1919.
Edward L. Miller.

now following orders: "I am just like a soldier now, Elta, others plan for me and I don't know just what happens an hour ahead." Orie admitted that he was "pretty helpless at first," but he was learning "a good deal in this kind of work that I should have known long ago."[9] Here he could not call on Uncle Ed Hostetler to do the manual tasks for him. In a few more days, Orie thought he would be able to assemble a complete auto by himself. Before Orie had the chance to prove his claim, Major Nichol issued new orders for which he was better suited: to help Lieutenant Bess check, organize, and inventory the relief supplies carried by the *Pensacola*. The cargo was placed helter-skelter in four warehouses. Bess had other things to do, so he put Orie in charge of organizing the warehouses. With Silas Hertzler, six Syrians, and an interpreter, Orie got to work. The next day, Orie had ten local workers and the following day, thirteen.

Until transferred elsewhere, all the men were engaged in transporting goods to various relief operations in the Beirut City District. David Zimmerman, unlike Orie, was adept with his hands and became a construction engineer. Ezra Deter continued working in transport; William Stoltzfus and Silas Hertzler were assigned to oversee orphanage work in Sidon on the coast, twenty miles south of Beirut;[10] Frank Stoltzfus became assistant director of an orphanage in Jerusalem, 150 miles south of Beirut; and Chris Graber was given the responsibility for a refugee camp and the industrial project in Aleppo in northern Syria, some 200 miles to the northeast.[11]

Every morning, a queue of women and children appeared at Red Cross headquarters for food or clothing. There seemed to be no end of need. In Beirut, where the imperial French and British were resented, Americans were welcome. It gave Orie "a peculiar feeling" to be respected just because he was American.

Lieutenant Bess gave Orie the additional task of dispatching supplies to Red Cross institutions beyond the city. As orientation to his new role, Orie accompanied the transport of freight to the various distribution points. First, he visited the Red Cross industrial shops at Keifer Shima, where he observed 750 women and girls at work, knitting, spinning silk, carding wool, making baskets, and sewing clothes. Many walked several miles morning and evening to earn fifteen cents per day. Daily, fifty more applied for work. Orie learned that in the month of February, the

The American Committee for Relief in the Near East poster (right) was based on the photograph of an Armenian woman and her children (left). Bain News Service and www.armenianpages.com.

Red Cross assisted twenty-five thousand people, a commentary on the great need.

The poverty and diseases were appalling. "Many have only patched up rags for clothes, some only gunny sacks," he wrote to Elta in February. "Some scratch for particles of food out of the dirt in the streets." Of all the diseases, skin diseases of the scalp were "the most hideous looking." Often, he observed "men picking the cooties out of their clothes. It gives me a creepy feeling . . . 7,000 miles from home."[12]

Across the seven thousand miles in Akron, Elta was lonely, imagining what might be happening to Orie and then "indulging in a little cry." Did Orie think her foolish? "Well I am as I am, as you used to say." To keep her company, her father sometimes spent the night at Elta's house. She was starting an accounting book "of my money matters, so [I] can show you when you come home—and also for my own convenience." Believing that a mission assignment for both her and Orie was on the horizon, Elta decided to attend the spring term at Bethany Bible School, a Church of the Brethren institution in Chicago. Knowing Orie would be pleased, and after consulting her parents, Elta joined sister-in-law Ruth Blosser Miller, wife of Orie's brother Ernest and a full-time Bethany student. Lois would stay with Orie's family on Cloverdale Farm.[13]

On the job in Beirut, Orie was irritable and impatient. Supplies he was to ship out were buried deep in warehouse stacks. He confessed to Elta that "when the natives work so slow[ly], I almost swear at them sometimes. . . . They couldn't understand me of course if I did, no more than I can [understand] them when they cuss me." A few days later, Orie hired and trained two Syrian bookkeepers to track the funds received and spent. About his own performance he wrote, "I know that my work on this job is appreciated."[14] Lieutenant Bess wanted to train Orie to take over his job—purchasing, storing, shipping, and distributing materials to Red Cross operations.

Orie observed that the Red Cross workers "smoke and swear [and] watch us peculiar Mennonites like hawks [to see] how we work, [and] how we treat the natives," who always "seem so slow, so careless, so dirty." Orie reminded himself that "Jesus lived among [such people] and loved them." The men who worked for Orie responded to his kindness. When they saw him anywhere in the city, they acknowledged him by waving. He was constantly mindful that the "church at home was depending on us." In addition to the expectations of the church were those of Elta: "When I think of you, your trust in me, your confidence that I'll make good here I have still an added reason for watching each word, thought and motion." He concluded his letter by admitting, "Sometimes I feel guilty when I think how I have left you, but I believe it was His will."[15]

Elta was not plagued by guilt, but she often felt "very sad" when thinking about the separation—she in Chicago, Lois in Middlebury, and Orie in far-off Beirut. On the other hand, when reading of conditions in the Middle East, Elta believed "that surely this sacrifice is made for a noble cause." She was also confident that Orie's service was "God's will." That did not remove her longing to be with Orie and to talk things over. She wished for faster transatlantic mail; after two months of separation, none of their many letters had arrived. "This is quite an experience to go through, perhaps it is good for me—at least it is a training in patience."[16]

THOUGHTS ABOUT FUTURE SERVICE

On March 16, the Mennonite workers in Beirut had front-row seats in a memorial service for the million or more Armenians massacred by the Turks in the recent war. They found themselves in "rather stately company" among French and English officers and Red Cross personnel. The ceremony was conducted in Armenian, except for an English-language description of the horrors suffered by the victims and an expression of gratitude for the civil and military assistance of the Allied nations.[17]

A few days later, the Beirut volunteers had reason to celebrate—finally, mail had arrived from home! Each received six or eight letters that had accumulated in New York before their overseas transit. Orie also felt a sense of satisfaction that the monthlong task of sorting, storing, and taking inventory of the *Pensacola* cargo was finished.[18]

Red Cross officials were also eager to know what the Mennonites were planning, since the agency was holding three "principal jobs" for them. The officials were expecting a shipment of a thousand cases of food and clothing soon, so they had to be ready to handle it. When the shipment from Egypt and the United States arrived a few days later, the volunteers and local workers transported everything to the warehouses. Orie had meanwhile worked up a new organizational system for the warehouses under his supervision.[19]

Near the end of March, Major Nichol called a conference of all Beirut personnel to lay out the future. By July 1, the Red Cross would transfer all relief work in Syria to Near East Relief. Major Nichol was to remain in charge, and most of the officers and workers would continue to do their current jobs under the NER. The Red Cross, however, would move to a new region. In the shuffling of assignments, Hertzler and the Stoltzfus brothers were dispatched north to Adana, a city by the Seyhan River in southern Turkey. Perhaps other Mennonite volunteers would follow.

Having now received the first of Elta's letters, Orie was pleased to learn that she was studying at Bethany. He had been thinking about future mission work in Beirut for both of them but then concluded it would be difficult to make a "long term impression," since the Presbyterian mission and the Red Cross were so well-established there. Orie thought the Red Cross "wasted too much money on fine hotel living, on equipment allowances, and on salaries for people who are not needed and do no work." The end of the war had left "immense sums of unspent money" in Red

Cross hands, and as a consequence they had become careless. Whatever their future assignments, Orie wanted Elta to come to Beirut to experience firsthand what he was describing in his letters. It would also be an opportunity for them to assess the city as a field of service.[20]

By the end of March, Elta was in Chicago taking sixteen hours of Bible and mission courses at Bethany Bible School. She enjoyed the company of her sister-in-law and fellow student Ruth Blosser Miller. Less enjoyable was leaving Lois with the Millers on Cloverdale Farm. As Elta was going, Lois was the one to offer comfort: "Don't cry, it is all right Mama."

In her March 24 letter to Orie, Elta included news of another shake-up at Goshen College. The Mennonite Board of Education was meeting that week to appoint a new president. D. D. Miller thought H. F. (Henry Frank) Reist would be chosen to replace India missionary George J. Lapp, who while on furlough in 1918 had replaced J. E. Hartzler. These round-robin presidential appointments, which would continue until the college closed in 1923, were an attempt to bring the school into line with church expectations. Further, Elta wrote, "I know some of the younger men of our church think that [they] do not have enough chance" to serve in leadership roles. They think the church is "not democratic enough and that a few men run [the] affairs of the church." What did Orie think? She also reported D. D.'s concern about the Mennonite volunteers serving in France under the Quakers: "They are changing their ideas, becoming free thinkers—entirely too liberal." Elta believed she could see evidence of that in a recent letter from Orie's brother Trueman, one of the "Mennonite boys" in France.[21]

A MISSION TO RUSSIA?

In Beirut, Orie was now in charge of Red Cross warehouses and all goods received and shipped. He was part of the network of support for five thousand orphans in the city. While the work was going well, Orie was dismayed by the long silence of Aaron Loucks and William Derstine, who had not kept the Beirut volunteers apprised of their progress in Constantinople. On their way home they suddenly appeared in Beirut, as though it were an afterthought. The two had been entirely unsuccessful in Constantinople. Although the NER had assured them of assistance, the New York office had not prepared the way with the Constantinople office. There would be no Mennonite relief unit. Orie was disappointed, but not surprised; he had "felt it coming." Still, the news "took the snap out of the boys."[22] He felt a bit sorry for Loucks and Derstine, having to report their failure to the church at home. Orie knew that the Lancaster Conference would be especially unhappy, since the promise of a separate Mennonite unit seemed a safe step in their cautious entry into a foreign field of service.

Major Nichol, however, was pleased that the Mennonites were staying in Beirut. He also admitted that Loucks and Derstine had "not been treated fairly." The New York office bore responsibility for their "bunglesome mismanagement" of the whole Mennonite venture.[23] Orie also learned that the British did not allow anyone into territory they had not already occupied, and in Constantinople there were too many workers with too little to do. More than anything, Orie feared that the home churches would be less inclined to support the current relief work or any future mission.

Orie had begun to dream about possibilities for service beyond the Middle East. Confident that the church at home was ready to add a third field to its existing missions in India and South America, he was thinking about Russia. The 1917 Bolshevik Revolution made it impossible to enter Russia now, but surely it would open in time. To Elta he wrote, "I want to obey the call and see this thing thru, God helping and I know you want to do it also." As Orie would do so often in the future, he was "praying out a probable plan of procedure." He could hardly wait for his brother Ernest and Jesse Smucker to arrive so he could discuss the mission with them, since he believed he could not "take any of the present boys" into his confidence.[24] Orie soon sent a "confidential" letter to Ernest so he too could dream and pray. Three days later, on April 9, Orie sent his proposal for relief and mission work in Russia to the Mennonite Relief Commission for War Sufferers in Scottdale, Pennsylvania, and to the Mennonite Board of Missions and Charities in Elkhart, Indiana.[25]

In his cover letter, Orie wrote of the American Mennonite Church and gave a rationale for maintaining the church's witness of service:

No one will deny that the spirit of giving and sacrifice manifest during the past year was encouraging. Many gave more freely because of our unpopular attitude on the war question. But there is no reason why this spirit cannot be enthused by new stimuli, nor why the church should go back to the old way of doing things. During the world's reconstruction period we can conscientiously help, and act positively, showing the world the sincerity and consistency of our profession.[26]

In Chicago, Elta had received the first of Orie's letters and diaries. She would keep them in the candy box Orie had given her in New York. Elta cautioned Orie not to "work too hard—really I mean it, it seems you always work about as hard as you possibly can, no matter where you are." But then, that is what she expected of Orie and what she liked about him. While Orie was inclined to hard work, Elta was softhearted and generous. "Money has a queer way of leaving one, just when you need it most. I am too sympathetic (that's me all over)." She had felt sorry for fellow student Harold Esch, who was trying to win fifty dollars by selling magazine subscriptions. "I paid no attention at first but as none of the others cared, I finally took pity and am now minus seventy-five cents."[27]

Orie confided to Elta that taking over Lieutenant Bess's job was a large undertaking, but he was happy that his past few years of experience with Miller Hess had prepared him well for it. His characteristic thrift and proficiency were evident. Since taking on the new responsibilities, Orie thought his efficient management would save the Red Cross about $1,700 a year.[28]

Orie was beginning to feel more and more at home in Beirut. He regularly attended a large Protestant worship service at the American College chapel, a congregation largely made up of occupying British soldiers and led by army chaplains. "I can worship there better than any other place even though I don't agree with all they do and say." Attending such a service in Lancaster County would be impossible, he told Elta. His comfort with ecumenical relations and his broader worldview had begun at Goshen College. Now he was learning to know some "really great" Presbyterians and was spending time with "a man who is considered to be the greatest Arabic scholar in the world." Orie reserved his greatest accolades for Major Nichol, whom he considered "one of the most talented and finest men I ever saw."[29]

The Presbyterian missionaries had noticed Orie too and had begun to talk to him about serving in their mission. American Protestant mission work in Syria had been established as early as 1819. The Presbyterian Board of Foreign Missions, formed by the union of two

U.S. Presbyterian bodies in 1870, took on responsibility for the Syria mission as well as for extensive missions across the Middle East. The Beirut mission was founded in 1833 as one of four main stations that collectively operated sixty-three "outstations" and several "substations." In addition to evangelistic work, the Presbyterians engaged in educational and medical outreach. Among the educational ventures was the Syrian Protestant College, which in 1920 became the American University of Beirut.[30]

One missionary was eager to talk to Orie after reading up on Mennonites in an encyclopedia and in *Tillie, the Mennonite Maid*. Orie griped to Elta that *Tillie, the Mennonite Maid*, a harsh, clichéd 1904 novel of Lancaster Mennonites, "seems to have preceded us everywhere." He had seen it on the *Pensacola* and in a missionary's library in Sidon. Maybe that was why people "looked at us rather cross-eyed at first." If we do nothing else, "I hope we may live down the wrong impression of our people created by this book." Orie was also "disgusted" by the inefficiency and waste of the NER, which was now taking control of Red Cross relief operations. He could see the problem as well as its cause; the agency was squandering its people, money, and supplies because it had no "definite policy."[31] In his later work with instructions and projects, he was always careful to create "definite policies."

Coincidentally, in Chicago, Elta went to see the play version of *Tillie, the Mennonite Maid* at the Blackstone Theatre. A. N. Wolf, in town on shoe business, invited Elta and Ruth Miller to dine at Hotel La Salle, where he was staying, and then took them to the show. Elta did not think it was wrong to attend a theatre as long as one didn't make a habit of it. When she heard *Tillie* was playing, Elta was disgusted, yet she was also "curious to know just what kind of people they make us out to be." She was not surprised by its portrayal of Lancaster Mennonites, but it fed into her own negative thoughts: "I am inclined lately to wonder about our wearing bonnets—whether after all we accomplish much good by doing so." Orie need not worry, though, that she would be wearing a stylish hat when he returned—"Oh no!" But on the streets of Chicago, their bonnets made Elta and Ruth feel conspicuous and self-conscious. "I often wonder wherein the power of good plain clothes lies."[32]

Elta observed at the Chicago mission, where she was teaching Sunday school, that plain clothes hindered the mission's success. "You would be surprised how really few members are here considering the [twenty-six] years the mission" has existed.[33] Changes were coming, however. Ruth's father had sent her a copy of a petition signed by every member of the New Stark Mennonite Church in Allen County, Ohio, against wearing the bonnet.[34] When Orie answered this letter, he said he would love to be part of a congregation like New Stark.[35]

In Chicago, Uncle Clarence Hess joined A. N. Wolf, expecting to clinch a $100,000 order from Linsheimer Stores. Before they left Chicago, Sears, Roebuck & Company entertained the Akron salesmen in the company's private dining room. After Chicago, the two were going on to Milwaukee, Pittsburgh, and Harrisburg. Hess and Wolf were also thinking about the future. What will Orie do when he returns from Beirut? Miller Hess was doing so well that A. N. wanted to buy another shoe factory in Denver, Pennsylvania. But he would not add a second factory to the business unless Orie came back to Akron.

ORIE PROMOTED

When Emir Faisal, the crown prince of Arabia, visited Beirut on April 30, 1919, the city welcomed him with rockets, cannon fire, firecrackers, banners, parades, and "yelling." Emir Faisal had represented Arab interests at the Paris Peace Conference of 1919, with T. E. Lawrence "of Arabia" as interpreter. Over Emir Faisal's protests, the victors of the Great War enacted the secret Sykes-Picot Agreement of 1916 that anticipated the defeat of the Ottoman Empire, and the Balfour Declaration (November 2, 1917) that promised a Jewish state. France and Great Britain divided the Arab states between themselves; the French became the overlords of Syria and the newly created state of Lebanon, including the Beirut District.[36] The artificial boundaries drawn without regard for the religious and ethnic identities of the people created the political instability still so evident a century later.

While the city celebrated the crown prince's arrival, Orie was working in the warehouse as usual. Congested city streets complicated his work by making the delivery of goods impossible. Of greater interest to Orie was the news in the *Middlebury Independent* (which had finally reached him, weeks later) that Elta and Lois had been to Cloverdale, and that Lois remained with the Millers while Elta went on to Chicago. It gave Orie "a funny feeling" to read about what Elta and Lois were doing in a public newspaper.

On May 23, Orie received by letter his formal appointment as quarter-master to the stores of Beirut District. Major James Nichol, deputy commissioner for Syria, signed the order. The new title was a military designation for the chief base supply officer, having the rank of captain or major. Quartermaster Miller would now buy all supplies foreign or domestic, sign all shipping orders, and oversee weekly expenditures of $3,000 to $5,000 for supplies from the local markets. He was quite confident that by making these purchases personally, he could save the agency money. To Elta he wrote that he did not share this "dope" with everyone, but only with her, since she was interested in everything he did.[37]

In addition to giving Orie more responsibility, Major Nichol was asking Orie's counsel. Of the newly arrived Mennonite volunteers, whom would Orie recommend for service in Beirut? Nichol was by now impressed with Mennonite volunteers, because unlike the others, "they willingly do anything that needs to be done, no matter whether it was in line with what we thought we should or should not do."[38] Orie hoped the church at home would realize the good and important work Mennonites were doing, even if they were under the administration of another organization. Despite Orie's wish that Chris Graber be assigned to Beirut, Graber was sent to Aleppo: "I like him very much and will miss him."[39]

A long queue of Armenians waiting for examinations at an Aleppo eye clinic. David Mann.

Though the two met as students at Goshen College, it was their shared experience in the Middle East that cemented a lifelong friendship.

Orie continued to ponder mission work in India or Russia, believing that future mission work for him and Elta would become clear in the next few months. "We have shown our willingness to be used and are now waiting upon Him to reveal to us His will," he wrote Elta. Yet despite Orie's enlarged duties in Beirut and his dreams of Russia, he was discouraged. "This trip has fed me up on all ideas of becoming a great or important personage. . . . I shall be perfectly content to slip into some inconspicuous corner and there do what little good I am capable of."[40]

Responding to Elta's reluctance to wear a bonnet on the streets of Chicago, Orie wrote back in June: "You know Elta, I haven't seen a bonnet for so long, I think I'd almost hug any women I'd see wearing one." Then he drew a parallel to the uniform he wore in Beirut. "I am proud of the fact . . . that I am a U.S. citizen. I can't go into any shop or store unless I hear someone saying, 'Americana?'" They identify me "by my helmet, style of clothes, and talk. Why should we be any more ashamed of our dress as Christians?" On the other hand, he saw no virtue in the bonnet over the plain hat such as most of the missionary women in Beirut wore. Recalling Ruth Blosser Miller's home congregation, he added, "Still I would like to be a member of the Mennonite church that first unanimously petitions to have the hat substitute for the bonnet."[41]

Again, Orie asked Elta to come to Beirut for several months so she could share his experience and so they could travel home together. He had been saving money from his $25 monthly allowance—$100 so far. If Miller Hess would declare a directors' salary as last year, he mused, it would more than pay for Elta's $800 ticket and souvenirs. "Maybe your father could come too and he could see about doing business here." As for saving money, every week he was saving the NER money. He was negotiating lower prices in the market and he was buying more himself, so that he could cut the commission of the regular buyer. But the work was taking its toll: "All of it together [puts] a nervous strain on me, especially coupled with the uncertainty of the future and my separation from my two loved ones."[42]

Elta, who was back in Akron after completing her term of study in Chicago, wished to see Beirut but was reluctant to leave three-year-old Lois again. Elta found her single-parenting role difficult. "I am doing the best I know how to train her well, but she surely needs a strict boss. . . . She is very dear and all that, but oh, she does want her own way, and if she can't have it she will throw herself down and scream and kick." Elta told Orie how she left Lois with Anna for a few hours and when she returned, she "found both Mamma and Lois crying." Anna's "nervous temperament" made it difficult for her to handle much stress, and Lois's demands were a challenge.[43]

COMMANDING OFFICER AND DIRECTOR OF BEIRUT DISTRICT

Orie had challenges of a different sort; he was now buying all food supplies for the mess hall at the American College, two hospitals, and an orphanage, about 150 people in all. With frugality ever in mind, he could save more money by buying supplies in larger quantities. He was also learning to know "nearly all the biggest wholesale merchants of Beirut," some of whom were very wealthy. While his success was pleasing his Beirut superiors, he knew he was failing others. Elta's parents "wanted and deserved a different kind of son-in-law." Any decision he and Elta would make that deviated from the past four years "will not be just as they wished." He was "very, very sorry about this . . . but I want to do right at any cost." In an echo of his floundering for direction at Goshen College, he lamented, "It is so hard to know just in what direction one's duty lies."[44]

In Boston on business, A. N. Wolf was thinking about Orie's future too. Writing to Orie on United States Hotel stationery, he reported on shoe sales. Then to the point: Orie was missed very much at home and church as well as at the factory. Now that his term in Beirut was half over, the company needed to know whether he was planning to return to the shoe company. "You can imagine how much work falls on Clarence [Hess] and me, and how important it is to have understudy's [sic] to take our places in case of sickness or death. For this reason we are very anxious to know whether you will come back and stay with us or not." Wolf said he didn't want to influence his son-in-law one way or the other, and he supposed he could not even if he was so inclined. But they had to have someone to step in if needed, because "if Miss Gehman would get married or Clarence should get sick it would put Miller Hess in *a heck of a fix*! Don't you think so?"[45]

Orie's response was not long in coming, nor was it what Father Wolf and Clarence Hess wanted to hear: They should replace him at the factory, because he was going to the mission field. Orie was feeling quite certain of his future. To Elta he wrote, "To your father, I realize, the decision will mean most by far, both in a business way and in the home. I hope he does not regret having sent you to Goshen where you met me, but I would not blame him very much if he did."[46]

A few weeks after his latest promotion, Orie's work was again enlarged. He was given Captain Doolittle's job of hiring and firing clerks and employees, "fixing" wages, checking payrolls, approving requisitions for clothing distribution, prescriptions for medicines, and handling mail and telegrams. Orie hired a pharmacist and moved the pharmacy into one of the warehouses. He now planned to spend four hours at the office and four hours in the warehouse, although his days were often longer than eight hours. If he could hire good local help beyond the current number of eleven, he believed he could handle the work. He underplayed his role when he told Elta, "The whole bunch makes quite an organization for one dumb Pennsylvania Dutchman to handle, especially after being here only five months."[47]

With his new responsibilities came a new title of commanding officer, and as such he was to sign all communications to the military authorities. The irony of signing orders as "CO" did not escape him. He was at the same time a commanding officer and a conscientious objector. "Perhaps the two indicates inconsistency," Orie wrote, "but I am glad Major Nichol trusts me as he does, and [I] want to work as hard as I can." The Mennonite volunteers were amused to discover Major Nichol's early impression of them: "*Pensacola* has come and left again, ten men have been left as workers but they don't seem to be our kind." Orie concluded, "If our stay here and [our] work puts a favorable stamp on [us] . . . in the minds of those with whom we [work] I feel the year has been worthwhile."[48]

In Akron, Elta and Lois moved to one of the Wolf farms on the west side of town in August of 1919. It was a good move for Lois, who "likes it so much. At home she runs away." On Sunday evening, Elta told Orie, she was with their "usual bunch." In the morning at Ephrata, Amos Horst had "preached a real good sermon, but then he finished it by giving a *lengthy* talk on plain clothes." She admitted she may be "so far in the wrong," but she found the detailed admonition "disgusting." They were good friends with Amos and Nora, and Elta did not want Amos to feel bad, but she didn't think the lecture was called for. She was sure Amos had her in mind, because "I wear my cape to teach Sunday school, but never other times." In a final note, she reported that D. D. had sent $30 as interest on the $500 loan Orie had given him.[49]

Orie was aware that the challenges of his work and the influence of his mentor, Major Nichol, were affecting his style and temperament. "Elta, I believe I am becoming more fussy about things. You know you always deplored the fact that I had not been enough so." Orie was sensitive about how others perceived him in his elevated status. His job had become rather "ticklish" since he was now directing the work of a dozen other Americans. Some were older than Orie and were quite certain they knew "more about running affairs" than he did. Several were clearly jealous. He told the major he did not want to lose friends because of his role. He did not flaunt his authority; as he told Elta, "My policy has been to take up the new duties as quietly as possible." Consequently, they would go first to the major with questions, and "invariably he refers them to me, advising them that I am in charge of the work here."[50]

The major was now consulting Orie on every detail, "not even raising a single salary without asking me about it." Orie wished he had A. N. Wolf to handle the finances and set up proper accounting practices. A "favorable stamp" was not long in coming in the form of even larger duties. In the fall, Major Nichol appointed Orie director of Beirut District, and as such, he was an assistant to Major Nichol "in his work of all Syria." Orie now had an administrative Syrian staff of seventy on the payroll. To fill a gap, Orie also became temporary cashier of the NER in Syria.

For Elta, the future was still uncertain. "Of course I know [Papa] asked you to tell [him] what you expect to do about the shoe company," Elta wrote. "I think he can hardly believe it [but] do not think he will say anything to anyone about it. He said tonight it would break his heart if we would leave him."[51] A. N. Wolf had not yet told Clarence Hess that Orie was not planning to come back to the company.

Perhaps A. N. Wolf was recalling Orie's earlier indecision about moving to Akron. Once again, Wolf was in an awkward situation. He and Anna did not want to prevent Orie and Elta from following a call to missions, yet they were "not in full sympathy." This put Elta in an awkward

Relief workers by the Sea of Galilee, October 1919 (*left to right*: B. Frank Stoltzfus, Ernest E. Miller, William Stoltzfus, Silas Hertzler, Jesse Smucker, David Zimmerman, Amos M. Eash, C. L. [Chris] Graber, and Orie Miller). MC USA Archives–Goshen.

place too. "Not that they aren't good to me . . . but the strain and uncertainty" of an unknown future was difficult. The sooner they decided, the better. "I would want a little training somewhere along the line of medicine and nursing." Elta once again had divided loyalties. "You know I am in sympathy with you in the work, and that I would be willing to go with you." But of one thing she was certain: "Before making our plans so sure we should talk it over with our parents and decide when we are all together."[52] When Orie was tempted to make a decision about their future while in Beirut, Elta repeatedly reminded him they must speak face-to-face.

A GROWING CALL TO MISSIONS

While Elta, Lois, and the Wolfs were eagerly anticipating his return in January 1920, Orie decided to extend his stay for two reasons. First, it would be better to stay until the focus of NER work shifted from relief to orphan care in mid-February. Secondly, he wanted to pursue his special interest in Russia by going to Constantinople and then to Odessa, perhaps by March 1. Knowing he would disappoint his Akron family, he wrote, "I am very sorry if you are displeased with the plan, but as I see it I would rather delay going into mission work by six months or a year than change these plans."[53] The priority of work and mission over family continued to characterize Orie's future.

Elta wrote, warning about their financial status. The company's promise of a $1,000 directors' bonus would not be given, after all. Their profits were less than expected, and Clarence did not think "Charlie," a new director, deserved a bonus. He was not pulling his weight. Elta was worried: "It is almost appalling when we think of what we have lost financially, this year." But also, true to form, Elta followed the concern with an affirmation: "I do not regret that you went into the work you did."[54] Elta also worried about Orie's safety amid newspaper reports of continued threats of war, since the Treaty of Versailles had not yet been ratified.

Reflecting on the sacrifice Elta was making in support of his mission, Orie wrote, "I know that not one woman in hundreds would allow her home to be broken up as ours has been." When he returned home, Orie promised, he would "be a truer and a better husband to you for it." Nevertheless, he informed his waiting family that he would serve seven weeks beyond his yearlong commitment, which he called his "second mile plan." He also reported that Acting President Bliss of American College of Beirut had made him an official offer to join the faculty and manage the college's business department. The opportunity prompted a reflective moment. He acknowledged that his life had been relatively easy so far, from being able to support himself through college through being given a home and position when he married Elta. In Syria, where he could have been placed in an isolated, primitive post, as was Ernest, with "peculiar old maids and cranky bachelors," Orie was given many advantages: regular mail, many comforts, coworkers at least "nominally congenial," and most important, Major James Nichol, a worthy role model. In reality, "as of yet I have made no real sacrifice of any kind." But surely that would come in the future. He was certain that he and Elta would not choose the easiest path available.

Orie's call to missions continued to grow stronger, and his plans became more specific: "I feel now I should come home early next summer," he wrote to Elta, "so that . . . we could leave again some time in the fall. . . . I am convinced more than ever of the intense need of both the church and the world for what the Christian missionary enterprise alone can contribute." He wanted to be "sensible and recognize" their obligations to the Wolfs, "but after thinking and praying it over hundreds of times as I have since over here, I feel we can and ought to spend the next ten, fifteen or even more years in that service."[55]

The year 1920 brought Orie even more opportunities. NER officials offered him a five-year term as director of all NER operations in the Syria-Aleppo District. He would be responsible for the care of eight to nine thousand orphans, direct the work of up to fifty Americans, and manage a monthly budget of $100,000. This was bigger than anything his "own church" could offer, but he assured Elta that he was not seriously considering this offer, because "I am still pretty much of a Mennonite."[56] William Jessup asked Orie to seriously consider mission work for the Presbyterians. And then there was the offer to join the American College of Beirut. Could Orie not be happy in Beirut?

On January 25, the one-year anniversary of his departure from New York Harbor, Orie fondly recalled the "memorable prayer service" in the Albert Hotel on the previous night with Elta, A. N. Wolf, and Martha Martin. The time seemed short when he thought of the work in Syria, but much too long to be separated from Elta and Lois. As for Elta's comment about the money they had lost, Orie responded: "Sometimes too I am almost appalled at the financial difference this year makes to us." Then surprisingly, he confessed his greatest weakness: "You know how I love money tremendously, probably it presents greater temptations to me than anything else. I get almost afraid of the temptation sometimes." For that reason, Orie was thankful for their current sacrifice for the cause of humanity.

By this time, Orie had given up the idea of going to Russia, because "for some unknown reasons, a few of the [Mennonite] boys . . . in France, are almost openly snubbing us out here." Orie had earlier speculated that the "hostility" resulted from the attitude of Mennonites at home, who were "plainly disappointed" by the attitude of the boys in France but were "everywhere . . . well pleased" with the NER volunteers. He could not understand the hostility, because all the workers in the Middle East bore "only goodwill" to those in France.[57]

In October 1919, the Mennonite Relief Commission had sent A. J. Miller, J. Roy Allgyer, and A. E. Hiebert to investigate possibilities for relief work in other parts of Europe. They explored Berlin, Leipzig, Dresden, Prague, Vienna, and in South Russia, Odessa and Kherson.[58] Whether the commission had decided on this exploration before Orie suggested it in his April proposal is not clear. In any case, Orie was not consulted. "They evidently consider Russia their find," so Orie was going to back off and do nothing to contribute to the apparent hostility. "Given the terrible need in Russia, it will be so sad if conflicts keep us from meeting that need."[59]

Earlier, Orie had been far more optimistic that cooperation in relief efforts such as that in the Near East would create unity at home. To Vernon Smucker he had written, "I feel that the various elements in the church who have in the past not always understood each other, will be drawn together in work such as they have never done before." Now, instead of dreaming about Russia, Orie turned his attention toward home. Little did he know how much Russia would become part of his life and ministry.

RETURNING HOME

In March 1920, Chris Graber joined Orie in Beirut. He assisted Orie in supervising the inventory of equipment and supplies on hand, and completed final weekly and monthly financial reports. The numbers showed that during the month of December, Orie had taken in $30,000 and spent $25,000. With Major Nichol, Orie made a tour of all facilities and projects, and the two assigned final responsibilities to other staff members. On the last day, Nichol sent his own stenographer to Orie's office to help produce the reports. When Orie left the office at four o'clock for the last time on March 7, six typists were still at work.

Major and Mrs. Nichol hosted a final tea. Then, on March 8, the Nichol family and all the Beirut workers accompanied Orie and Chris Graber to the harbor where their ship was waiting. The farewell on the pier was a scene Orie said he would never forget. If the words and emotions were any indication, Orie would be sorely missed in Beirut. Gifts for Orie included a gold watch.[60]

An NER interoffice memo informed Elta that finally Orie was on his way home. After arriving in Venice on the British steamship *Dalmatia*, they expected to spend ten days in Venice and two weeks in Switzerland, France, and Italy, and then leave France for New York about April 20. On the *Dalmatia*, Graber and Orie had first-class cabins. Orie liked Graber very much and found him a "splendid travel companion," even though Graber had not been well for some time. While crossing the Mediterranean Sea, the voyagers started a "systematic course" of readings, which they read audibly: medieval history, two novels, and Shelly's poems. Orie liked Shelly's verse, "I suppose because his mystical expressions agree so well with my own feelings sometimes."[61]

In Langnau, Switzerland, the travelers found lodging with Graber's cousin Jean Widmer. On April 4, a Sunday afternoon, Miller and Graber went to the home of Samuel Nussbaumer in Basel where they met three Russian Mennonites who told of the desperate suffering of their people in the Ukraine and elsewhere. The three men were part of the *Studienkommission,* a delegation on its way to North America to plead for an inter-Mennonite emigration and relief effort to help alleviate the dreadful suffering in Russia. North American Mennonites would hear a great deal more from this Russian delegation.

On April 5, Orie and Graber made their way through Europe and boarded *Le France* at Le Havre, France. The first-class accommodations were the best Orie had seen anywhere. Five days, 3,185 miles, and one major storm later, *Le France* docked in New York Harbor. Orie had been gone fifteen long months—the twelve-month assignment plus three more months of his "second mile plan" to ensure an orderly transfer of his responsibilities in Beirut.

SOMETHING OF A CELEBRITY

At home, Orie found himself something of a celebrity. In the next sixteen weeks, he spoke eighteen times to audiences from Akron to Middlebury, Indiana, and from from Knoxville, Tennessee, to Ocean Grove, New Jersey. His diaries, letters, and articles for the church press had made his a household name. He also had opportunity to speak to other audiences, but when invited by the NER to speak to other groups, Orie said, as he would so often in the future, that his first obligation was to the congregations "of our own church."

Orie was never eloquent. He gained a hearing not for the manner of his speaking, but for his message. In time, he developed his own vocabulary, which his first biographer called "Orieisms" and "Millerese." Sometimes his language was cryptic; at other times, he wrote endless sentences. Having earned an English major at Goshen College did not prevent Orie from inventing his own unorthodox semantics.[62] (For a sampling, see appendix A.)

His public speaking in Lancaster Conference churches raised the issue of the plain coat. At Groffdale, Noah Mack invited Orie to speak from the pulpit, so he could be seen and heard by the large audience. After the service, Mack told Orie that he was causing a problem for conference leaders. "The people want to hear, yet your attire violates our standards." Orie understood the problem, but he had a problem of his own. He had to think of his business and the retailers to whom he sold shoes. For this, his business suit was more appropriate. Would Mack recommend wearing two suits—a business suit for work and a plain suit for church? "Well," answered Mack, "you have to start somewhere."[63] Orie was not ready to start then and there. Given his ecumenical relief work in Beirut, he may have been even less inclined than before to adopt Lancaster standards.

Orie's Beirut experience had shaped him in ways he could not have anticipated. He had told Elta that as quartermaster, commanding officer, and director of Beirut District relief efforts, "many unique and baffling problems" came to his attention every day. As a result, "I am learning to think more clearly, and decide more positively. I am almost shocked sometimes at the quickness in which I make very important decisions. It must be done, or others simply pile in and the work gets clogged."[64]

The decisive Orie had been born. His snap, on-the-spot decisions characterized his future work. Even his disposition may have changed: "I have even learned to get real cross when necessary. I don't believe you'd know me if you would step into the office at times," he had written to Elta. "I don't want to brag for I do make a fearful number of mistakes, but I am developing along a few lines I think where I was weak before."[65]

Aside from sharpening his administrative skills under the guiding hand of Major James Nichol, Orie had caught a larger vision of the world. It was a world of suffering caused by a devastating war that had engulfed the world. Amidst the ashes of that war, Orie participated in bringing a measure of relief by feeding the hungry, clothing the naked, and caring for the stranger. Such service had been embedded in Mennonite theology and practice since the beginning of the Anabaptist movement.

But Orie had also learned in Beirut that Mennonites were not the only ones who had a heart for such ministries. The thirty Mennonites who served in Syria, Turkey, and Palestine were only a small part of a larger interfaith and international relief effort in the Middle East. He had worked alongside Islamic Syrians, sung and prayed with American Presbyterians, bargained with Egyptian merchants, and negotiated with British military officers. In Beirut, Orie's ecumenical and global impulses, if not sparked, were fanned into flame.

Chapter 5
Terrible Beyond Description: 1920–1921

"I am too close to all this misery and suffering to talk much about it, my mind is all a daze. I have thot nothing, dreamt nothing it seems for weeks . . . but poor, starving, sick miserable humanity."

Amid speaking engagements and shoe sales (yes, Orie was selling shoes again), Middle East relief work was ever on Orie's mind and agenda, even as his passion for Russia was rekindled. Having won the confidence of Major James H. Nichol in Beirut and NER general secretary C. V. Vickery in New York, Orie was helping recruit young Mennonites for NER work in Syria and Turkey. In recruitment, Orie was careful, and in the case of one young couple, immovable. Nellie Miller, who was already serving in Constantinople, was eager to have Cleo Mann, her fiancé, join her in Beirut. C. W. Fowle, NER managing director of Beirut District, sent an urgent request for Mann to New York, Scottdale, and Akron. Cleo was eager to serve, but Orie believed him too young and refused to bend, to the great disappointment of both Nellie and Cleo.[1]

Orie also worked with Wilbur Thomas of the American Friends Service Committee to secure U.S. visas for the Russian Mennonite *Studienkommission*, or study commission. The *Studienkommission* was formed by Mennonites in South Russia to represent all Russian Mennonites. By coincidence, Orie and Chris Graber, on their way home from Beirut in April 1920, had met three of the four delegates in Basel,

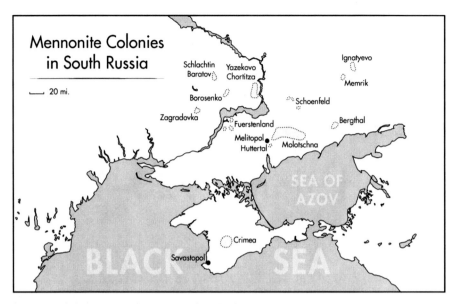

Mennonite colonies in South Russia. Reuben Graham.

Switzerland. When their visas were granted and the delegation arrived, Orie hosted them in Akron and introduced them to Lancaster Conference leaders.[2] The delegation then moved to Mennonite communities farther west in the United States and Canada.

MC Mennonites were learning more about their brothers and sisters in Russia. Mennonites had been living in Russia since 1788, when the first Dutch-Prussian Mennonites migrated to the Ukraine and a year later founded the "Old Colony" of Chortitza along the Dnieper River, on land Russia had gained by conquest over Turkey.[3] In 1803, a second wave of immigrants established the Molotschna Colony, one hundred miles farther southeast. By 1835, about six thousand were living in sixty villages in Molotschna.[4] In self-governing communities, the German-speaking settlers grew and prospered, particularly those who settled on the rich soil of Molotschna Colony. When additional land was needed, the colonies spawned daughter colonies. Entrepreneurs developed industries that produced a wide range of agricultural implements.

In 1870, an imperial edict rescinded or curtailed the special privileges that had drawn Mennonites to South Russia eighty years earlier. Under increased pressure to *russify*, or assimilate, eighteen thousand immigrated to the prairie states of the United States and the provinces of Canada between 1874 and 1880. As the immigrants passed through Pennsylvania,

Lancaster County Mennonites hosted them in their homes and contributed significant amounts of money in gifts and loans. These contacts formed the basis for future relief and immigration efforts.

Those who remained in Russia accepted forestry work or medical work in the Red Cross as alternatives to military service. They themselves shouldered the financial burden of alternative service in whatever form it took. This Mennonite cooperation with the government in Russia would later become something of a model when the historic peace churches began planning for Civilian Public Service (CPS) during World War II.

Economic growth in Russia continued. Through industry and innovation, landed Mennonites in South Russia built large estates, and entrepreneurs built mills and factories. In the Halbstadt district in 1908, for example, there were 191 industrial and commercial establishments.[5] Mennonites in South Russia also established educational institutions for all ages, including schools for women, teachers, and the deaf, and for business. Conscious of social needs, they built and managed charitable institutions such as orphanages, hospitals, and homes for the elderly. They sent missionaries to Indonesia. By World War I, Mennonites had spread to Siberia and many other places in the Russian Empire. No one could have

Gerhard Weiss farmstead in Blumenort, Molotschna. Canadian Mennonite Board of Colonization Photograph Collection.

imagined that this golden era, at its zenith in 1914, would end in tragedy and terror with the coming of war, revolution, and famine.

During World War I, armies crossed and recrossed Mennonite lands. When discontent and poverty sparked the 1917 Bolshevik Revolution, Mennonites again suffered the destructive forces of war. They were caught between the Red Bolshevik Army and the anticommunist White Army, and targeted by anarchists. Drought, famine, and disease followed. The typhus epidemic killed thousands, and an Asian cattle plague killed off most of the cattle—their source of milk and meat.[6] Raids by armies and anarchists took "virtually all movable assets . . . including livestock, grain, hay, wagons, food, bed linens, and wood."[7]

This was the crisis that prompted village representatives of the Molotschna Colony in late 1919 to appoint the *Studienkommission* to seek the help of European and North American Mennonites. Their primary objective was emigration, and the second, relief. Two teachers and two businessmen were chosen to represent the colonies. Abraham A. Friesen and Benjamin H. Unruh were teachers at the Halbstadt business college, C. H. Warkentin was a merchant in Waldheim, and John J. Esau was an entrepreneur who had been mayor of Ekaterinoslav but was now living in Berlin, Germany. On New Year's Day of 1920, Friesen, Unruh, and Warkentin—later joined by John Esau—left the Ukraine with the retreating White Army, crossed the Black Sea to Constantinople, traveled through Western Europe, arriving finally in New York on June 13.[8]

NEVER A "CAUSE IN WHICH I SO THOROUGHLY BELIEVE"

In the spring of 1920, Orie returned from a long business trip in time to travel with Elta to Johnstown, Pennsylvania, to attend meetings of the Mennonite Board of Missions, and then to Scottdale for a meeting with the Mennonite Relief Commission for War Sufferers. At both meetings, Orie urged leaders to make Russia a priority.

From Scottdale, Orie wrote about his future with Miller Hess. To his brother Ernest he wrote that he had his partners' "reluctant permission" to take a four-month leave and that his job would be secure.[9] But a day later, Clarence wrote that an extra salesman for the next season was absolutely necessary and asked Orie to declare his intentions. Orie responded: "It does not seem possible to open Russia work now unless I stay by my promise" (to be available for service there). "Does your wire mean my acceptance would sever my past relations with the firm or would you endeavor to secure a temporary salesman?"[10]

Then to Elta: "I see more than ever since I am here, how very important my accompanying the first group would be." He reported an upcoming "small conference" to consider forming a united inter-Mennonite relief committee to assist Mennonites in Russia. Orie himself was to be one of seven delegates from "our branch." The others were to be Aaron Loucks (Relief Commission chair), D. H. Bender, "Papa" (D. D. Miller), Sanford C. Yoder, John Mellinger, and "probably, Noah Mack." To Elta, he declared that there would never be a "cause in which I so thoroughly believe than this . . . and I do hate to give it up." But he was wavering. Regarding Miller Hess, he wrote that "if my place cannot be held open . . . I expect to turn this matter down unless you should give your advice to the contrary."[11]

MISSIONS OF MERCY TO RUSSIA

While MC congregations, through the Mennonite Relief Commission for War Sufferers, focused on relief work in France and the Middle East between 1917 and 1919, various other Mennonite groups had rallied to gather and send supplies to relieve the suffering in Russia. The Krimmer MB church on the West Coast was the first to get aid into Russia, in June 1919. Martin B. Fast, William P. Neufeld, and B. B. Reimer from Reedley, California, organized a relief committee and collected nearly $44,000. At great risk, Fast and Neufeld delivered in person the contributed funds and clothing to Mennonites in Siberia, not yet under Soviet control. This mission of mercy, said Fast, "brought great joy to many a sad heart."[12]

Upon their return, Fast and Neufeld reported "in graphic words" to audiences who "streamed together in large numbers." Their reporting on January 4, 1920, in Hillsboro, Kansas, led to the formation of the Emergency Relief Committee of the Mennonites of North America, representing GC, MB, and Krimmer MB groups. When access to Siberia was cut off, the Emergency Relief Committee shifted its efforts to Austria and Germany.[13]

When the United States entered the war, American Mennonites were shaken to discover they were suspected of favoring Germany. It was true that many of them spoke German and refused to join President Wilson's war to "make the world safe for democracy." It was true that they refused to answer the bugle call to arms, not because they were disloyal Americans but because they knew that peace could not be won by violent means.

It was also true that farmers—including Mennonites—produced much-needed food for the Allied soldiers in Europe at inflated prices. In an effort to show goodwill and make a positive contribution to humanity, Mennonites looked to the needs of those suffering the ravages of war in Europe. Mennonite volunteers serving under the Quakers in France were also looking eastward. A delegation exploring needs in Central Europe and Russia found an "appalling need for clothing, bedding, hospital supplies, fats, and milk."[14]

In response, the Relief Commission acted to send a unit to Russia as soon as the logistics could be arranged.[15] On June 24, the commission appointed Orie Miller and Arthur Slagel as an advance team to work from a base in Constantinople. Slagel, from Flanagan, Illinois, had graduated from Goshen College and was teaching music and Bible at Hesston College. Orie, as team leader, would investigate the best port of entry to Russia, coordinate efforts with Mennonites in South Russia, and put wheels under the relief operation. After accomplishing the tasks assigned, presumably in four to six months, Orie would return home. Slagel and a third volunteer would carry on relief operations for a longer period of one year. Soon Goshen College student Clayton Kratz, from Blooming Glen, Pennsylvania, agreed to become the third member of the unit.[16]

On July 13, the Russian delegation met with area Mennonites in Newton, Kansas. They requested a coordinated effort of North American Mennonites, rather than having to deal with the complexity of multiple committees. Heeding the *Studienkommission*, the assembly appointed a Committee on Information with P. C. Hiebert as secretary and MB representative, and D. H. Bender as a Kansas MC representative. A week later, on July 19 and 20, the *Studienkommission* drew large crowds in Hillsboro, Kansas, as they reported again on the dreadful suffering in Russia. Their witness stirred people's emotions and prompted a strong response. During those days, the members of the Committee on Information convened in Hiebert's home and agreed to issue a call to all Mennonite groups to send representatives to a meeting in Elkhart, Indiana, a week later, on July 27. Bender issued the call.[17]

The idea of an inter-Mennonite relief effort was not new. In response to the 1896–97 famine in India, the Mennonite Church had organized the

Home and Foreign Relief Commission, which included American Russian Mennonites as members and officers. Press releases at the time called it an all-Mennonite project. After the three major Mennonite groups established their own missions in India, the inter-Mennonite character of the commission faded, and in 1906 it disbanded.[18]

A decade later, when a resurgence of interest led to the formation of the Mennonite Relief Commission for War Sufferers, MC leaders were less eager to cooperate with "unlike-minded" Mennonites. But the initiative of American Russian Mennonites in Kansas called on their reluctant MC counterparts to cooperate. The January organization of the Emergency Relief Commission in Hillsboro was clearly a prelude to the birth of Mennonite Central Committee (MCC) seven months later. James Juhnke has argued that January rather than July, and Hillsboro rather than Elkhart, should be considered the actual founding of MCC. Since Mennonite Brethren and GC Mennonites had already joined their efforts, the Elkhart meeting could be seen as an invitation to the Mennonite Church to join the union.[19] Perhaps the best approach is to consider multiple points of influence in MCC's founding.

"A MISSION OF GOODWILL AND LOVE"

The "small conference," as Orie called it, convened at the Prairie Street Mennonite meetinghouse in Elkhart on Tuesday, July 27. MC representatives were in the majority, ten of the thirteen in attendance:[20] Aaron Loucks, D. D. Miller, and Levi Mumaw, officers of the Relief Commission; Sanford C. Yoder, moderator the MC General Conference; D. H. Bender, Hesston College president and the only one of the ten who attended the prior Kansas meetings; Eli G. Reist, treasurer of the Eastern Mennonite Board of Missions and Charities (EMBMC); the others were of the next generation—Orie Miller, Vernon Smucker, Arthur Slagel, and Ernest E. Miller (Orie's brother).[21]

Also in attendance were P. C. Hiebert and W. J. Ewert from Hillsboro, Kansas, and H. H. Regier of Mountain Lake, Minnesota. Hiebert, an MB, was chair of the newly formed Emergency Relief Commission of Mennonites in North America; Regier and Ewert were GC Mennonites. The most important person present was a guest, Abraham A. Friesen of the Russian *Studienkommission*. While Friesen was in Elkhart, his three colleagues were meeting with Mennonites in Kansas and Oklahoma.[22]

Since MB and GC Mennonites in Kansas had combined their forces in the January meeting at Hillsboro, the question at hand was whether the MC commission would join them. MC leaders, primarily from Indiana and Pennsylvania, had less interaction with the American Russian Mennonites and tended to focus on the cultural and theological differences that separated them. D. H. Bender, president of Hesston College in Kansas, was an exception, having had many more occasions to interact with GC and MB groups.

The MC delegates were surely mindful of editor Daniel Kauffman's warning in the previous week's *Gospel Herald* against forming an unequal yoke with other Mennonites who were not in "full obedience" to the teachings of Christ. An organizational unity of Christians without a common spiritual union was not genuine, Kauffman wrote. Nor could a union that ignored even "one jot or tittle" of biblical nonconformity be a true union. While Kauffman's implication that the Mennonite Church was the only body that was fully obedient to the Scriptures sounds arrogant, his concern was for a carefully guarded four-hundred-year-old Swiss distinction between the church and the world. In the early twentieth century, MC leaders nurtured the doctrine of nonconformity to the world, symbolized by plain dress as a mark of identity and as a hedge against modernism.[23]

Plainly clad D. D. Miller opened the Elkhart meeting with Scripture reading and prayer. The assembly selected two officers to conduct the day's business: D. H. Bender, chair, and P. C. Hiebert, secretary. All agreed to hold a public meeting that evening, where *Studienkommission* member A. A. Friesen could present to a larger audience a firsthand report of the dire needs in Russia. Aaron Loucks, Relief Commission chair, reported their readiness to send food and clothing to Russia, accompanied by three "advance workers." The NER and the Red Cross had recommended a southern approach into Russia from a base in Constantinople.

In the afternoon, during the second session, the inter-Mennonite assembly resolved any remaining resistance and reached an accord:

Resolved, that we, the representatives of the several branches of Mennonites assembled at Elkhart, Ind., this 27th day of July 1920, deem it well and desirable to create a Mennonite Central Committee, whose duty shall be to function with and for the several relief committees of the Mennonites in taking charge of all gifts for South Russia, to make all purchases of suitable articles for relief work, and to provide for transportation and the equitable distribution of the same.[24]

It was, in the words of Aaron Loucks, to be a "mission of good will and love."[25]

In further action, the group appointed a temporary executive committee of P. C. Hiebert to represent MB churches; H. H. Regier of Mountain Lake, Minnesota, to represent GC churches; and Levi Mumaw of Scottdale, Pennsylvania, to represent the MC branch. In the third session, at six in the evening, emigration (from Russia) was the main agenda. The group appointed a committee on emigration and considered calling a meeting of all Mennonites to consider the emigration "problem." Then in the public session at the Prairie Street Church, A. A. Friesen described the catastrophic conditions in Russia caused by the world war, revolution, civil war, disease, and famine.[26] Some "350 Mennonites had been hanged, shot, burned, or killed" by the time the delegates left the Ukraine.[27]

On Wednesday morning, the temporary committee chose P. C. Hiebert as chair and Levi Mumaw as secretary-treasurer. Mumaw was to contact the secretaries of all Mennonite relief committees to invite representation on the new Mennonite Central Committee.[28] Further, they resolved to call a meeting in Chicago in September to make MCC a permanent organization with broader representation and to launch "regular work."[29]

As with many great events, folklore and disparate memories accent the written record—or in some cases supplant it. There are two MC memories about how the reluctance to cooperate was overcome, with D. H. Bender and Orie Miller as the actors. Apparently, the strongest resistance came from the reluctant Aaron Loucks, Relief Commission chair and Mennonite Publishing House manager, who would have to report to Daniel Kauffman back in Scottdale. Between sessions on Tuesday, Bender took Loucks aside and persuaded him to cooperate.

The other memory comes from Orie Miller. As Orie looked on, he observed how the group found it impossible to "structure anything." They had "never worked together before . . . and did not know how to get started now." Someone asked whether Orie, the only one with experience in foreign relief work, would be willing to go to Russia. Emotions became intense. About noon, Orie broke down and wept, as he would do in future crises. Yes, he would go, but only if he were to be sent by one committee. It was difficult enough to represent one committee. To work for multiple committees would be intolerable. The "bawling spell," as Orie called it, added the final emotional stimulus to organize the inter-Mennonite union.[30]

Mennonite Central Committee, its name an ironic parallel to that of the Central Committee of the Communist Party of the Soviet Union, was born a fragile infant. Its parents were barely acquainted and struggled to build trust. Not all were convinced this child should have been born, and no one could be sure it would survive. It was not the result of an intense love affair but was a tentative relationship born of obligation and great need.

Deeply embedded in the Mennonite DNA is the call to care for the sister and brother in need as well as to serve those beyond the community of faith. Mutual aid and service to neighbor are not the means to salvation, but rather a distinguishing characteristic of Christ-followers, an expression of "true evangelical faith." Because siblings and cousins in Russia were in great need, American Mennonites overcame their differences to create an incarnation of love and compassion called MCC. The 1920 Elkhart meeting was the culmination of multiple origins, a fortuitous convergence of charitable impulses.

Two days after the July meeting, the *Gospel Herald* carried the news that Orie O. Miller and Arthur Slagel were going to Russia via Constantinople. Orie as unit director was to "establish working policies," as he often put it. Slagel and a third member were to serve for a longer term of a year. The "Relief Notes" column appears to be the report of the Relief Commission rather than the newly minted Mennonite Central Committee, since MCC is barely mentioned.[31] Though editor Daniel Kauffman agreed to carry news of MCC's work, Orie remembered that it caused him "pain" to do so.[32]

The size of the "small conference" in Elkhart belied its significance. James Juhnke has proposed that the meeting "was the most momentous meeting in North American Mennonite history."[33] The resulting Mennonite Central Committee may be the most significant inter-Mennonite organization in Mennonite history. The convergence of American Russian Mennonite initiative and MC momentum in appointing Orie Miller,

Arthur Slagel, and Clayton Kratz was fortuitous. Guy Hershberger has said it would be "difficult to overestimate" MCC's significance for those who received aid as well as those who gave it. John A. Lapp, MCC executive secretary emeritus, has said that "MCC was the first and likely continues to be the strongest institutional expression of inter-Mennonite cooperation."[34] And Robert S. Kreider, long affiliated with MCC as an administrator and member of the executive committee, has called it the "most beloved of Mennonite institutions."[35]

"THINK OF US AS YOUR SERVANTS"

On Wednesday, September 1, 1920, Elta Wolf Miller once again watched Orie disappear over the Atlantic horizon. She, Clarence and Gertie Hess, and Levi Mumaw, secretary-treasurer of MCC, traveled with Orie to New York Harbor where Orie boarded the SS *Providence*.[36] His companions were Arthur Slagel, a member of the Hesston College music faculty from Flanagan, Illinois; and Clayton Kratz, a Goshen College student from Perkasie, Pennsylvania. Kratz was a campus leader and an excellent student. He was president-elect of the Young Peoples' Christian Association, the most active of student organizations. Kratz interrupted his college training to accept the call to service in Russia.

In a farewell message written in New York City just before departure, Orie said:

> Brethren Slagel and Kratz unite with me in expressing our deepest appreciation of the interest shown by the church in us and the work to which we have been called. . . . We wish [for] your prayers, your sympathies, and support, suggestions and criticisms. . . . A constant effort will be made to keep the home people informed in a clear and understandable way of disposition being made of your money and clothes. Think of us as your servants in their distribution that all may be done to His honor.[37]

Although World War I had ended in 1918, international conflicts abounded: Ireland was engaged in a war for independence from Britain; right-wing fascism was on the rise, soon to emerge in Italy as the totalitarian National Fascist Party under Benito Mussolini; and revolution was shaking Russia. At home, the U.S. Senate refused to ratify the Treaty of Versailles, rejected Wilson's League of Nations, but enacted Prohibition. America rebuffed Progressive Era activism, retreated into isolationism, and in a resurgence of nativism, embraced the Ku Klux Klan and closed U.S. ports to immigrants.

The American Mennonite population was about 80,000, with the Mennonite Church comprising 35,000 members, the General Conference about 20,000, and Mennonite Brethren and other related groups the remaining 25,000.[38] The Canadian Mennonite population stood at 58,874.[39] In the Soviet Union, toward which Orie, Kratz, and Slagel were traveling, Mennonites numbered about 100,000.

Parting was more difficult for both Orie and Elta than his earlier departure for Beirut in January 1919 had been. "The first night at home for a while I could hardly bear it—to think of you going so far away again," Elta wrote. She was, however, fully supportive of the mission. "I am happy feeling we both understand each other perhaps as never before and knowing that you care. You can have the assurance that my thoughts are continually with you."[40]

Again, Orie penned his observations in his daily diary. Of Kratz he said, "I surely like him. He is quiet, eager to learn, anxious to do his very best in the work." As for Slagel, Orie believed he would "make a good worker, [was] thoroughly consecrated to this work," and had "a fair amount of tact." Orie decided he would be most effective as team leader by waiting for Kratz and Slagel to come to him rather than asserting himself. Kratz came to Orie's room often, but Slagel rarely. He and Slagel were different enough that Orie doubted the two would ever be close.

Of course, Orie was thinking of those he had left behind. Daughter Lois was about to turn four and was puzzled by Elta's occasional tears. Orie wanted full reports on Elta's life and Lois's training. "I am conscious of what a sacrifice it means to you to have our home broken up in this way, and am oh! so thankful that our mutual convictions about life and its duties made this decision possible." He knew their "mutual convictions" were not shared by A. N. Wolf and Clarence Hess, his business partners.[41]

A. N. Wolf thought Orie should be content with his fifteen months in Beirut. He did not doubt the need in Russia, but did not see why Orie should be the one to go. Both Hess and Wolf said they would no longer "count on" Orie—they would find someone else to do the bookkeeping and the selling. "That did it for Elta," who thought Hess and her father were being unreasonable. "She decided then and there" that Orie should go. Eventually, Hess began to understand Orie's call to serve humanity in need, but not Elta's parents; they "were just beat."[42]

In his first letter to Orie, A. N. Wolf apologized for his attitude. "If I have said or done anything about your going across [the Atlantic] that hurt your feelings I surely ask your forgiveness. I may have been radical on some points, but you know we do not always look at things alike." Writing from Sheboygan, Wisconsin, Wolf was sure Orie would have a more pleasant time crossing the Atlantic than if he were on the road in the United States trying to sell shoes "when there is no business." Finally, Wolf wished Orie the "choicest blessings" and said he missed him very much.[43]

From home in Akron, Elta wrote happily that she was wearing the watch Orie had given her in New York and that it kept perfect time. She was not happy, however, when wristwatches became the target of Amos Horst's preaching at Ephrata. He considered them jewelry, and like the new wire bonnets currently in fashion, far too worldly. Nor was Elta pleased that her relatives insisted she sleep in their homes and not in her house alone, but their insistence was stronger than Elta's resistance.[44]

IN CONSTANTINOPLE

On September 27, 1920—the day the MCC board was meeting for the first time in Chicago—the *Providence* steamed through the Dardanelles and into the Sea of Marmara, then into the Bosphorus Strait to dock at Constantinople, the former capital of the great Byzantine Empire. Named for Emperor Constantine, the city spanned the strait to occupy the continents of both Europe and Asia. The grand city of Emperor Justinian, who built the world-famous Hagia Sofia, the Church of Holy Wisdom, had strategic access to the Black Sea on the north, and the seas of Marmara, the Aegean, and the Mediterranean to the south.

Orie expected A. J. (Alvin J.) Miller, Red Cross volunteer from Grantsville, Maryland, to meet them at the dock, but was disappointed. Before long, the driver of a Near East Relief car saw the newly arrived volunteers "hanging over the railing" and took them to the Red Cross office. There they learned, to Orie's consternation, that A. J. Miller had recently gone to Paris. Next, they went to the headquarters of the NER. Orie explained their mission to NER director Colonel J. P. Coombs, who promised his assistance. They visited Leon Myers of Lancaster, Pennsylvania, who had arrived in February 1919. He was managing the maintenance

Near East Relief service center in Constantinople. Public domain.

of the NER's thirty-two cars and supervising the work of their mechanics and drivers.

At every turn, officials—the American vice consul, an aide to Admiral Bristol, the Red Cross, and NER—assured Orie that it was possible to enter Russia as far as Melitopol and perhaps to Halbstadt in Molotschna Colony. Having learned of the complexities of international relief work in Beirut in 1919 and 1920, Orie knew that success depended on a coalition of agencies, governments, and even the military. His familiarity with the Red Cross and the NER and their officials served him well now.

Orie met with Colonel Coombs to plan their strategy. They decided Slagel should remain in the city and manage NER warehouses until needed in Russia. Carrying letters of introduction from the American consulate, Orie arranged meetings with Red Cross major Robert Clewell and Admiral Mark Lambert Bristol of the U.S. Navy, who was high commissioner for Turkey.[45]

Orie found Coombs, Bristol, and Clewell all sympathetic to his cause and each promising to help the Mennonite mission. Admiral Bristol arranged for Orie and Kratz to travel on an American destroyer to Sebastopol. The admiral introduced Orie to Mr. Whitmore, who had spent the last fourteen months in South Russia and was well acquainted with the Mennonites there. He too promised to help.

On Sunday, October 3, armed with Russian visas, letters of introduction from Admiral Bristol, advice from the admiral on doing relief work in South Russia, and $4,000 in British pounds and American dollars, Orie and Kratz boarded the American destroyer *Whipple*. The destroyer, designed to escort larger ships, had a crew of 130 and was equipped with four-inch guns.

The two Mennonites were assigned to officers' quarters. The irony of nonresistant Mennonites traveling with naval officers aboard a ship of destruction surely did not escape Orie. But such irony did not prevent him from making a pragmatic decision to use a destroyer to fulfill their mission of compassion. He and Kratz found the crew to be sympathetic and free with advice. They made a short stop at Batum, the Georgian seaport city, where Joseph Stalin had organized labor strikes twenty years earlier, then continued. The *Whipple* was well on its way to Sebastopol when a storm hit, giving Orie "a fierce headache and a lumpy feeling in the stomach."[46] Kratz seemed not to suffer. The storm gave the captain occasion to explain that the Black Sea's name came not from the color of the water, as many assumed, but from the region's infamous winter weather.

THE DREADFUL SPECTER OF STARVATION

On the northern shore of the Black Sea lay the object of their mission. Like much of Europe, the Russian Empire had suffered the ravages of World War I, the folly of vainglorious royalty. Russia, the Goliath among European nations, had aligned itself with the Allies—England, France, Italy, and Japan (and eventually the United States, Canada, and others) against the Central Powers—the empires of Germany, Austria-Hungary, and the Ottomans (and later, others). Imperial Russia under Czar Nicholas II was ponderous, inefficient, ill-prepared, underequipped, and plagued by disasters, massacres, and uprisings—culminating in the revolution of 1905.[47] Czar Nicholas II was deposed during the March Revolution of 1917, ending three centuries of autocratic Romanov rule. After a few months of a provisional government with Alexander Kerensky as prime minister, Vladimir Lenin and the Bolsheviks seized power in the October Revolution of 1917. Russia withdrew from the Great War with the signing of the Brest-Litovsk Treaty on March 3, 1918.

The ultimate result of the 1917 revolutions was the birth of the Soviet Union, the world's first communist government, under Vladimir Lenin. Civil war between Lenin's Soviet Red Army and the anti-Soviet White Army raged for three years. Roving bands of anarchists, among them Nestor Makhno and his Black Army of thousands, marauded Mennonite villages and estates, adding to the chaos as they looted, burned, raped, and killed at will. *Kulaks*, landowners and people of means (which included Mennonites), believed to have profited at the expense of peasants, became "enemies of the people."

About 400 Mennonites were shot and 800 children were orphaned between 1918 and 1921—all at the hands of Nestor Makhno and his guerillas. In Chortitza Colony, four Mennonite villages were demolished: Eichenfeld, Ebenfeld, Steinbach, and Altona.[48] The men disappeared—were shot or deported—and those who survived moved to other villages.[49] In addition to the violent bloodshed, soldiers brought typhus and cholera that spread in epidemic proportions. Of 11,016 Mennonites in eleven Chortitza villages, 917 died from typhus, 24 were killed, 668 were orphaned, and 17 women in the village of Rosenthal were raped.[50] In the aftermath, syphilis and bitter memories remained.[51]

While stories of Makhno, now a Ukrainian folk hero,[52] are legion, there were also other perpetrators. The Gabselinovih brothers and their thugs rampaged through Mennonite villages in Bashkir in 1919. Local peasants, who resented Mennonites with the best land and greatest wealth, supported the Gabselinovihs.[53] Desperation drove some to abandon core convictions, and as a result contributed to the fragmentation of Mennonite community.

"Food dictatorship," the senseless, forced requisition of food and grain, was another means of control over *kulaks*, the so-called "class enemies of poor peasants." In the Keppentalskiy region of Samara in the Volga River region, also home to Mennonites, for instance, all flour was confiscated in 1920, compounding famine conditions. Wheat production dropped to almost nothing.[54] This, on top of the looting and pillaging of villages, hastened the downward spiral to the famine of 1921. Consequently, many died of hunger—most villages, including those of the Mennonites, reported ten to twenty deaths. In Neu-Halbstadt fifty-six starved to death.[55] From one who was there comes this tragic testimony:

The storms which broke over us began, as you know, with the Liquidation Laws. . . . They raged over us with destructive fury during the civil war and through the fearsome all-prevailing specter of death by starvation, drove every robber band to one's door, so that our life became far dearer to us than our devastated goods and chattels. These [words] are verified by the empty granaries and cellars, the many uncultivated fields, the many fresh grave mounds, the camps of the emigrants in the ports.

Because help still did not come and the situation steadily grew worse, many a person who had his last morsel before him logically concluded: If I can expect death from hunger here at home . . . it is wiser to go in a direction where help can reach us earlier, and where the outstretched arms of the dear brethren from abroad are in a better position to rescue us from the clutches of that dreadful specter, death by starvation.[56]

This was the heartrending, chaotic crucible that Orie Miller, Clayton Kratz, and Arthur Slagel entered in October 1920. The "dear brethren from abroad" were trying to bring food and clothing, but the advance of the Red Army was threatening the effort. When Miller and Kratz crossed the Black Sea, the Soviet Reds controlled most of Russia. The White Army, the armed forces of South Russia under the command of General Pyotr Nikolayevic Wrangel, struggled to hold what was left of the Ukraine and the Crimea, where most of the Mennonite colonies were located. Wrangel's coalition government welcomed the relief efforts of the American Mennonites, but a Red victory would close the door to Russia. By October 1920, a White defeat was imminent but still, the determined relief workers pressed forward.

The *Whipple* docked at Sebastopol (now Sevastopol) on the southwest coast of the Crimean Peninsula, the base for the Russian Black Sea naval fleet. When the Mennonite relief workers arrived, they introduced themselves to Admiral Newton Alexander McCully and to Acting Director Ridden of the Red Cross. With Director Ridden, they arranged to purchase Red Cross supplies. For permits to travel inland, they went to the office of Colonel Svengizoff, General Wrangel's chief liaison officer, and were then directed to the office of the American Foreign Trade Corporation where they registered the American Mennonite Relief Mission, as Mennonite relief efforts were known in Ukraine and Constantinople.[57]

Their first two days in Sebastopol were busier than any Orie could remember, "running from one office to another, and getting one permit after another." Finding lodging was yet another challenge, since the city was "full & overflowing with Wrangel officers & soldiers." They finally found lodging in the home of Kornelius Hiebert, whose name they brought with them from the United States. Mr. Tverakoy of the Ministry of the Interior, representing the Wrangel government, received the two volunteers "very kindly" and promised to supply a guide, interpreter, and free rail transportation.[58] Given the many promises of help in Constantinople and Sebastopol, it appeared as though the task of organizing the American Mennonite Relief Mission was proceeding smoothly and successfully.

From Akron, Elta said the newspapers were carrying little news of Russia, since the people were more interested in the baseball World Series and the presidential campaign. But there was plenty of other news. "Papa" Wolf was discouraged because of the "very dull" business in the South, and Orie's parents had purchased Brookside Farm, across the road from the Forks meetinghouse, from Uncle Mose Miller. Elta was going to stay with friend Ada Leed in Lititz, since Ada's husband, Jack, was gone on business.[59]

Elta marked a moment in history, the passage of the Nineteenth Amendment, but she remained a spectator rather than an actor. On November 2, she wrote, "Orie, I guess I missed it today. I should have voted for a president when I had the chance. When I first heard that women could vote I tho't surely I would, but now that the time has come I didn't after all." Perhaps she heeded the action of the Board of Bishops two months earlier: "No member permitted to exercise privilege of voting under national law of women's suffrage."[60] Without Elta's help, and apparently without the vote of Lancaster Conference women, Republican Warren G. Harding won a landslide victory over fellow Ohioan, James M. Cox.

THE BLIGHTING EFFECTS OF WAR

Miller and Kratz, in the company of their female multilingual interpreter, Dr. Monastery, boarded a train for Melitopol, just south of Molotschna Colony. Chortitza Colony was to be Orie's next destination, as they wanted to visit as many Mennonite villages as possible. They carried with them letters of introduction from Kornelius Hiebert to Mennonites in the Crimea and Molotschna. The train steamed northward through the Crimea to the South Russian province of Ukraine. With each stop, more passengers climbed aboard until the train had almost as many on the roof and hanging on to the sides as inside. Most appeared to be refugees, probably returning to homes recently liberated from the Red Army by Wrangel's White Army.

On October 10, in the trade city of Melitopol on the Molotschna River, Dr. Monastery hired a "rickety" carriage to take them the three miles to Jacob Neufeld's mills. Neufeld had also been appointed a member of the *Studienkommission* but had been denied a visa. Along the way, Miller and Kratz began to see the suffering they had come to relieve, though not yet at its worst. Orie recorded the scenes in his diary:

> I never saw a poorer looking town. A few Wrangel motor cars and trucks lumbered along on the poorly paved street. 90 per cent of the people outside of the army and even most of these seemed to be literally in rags. Windows in buildings were broken and not replaced. Horses are skinny and few, and the poorest kind of harness. On the way down we met a bunch of Bolshevik prisoners, mere boys, with their coarsely woven gray uniforms. Probably one woman out of four had shoes that at least looked like leather, the rest had none or cloth ones. Children are mostly barefoot.[61]

At the mills, they met Jacob Neufeld. Of seven mills, Neufeld had only one working mill left, but it was large enough to employ seventy-two men. Everything they produced went to feed Wrangel's army. In the Neufeld home, Miller and Kratz reported on what Mennonites in North America were attempting to do. Neufeld said that in the last three years, Melitopol had been in Bolshevik hands eighteen times, and each time liberated by Wrangel.[62]

On Sunday, they attended the Mennonite worship service in Melitopol in "a very beautiful building" only a short walk from Neufeld's home. Some members of this congregation had died during a Makhno "reign of terror" in the spring of 1919.[63] Orie, having been asked to speak, did so for about twenty minutes "in German such as I could command." He reported on North American Mennonite efforts to deliver food and relief supplies. Congregational leaders reported that the greatest needs were farther north at Alexandrovsk and Chortitza and that relief should be directed there first.

Ohrloff Zentralschule (Ohrloff Central School) in better times. Mennonite Heritage Centre.

On the way to Halbstadt on Monday, Miller, Kratz, and Monastery stopped in Ohrloff, where in a peasant's house they were given milk to drink, and visited a Mennonite school for the deaf and hearing impaired, the Mennonite hospital, and the Ohrloff Central School. The visitors could see "evidences of their past prosperity, but the war had left its blighting effects everywhere." At Halbstadt, the administrative center of Molotschna Colony, Wrangel's soldiers crowded into homes, and Bolshevik prisoners filled yards and sheds.[64]

Here, elder Abraham Klassen was their host. In meeting with Mennonite leaders, Miller and Kratz attempted to assess what was most needed, asking such questions as where supplies could be purchased and where Kratz could be most effective. Elder Klassen introduced the two to a variety of Mennonites in Halbstadt. At the home of Miche Goossen, they delivered a letter from her fiancé, A. A. Friesen, *Studienkommission* member now in Canada. At the home of Johann Peters, they learned that their host was president of a new relief committee that was attempting to receive supplies from Holland and America. In the afternoon, the Americans met with the Halbstadt relief committee, where they discussed details of relief operations. The committee members made "many useful suggestions" in a spirit Orie thought was "splendid."[65]

In the days that followed, Miller and Kratz met with the *Mennozentrum*, the executive committee of Molotschna Colony; saw more Mennonite institutions; and collected still more information. The generous spirit and unselfish nature of the people of Halbstadt impressed Orie; they wanted relief supplies to go first to those elsewhere, where the need was greater. The members of the *Mennozentrum* expressed their profound thanks to American Mennonites who were coming to their aid. "I shall always remember seeing the Americans for the first time in the yard of the district office in Halbstadt and even having the opportunity to chat with one of them," remembered Heinrich Goerz. "To us they seemed like beings from another world."[66]

THE ABDUCTION OF CLAYTON KRATZ

The road to Alexandrovsk, their next destination, ran parallel to the battlefront. Destruction was visible everywhere. They saw hundreds of the reported twelve thousand dead horses, some partly consumed by dogs. There were "hundreds and hundreds" of graves of fallen soldiers, and mass graves in trenches. They stopped for the night in a German village where they heard more stories of deprivation and suffering caused by occupying armies. Eleven times the village had been occupied by one army or the other, each time soldiers taking what they wanted. The people were "all extremely sad and pessimistic, and felt utterly hopeless in their misery." They were "in constant fear of plunder, robbery and rape. Roving bands on horseback under a Father Maknov [*sic*] were the special terror of many."[67] Thousands had died here the winter before from the typhus spread by soldiers. The next day, Orie, Clayton Kratz, and Dr. Monastery drove four more hours to Alexandrovsk by the Dnieper River, in Chortitza Colony.

Clayton Kratz, 1920. MC USA Archives–North Newton.

Ten percent of the colony's population of twelve thousand had died in a period of three months. Everywhere there was an "extreme lack of medical supplies, clothing, bedding, soap, and farm equipment." Large, once-productive Mennonite factories now stood silent. In Alexandrovsk, Miller and Kratz met Abraham Koop, proprietor of one of the largest producers of farm machinery with factories in Chortitza, Einlage, and Alexandrovsk, which had by now been nationalized.[68]

Also in Alexandrovsk, Orie visited Commanding General Pasenov of the White Army, who said the emissaries were three days too late to visit the villages of Chortitza Colony. Soon the territory beyond the Dnieper would be evacuated, so they could proceed no farther. General Pasenov gave Kratz and his host, Johann Peters, travel passes to "ensure" their safety. Back in Halbstadt, Miller and Kratz again met with the local relief committee to plan for relief operations, even though "all of us felt that probably the time had not yet come when these plans could be carried out."[69]

Before retiring for the night, Miller and Kratz together read Psalm 91, which spoke of God's protection in the midst of danger and destruction. Never before had Miller and Kratz been so vulnerable to terror, arrows, and pestilence as that night in Alexandrovsk. Never before had they seen destruction and waste such as that which lay around them on all sides. Never before had they had more reason to seek refuge "under the shadow of the Almighty" and "trust in the fortress of the Most High." That night both rested in the confidence of God's deliverance and salvation—the promise of the psalm.

Forever after, when Orie read Psalm 91, he could not do so without feeling the pathos of that night in Alexandrovsk.[70] Later in the night, Orie was awakened by endless streams of retreating soldiers, horses, wagons, and guns that continued into the next day. One regiment marched to the tunes of a band; some sang "Russian war songs that sounded thrilling in the early morning hour." Midmorning, the visitors were advised to leave. The commanding general had ordered seats on the train to Melitopol and Sebastopol for Orie and Dr. Monastery, believing their exit was secure. Kratz and Johann Peters accompanied Orie and Dr. Monastery to the Alexandrovsk station. It was October 16, the last time Orie, or any other North American Mennonite, would see Clayton Kratz.[71]

Despite the Red Army's swift advance, Kratz believed that as an American relief worker he would not be harmed, so he chose to stay in Halbstadt. Nevertheless, Kratz and Johann Peters were arrested and released when local Mennonite leaders, risking their own lives, pressed the military *commissar* to release Kratz. Two weeks later, Kratz was again abducted near Fürstenwerder, about ten miles southeast of Halbstadt.[72] With the Red victory came local and regional governing soviets, or councils. Lacking accountability, nothing prevented the *commissars* from lining their own pockets, plotting revenge, or arbitrarily brutalizing the populace.

Without as much as an overcoat, Kratz was spirited away. Local Mennonites tried to track him but without success. G. A. Peters of Halbstadt, who was the last Mennonite to see Kratz, was of the opinion that he was to be sent home by way of Charkof (now Kharkov), Moscow, and Sweden, and that he most likely died of disease rather than by maltreatment or execution. The report of the region's military *commissar*: "Disappeared in Charkof."[73]

Since then, there has been much speculation about the manner of Kratz's death. Subsequent relief workers, Arthur Slagel, A. J. Miller, and C. E. Krehbiel, investigated the abduction in the years between 1920 and 1926 without satisfactory results. But in 2000, Krehbiel's diary surfaced with additional details. "Mrs. Dyck" told Krehbiel that Grigori Saposhnikov, who had lodged in her house, had killed Kratz. Krehbiel's diary adds another account: Johann Wall learned from Charkof records that Kratz was arrested by "Bagon" at Halbstadt on charges of spying. From Halbstadt, Kratz was taken to Bachmut, Krakow, and finally, back to Alexandrovsk, where he was shot.[74]

In 1925, Wilbur Thomas of the American Friends Service Committee in Philadelphia, and William Dodd and Charles Vickery of the NER in New York City made inquiries into Kratz's abduction. Through the Quakers' Moscow office, Thomas pursued a rumor that Kratz was doing forced labor in a Siberian mine. This round of correspondence brought further reflections from G. A. Peters, by now a teacher in Herbert, Saskatchewan. Peters's account bore some parallels to that of Krehbiel's diary: After pursuing Kratz's trail through numerous villages, they had come to Fürstenwerder "where hundreds of prisoners were kept." There they "dared to interview" the chief of the "terrible *Cheka*" (an early version of the KGB, the main Soviet security agency), who told them that the "suspicious American" was sent to the main *Cheka* station in Bachmut. Then he added, "If your American is not a spy sent by capitalists of his country you may be sure we shall not do him any harm . . . we shall set him free." Peters wrote, "These were good words, but nobody—not even the speaker himself—did believe them. Who can trust a Bolshevik!"[75]

Whatever his fate, Kratz has not been forgotten. A marker in the Blooming Glen Mennonite Church cemetery in Bucks County, Pennsylvania, notes his birth and mission to Russia. A Goshen College dormitory bears his name, as does the Clayton Kratz Fellowship, a business and service organization based in Souderton, Pennsylvania. Continued interest in Kratz's story has generated further investigation, a biography, and two separate video productions.[76] Orie counted Kratz as a modern Mennonite martyr, MCC's first. Though some thought Orie had used poor judgment, he did what he always did—make the best decision possible with the information available. He later wrote that Kratz's arrest was "one of the dear prices that our church seemingly had to pay to do its relief service."[77] Late in life, Orie told Lancaster Conference moderator David Thomas that the modern church was too careless with money and too careful "that we have as few martyrs as possible in our Mennonite brotherhood. In my day we would send . . . folks [everywhere to] open fields for the gospel."[78]

"TOO CLOSE TO THE MISERY"

When Orie and Clayton Kratz had parted at the Alexandrovsk train station on October 16, 1920, Orie noticed an observation balloon hovering overhead. The cannon and gunfire seemed louder and closer, making it evident that the station was the target. Orie and Dr. Monastery boarded the train loaded with doctors, nurses, and wounded soldiers. Shells landed and exploded very near them, wounding one man standing close by. Shells damaged the rails, prolonging the wait. After thirty minutes, "which seemed like hours," another track was cleared and the train moved out. A number of the medical attendants were young Mennonite men doing noncombatant duty in the "sanitary service of the army."[79]

Alexandrovsk was heavily bombed that day. Bolsheviks broke through the eastern line and marched toward Melitopol, but were captured by a White regiment. A cavalry troop broke through the western line intending to cut the rail line between Alexandrovsk and Melitopol, but was held off. Despite the dangers, Orie and Dr. Monastery made it back to the Neufeld home in Melitopol.

In Melitopol, Orie negotiated the employment of three young men as links to the interior: a courier, a mechanic, and a doctor/inspector/ diplomat. Orie would need to negotiate releases from the army for two of the young men, one of them Neufeld's son. Orie set their salary at six dollars a month. The courier and the driver were to make weekly trips between Sebastopol and the interior.

When all was arranged, he and Dr. Monastery boarded a special military train for Sebastopol, sharing a coach with two Russian Red Cross nurses, two colonels, and their "servants." While waiting in Sebastopol for transport across the Black Sea, Orie secured warehouse space from the American Foreign Trade Corporation and worked out an arrangement for ordering supplies. Orie, with assistance from Dr. Monastery and Kornelius Hiebert, purchased supplies in local markets to send to Kratz. Orie then reported to Admiral McCully, had long conversations with Major Ridden about working procedures, rented office and living space for a Mennonite headquarters in Sebastopol, and (not realizing that Kratz had been abducted) left $1,200 for Kratz's use at the American Foreign Trade office. Finally, he ordered the promised equipment for the hospitals in Ohrloff and Halbstadt, then boarded the SS *Constantine* to return to Constantinople.

While on the Black Sea, Orie wrote to Elta: "The whole past three weeks was one sad story of suffering, want, murder, rape, and all those things that go with war. It would take books to tell all that we heard, and most of it too sad and horrible to try to remember."[80]

Arriving in Constantinople on October 27, 1920, Orie and Arthur Slagel began planning for Slagel's departure for Russia with a load of supplies. They bought cloth, sewing machines, thread, needles, milk, soap, bed linens, and a one-ton Ford truck. Perhaps mindful of the theft of $100,000 worth of supplies from the NER warehouses in Derindje, reported in the September 12 *New York Times*,[81] Orie went by boat the fifty-five miles to Derindje "to hurry along" the first shipment of American supplies.

When strong wind overpowered the small motor, Orie, impatient to get the job done, asked to be rowed ashore where he took the train to his destination. Back in Constantinople, Orie hired a small barge and a

tugboat to take the supplies out to a Greek freighter in the harbor and got
them loaded. On November 9, after numerous delays, Slagel was off to
Sebastopol with the first load of supplies. Orie was pleased with the way
the NER helped expedite the shipping of supplies.

Orie was unhappy, however, that the New York office of the NER
had not sent the October allotment of funds on time, nor had the promised Mennonite workers arrived in Constantinople. He cabled the NER
in New York and complained to Levi Mumaw at Scottdale. He had made
promises to Mennonites and officials in Russia, so he was obligated to
fulfill them. He had "mountains of work" to do! Could Mumaw send
four more volunteers "right away"?[82]

In November, Orie attended a meeting in the American Red Cross headquarters with representatives of all relief agencies in the city. An executive
committee was formed, with Orie representing American Mennonites, to
coordinate their combined efforts. He learned about the many projects
in the city of Constantinople: hospitals, schools, orphanages, industrial
schools, and professional training and settlement houses. There he met
Baroness Olga Michailovna, the wife of General Pyotr Wrangel, who was
much interested in the welfare of Russian people.

Rumors of Wrangel's retreat and impending defeat reached
Constantinople.[83] Russia's recent armistice with Poland allowed the Red
Army to focus on the White Army, forcing Wrangel back into the Crimea.

On November 13, Orie, along with Baroness Wrangel and Mr. Griffen
of the American Foreign Trade Corporation, boarded a destroyer at
Constantinople to return to Sebastopol. The baroness was somber, given
the news of the probable defeat of her husband's forces. There was enough
worry to go around. Mr. Griffen fretted about his $97,000 worth of goods
at Sebastopol. Orie was troubled about Kratz, having heard nothing from
him since they parted at Alexandrovsk; he worried about Slagel's supplies
worth $30,000, and about his newfound Mennonite friends in Russia.

A late-night cable confirmed their worst fears: the Bolsheviks were in
the Crimea advancing toward Sebastopol. Most Americans had fled the
city, and parts of the city were burning. The next morning's wire carried the news that Wrangel had given up hope of holding out against
the Reds. All were to evacuate the city. As though confirming the recent cable, ships and boats "just as full as they could be" with refugees,

including Mennonites, fleeing Sebastopol steamed by them bound for Constantinople.

Indeed, on October 29, General Wrangel had issued a statement to the Russian people:

> I have done everything that human strength can do to fulfill my duty to the Army and the population. We cannot foretell our future fate. We have no other territory than the Crimea. We have no money. Frankly as always, I warn you all of what awaits you. May God grant us strength and wisdom to endure this period of Russian misery, and to survive it.[84]

When Orie reached the Sebastopol Harbor, he found it full of ships. Small boats with refugees and baggage were rowing from one ship to another seeking room to board. Upon pulling alongside an American destroyer, they learned that the American Red Cross warehouse had been looted and burned. About nine hundred tons of relief supplies had been destroyed. The captain went ashore to learn that the Bolsheviks were not yet in the city and that the four men aboard would have a few hours to look after their concerns.

Orie went immediately to Admiral McCully's office in Sebastopol, where he learned that Clayton Kratz was in Bolshevik territory with no way of escape. The admiral, however, was confident Kratz would be all right, saying that recent reports of a Red Cross worker killed had been only a rumor. Any Mennonites in the city were welcome to leave on the admiral's ship, and Orie could arrange with the Red Cross to transport any remaining Mennonites to Constantinople. McCully thought it likely that Slagel's ship had been warned of the Bolshevik victory and would return to Constantinople with the American Mennonite Relief supplies, which included the Ford that had arrived just two days earlier.

Orie went to Hiebert's house where he found everyone subdued and somber. A block away was the Kiest Hotel where Wrangel had given his farewell speech to his troops, saying that he hoped for a time when they could go back and rebuild Russia. At five o'clock on October 23, Orie's ship left Sebastopol, a city whose future was "too horrible to imagine." Orie had done "all that we know to do," and now he "must trust Him to protect the boys and save the supplies for use in this great need."[85]

Back in Constantinople, Orie called on the American Foreign Trade Corporation to inquire about any loss of supplies, dispatched Dr.

Monastery to write her report on funds used in Sebastopol, was called to the embassy to declare unpledged funds that could be directed elsewhere, discussed with Mr. Whitmore a house they could rent for 250 refugees, and heard the latest reports on the number of expected refugees.

The next day 2,400 wounded soldiers were admitted to city hospitals, and 6,000 with less serious injuries were being cared for on six ships anchored in the harbor. The day after that, 10,000 refugees arrived, many of them family members of retreating soldiers. Orie promised food assistance to 150 Lithuanian refugees for their journey home. Slagel wired Orie to report that he and the supplies were in Constanza, Romania. Orie wired orders to Slagel to get the supplies back to Constantinople.[86]

The next day Orie (representing MCC), officials of the NER, and the Russian YMCA agreed to open another children's shelter. Then Heinrich Schroeder from Halbstadt appeared in the city, bringing a letter from twenty-one Mennonites marooned on ships in the harbor, asking for care. After a search, Schroeder and Orie found the young men on board the *Sczaritz*, one of sixty-two ships in the harbor that were carrying more than 100,000 desperate refugees.

When they boarded the *Sczaritz*, they could scarcely move through the overcrowded ship. Orie and Schroeder retrieved the twenty-one Mennonites from the *Sczaritz* and found a house for their lodging. While working to improve the living conditions in what became the first Mennonite home for men, administered by Orie and the Mennonite volunteers, they found a refugee with good English-language skills and employed him to teach the twenty-one Mennonites English in preparation for emigration to the United States or Canada. As more Mennonites (and Lutherans) were found, they were added to the homes. In addition, MCC volunteers also later founded and operated homes for women and children.

Among the Mennonite refugees was Jacob Huebert from Schoenwiese, Chortitza Colony, who had worked as a medic in the White Army. He had observed Orie and a colleague, likely Schroeder, paddling a small boat around the ships in the harbor calling for Mennonites through a megaphone. "How they all wished to be Mennonites!" Huebert recalled. He also long remembered the hospitality offered in the Mennonite home for men. Huebert was one of "the 62," a group of young men who were later granted entry into the United States.[87]

To Elta, Orie wrote,

I have seen sights that I shall never be able to forget. As I sit here and think of
the 70,000 refugees living out here in the harbor on boats, with no country
and no place to go, I shudder all over. . . . I am too close to all this misery
and suffering to talk much about it, my mind is all a daze. I have thot nothing, dreamt nothing it seems for weeks . . . but poor, starving, sick miserable
humanity."[88]

On November 29, 1920, Orie sent a telegram from Constantinople to
Levi Mumaw at Scottdale: "Present refugee situation here and vicinity
terrible beyond description. Our unit organized to administer any funds
given by our people for this purpose. . . . With supplies still untouched
suggest previous order of supplies with December budget be cancelled and
funds sent instead. Old clothing shipment badly needed."[89]

From afar, MCC chair P. C. Hiebert was observing Orie's efficient work.
"The promptness with which Orie Miller can adapt himself to changing
situations is above the ordinary," Hiebert wrote to Levi Mumaw. "I realize we certainly have a first class man in him for this difficult work. He
grows in my esteem with every new report."[90]

"MOUNTAINS OF WORK" IN CONSTANTINOPLE

While to P. C. Hiebert, Orie's worked appeared efficient, Orie was becoming impatient. He wished for Slagel's return and for A. J. Miller's arrival
to share the load. To Elta, he registered his frustrations: "So many more
things could be done right now so terribly necessary if only personnel
were here. Three months gone already and still [I have] no help. I want to
come home by February 1. . . am ready to turn the work over to someone
else, but plainly can not leave now until a proper person arrives to take
it. I am tired and have lived under severe strain for the past two months,
and just long for a little let up, but none is in sight."[91]

There was still no word from Clayton Kratz. To Elta he wrote, "I know
by repeated cables I get concerning him that his folks worry terribly."
Even though he and Kratz had met only a few months earlier, Orie wrote,
"We were constantly together. Our aims, ideals, purposes and plans were
the same. They were unforgettable months."[92]

By December 2, the twenty-one "boys" in the Mennonite home had
become forty-six, then fifty-two. Orie was finding various kinds of work

for them—one in his office, twelve cleaning the home, and five others were organizing the home. He had begun applying for U.S. passports for the men, ten each week. The bureaucracy was infuriating. "I never was in a place where one has to fight to get things done like here . . . in a land of backsheesh and a city of crooks. [It] almost drives one wild at times."[93]

He opened a new orphanage, and by cable he asked for Vinora Weaver to come immediately to manage it. Orie's days were filled with "annoying little details."[94] Ten days later, he was "agreeably surprised"[95] to see Slagel return with the supplies, but perturbed by the difficulty Slagel had getting the supplies cleared through customs. Only three cases of shoes and three sewing machines had been lost, but losses in freight and insurance amounted to $1,300. Another welcome surprise a few days later was the appearance of Mennonite volunteers John Warye, Joe Brunk, and Frank Stoltzfus. With new volunteers in place and systems well-organized, Orie took a three-week leave. With John Warye as his traveling companion, Orie visited cities around the Mediterranean, with Beirut as the final destination.

Toward the end of January 1921, Orie was back in Constantinople. The Mennonite home, managed by Stoltzfus, was now occupied by one hundred Mennonite (and some Lutheran) men, and the orphanage by more than one hundred children. Orie was again disappointed to learn that Vinora Weaver and Vesta Zook still had not arrived to manage the orphanage and keep the books. Two days later, on January 29, he was delighted to see the long-expected A. J. Miller appear. After the two discussed the work and policies of the Mennonite projects, A. J. agreed to oversee the work in Constantinople—and to begin the painstaking process of getting into Soviet Russia as soon as possible. Orie was greatly relieved.

In the next two weeks, Orie gathered the Mennonite volunteers to discuss policies that would guide their work, which he would then report to the MCC executive committee back home. Sixty men were transferred to a second Mennonite home located at Yeni Kuey, six miles north of Constantinople and two miles above Robert College, overlooking the Bosphorus Strait.

Orie filed claims against the Russian Steam and Navigation Company to cover the loss of goods shipped to Sebastopol, and to recover customs paid on the American shipment. He cleaned up longstanding accounts with the NER and organized a more efficient system of bookkeeping. He spoke to the men at the Mennonite home for the last time and reviewed agreements with them for paying back to MCC the cost for their maintenance in Constantinople.

He had explored the needs in South Russia, had met Mennonite leaders in several communities, and had arranged for the distribution of relief supplies to South Russia through Sebastopol. But the victory of the revolutionary Red Army over Wrangel's White Army had unraveled all his attempts to get aid to Mennonite communities in Russia. For now, Mennonite aid efforts were limited to Constantinople. He told Elta, "I have done the thing in the best way that I could, and left . . . with a clear conscience."[96]

Other Mennonite relief workers—A. J. Miller, Arthur Slagel, Frank Stoltzfus, Joe E. Brunk, Vesta Zook, and Vinora Weaver—continued the work in Constantinople. Additional ministries included a hospital, a children's shelter, a Russian women's home, distribution of clothing, and loans for transportation. From its beginning in October 1920 to its conclusion in July 1922, MCC's work in Constantinople cost a total of $200,738.[97]

CONTACTS WITH EUROPEAN MENNONITES AND QUAKERS— AND AID TO RUSSIA

Orie left Constantinople on February 9, 1921. He apologized to Elta for his indefinite return plans—he had not been sure when he could leave Constantinople, and MCC had insisted he consult with Swiss, German, and Dutch Mennonite leaders on his way home. That would take an additional ten days. "In a short time . . . we can talk over these misunderstandings together and they will probably clear up."[98] At least he hoped so!

The Orient Express took Orie through the Balkan States to Milan, Italy, and through the St. Gotthard Tunnel to Basel, Switzerland, where he visited Elders Nussbaumer and Goldsmith. He went on to Mannheim and Ludwigshafen in Germany to consult with the European Mennonite relief committee. With the support of Dutch and American Mennonites, they were helping Russian Mennonite refugees, resettling those who wished to remain in Germany.

Orie then went to Ingolstadt and Helmansberg to see Michael Horsch, the elder of the Ingolstadt congregation. Horsch, also the head of the South German relief committee,[99] explained their work of feeding twelve thousand people in eighty-five villages. In Munich, Mennonites were assisting two thousand people. In Berlin, Orie consulted the American consulate about the emigration of Mennonite refugees from Constantinople, and met with the Lutheran Relief Committee to arrange the same for the Constantinople Lutheran refugees. After meeting with both relief committees, Orie concluded, "Bolshevist Russia is just as much of a conundrum from Berlin as from Constantinople. The nearer one is to Russia, the more puzzling the whole situation seems."[100]

At The Hague, B. H. Unruh met Orie and traveled with him to Amsterdam to meet with the Dutch Relief Committee. After hearing about the work in Constantinople, the committee agreed to "arrange the diplomatic end of the work" to get Mennonites out of Constantinople. They would also advance funds to help pay the expenses of the refugees at the two Mennonite homes.[101]

In London, Orie consulted the secretary of the Friends Society in England. Mr. Nicholson hoped his own upcoming meeting with prime minister Lloyd George would result in diplomatic and financial assistance for the emigrating Mennonites. Orie learned that both the British and American Friends had representatives in Moscow, and that their supplies were going into Russia through the Baltic seaport of Riga, Latvia. The Quaker officials were optimistic that they could also help get Mennonite workers and supplies into Russia by the same route.

It was left to A. J. Miller, who became director of MCC's American Mennonite Relief Mission, and Arthur Slagel to find a new route into Russia. After eight months of futile efforts, A. J. learned that Herbert Hoover's American Relief Administration (ARA) was negotiating with Soviet officials to deliver relief supplies from the north through Riga, Latvia. In Paris, he called the ARA office in London, then traveled there by plane—surely the first air travel by an MCC worker. Then he traveled to Moscow where daily and persistently he lobbied high Soviet officials. Finally, on October 1, 1921, A. J. Miller and the president of the Moscow Soviet signed a contract that permitted MCC to operate under the umbrella of the ARA.[102]

Hungry Ukrainians receiving food. MC USA Archives–North Newton.

That was not enough. A. J. Miller also had to negotiate a contract with the Ukrainian Socialist Soviet Republic, which he did on October 21, 1921. Still, bureaucratic and political snags prevented the delivery of desperately needed relief supplies. Not until Christmas was the first food delivered to settlements in the Volga region. Not until March 1922 could Arthur Slagel begin feeding the hungry in the Ukraine—in Chortitza on March 16, in Halbstadt on March 20, and in Gnadenfeld on March 25— more than two years after Orie arrived home from Constantinople.[103] Though much delayed, Mennonite relief efforts saved "thousands upon thousands" of lives.[104]

RETURN TO AKRON

On March 1, 1921, Orie left Liverpool on the SS *Cedric* for New York, his fourth transatlantic journey. His dream of using relief as an entree to mission work in Russia remained unfulfilled. Even the first step, gaining entry into Russia with relief supplies, had been impossible. One wonders how Mennonites in the prospective mission field of Russia would have responded to American Mennonite mission efforts. How much did Orie know about his spiritual cousins when in the spring of 1919 he sent five copies of his proposal to the five who knew him "as well as any other five people"?

But the mission work in Russia was not to be. Having, indeed, explored a bit of South Russia and having seen the way blocked by the communist takeover, Orie returned to Akron. He resumed his place in Miller Hess, and from Akron Orie tirelessly promoted the work of MCC and Mennonite mission boards in the Lancaster Mennonite Conference and the Mennonite Church.

The double lenses of service and mission increasingly characterized Orie's worldview. Both were essential, and in his mind, service led naturally to mission. As twentieth-century Mennonites developed increasingly dichotomous views of service versus mission, peace versus evangelism, Orie persistently advocated for and embodied the unity of word and deed.

Chapter 6
Patterns of a Calling: 1921–1929

"Where the administrative gift tends to become noticeable and prominent anywhere, it's a pity, because it's not intended to be that."

When Orie returned from Russia in 1921, it was to a troubled church. Mennonites were caught up in a theological crucible, which included premillennialism, resistance to modern cultural change, and the fundamentalist-modernist debate. Fundamentalism, which emerged in the wake of World War I, was a militant protest against liberal theology and social, cultural, and intellectual changes. Modernists believed it possible to reconcile recent discoveries in history, science, and religion with Christian faith. Fundamentalists attempted to safeguard traditional views of biblical inspiration and authority against Darwinism and higher critical methods of Bible study. Essential "fundamentals" of doctrine included inerrancy of Scripture, the virgin birth, Christ's bodily resurrection, and the historical reality of his miracles. One result of the turmoil was a realignment of American Protestantism into "mainline" liberal Christianity on the one hand, and evangelical and fundamentalist churches on the other.

Further, as Paul Toews writes, Mennonite fundamentalism was an attempt to correct the influence of the evangelical renaissance promoted by John Funk and John S. Coffman during the last half of the nineteenth century. The church had embraced the modern missionary movement and moved in the direction of American Protestantism and cultural modernism.

New forms of worship, loss of the German language, a relaxing of traditional symbols of nonconformity, and trends toward higher education were signs of danger in the view of conservatives and fundamentalists.[1]

Though Mennonites didn't fit either camp, modernism seemed the greater danger. Both GC and MC leaders sought to clarify Mennonite orthodoxy in several confessional statements. MC leadership took two defensive moves. The first was the adoption of a new doctrinal statement in 1921, and the second was the temporary closing of Goshen College in 1923. A third, which had implications for Orie, was the strident reaction of Lancaster fundamentalist conservatives to his peace advocacy as chair of the Peace Problems Committee. In reaching across denominational lines to cooperate with the historic peace churches (Friends and Church of the Brethren), they believed Orie was leading the church dangerously close to worldly pacifism, a far cry from biblical nonresistance.

Orie had witnessed the explosive debate in the Mennonite Board of Education meetings at Goshen College in October 1914. The forceful George R. Brunk I of Virginia had interrogated science and Bible faculty on their views on such matters as evolution, creation, inspiration of the Bible, and historical-critical methods of Bible study. Reflecting the militant spirit of fundamentalism, Brunk pressed for decisive and unequivocal statements of orthodoxy. The debate went on all evening and into the next morning without resolution. While D. D. Miller had been discouraged by the dynamics of the encounter with Brunk, Orie could hardly wait to get involved. He would now have his opportunity.

The concerns and language of the Brunk confrontation in 1914 reappeared in the form a doctrinal statement intended to "safeguard" the church from modernism. In August 1921, the MC General Conference at Garden City, Missouri, endorsed a statement on *Christian Fundamentals*. It was a near word-for-word copy of the Virginia Conference's confession written by Brunk, J. B. Smith, and A. D. Wenger, and adopted in 1919. Having fortified the conference against liberal heresy, Virginia leaders wanted the denomination "to take decisive and scriptural action in unmistakeable [*sic*] terms opposing the tenets and delusions of the new theology."[2]

According to the preamble of *Christian Fundamentals*, modernism was threatening the "particular doctrines of the church," and so a restatement of the traditional 1632 *Dordrecht* (Holland) *Confession of*

Editorial cartoon of the state of Mennonite education. E. G. Gehman, *Sword and Trumpet* (April 1930).

Faith was considered necessary.[3] The doctrinal statement of eighteen *Fundamentals* claimed not to "supersede" the eighteen confessional articles of *Dordrecht*, but it nevertheless came to the fore, restated theology, and shaped the debates of the 1920s.[4] In particular, it highlighted the key issue in the current debate—the authority of the Bible—by beginning with the following claim:

> We believe in the plenary and verbal inspiration of the Bible as the Word of God; that it is authentic in its matter, authoritative in its counsels, inerrant in the original writings, and the only infallible rule of faith and practice.[5]

The 1921 Garden City assembly, following the Virginia Conference, appropriated the language of fundamentalism and accepted new definitions of orthodoxy: "plenary and verbal inspiration," "inerrant," and "infallible." Ironically, the Bible's own definition of inspiration as "profitable for doctrine, for reproof, for correction, for instruction in righteousness"[6] was no longer adequate. New battle lines were drawn, with fundamentalist conservatives defending the Bible in the new language against liberals who seemed to deny its truth. Twentieth-century North Americans assembled at Garden City did not differentiate between the two testaments, thus indicating a "flat book" reading of the Bible where all parts appeared equally authoritative.

The *Christian Fundamentals* adopted at Garden City reflected the MC swing to the right. The statement set the terms of the debate and played a part in the closing of Goshen College. The college served as an institutional lightning rod during the storms of the turbulent twenties. Moreover, the tone of the debate was often harsh, accusatory, and militant.

Indiana-Michigan Conference leaders had, by this time, also adopted more inflexible, conservative tones. It was a shift from the more moderate and flexible attitudes of earlier years. As a result of the 1916 merger of the two Indiana-Michigan conferences—Mennonite and Amish Mennonite—Amish Mennonite congregationalism soon gave way to centralized conference authority. D. D. Miller and other Amish Mennonites had advocated for conferring over legislating as the function of the conference, but had nevertheless quickly adapted to legislation after the merger. Conference minutes reflect the change. At the turn of the century, ministers carried issues home for "congregational discernment." In the 1920s and after, conference actions typically reported, "The decisions of the Executive Committee shall be final."[7]

In May 1923, the conference executive committee, which included D. D. Miller, removed Wilbur Miller—D. D.'s son and Orie's brother—from his office as pastor at Forks because he had been unwilling to sign a pledge of loyalty to conference standards. The main issue for Wilbur seemed to be the ban on life insurance. In June 1923, the conference appointed a committee of eleven to enforce the conference discipline in matters of "nonconformity"—plain dress and a ban on life insurance. Particularly troublesome was the trend of women wearing hats in place of the plain bonnet. Nevertheless, it was not the special committee but the executive committee that "summoned" six ministers for examination in August. As a result, the committee revoked the ministerial credentials of five of

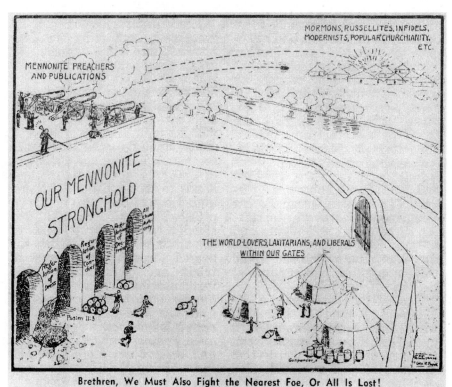

Brethren, We Must Also Fight the Nearest Foe, Or All Is Lost!

Editorial cartoon of the threat within the walls. *Sword and Trumpet* (July 1944).

the six ministers. The disciplined ministers believed that such matters of nonconformity were congregational issues, not agenda for heavy-handed conference leaders. During this tumultuous time, about four hundred members withdrew their membership from Indiana-Michigan Conference congregations and four congregations affiliated with the GC Mennonite Central Conference District Conference.[8]

GOSHEN COLLEGE CAUGHT IN THE STORM

The leaders of the Mennonite Board of Education and the Indiana-Michigan Conference, in whose territory Goshen College operated, used their influence to close and remake the college. Orie had hoped drastic measures could be avoided. In 1921, when D. D. Miller mentioned the possible closing, Orie was thoroughly disappointed: "It seems to me the last thing that should be thought of is to close the school. . . . There must be some way out."[9]

By March 1923, however, he was persuaded otherwise. Writing privately to his father, Orie played out a radical solution:

> Personally it seems to me that the time is past to think of it being possible for
> any individual to step in at Goshen College and attempt to work with both
> sides on the present issues. . . . Even if [Daniel Kauffman] should succeed in
> getting the faculty together, which he feels he can, and if he should succeed
> in drawing enough students to warrant having a college it does not seem wise
> to me for the Board to continue at Goshen. The bitter feeling which would
> exist in the minds of all those on the other side would continue thruout this
> whole generation. Might it not be better for the Board to offer to sell the in-
> stitution either to the Central Illinois Mennonite Church or to a local Board
> of Trustees which might be created to take the institution over? The selling
> price ought to be enough to cover not only the debt of the Board but also
> all the annuities on which the Board is paying interest and a nice tidy little
> sum besides.
>
> Personally I would favor such a transaction only if the Board would then
> at once proceed to establish a college and bible school at some other place
> in the Central States, perhaps some place in Ohio. I believe that with the
> proceeds that could be gotten from Goshen and by starting a new institution
> . . . the Board might be able to have a school ready for this coming fall. . . .
> I think it would be very unwise for the Board to sell the school unless they
> would intend to open another just as soon as possible.[10]

Orie was appointed to a committee on June 18, 1923, to consider whether the embattled college could or should continue to operate. Serving with Orie were Daniel Kauffman, influential editor of the *Gospel Herald* and current college president; Sanford C. Yoder, MBE president; and Albert J. Steiner, an alumnus of Elkhart Institute.[11] At thirty, Orie was the youngest member of the committee and the only Goshen alumnus.[12]

Orie had reached an understanding with Daniel Kauffman that spring. As the most powerful leader in the church, Kauffman had been appointed president in a last-ditch effort to save the college. Orie and his friend A. E. (Amos) Kreider had been sorely disappointed when Kauffman was not able to bridge the college-church chasm. Orie came "the nearest to losing heart" as a result. Later, Orie recounted a deep conversation about the crisis with Kreider as the two of them walked across the campus and beyond. Amos believed the conservative leaders were good men and meant well but were simply unable to accommodate needed change. The old leaders would never accept such things as musical instruments, photography, and non-Mennonite speakers in Mennonite schools. What should they do?[13]

"Well Amos Kreider was quite impressive," Orie recalled. "He had decided that he would not make trouble and so he'll drop out" of the debate. When the two parted, Orie went back to campus to see President Kauffman. Orie told him about his conversation with Kreider and said, "Dan, you can't stand a piano or an organ in the home, and I have one." He pointed out other issues on which they differed, and then asked, "Are these differences going to be a frustration to us the rest of our days? Can we ever work together?" Kauffman understood and assured Orie that they could and would work together. According to Orie, he "never went back on his word."[14]

Orie had many more opportunities to share board and committee work with Kauffman. Beginning in 1921, Orie attended a plethora of MBE and Goshen College committee meetings. He was appointed or elected to serve on a nominating committee, faculty committee, finance committee, a special committee to arrange the board's accounts, and a Committee on Recommendations where he served with his father. Recognizing his uncommon fiscal acumen, the board executive committee appointed Orie on June 30, 1922, to be its financial agent. By virtue of this appointment he became a member of MBE's executive committee.[15] This office gave him considerable influence and placed him in the center of the church-college controversy. In 1914, Orie had wished for such a place!

In 1923, the MBE surreptitiously appointed Orie to represent Lancaster Conference. The conference itself had not appointed, nor would it appoint, a representative to the board. An action of the Lancaster Conference Board of Bishops in 1930 reflected their attitude: "Decided to not approve of worldly tendencies at Goshen College, neither do we approve of our young people attending nor supporting it."[16] Orie served on his own merit, though the board found it convenient to list Lancaster as a participating conference.

With the educational crisis reaching its zenith, Orie's friend Amos Kreider, Orie's father, D. D. Miller, and D. A. Yoder (the next MBE president) called a special meeting in Goshen for April 4–6, 1923. There the

Kauffman-Yoder-Steiner-Miller Committee on Recommendations coun-
seled the board to close the college:

> Because of existing conditions brought on by dissatisfaction between the
> different elements in the church generally, found especially prominent within
> the conference district and local congregation where Goshen College is lo-
> cated and reflected acutely within the institution, it seems impossible to the
> Board to plan for the continuance of the institution for the coming year.[17]

At the annual meeting that followed on June 18, 1923, the MBE accepted the committee's recommendation to close the school. Aaron
Loucks, publishing manager of Mennonite Publishing House in Scottdale,
believed it had to be done. When Amos Kreider, the sweet-spirited business manager and head of the Bible department, asked questions, Loucks
scolded him harshly, characterizing him as a "young upstart who doesn't
understand the facts of life."[18] It is unfortunate that Loucks and others
of his generation could not embrace the new generation and mediate the
differences. The church elders lacked the sorely needed generous-spirited,
seasoned, pastoral guidance to affirm and correct young leaders, who
were equally committed but inspired by new dreams and larger visions.

The MBE appointed young Orie Miller to a new Administrative
Committee, responsible to oversee the transformation of the "old
Goshen."[19] The committee elected Orie secretary. At age thirty, Orie held
one of the most responsible and influential offices of the church.[20] With
the office came the responsibility to interpret the actions of board. "I do
not think anyone could feel worse about the closing of the institution than
I," Orie wrote to alumnus and former faculty member Frank Smucker at
Tiskilwa, Illinois. He recalled his five years as a student and three years
on the faculty: "I know that if the college could continue to do for other
young people in the church what I feel it has done for me, no sacrifice
would be too great to have it continue."[21] To his friend Vernon Smucker,
a fellow alumni representative on the board, Orie wrote, "What do you
feel that our attitude should be towards the problems that are coming up?
I frankly confess that I am unable just at present to think my way thru
the whole business. I do not know just what we should or might do."[22]
Smucker raised a larger question, "Would things go smoothly even if we
succeeded in solving the real problem at the college, or would there still be

the old difficulty of securing harmonious relationship of the college with the church in general?"[23]

Despite Smucker's larger question, Orie thought that the board had little choice. As he would do consistently in the future, Orie sided with the church. Whether leaders were wise or shortsighted, the church was the only legitimate discerning body. Mutual accountability was the genius of the Anabaptist view of church, harking back to the rule of Christ: "Where two or three are gathered, there am I in the midst of them." All other institutions were servants of the church.

AN IDEAL MENNONITE COLLEGE

Writing from Union Station in Kansas City, Missouri, later that year, Orie reflected on his recent visit to Hesston College. After a meeting of the Mennonite Colonization Board in Newton, Kansas, president D. H. Bender had persuaded Orie to spend the evening at Hesston. The visit prompted Orie to write to Elta, "I always enjoy the fine spirit at Hesston [College]. I wish somehow at Goshen we could get the same spirit and loyalty plus the culture and broad mindedness and scholarship that Goshen has stood for in the past. That in my mind would be the ideal combination for a Mennonite college." He continued his musings as he boarded the train to sell shoes in Nashville and New Orleans.[24]

Later that summer, the MBE persuaded its reluctant president, Sanford C. Yoder, to shoulder the heavy burden of reshaping Goshen College as its chief executive officer. As president, Yoder described Goshen's mission as offering a "broad general education under strong Christian influences, and in full harmony with the distinctive as well as the fundamental doctrines of the church which founded it."[25]

Among Yoder's first responsibilities was to recruit new administrators and faculty. He set his sights on J. D. Charles, dean at Hesston College, and Orie Miller. Having served often as a teacher of the Special Bible Term at Hesston, Yoder knew its faculty well. He pressed J. D. Charles to move to Goshen, saying he would refuse the presidency if Charles would not join his administration as Goshen's dean. Unfortunately for both schools, Charles died of cancer in the summer of 1923 at the age of forty-five. Yoder then set his sights on Noah Oyer, Hesston's new dean. The multitalented Oyer had served nearly every role, from maintenance to teaching. Hesston administrators had groomed him to head the Bible department and had made him dean. Nevertheless, Oyer was ready to move to Goshen.[26]

Orie Miller, however, was not. Yoder wanted Miller to become the business manager. Writing confidentially, Yoder wanted Miller to be ready for the call and to discuss it with Elta. If called, Yoder hoped Orie would "give a definite reply." Orie would be good for the office, Yoder thought, because he "would be able to hold more of the pledged money than anyone else."[27] Orie said no, having earlier declined a similar invitation from former acting president I. R. Detweiler.[28]

From Akron, Orie rallied alumni to support the college. Writing as chair of the alumni fundraising committee (which also included S. W. Witmer and H. S. [Harold] Bender) in August 1924, Orie explained that they were charged with the responsibility of helping "the management" raise funds. Since Bender was studying in Europe, Miller and Witmer had composed the letter. In a controversial move, President Yoder and the board had acted to liquidate Goshen's alumni endowment fund of $25,000. Now Orie's committee was asking donors for permission to redirect those funds from endowment to general use, as needed by the new administration. Miller and Witmer signed off as "Yours for a better and bigger Goshen College."[29]

The church-college tango had tipped in favor of the church, but by no means was the future of Goshen College assured. Many alumni were loyal to "old Goshen" and were skeptical and cynical about its transformation. For decades to come, college administrators and church leaders would continue to ponder and debate the role of Mennonite higher education.

NEGOTIATING ON BEHALF OF "THE 62"
After Orie's return from Russia in 1921, he promoted ongoing relief efforts tirelessly and persistently. In 1922, Lancaster congregations and individuals through Eastern Mennonite Missions contributed $73,426; in 1923, $72,889; and in 1924, $90,486. Line items included the NER, German relief, Russian relief, Fordson tractor fund for Russia, passage money for Constantinople refugees, Canadian immigration, and loans to immigrants.[30]

With typical optimism, Orie imagined that in the 1920s his "whole life work" would be clarified, and he would enjoy his most productive period thus far. He and Elta had by now decided that overseas mission work was not in their future, but rather their work was "to be right in Lancaster County."[31] Orie informed the officers of the Mennonite Board of Missions—J. S. Shoemaker, G. L. Bender, D. D. Miller, and Levi Mumaw—of their decision. Board president J. S. Shoemaker had been observing Orie's focus on relief work and assured him that the church was vitally interested in his work, as evidenced by the many prayers and contributions on his behalf.[32]

Orie reported in person to the MCC meeting on June 7, 1921, in Lancaster. There, because of the demands on secretary Levi Mumaw and because of Orie's "special fitness and experience," he was appointed assistant secretary of MCC, an office he would hold until replacing Mumaw in 1935. Also on the agenda was the invitation of Herbert Hoover, director of the American Relief Administration, to all relief organizations to a consultation in Washington, DC, on August 24. Further, Hoover invited the groups to work under his administration's umbrella. The ARA's agreement with the Soviet government helped open the door to Russia that A. J. Miller and MCC had been seeking. In addition, Hoover's organization handled many of the logistics, making Mennonite operations more effective and efficient. Mennonites found Hoover and his staff to be "fair and accommodating," and they enjoyed "cordial" relationships.[33]

In Akron, Orie—along with Levi Mumaw in Scottdale, Maxwell Kratz in Philadelphia, and P. C. Hiebert from Hillsboro—focused on the immigration of some two hundred Russian Mennonite refugees who had fled to Constantinople. The émigrés had found shelter in the Mennonite homes in the city and above the Bosphorus Strait in Yeni Kuey, a suburb of Constantinple. While working in Constantinople, Orie and other relief workers had begun preparing the refugees for life in the United States or Canada by arranging English-language lessons and by applying for passport permits. Before leaving, Orie had already sent eighty-one applications to the U.S. State Department.

On September 1, 1921, sixty-two (later referred to as "the 62") of the eighty-one applicants landed on Ellis Island to an unwelcome reception. For six weeks, immigration officials detained them behind barred windows and locked doors. There were multiple problems; they carried no money, had no tickets beyond Ellis Island, were not sure of their destination, and neither the Department of State nor the Labor Department knew much about MCC.[34]

With his usual persistence, Orie went to work. He traveled to New York City several times and to Washington, DC, five times in an attempt to unravel bureaucratic red tape. The detainees were aware of the efforts on their behalf. One of them, Gerhard Lepp, wrote a note of appreciation in the language he was learning: "We learned . . . that you have been again three days in Washington in our sake. You spend your best time for us. We are sitting behind gated windows and locked doors, young and strengthful and impossible anything to do."[35]

As a guarantee that the penniless men would not become a burden to the federal government, the Labor Department required six-month bonds of $500 for each. Signing for the loans were Joseph Bechtel, a wealthy Mennonite builder in Philadelphia; William Derstine, who had accompanied the relief workers to Beirut in 1919; and A. N. Wolf, Elta's father. This, said Philadelphia attorney O'Donnell, gave the Labor Department the legal protection it needed to grant admission to the country. If in six months the immigrants were productive earners, the bonds could be cancelled. MCC and individual lenders carried a debt of about $150,000 for the refugees' maintenance in Constantinople and transport to New York. Railway fares to final destinations would require an additional $4,000.[36]

On October 13, the émigrés finally arrived in Lancaster County, where Orie found temporary hosts. Three days later the men were on their way to more permanent homes and employment in Pennsylvania, Ohio, Virginia, Indiana, Illinois, Iowa, Kansas, South Dakota, Minnesota, Mississippi, Nebraska, and California.[37] Orie kept one man, Gerhard Lepp, at Akron to help with "detail work" of corresponding with the men, requesting and compiling monthly reports.[38] Another, Jacob Huebert, remained linked to Orie in other ways. Huebert went to Columbiana, Ohio, where he eventually married Grace Lehman. Grace's sister Esther married Albert Wolf Miller, Orie and Elta's oldest son. Huebert, an accomplished musician, played the cello for the Youngstown, Ohio, symphony for thirty-three years. When he and Grace came to Akron annually to visit Albert and Esther, Huebert tuned Elta's grand piano, and on at least one occasion, Huebert played a cello recital in the Miller home.[39]

Another arrival, a widow with three children, illustrates Orie's personal stake. The four landed on Ellis Island, but due to poor timing and the lack of a communication channel to Akron, they were deported. The discouraged family recrossed the Atlantic to an unknown fate. When the ship stopped at the port of Cherbourg, France, a cable from Orie awaited the captain. Orie ordered the captain to send the four back to New York as soon as possible. Orie paid for the tickets.[40]

The story of Orie moving heaven and earth on behalf of "the 62" demonstrates his typical dogged determination. Some, however, thought the widespread news reports focused "unduly" on these few. But for Mennonites in the Ukraine and the Crimea, the success of "the 62" was a bright gleam of sunlight shining in the darkness of despair. It gave hope for their own deliverance.[41]

MORE COMMITTEES AND A NEW SHOE COMPANY

That's not all Orie was doing. In addition to his involvements with Goshen College, the MBE, and refugee settlement, Orie took on three more institutional affiliations and offices in the 1920s: chair of the Young People's Problems Committee (1921–37); financial agent and member of the MBE executive committee (1922–55); and the MC Peace Problems Committee, which he would serve as executive secretary (1925–53). It was an era of identifying tasks as problems—appropriate for the troubled twenties.

Since Orie's work with Mennonite institutions was unpaid, and since he and Elta had decided to remain in Akron, returning to work at Miller Hess was Orie's best option upon his return from Russia. The company provided economic security. As a partner, he received dividends of $10,000 annually plus a comfortable salary. Despite their consternation about Orie's desertion when he went to Beirut and Russia, Clarence Hess and A. N. Wolf took him back. They had not found a replacement for Orie. Besides, he had proved his worth, and Hess and Wolf had to admit that business was better when Orie was involved. So once again, Orie traveled by rail to the major cities of the East and the Midwest where Miller Hess had accounts, to take orders for the fall season. He also expended significant time and energy recruiting new retail customers to carry the company's children's and young women's shoes.

In 1922, Miller Hess added a second factory to the business, this one in Denver, Pennsylvania, about nine miles north of Akron on the northern edge of Lancaster County. Hess and Wolf hoped the addition of the "A. N. Wolf Shoe Company" would provide enough challenge to keep Orie at home. The reward for Orie was immediate—his income doubled. "Home" was a relative term, since that year Orie spent 127 days on the road and seventy-six nights in a Pullman sleeper car.[42] Typically, Orie arranged his travel schedule to coincide with committee and board meetings. When a frugal Mennonite board member questioned Orie's unnecessary expense of a sleeper car, Orie suggested the man do the same next time, so he could make a better contribution to the meeting. After sitting upright in his train seat during the night, the frugal colleague had arrived rumpled and tired, whereas Orie came to the meeting rested and alert.

ALBERT AND DANIEL JOIN THE FAMILY

On January 29, 1922, Orie went to the NER offices in New York City to accept a medal for meritorious and humanitarian service in the Middle East, an honor he never seemed to mention to anyone. Surely the most significant event of 1922 for Orie was the birth of Albert Wolf Miller on March 18. Albert, Orie and Elta's second child and first son, was named for his grandfather Albert N. Wolf.

While on the road for business and committee meetings, Orie often reflected on work and family life. After Daniel Wolf Miller was born on February 16, 1924, Orie wrote to Elta from the Washington Hotel in Portsmouth, Ohio: "I must simply say that I believe I like you just a bit better than I ever did before and a great deal more than any other mortal I know. I have thanked God hundreds of times for you. . . . And we both love the kiddies. . . . I surely am glad for them, and hope for their sakes that we are made of the proper parent stuff."[43]

From Spencer House Hotel in Indianapolis, Indiana, Orie wrote of his concern for Elta: "You must take things easy for a while. . . . You've done your share in bringing us such a nice boy [Dan] and in just mothering him and the other two now." The astute MBE financial agent then wrote of his philosophy of personal and family priorities:

I don't believe in spending money for flashy clothes, fancy autos, on things to show off in any way, but as long as things go well with us financially, we want to spend on anything that makes the home more homelike for the kiddies and which will make it easier for you to be a good mother to them. We'll just have them with us once. Soon they grow up and are gone. We want to do all we can to make their memories of it pleasant & happy ones.

Considering Elta's well-being, Orie imagined, rather unrealistically, that she would have time for leisure: "During the coming years you ought

Wolf and Miller families, ca. 1928 (*back row, from left*: Anna Wolf, Elta, A. N. Wolf, Orie with John; *front row*: Dan, Albert, Lois). John W. Miller.

to have much time for reading and for companionship with them. If one is always all tired out that cannot so well be done."

In September, writing from the Robert Morris Hotel, Philadelphia, Orie reflected on his own role as a husband and father:

> I guess I am not much of a husband to leave you alone with the children so much. I have always tried to be one, but sometimes one forgets the importance of some of the apparent little things connected with a Daddy's & hubby's job. I am resolved to try harder than ever. . . . I know I do not always act my appreciation. . . . I get these spells sometimes lately. It seems I make so many mistakes and accomplish so little along all lines. But enough of this chatter.

A "hot, blue, and tired" shoe salesman collapsed in his Hotel McAlpin room in New York City in July 1926. Not only was Orie tired, he was also "in a daze" over a recent crisis at Miller Hess. Apparently, Clarence Hess and the board had a falling out. The board overruled Hess, a founding partner, and was not clear whether Hess would stay with the company. While it might be easier to go forward without Hess, Orie hoped "with all his heart" that Hess could "adjust himself to the policy now adopted by the board. . . . I personally want to leave no stone unturned" in finding a way for him to stay with the company. Orie prayed that they could "learn the lessons the events were intended to teach them."

From the Chittenden Hotel in Columbus, Orie reported that a buyer would like to handle their shoes, but preferred styles that Miller Hess could not or would not—"in our slow Pennsy Dutch fashion and policies"—produce. Nevertheless, business was good—better than it had been for the last three or four years. As was often the case when Orie was on the road, he considered his place in the family as husband and father. He imagined a time when he could "arrange life" to spend more time at home. Still, he was "very very happy in my family life, my Christian experience and in the work He is giving me to do."

While in Chicago in September 1927, Orie visited his brother Wilbur, a casualty of the Indiana-Michigan Conference cleansing of 1923–24. Though Orie was glad Wilbur carried no bitterness, he was distressed by the loss to the church: "Knowing his ability and the opportunity for service in the church that he had, I could cry at the way he passed it up." Orie's expressed regret was not in the conference's handling of Wilbur and the other dissidents, but that his brother had chosen to leave the MC denomination. It was good that he was maintaining his membership in a GC congregation in Nappanee, but "his passion for service thru the church" had been lost.

Orie imagined he had inherited his father's respect for the church and its "orderly process," aside from what was right or wrong. Wilbur, on the other hand, valued principle over process, as revealed in a conversation between the two after the conference's winnowing. Wilbur chided his older brother for not speaking his mind. "Orie, you and I believe alike." The difference is "I say what I think and you won't." In response, Orie said, "Well, Wilbur, let's assume that is the case—that you and I both see nothing wrong with life insurance. We set ourselves in a row of churchmen here—there are ten of them and two of us. They think it's wrong and you and I think it's right. So what does that say? Does that make it right or wrong? Here are these ten—on other things we agree, but on this we differ. Whether right or wrong, I see no reason why I can't work with the ten even if what you say is true."[44]

This attitude did indeed characterize Orie's loyalty to the church despite any differences of opinion.

CALLED TO BE AN ADMINISTRATOR

Like a magnet attracting metal, Orie continued to attract offices and duties. In 1924, in addition to fundraising for Goshen College, he was appointed to the executive committee of the Mennonite Colonization Board. He offered privately to John Mellinger to help launch a missionary paper, and Mellinger made Orie the founding editor of the *Missionary Messenger*, the periodical of EMM. Mellinger's paradoxical quip summed up Orie's productivity: "If you need to get something done, ask Orie Miller. He is busy and he will have time to help you."[45] In 1925 (August 5), Orie was elected vice president of EMM, an office he would hold until he became secretary in 1935, serving until retirement in 1958.

It was in this stage of life, at age thirty-three, that Orie began to see a pattern emerging that gave him a sense of direction. By now, he had passed through the lot at Ephrata church three times without being chosen for ministry: in 1918, when Amos Horst was chosen minister; in 1922, when Abraham A. Landis was ordained deacon; and in 1923, when Landis was again ordained, this time as minister.[46] The lot confused and frustrated Orie, since he had always believed he would be called to be a minister and missionary. All the other assignments that came his way seemed to him to be "one unrelated thing after another."

But in 1925, he began to see the pattern of his calling as a lay leader with a gift for administration. It was, as he often said, "the next to the last one in 1 Corinthians 12:28." Orie believed that an administrator should work behind the scenes, "and where the administrative gift tends to become noticeable and prominent anywhere, it's a pity, because it's not intended to be that." At age thirty-three, Orie the administrator had at last come to terms with his gifts and his life work.[47]

THE PEACE PROBLEMS COMMITTEE

In 1925, Orie became the "highly active" and "aggressive" secretary and treasurer of the Peace Problems Committee, a role he continued to hold until 1953.[48] The committee was the successor to the Military Problems

Committee of 1907–19. When in 1925 the PPC considered disbanding since the Great War had ended six years earlier, Orie argued it should continue. During a break in the 1925 Mennonite General Conference at Eureka, Illinois, Orie walked with Aaron Loucks "down the road" as they discussed the future of the committee. While Loucks said it looked as though their work was "about done," Orie countered, "There is another war coming and the work is only beginning." Orie admired the Quakers for the strength of their peace witness and believed Mennonites should show similar strength. Rather than disbanding the committee, Orie argued, it should be enlarged and strengthened. The next day, the conference did, indeed, act to enlarge the PPC and appointed Orie as a member. The committee then organized and selected Orie as secretary and treasurer—essentially the role of an executive.[49]

The PPC was the MC expression of a wider ecumenical peace movement seeking to redress the church's failure to oppose the unprecedented barbarism of World War I. The shocking disillusionment of the war also sparked secular international peace movements, such as the World Peace Alliance, with a goal of ending war through political persuasion.

Orie had a channel of communication to his Lancaster Conference constituency, and he used it. In the November 15, 1925, issue of the *Missionary Messenger*, Orie's editorial highlighted the "aggressive peace work" of the PPC. Since the editor of this paper also "happened to be" the secretary of the committee, Orie hoped the readers would "understand and pardon" his taking some space to promote the committee's work and to "appeal" to readers for their "prayers, interest and help."[50]

The committee's purposes included making "official protests" and keeping an eye on legislators who promoted "universal military training" or militaristic courses in public schools. A month later, the editor noted a three-day ecumenical conference on peace and war in Washington, DC. Delegates from twenty-eight denominations all agreed that the teachings of Jesus were against war, but they could not agree on what the church should do about it. Though that was disappointing, Orie reported that the conferees had agreed to initiate a "nation wide campaign thru churches against war."[51]

That was the last hurrah for Orie's bully pulpit on peace activism in the Lancaster Conference. Further issues of the *Messenger* avoided mention of the PPC's aggressive peace advocacy. Minister John H. Mosemann Sr.

and other conservative leaders of the conference had objected and Orie relented. The *Gospel Herald*, however, gave him a wider audience.

In an October 7, 1926, *Gospel Herald* article, Secretary Miller outlined the peace committee's role and objectives:

> 1) The education of our own people to a clearer understanding of the true basis of our belief in the doctrine of non-resistance; 2) To keep in touch with such pending legislation in both the U.S. and Canada . . . which might affect us . . . and to keep the proper bodies in the church advised when official protests or statements of our position could appropriately be made; and 3) Let others know our position . . . and our basis for such a position. In this the work of the committee is missionary.

Orie hastened to say for the sake of critics like Mosemann, now a bishop, that the committee "has no sympathy with . . . any peace movements" that divorce peace from Christian faith.[52]

Then Orie reported the thinking, actions, and findings of the committee—in ten full columns. He framed the work of the Peace Problems Committee in an exposition of Scripture, from Jesus to Paul, and in a broad sweep of church and Anabaptist-Mennonite history. He identified other Christian groups that had taken similar positions on peace, such as the Brethren and Quakers. He was encouraged to see "many others" who were coming to embrace nonviolence, although Orie believed that "our group of Christians" had been more consistent than any other.

He also thought "we have been largely content to hold this light for ourselves and our children." Isn't it a bit strange, he asks, that in the four hundred years of our existence, "not a single book has been written" to explain to others our convictions on peace? Is it not also "strange that even today we have very few individuals who have thought thru the implications of this principle" of peace for humanity in general? Many others were "longing for a better way" to avoid the massive suffering caused by war. Mennonites could offer a "presentation which will at least compel the respect of such groups, and even of others who pessimistically insist that these ideals of Jesus are too ideal and impractical" for the modern world.[53]

Secretary Miller then reported the committee's study of other peace movements as well as Mennonite practice and teaching. While there was general agreement about nonparticipation in war, litigation, and politics, there was a wide divergence of opinion about sharing these views with others. While some believed that lasting peace could come only through changed hearts, others believed the time was right to persuade nations to ban war. Some feared that an aggressive peace program would lead to unholy alliances and compromise of essential doctrines. It was true that what editor Daniel Kauffman had recently cited as "a strange lineup" of divergent groups such as anarchists and modernists did exist. Of concern to Orie and the committee was the dearth of Mennonite nonresistance teaching in print during a time when younger people were expressing interest in the topic. In closing, Orie invited criticisms, support, and contributions.[54]

To meet the first objective of educating "our own people," the Peace Problems Committee sponsored study conferences and assigned scholars to interpret and promote Mennonite peace theology and practice.[55] Orie and the committee began meeting informally with the Church of the Brethren and the Quakers, which evolved into the more formal Continuation Committee of the Historic Peace Churches (CCHPC). After becoming chair of the PPC in 1924, Orie and the committee invited several scholars to write educational peace literature.

In October 1925, during Guy F. Hershberger's first year of teaching at Goshen College, Orie stepped into Hershberger's office for a conversation. At a recent peace conference, Orie had seen nothing at all written by Mennonites. That needed to change, so Orie approached Hershberger about doing "something about this." Hershberger agreed, and "that was the beginning of it"; this assignment launched Hershberger's prolific writing career on peace themes, culminating in his landmark *War, Peace, and Nonresistance*, published in 1944. Hershberger also began attending peace conferences and giving voice to Mennonite perspectives on peace.[56]

DIALOGUE WITH MOSEMANN AND HORSCH

As secretary of the Peace Problems Committee, Orie carried on a constant stream of correspondence. While nurturing and encouraging such writers as Guy Hershberger and Edward Yoder, a Hesston College teacher, he also fielded the concerns of eastern conservatives and fundamentalists. He had his longest exchanges with John Horsch of Scottdale and John H. Mosemann Sr. of Lancaster. Horsch and Mosemann objected to the PPC's interactions with liberals of secular peace movements because they threatened the MC separatist identity. While Horsch grounded his peace writing in historical Anabaptism, Mosemann added a dispensationalist framework in which peace was relegated to the future millennial rule of Christ. According to this theory, trying to make peace worked against the purposes of God, and perhaps even delayed the second coming of Christ. Of Mennonite proponents of such thought, Mosemann listened to Horsch, George Brunk, and J. B. Smith. He subscribed to magazines of the Plymouth Brethren and their most influential leader, John Nelson Darby, the source of dispensationalism. Mosemann was an ardent admirer of fundamentalist evangelical ministers.[57]

Dispensationalism redefined history as seven ages, or dispensations, each with unique divine purposes. Such a theory diminished the role of the church, projected the Sermon on the Mount into a future age, identified the kingdom of God with a future Jewish state, and insisted on a literal interpretation of apocalyptic writings such as Daniel, Ezekiel, and Revelation.[58]

Church papers carried on the debate. The *Gospel Herald* published articles by the PPC advocating peacemaking and witnessing to government, as well as counterarguments by conservatives who considered world peace illusory. Orie's "old Goshen" friends Vernon Smucker (with whom he exchanged twenty-nine letters in ten months in 1929) and Lester Hostetler, editors of the MC *Christian Exponent*, took up the activist argument against eastern conservatives. Hostetler, for example, in a February 1926 issue of the *Christian Exponent*, challenged John Mosemann's denunciation of peace movements. Mosemann had decried modern peace movements as "nothing less than a Satanic delusion." Hostetler, on the other hand, argued that the committee was proclaiming the "Gospel of Christ." Hostetler asked whether war was ordained of God or "the result of man's folly and wickedness."[59]

Mosemann objected to the Peace Problems Committee's fraternization with "liberals" of the ecumenical Continuation Committee of Historic Peace Churches (CCHPC). These liberals included other branches of Mennonites, the Quakers, and the Church of the Brethren. Beyond these peace churches were the even more objectionable secular societies such as the Fellowship of Reconciliation (FOR) and the World Peace Alliance. In Mosemann's view, it was useless to work for world peace when Jesus predicted there would always be wars and rumors of wars.

Some Mennonites were absorbing dispensationalist theology from such schools as Moody Bible Institute in Chicago and Dallas Theological Seminary. Perhaps most influential of all was the *Scofield Reference Bible*, first published in 1909. Lancaster Conference bishops in 1930 warned against the alien teachings of the Scofield Bible, as did the Franconia Mennonite Conference, but Mosemann argued in its favor.[60]

Orie responded to Mosemann in his usual measured tone, asking him "for the privilege" of discussing their differences in person. Orie proposed several meetings to "talk through" their divergent views. Mosemann doubted their conversations would be useful, unless Orie could "enlighten me from a viewpoint that is scriptural." In that case, "I shall be glad for your assistance."[61]

Mosemann did not appear at the appointed time, but instead, on August 16, 1926, posed fifteen questions by letter for Orie's consideration. Orie responded respectfully, arguing that it was the duty of Christians to work for a better and more just world. Is it not a "Christian's business to do His will, to do his commandments, to love his neighbor as himself, to lift him up before a lost world in need of Him, etc. etc. and God will see that whatever program He has for this world is carried out?"

Then Orie had some questions for Mosemann. As for Mosemann's claim that working for peace would delay the second coming, would not increasing the number of disciples have the same effect? Was not the work of the Peace Problems Committee consistent with historic Mennonite belief and practice?

Regarding Mosemann's fear that Orie would be unduly influenced by liberals, Orie assured him that no one who knew him could possibly question his commitment to fundamentalism. Nor did such interaction compromise him on questions of orthodoxy. On the contrary, it had the opposite effect, giving Orie the opportunity to present the Mennonite "orthodox Peace and Nonresistance position."

Orie said further that he had been encouraged by his colleagues and his bishop to continue with his work, although he assured them that he "would act subject to their wish in the matter." But until "someone shows me from the Scriptures that the course is wrong, or as a matter of Church polity it will do harm or that it is inconsistent with our profession otherwise, I know nothing to do but follow conscience in the matter and continue to maintain the attitude toward those over me in the church as I have tried to."[62]

"BROTHER ORIE IS A DANGEROUS MAN"

On December 27, two days before an important peace conference at Elizabethtown (Pennsylvania) College, Mosemann complained vociferously in a letter to Orie about his association with such dangerous people as former Goshen College president Noah E. Byers. Since Orie's name appeared with that of Byers on the letterhead of the Continuation Committee of the Conference of Pacifist Churches, "Can you blame any one for believing that your sympathies run strong toward the old Goshen ideas of world progress, world betterment and world improvement? Is not this conclusion justly drawn?"

Then he threatened Orie at a point of vulnerability: "In my judgment, it cannot but impair your own usefulness among us in the East. Trusting you will give this matter your earnest consideration, as your connection with this affair can rightly be regarded as being reactionary, and a return to your former Goshen ideals and colleagues."[63]

Mosemann got Orie's attention. Before moving to Akron, he and Elta had talked often about whether it would be possible for Orie as a mid-westerner and a Goshen College graduate to be active in the Lancaster Conference. He had done well. The conference had allowed his name to stand as a candidate for minister at Ephrata in 1918. He had been elected vice president of the conference's mission board, and he had become founding editor of the *Missionary Messenger*. Now Mosemann was threatening Orie's continued service.

Orie quickly backpedaled. Immediately, he sent a telegram to Richard R. Wood, chair of the Continuation Committee of the Conference of Pacifist Churches. He would not be coming to the two-day peace conference at Elizabethtown College after all. He cited "family circumstances" as the reason that made his attendance "inadvisable." Seven days earlier, Elta had given birth to John Wolf Miller, their fourth child and third son. Typically, such a family event would not have hindered his committee and church work.[64]

On the same day, Orie wrote Wood a letter with a fuller explanation. Not only was he skipping the meeting, he was also resigning as a member of the committee. "During the past few days," he wrote, "circumstances have arisen which prompt me to ask that I be dropped at once as a member of your committee." And further: "My own interest in the way of doing everything possible to spread the Peace idea as lived and taught by Jesus are [sic] as deep and keen as ever." As secretary of the PPC, Orie wanted to stay abreast of what Wood's committee was doing and would and will "be glad to reciprocate this courtesy at all times." Orie promised to drop in at Wood's office in the near future to explain in person.[65]

A disappointed Richard Wood responded, challenging the wisdom of Orie's decision. He had found Orie's advice to be "very valuable," and he had found Orie's company "always pleasant." Wood urged his Mennonite friend to reconsider his decision.[66]

To John Mellinger, Orie later recalled his reaction to Mosemann's scolding: "I felt like I did when I was twenty years younger and my father dealt with me. It was embarrassing." Mellinger, who gave Orie's speech at the Elizabethtown conference, reprimanded him for staying home. "But you didn't get a letter like I did!" Orie said.[67]

Mosemann, however, was pleased. "It is with deep gratitude in my heart to God that I learn of your decision and the long step you have taken in the right direction. You will naturally feel that you are suffering a distinct loss, but as time goes on you will have discovered that it has been great gain on your part and the cause of Christ as well."[68]

To E. L. Frey of Archbold, Ohio, chair of the PPC, Orie explained that he had taken the warnings of Mosemann and others to heart. Orie no longer had anything officially to do with the Continuation Committee, but he did not believe "that this should stand in the way of having representatives of our Committee attend . . . these meetings."[69]

Ever pragmatic, Orie continued his "aggressive" leadership of the PPC without official membership on the Continuation Committee of the Conference of Pacifist Churches. He thought he had appeased Mosemann, but Orie was wrong. In fact, the elder bishop had been less than transparent with him. Mosemann told John Horsch,

> I am more convinced that brother Orie is a dangerous man. . . . That man gets machinery in motion that will take some power to stop in course of time if allowed to proceed. I do not understand why others are so blind that they cannot see the outcome of these things. . . . I think most people consider Orie a very good sound harmless brother.

Mosemann said it had become clear in Orie's correspondence that he was "a reactionary" member of the "old Goshen College crowd." It was the threat of losing his place of influence in Lancaster Conference that had "apparently" moved Orie to resign from the Continuation Committee. Mosemann was planning to warn George Brunk of Orie's danger to the church.[70]

Orie's deference to Mosemann continued. As historian James Juhnke aptly phrased it, Orie's language was "perfectly keyed to the 'old Mennonite' traditional ethos of humility."[71] To Mosemann, Orie wrote,

> I am sure I want to do right, and try to serve obediently and submissively the Master and His Church. Will you pray for me that I may be kept more faithful and more watchful yes and more humbly submissive in life, attitude and mind? I appreciate the confidence that fellow workers in the Church have and have had in me, and certainly pray that I may merit its continuance.[72]

Nevertheless, Orie's enthusiasm for his peace work never wavered. He continued attending peace conferences, writing reports for publication, and writing letters. In 1928, he wrote at least forty-seven letters for the Peace Problems Committee. The PPC and the Continuation Committee of the Conference of Pacifist Churches remained active until 1931. In 1935, with the threat of Nazism on the horizon, the PPC was reactivated and conversations with the historic peace churches were renewed.

BIBLE IN ONE HAND, NEWSPAPER IN THE OTHER

Orie carried his many responsibilities with surprising composure, but to Elta, he always bared his soul. "Elta, I feel about half blue and homesick and altogether lonesome for you this evening," Orie wrote from Hotel La Salle in Chicago. "Sometimes the burdens & responsibilities seem heavier than at others." As a husband and father he provided well, but his presence at home was minimal. "I know I ought to be at home more, but there are so many, many demands all the time, and they seem to be clear calls to duty that one hardly knows what to do or say sometimes. I want to spend more and more time in intercessory prayer and in learning to know His will in the demands that come. If He calls, He will of course give both of us the strength and grace to carry thru."[73] Was not his presence at home also a calling?

Just after the New Year of 1929, Orie noted the beginning of a practice that became deeply ingrained in his daily schedule. He and twelve-year-old Lois decided to read the Bible through in a year—three chapters a day and five on Sunday. From the Statler Hotel in Boston, Orie wrote to Elta, "Now we'll see whether she [Lois] or I can stick to our resolution best." Orie decided to begin with the Book of Job.[74]

In countless future conversations with colleagues and protégés, Orie described his reading practices (in a formulation later attributed to Karl Barth) as the Bible in one hand and a major newspaper, such as the *New York Times* or the *Wall Street Journal*, in the other. It was not enough to read one without the other, because each illuminated the other. The Bible provided the prism through which he saw nearly everything. Orie had "hidden the Word in his heart," and he applied Scripture to most everything.[75] Often his first response to a problem or event was a biblical allusion. "He owns the cattle on a thousand hills" was his response to the challenge of raising a monumental amount of money to move several thousand refugees to South America. The *Wall Street Journal* was the lens though which he saw the world—international events or trends and financial markets. Reading the trends often informed his decisions about new service or mission opportunities.

Throughout the 1920s, Orie never lacked for opportunities. The various letterheads on which he carried out correspondence are a testament to his many involvements: the Peace Problems Committee, Eastern Mennonite Missions, *Missionary Messenger*, Mennonite Board of Education, Young People's Problems Committee, Mennonite Colonization Board, and Mennonite Central Committee. Then there were the letterheads representing his employment: Miller, Hess & Company and A. N. Wolf Shoe Company.

FEEDING THE HUNGRY

The ultimate MCC report on relief work in Russia, titled *Feeding the Hungry*, was published in 1929. P. C. Hiebert, MCC chair, did the majority of the work, but Orie is listed as coauthor. As such, Orie suggested the organizational structure, wrote a chapter, and proofread the manuscript. As well, both Arthur Slagel and A. J. Miller did significant work. Other relief workers—C. E. Krehbiel, G. G. Hiebert, D. M. and Barbara Hofer,

P. H. Unruh, Howard C. Yoder,
and Dan Schroeder—also contributed portions.

When relief operations in Russia
closed in 1925, many assumed the
work of MCC was finished. P. C.
Hiebert and Orie Miller were not
among them. Already on August 9,
1923, Hiebert issued a call to all
Mennonites to make MCC a long-
term agency in order to respond to
future emergencies. Unspent funds
could be applied to other needs. In
his open letter, Hiebert asked the
readers of Mennonite periodicals
whether it would not be beneficial

P. C. Hiebert, MCC chair 1920–53 and principal author of *Feeding the Hungry*. MC USA
Archives–North Newton.

to make MCC a permanent organization. "Is our mission as a peoplehood
finished? Does God say, 'Enough, Now you may quit?'"[76]

In February 1924, Orie sent several suggestions to the MCC executive committee about how a continuing agency might be organized. The
Lancaster Conference leaders were "in entire accord" with Hiebert's invitation, except that they wanted to hold their own funds until a need
arose. In that event, they would like the freedom to choose whether to
participate.[77] A preliminary meeting of those interested in a permanent
organization met in Chicago on December 30, 1924. Since MCC had no
authority to act beyond its Russia mandate, the gathered men organized a
new agency, the American Mennonite Relief Commission. To Orie's great
disappointment, the MC Relief Commission for War Sufferers chose not
to cooperate. Nevertheless, Orie and Levi Mumaw served as members-at-
large and were welcomed to the table. The next meeting was to coincide
with MCC's final meeting.[78]

On August 1, 1925, MCC's executive committee, meeting in
Philadelphia, acted to close the work in Russia by October 1.[79] As it
turned out, MCC was unable to close the books and write a final report
until A. J. Miller finalized operations in Russia and returned home. Miller
did not leave Russia until July 12, 1926, and did not arrive in New York

Feeding the Hungry
Russia Famine
1919--1925

American Mennonite Relief Operations under
the auspices of
MENNONITE CENTRAL COMMITTEE

P. C. HIEBERT, A. M.
Chairman of the Mennonite Central Committee
Author—Editor

ORIE O. MILLER, A. B.
Assistant Secretary of the Mennonite Central
Committee and Relief-Worker. Associate Editor

Scottdale, Pa.
Mennonite Central Committee
1929
All rights reserved.

Title page of *Feeding the Hungry*, the MCC
report on relief work in Russia.

until May 21, 1927. For that reason, the publication of *Feeding the
Hungry*, authorized in 1924, was
delayed until 1929.[80]

Feeding the Hungry helped in-
still MCC and its work in the hearts
and minds of North American and
Russian Mennonites. From its
birth in 1920 to its closing in 1926,
MCC spent $1.3 million to "com-
fort the afflicted and feed the hungry." Mennonite contributions to
all relief organizations during this
time totaled more than $2.4 mil-
lion.[81] In the face of a new crisis
in Moscow, the deeply ingrained
positive perception of MCC made
its rebirth seem logical. The relief
agency's most productive period
was still to come.

Chapter 7
Mission as Necessity: 1930–1939

"I believe our missionaries are going to do good work in foreign fields . . . if they can shake off, mentally at least, the traditional attitudes towards other . . . groups. One doesn't need to compromise in principle or simply molly coddle other folks, but one must give them the same rights to interpret Christianity's basics as one reserves for oneself. Sometimes I get shivers on just this point."

On the road for Miller Hess and A. N. Wolf shoe companies, Orie saw economic distress in nearly every city he visited. In Cincinnati in a single month, 799 new families appealed to the charitable organization, the Community Chest. Detroit had "police watching all entrances to the city to keep outside unemployed from coming there for jobs & then becoming subjects of charity." Daily, Orie heard and read stories that "make one sick at heart." St. Louis was no exception. "Everywhere, it's the same story of unemployment, bread lines, [and] distress."[1]

In 1930, the United States and the Western world were in the early stage of the decade-long Great Depression. Wartime demand for food and subsequent high prices had boosted agricultural production, and by the end of the 1920s there was a worldwide agricultural surplus. Consequently, in 1929 the price of wheat fell to its lowest level in four hundred years. Furthermore, the post–World War I economic boom in all sectors led to exuberant speculative spending and investment. When optimistic investors who held overpriced stock faced the inevitable, they began pulling out of the stock market. Panic selling at any price led to the infamous October 1929 stock market implosion. The ripple effect of the U.S. crisis encircled the globe, destroying the intricate international, commercial, and financial matrix.[2]

Consumer spending fell dramatically, businesses failed, and unemployment soared. Production spiraled downward until, in 1932, the national industrial production dropped to half the 1929 level. Personal income plummeted and thousands lost life savings. By 1933, twelve to fifteen million were unemployed and nearly half of the nation's banks were closed. Ironically, president Herbert Hoover, the mastermind of the successful American Relief Administration efforts in Russia, presided over this American crisis—the steepest and longest economic slump in U.S. history.[3]

SHOE COMPANY PROSPERITY

In striking contrast, the prospects for the A. N. Wolf company in Denver, Pennsylvania, "never was brighter," and Miller Hess in Akron was "picking up every day." The two companies produced quality shoes at lower prices. If people could afford shoes at all, they chose products made by such companies as the efficient "Mennonite" factories in Lancaster County, Pennsylvania. In comparison to the pain of millions, Orie and his partners could "feel most happy."

While staying at the Hotel Baltimore in Kansas City, Missouri, in 1930, Orie noticed three airline offices. Business travel by air seemed to be catching on, but since Orie's territory was Kansas City and eastward, it did not seem practical to use air travel. Still, the seeds of opportunity were planted, and before long he began pondering the possibility of expanding his sales territory westward.

By the spring of 1931, business for the Lancaster companies was even better. From Saint Paul, Minnesota, Orie reported mailing in sixteen cases of A. N. Wolf "welts" and twenty-two cases of Miller Hess "McKays"— more than he had expected. A welt shoe had a rubber cushion stitched between the insole and leather upper, with the stitching visible on the outside of the shoe. A McKay shoe had a patented type of stitch requiring

Miller family on the way to a vacation, 1930 (*back row, from left*: Orie, Elta, Lois, Albert; *front row*: John, Dan). John W. Miller.

a specialized machine to sew together leather uppers with the outsole and insole, with the stitching inside the shoe.

Orie had also picked up two new customers. "The outlook for our business at both factories certainly continues to look good and the shoes they make surely do please the trade." In an attempt to make up for his many absences from home, Orie suggested that Elta lighten her load: "Since things look good I want you to use a little [money] in making your routine easier wherever and in any way you can, whether in getting more help or in making things more convenient."

Business was good in Dayton, Ohio, too. There Orie sold twenty-eight cases of McKays and nine cases of welts. "It begins to look as if our customers would soon snow us under with orders. I get cases on nearly every one I call. . . . I never before had such an experience."[4]

THE VOICE OF EASTERN MENNONITE MISSIONS

In July 1931, Orie's attention was turning southward to South America and an upcoming MCC mission to Brazil and Paraguay to help Russian Mennonites who had settled there. "The burden of the coming task is . . . resting more & more heavily on my heart, as the time approaches," he told Elta. His anxiety added intensity to his prayers: "Am praying mightily for full submission to His Will & for sensitiveness to His leading." He had reported the assignment to the readers of the Eastern Mennonite Missions paper, the *Missionary Messenger*, of which he was editor.

When John Mellinger, president of the EMM board, appointed Orie as editor of the *Messenger* in 1924, he immediately put Orie to work promoting the work of the board. Editor Miller published the first four-page issue of the *Messenger* on April 15 of that year. "Forward" is the one-word aim of the paper, Orie wrote, echoing John Mellinger's use of the word. "We want this to be a definite move forward in the cause of Missions in this conference district." It will be progress if we can "regularly get a little clearer glimpse of the Harvest Field thru [*sic*] the pages of the *Messenger*." In addition to mission topics, the paper became the major source of relief news; the editor was not shy about publishing a continuous flow of refugee needs.[5]

Since 1922, the wary but generous Lancaster Conference had been helping to fund relief efforts, first through the NER in Syria and Armenia, then via MCC in Russia. Though Lancaster Conference leaders mistrusted the inter-Mennonite MCC, the service of Lancaster volunteers prompted many to follow their exotic adventures.

In its second year, the *Messenger* expanded from four pages published quarterly to ten published monthly; then to twelve pages. After fundamentalist conservatives such as John H. Mosemann Sr. vigorously objected to Orie's promotion of Peace Problems Committee work in the *Messenger*, editor Miller focused on relief and missions—still controversial for some.

The January 15, 1926, issue of the *Messenger* featured the "unoccupied" mission fields in Africa, the beginning of a growing emphasis on that continent. The editor also noted that he had been to Washington, DC, as directed by "Mennonite Central Relief Commission," an organizational name that alluded to the former MC relief commission and downplayed MCC. Orie's continuing challenge was to promote the work of MCC in the midst of a conference where many disapproved of MCC's inter-Mennonite character and its apparent lack of accountability. In the nation's capital, Orie called on the chair of the American Red Cross to discuss "relief needs in the world" and to establish the Red Cross as the conduit of information to MCC about disasters requiring emergency relief. There he learned of an immediate need in northeast Pennsylvania for clothing for impoverished children, whose coal-mining fathers were striking for better pay and safer working conditions. The EMM executive committee sent an investigator to assess the need and called on women's sewing circles for the clothing. Lancaster Conference women made and gathered 1,245 pounds of clothing, valued at $1,200, to ship through the Red Cross to Mount Carmel, Pennsylvania.[6]

In the April 15, 1926, issue, editor Miller asked, "Should we undertake a foreign missionary effort?" Knowing that a bishop carried more weight than an editor, Orie was quoting a bishop from a recent meeting. The editor reasoned that they were already "liberally" supporting mission work in India and Argentina, sponsored by the Mennonite Board of Missions and Charities at Elkhart, Indiana. Numerous Lancaster people were among those missionaries. Was it not time to launch our own foreign work?[7] The *Messenger* also reported on the action of the MC General Conference meeting in Kitchener, Ontario, to disband the Mennonite Relief Commission for War Sufferers, which had turned down further cooperation with MCC. A new MC Mennonite Relief Committee would function under the organizational umbrella of the MBMC. In addition to Eli G. Reist, Lancaster Conference treasurer, the members were D. D. Miller, S. C. Yoder, Aaron Loucks, and Levi Mumaw—who had all served the former commission.[8]

DAVID TOEWS AND THE CANADIAN MENNONITE BOARD OF COLONIZATION

In subsequent issues of the *Missionary Messenger*, Orie continued to publish reports on the Russian Mennonite migrations to Canada. In response, the Lancaster Conference shipped to Rosthern, Saskatchewan, and Altona, Manitoba, 8,877 garments, weighing 7,463 pounds and valued at $6,668. Ironically, as Russian Mennonites were immigrating to Canada, Old Colony Sommerfelder Mennonites of Russian origin were emigrating from Manitoba to Paraguay. The *Messenger* carried the report of A. J. Miller, director of MCC relief work in Russia, that the work in Russia was essentially finished. The Lancaster Conference had in six years given $50,000 to MCC's relief work in Russia. From Canada, David Toews reported that 18,098 Russians had arrived since July 1923.[9]

But who was David Toews? How could Lancaster Mennonites trust someone who lived so far away and whom they had never met? In 1927, Orie went to Rosthern, Saskatchewan, to investigate Toews and the Canadian Mennonite Board of Colonization. As a result, Orie could report to the conference that he had full confidence in "Brother Toews

David Toews, known as the "Mennonite Moses." Mennonite Heritage Centre.

and his associates, and in the efficiency [sic] and business-like way in which they carry forward this program."[10]

Elder David Toews of Rosthern, Saskatchewan, was the gifted chair of the Canadian Mennonite Board of Colonization, founded in October 1922. Toews, as persistent as Orie Miller, kept needs ever before all constituents, including the less ardent American Mennonites. More cooperative than most Mennonites south of the forty-ninth parallel, Orie did not hesitate to ask for stronger support. In the inaugural issue of the Messenger, editor Miller said he was gratified, but not satisfied, by the level of support from Lancaster: "Surely we can do better next year." After all, $80,000 from ten thousand members was only an average of eight dollars per member. Lancaster Mennonites had the capacity to give more. "Can we really say we believe in Missions unless we do?"[11]

Indeed, by the end of the 1920s, David Toews, sometimes called a "Mennonite Moses," had helped lead a Mennonite exodus of twenty-one thousand immigrants from Russia into the Canadian "promised land." Much had been accomplished, but it was not enough for Toews. Addressing the twenty-fifth General Conference (GC) Mennonite assembly in Hutchinson, Kansas, in August 1929, Toews lamented the thousands of others who had not escaped Russia: "How many more could have been brought out, if our people in the United States would have stood united in our support, I cannot estimate." American Mennonites had been lukewarm in their assistance. Lancaster Conference Mennonites, largely through Orie Miller's advocacy, had done better than most. Even in Canada, there had been far too much malice and mistrust. But Toews and the Board of Colonization had stubbornly refused to give up; the work was far from finished. Neither the board nor its chair could rest until the

Refugees, bound for Canada, leaving the Chortitza train station on July 2, 1923. Mennonite Heritage Centre.

more than $1.2 million of the *Reiseschuld*, or travel debt, was paid to the Canadian Pacific Railway for transporting the Russian Mennonite arrivals to their Mennonite host communities.[12]

A NEW CRISIS IN MOSCOW

The December 1929 *Messenger* informed its readers of a new crisis brewing in the Soviet Union. Thousands of refugees were camped in and about Moscow in a "final desperate attempt to emigrate."[13] After Lenin's death in 1924, Joseph Stalin worked to outmaneuver his rivals for control of the party and the Soviet Union. In 1927, he achieved his goal and initiated his "five-year plan" to industrialize and collectivize the Soviet economy. This disastrous policy enacted the confiscation of private property, religious repression, and a systematic program of extermination of Soviet citizens in Siberia—and sparked a new wave of emigration.

In late 1929, when news of exit visas granted to seventy Mennonite families circulated in the Mennonite colonies, some thirteen thousand hopefuls rushed to Moscow—leaving crops unharvested in the fields. Finding shelter in *dachas*, or summer cabins, on the outskirts of the city, they pressed officials for permission to leave. Ruthless Soviet *Cheka* agents terrorized, arrested, and deported many. Sympathetic Germans, who felt an affinity for the German-speaking Mennonites, lobbied the German

government to grant temporary asylum. After a "storm of secret communications" between Berlin and Moscow, and the advocacy of Benjamin H.
Unruh, a teacher from Karlsruhe, Germany, and member of the 1920
Mennonite *Studienkommission,* Germany agreed to receive 5,671 of the
Moscow Mennonites.[14] German president Paul von Hindenburg offered
hospitality and personally contributed $50,000.[15] Further, the German
government would provide the transatlantic transport on credit if a host
country could be found.

David Toews renewed his appeals to the Canadian government to re-
open its borders. Canada, in the midst of the Great Depression, took only
1,829 people—those with good health and financial means. What of the
others? Eastern Mennonite Missions and the Lancaster Conference bishop
board authorized the immediate use of the $5,000 in the Emergency
Relief Fund for the refugees. They also recommended that the dormant
MCC be called back into service as the proper agency to handle the crisis.[16] That Lancaster Conference leaders believed MCC should handle
the relief emergency shows a remarkable measure of acceptance of the
inter-Mennonite organization still located beyond conference borders in
Scottdale, Pennsylvania. On the other hand, it was easier to assign the
responsibility elsewhere than to handle it themselves.

A NEW MCC MANDATE

The rejuvenated MCC recommended Paraguay as a destination for the
Russian Mennonite refuges.[17] Paraguay's government had granted special privileges to Old Colony Mennonites from Canada, who established
the Menno Colony in 1927. Paraguayan Law 524 of 1921 granted them
special privileges, including military service exemption, self-government,
religious freedom, and the freedom to manage their own German-
language schools.[18] When MCC inquired about receiving the Moscow
fugitives, Paraguay answered, "If they are Mennonites, let them come."[19]
Benjamin H. Unruh and Harold S. Bender in Europe, the German government, and MCC officers in Scottdale and Akron managed the trek
to the forbidding Paraguayan Chaco. Menno Colony and Corporación
Paraguaya also assisted.[20]

In 1930 and 1931, a total of 1,576 immigrants from Moscow via
Germany established the Fernheim (Distant Home) Colony in the
Chaco. Fifty-seven from Poland and 373 from Amur via Harbin, China,

followed.[21] Though Brazil refused to grant exemption from military service, 2,229—with travel assistance from the German government—made it their home. A few others went to Argentina and Mexico.[22] When MCC called on Lancaster Conference leaders to raise $20,000 to help two hundred families settle in Paraguay, they accepted the challenge. Orie kept the conference posted on the refugees' progress.[23]

In the January 6, 1931, quarterly meeting of the EMM, vice president Orie Miller called the meeting to order. He read yet another appeal from David Toews for clothing and reported on the status of settlement in Paraguay. Further, he gave a "heart-wrenching account of the sentencing of Mennonites to a Siberia prison camp," and told of the thrilling flight over the frozen Amur River to Harbin, China.[24] When Stalin's terror reached to the Amur region, some Mennonites quietly and courageously crossed the frozen river on horse-drawn sleds. Their hardships did not end in Harbin, but they had escaped the Soviet nightmare.[25]

In a July 13, 1931, meeting of EMM, Orie reported his plans to visit South America. As a show of support, the Lancaster Conference assembly passed a resolution: "Since our Bro. Orie Miller expects to leave in August to visit these brethren in Brazil and Paraguay to help them solve their problems, Be it resolved that we wish him God's blessing on his journey and his labors." The assembly stood in a visible expression of support for the resolution.[26]

MISSION TO THE PARAGUAYAN CHACO

Having been thus commissioned, Orie set off on August 8 from Pier 64 in New York Harbor on the SS *American Legion*. It was Orie's first mission to South America, a trip he would repeat, by his count, thirty-some times. The next day, Orie wrote a letter for the *Messenger*, recalling his previous journeys to Beirut and Constantinople: "Now for the third time we find ourselves on the briny deep, cut off from homeland, loved ones, and friends." Orie took care, as always, to identify his MCC mission as an expression of the church. He expressed gratitude for the promise of prayer. "Indeed effective intercession is in itself efficient service."[27]

Orie's mission was to find out how best to assist Mennonite immigrants recently arrived from Germany. The challenges he would encounter were formidable. The Russian and Polish Mennonite fugitives had made their long journey halfway around the globe to the Gran Chaco of

Paraguay—an inhospitable tropical place far from everywhere. It looked more like a wasteland than a promised land. Half the battle had been won—escaping communism and enduring the transatlantic transport. The other half remained—surviving the "green hell" of the Chaco, or *el infierno verde*, as Paraguayans have called it. Small wonder that Orie was approaching this mission with "fear and trepidation."

In the Gran Chaco, the immigrants started from scratch. It was hot—often over one hundred degrees Fahrenheit. It often forgot to rain. Mosquitoes were monstrous. The cattle refused to eat the bitter grass. Many of the wells the settlers dug were too salty to drink. They lived in tents until they could build adobe shelters with grass-thatched roofs. Their debt for the land weighed heavily on their shoulders. Corporación Paraguaya, MCC's agent, reneged on its promises to assist the settlers. The colonists had to build their own roads. They had no doctors, so illness often meant death. A typhus epidemic killed almost one hundred.

When the colonists cleared brush from the land, they learned by trial and error what crops could be cultivated. Error meant hunger. Some years grasshoppers destroyed what did grow. When they were able to produce enough crops to sell, the markets in Asunción were so far away that produce spoiled by the time they got it there. The route was daunting. Colonists traveled the first sixty miles by oxcart to "End Station" at "Kilometer 145," the western terminus of a narrow-gauge freight railway. By rail, they traveled the 145 kilometers, or 90 miles, to Puerto Casado on the Paraguay River. There they boarded ancient steamers to travel the remaining 174 miles down the river to the capital city of Asunción. The return trip upriver took even longer.[28] A Fernheimer later reflected: "We knew we would be poor," but did not know we would be "poor so long."[29] This was the Fernheim Colony Orie encountered in the fall of 1931.

From aboard the SS *Burma* on the Paraguay River, Orie wrote that he was 1,100 miles from Buenos Aires, Argentina, but still 500 miles from Puerto Casado. This meant that the Mennonites in the Chaco lived "about as far from the Ocean as the state of Colorado is from the Atlantic." The trip up the river was about the distance between New York and Colorado. When he arrived in Asunción on Monday, September 14, G. G. Hiebert from Brazil and Mr. Vebber of Corporación Paraguaya were waiting for him. Hiebert had long been anticipating Orie's arrival. Within an hour of landing, Orie "was in the thick of the details and problems that brought me here." It was "a long mixed up and . . . sad story."[30] He was heartened, however, by U.S. ambassador George Post Wheeler, who gave Orie a "splendid" reception. Orie found Wheeler to be sympathetic and willing to do what he could for the Mennonites in the Chaco.

MC missionaries in Argentina, T. K. Hershey, J. W. Shank—both Lancaster natives—and Jacob Hiebert of the Chaco took him to the offices of Corporación Paraguaya and to see Webster Browning, a Presbyterian missionary. Browning, the author of several books Orie had on his shelf, was a storehouse of knowledge about South America. He and everyone else seemed to know about Mennonites since the recent movement of Russian Mennonites to Brazil and Paraguay.

Orie noted that the capital city of Asunción was founded in 1537 and had a current population of ninety thousand. He was surprised to see so many U.S. products "on display everywhere." Most of the people he saw on the street were indigenous, but here and there he observed the "fair complexion of the Nordic."[31] On September 16, Orie and the two Hieberts boarded the screw-propelled, gasoline-powered boat that was to take them up the Paraguay River to Puerto Casado. They made a brief stop in Concepción, one of the oldest cities on the continent.

Two days after leaving Asunción, they arrived in Puerto Casado, a town of several thousand—all employees of the Casado Company and their families. Orie called on Jose Casado to review the details of the contract MCC and the immigrants had made with Corporación Paraguaya, and to arrange transport to the colonies. Orie was surprised by the size of the Quebracho processing plant, which boiled wood chips to extract tannins used to tan hides in making leather. Daily, the plant produced 800 fifty-kilogram sacks of the extract. On Saturday, they boarded the narrow-gauge freight railway for End Station at Kilometer 145. On the way, Orie observed cheerless vistas: "Open camps and thick, thorny brush; peon workmen; dirty and miserable human beings; and wretched shanties."[32]

At Kilometer 145, the travelers drank coffee and then went farther into the Chaco in Casado's Ford truck. Four hours later, they arrived at the villages of Hoffnungsfeld and Wiedenfeld in Menno Colony—the settlement of Old Colony Canadians. In the evening, they arrived "tired, dirty, and sore" in the village of Lichtfelde, Fernheim Colony. On Sunday, September 20, the visitors were among the 150 people who gathered for

"Bible meetings" under a tent in Auhagen. Two village choirs sang hymns and a minister gave a lesson from Romans 8. In the afternoon, the colonists heard Orie and G. G. Hiebert report on their mission, and more generally, on the life of Mennonites in Brazil and in North America.

On Monday, Orie spent the entire day until midnight with Peter Isaacs, Jacob Hiebert, Franz Heinrichs (who became Fernheim's first *Oberschulz*, or administrator), Johann Funk, and a few other colony leaders. Orie and Hiebert were "getting the lay of the land" for the next day's meeting with all colony leaders. On Tuesday, September 22, the two emissaries met with 150 men in the Kleefeld schoolhouse. The agenda: closer relations with Mennonites in Brazil; the price of land and the survey; the hospital and sick fund; need for clothing; the cotton gin; horses; and further immigration.

The villages of the colonies were well-organized but lacked an umbrella organization to enable buying supplies and selling produce collectively. As the story was told later, Orie and the leaders of Fernheim sat together and wrestled with the challenges of economic survival. The problems seemed so insurmountable that at one point Orie excused himself from the circle. He found a private space behind a tree where he broke down and cried, a response reminiscent of the "impasse" at the Elkhart founding of MCC. Orie returned and the conversation resumed. Out of their struggle emerged the idea of forming a cooperative—the major key to their economic survival and success.[33] The cooperative gave colonists power to negotiate better prices for bulk purchases and sale of products.

By evening, "everyone was happy"—about the long-awaited rain, if not the meeting. Orie's assessment of the challenges was that some things "were bright enough, others much brighter than at any time hitherto since they are here," but the overall condition was "simply heartrending."[34]

The next week, Orie visited Menno Colony and each of the twelve Fernheim villages where he met with leaders, preachers, and teachers and visited in homes. He was taken to see widows, orphans, the sick, and the unfortunate. Conversations regarding difficulties were "frank and open." Orie participated in discussions about teachers' salaries, school organization, and whether to accept the government's offer of Spanish-language instruction for teachers in Asunción. On Sunday, 250 people from three villages met to hear a sermon, Hiebert's report on Mennonites in Brazil, and Orie's forty-five-minute "talk" on the U.S. church and mission affairs.

On Monday, September 28, a meeting was called to adopt a charter and constitution for the cooperative. Orie helped to determine the needed equipment and money for new arrivals, paring down the previous estimate of $600 to $200. Then Orie went with preacher Heinrich Friesen to see the site of the city (later called Filadelfia) that was to be the administrative center of Fernheim Colony. The city plan had been drawn and the streets and roadways were under construction. "Sentimentally," Orie noted in his diary, "the visit was most interesting, ours being the first auto [to use] the main street of the city."[35]

Bender and Miller Streets (named for Harold S. Bender and Orie O. Miller), Filadelfia, Fernheim Colony, Paraguay. John E. Sharp.

Of even greater sentiment would have been *Millerstrasse* named for him, but Orie failed to mention this in his diary and in his letters to Elta. He must have seen it, since it appeared on the original 1931 city map as an east-west street along with *Unruhstrasse*, named for B. H. Unruh, and *Hindenburgstrasse*, in honor of German president Paul von Hindenburg. There was yet no street named for Harold Bender.

On Thursday, September 29, Orie was taken to see the Lengua Indian tribe. He saw them as "most primitive" with a language of fewer than seven hundred words and having "child minds in every way." Women were making rope from cactus leaves, and the chief showed how to rub sticks together to start a fire. The Lengua worked mainly for the Mennonites and as a result were learning Low German and taking German names. Orie wondered what the Lengua thought about the development of land that had been "theirs since humans first came to this continent."[36]

The Polish Mennonites occupied the village of Rosenfeld. They were proudly independent, but wanted Orie to work out their part in the cooperative. On the last afternoon of his visit, Orie saw the printing plant and talked over problems in the publication of the *Mennoblat*. He had a final meeting with Heinrich Friesen and Peter Isaacs to discuss the orphan and widows fund. At the schoolhouse that evening, the colony had a farewell

Orie (*left*) and colony administrator, Jacob Siemens, 1939, Filadelfia, Fernheim Colony. Koloniehaus Museum.

service for Orie and Jacob Hiebert. A choir sang, the congregation sang, Preacher Friesen preached, and Orie and Hiebert spoke—"all in all a service which will not soon be forgotten."[37]

RETURN TO AKRON

Three weeks after leaving Asunción for the Chaco, Orie was back in the Paraguayan capital. To Elta he confided that "never before in my life have I been confronted with a more difficult and tangled mess." And he had points of comparison in Beirut and Russia. He was certain MCC would "unanimously confirm the steps I have had to take." The colony leaders had "seemed unanimous in their appreciation." Orie had found Jacob Hiebert very helpful in understanding the "psychological under current" in the colonies. Despite the apprehension he had felt when entering the Chaco, Orie could "still say and see and feel that the Lord wanted me to do this service."

While in Asunción on October 7, Orie was on hand to welcome an additional group of fifty-three immigrants. Reporting to *Messenger* readers on October 9, Orie was still too close to the Chaco sojourn to report comprehensively. The twelve days in the Chaco were still a jumble: "Just now the mind picture is still a bit confused," but prominent impressions were

Orie and Elta's children ca. 1934 (*from left*: Bob, Lois, Dan, Albert, and John, on his pony). John W. Miller.

"dust, mud, Indians, cactus, Paraguayan soldiers, oxen, and the thrill of witnessing the beginnings of 'civilized' living" by the Indians.[38]

Orie returned to New York on November 18, after an absence of fifteen weeks. His arrival had been delayed three days due to a landslide in the Panama Canal.[39] Upon his return, Orie asked to be released as *Missionary Messenger* editor—a rare move for Orie, who rarely gave up anything as he took on committee upon committee, and board upon board. He did, however, retain a place at the editorial desk as associate editor. J. Paul Sauder, the former associate, became the editor.[40]

THE EFFICIENCY OF AIR TRAVEL

Orie Miller, MCC liaison to the Mennonite colonies in South America and associate editor of the *Missionary Messenger*, also had to earn a living. And his family was growing—on August 8, 1930, Robert Wolf Miller was born, the fifth and the last child to join Orie and Elta's family. Fortunately, despite the dramatic drop in national industrial output, shoe sales in Akron and Denver were booming. From the Copley-Plaza Hotel in Boston on January 13, 1932, Orie reported higher than average sales of ninety-nine cases. In March, he was expecting even higher daily sales since he was getting into "better territory" west of Kansas City.

He now saw the benefit of air travel for business. On the last day of March 1932, Orie took his first flight from Kansas City, Missouri, to Omaha, Nebraska, on American Airlines. He told Elta that he was the only passenger, "aside from a stowaway whom I found in the lavatory." Airline security measures still lay in the future! As was his style, Orie noted the numbers: "The plane maintained an altitude of around a thousand feet and an average speed of about 115 miles per hour. The riding was much smoother than on a train and enabled me to see the folks in one day that took me two on my last trip." He was clearly appreciating the increased efficiency.

An instruction card, which he enclosed in the letter, introduced the novice to the protocol for flying. When boarding, passengers were given cotton and chewing gum. "Each serves a purpose." A ball of cotton in the ears would "reduce the noise of the powerful motor." The gum "will keep your mouth moist and tends to keep a tense sensation from the ears when ascending and descending." In addition, "swallowing corrects the variation in air pressure." Passengers were not to be concerned when the plane banked on turns; it was similar to the banking of curves on a highway. When preparing to land, the pilot, lacking control towers, banked as he circled the landing site "to make sure the field is clear." A final warning: "Under no circumstances should passengers throw or drop objects from the plane" because doing so "violates Federal Law and endangers life and property" of those below. Indeed![41]

MANAGING COLLEGE BUDGETS

In his role as financial agent for the MBE, Orie presented systematic Depression-era plans for both Hesston College and Goshen College. In 1933, he advised the Hesston College Local Board (of directors) to pay faculty salaries according to degrees held. Teachers could expect a monthly check if that much money was available. If funds were short, the checks were to be prorated. If at the end of the fiscal year, there was a surplus, faculty would be paid, again on a prorated scale. There was, however, only a three-year window; at the end of three years, unpaid salaries were to "be considered closed."[42]

Goshen College was also in crisis mode. Student enrollment was down and money was short. A year earlier, in July 1932, president S. C. Yoder had sent Orie a dire telegram: "We can't keep going beyond August 1;

what course shall we take?"[43] In January 1933, a faculty committee proposed hiring C. L. (Chris) Graber to assist Yoder in fundraising and managing finances. Despite Orie's reluctance, the MBE approved the plan and hired Graber as "financial executive and field representative." Orie wanted to cut costs, not hire new personnel, but dean Harold Bender had been persuasive. Graber, lacking confidence in Yoder's ability to lead, insisted as a condition for his hiring that

Orie reading the newspaper in the kitchen, 1930s. EMM.

the board appoint an administrative committee with Orie Miller as chair. Orie wanted "desperately to see Goshen College survive and so he kept on writing these [personal] checks."[44]

Graber hoped that Orie would eventually become president, and apparently Orie gave it some thought. Bender, however, was adamant in advising Orie to stay where he was. The church had far too few businessmen like Orie, who channeled talents and dollars to the church.[45] The new administrative arrangement worked well. Yoder, Bender, and Graber ran the college, and Orie used his considerable influence to promote the welfare of the institution. He was also a steadying force in balancing the occasional impetuosity of the forceful Bender and the enterprising Graber. With this team in place, Goshen's fortunes began to improve. In 1936, Goshen ended the year with a small surplus, and the fall looked promising with 310 students, the best student enrollment ever.[46]

A consequence of Orie's role as chair of the administrative committee was that Bender had to submit to the chair's decisions. While writing his dissertation and studying for doctoral examinations at the University of Heidelberg in the summer of 1935, Bender wrote to ask Orie's permission to extend his stay in Europe to do some writing. Orie said no: "I would strongly urge that you plan to return just as soon as you can after your work in Germany is completed . . . with the idea of taking up at once on your return such of your teaching load as can be assigned you."[47] Surely Bender was annoyed.

"WORLD EVANGELISM, AN IMMEDIATE NECESSITY"

The evangelical influences that ignited fundamentalist battles against modernism also shaped views toward missions. Mission advocates were inspired by valiant individuals who left home and hearth—and often the communal sense of accountability built on Matthew 18—to preach the gospel to a "lost and dying world." Revivalism bred not only more fervent expressions of piety, but also a more individualistic view of salvation. The theme of the gospel song, "My God and I," often became more compelling than the key biblical text "Where two or three are gathered." Individuals who were "saved" could be free to express their piety apart from the communal embrace and the lagging cultural "bondage" that sometimes characterized traditional communal life.

In midwestern conferences, individual initiative and more aggressive outreach had come with the "quickening" influence of John F. Funk and John S. Coffman in Elkhart, Indiana. Lancaster Conference, more traditional than many, was working to maintain a balance between accountability and outreach.[48] In the transition, some plowed ahead despite the effect on the church. Some who mounted campaigns for change threatened conference unity and could be relieved of their membership, or they could choose to leave for more "enlightened" evangelical congregations. Others, who gently prodded the church while remaining respectful and accountable to church authorities, were more effective. Two especially effective agents of change in the decades of the twenties and thirties were John H. Mellinger, who was "humble while he was aggressive," and Orie Miller, who was "a surprising combination of personal initiative and submission to church authority," to use John L. Ruth's characterizations.[49]

Since the 1920s, the theme of mission work in Africa had been gathering steam in Lancaster Conference. The *Messenger*'s editors, apologists for the cause, tracked the momentum. Beginning in 1927, the editors mentioned Africa in nearly every issue. Facts about Africa reprinted from the *Missionary Review of the World* appeared in the October 24, 1928, issue.[50]

At EMM's annual meeting at Gingerich's Meetinghouse near Lebanon, Pennsylvania, in March 1929, the assembly took cautious action. The assembly resolved to "take note of a seemingly growing conviction within the brotherhood that in our developing missionary interests, the unreached portions of Africa" ought to be considered. Having heard that the Board of Missions and Charities at Elkhart, Indiana, was considering work in Africa, chair Mellinger was instructed to inform that board of "our interests and sympathies in this matter." Any action on their part to enter Africa "would find hearty support from our constituency."[51]

At a meeting at East Chestnut Street church in Lancaster City on July 14, 1930, EMM put forward a proposal to establish a mission in Africa, pending conference approval. The matter was referred to the Board of Bishops, which deemed it prudent to delay action.[52] By October 1, 1930, conference leaders were ready to move ahead:

> Therefore, we, as a Board of Bishops feel that since the matter has been considered by us with that end in view from the beginning, we unanimously favor the starting of a mission in Africa under the Eastern Mennonite Board of Missions and Charities, subject to further joint action of both the bishop board and the Eastern mission board, and the leading of the Lord.[53]

Yet in the December *Messenger*, assistant editor Orie Miller reported the cautious words of a bishop regarding the communal mind: "Before there can be assurance of success in undertaking such a venture, there must be a common mind, purpose, policy and a unity . . . among the forces at home." As to financial viability, "all agree we have the necessary resources."[54] When the MC Mission Board (Elkhart, Indiana) lacked the resources to open a mission in Africa, the initiative remained in Lancaster Conference hands.[55]

In May 1931, the editor spoke forthrightly on the "Necessity of Foreign Missions." It is "not a novelty, but a necessity," for "without the Gospel they are LOST." Furthermore, "World Evangelism is an immediate Necessity."[56] The *Messenger* cover of August 14, 1931, featured an outline map of Africa, and in December, a detailed map of the "Dark Continent." EMM president John Mellinger, though passionate about a mission in Africa, assured readers: "There has been no rushing in. Instead the way has been shown step by step this far." Nevertheless, the twelve members of the bishop board and the twenty-five members of EMM appointed an examining committee to screen applicants.

FINDING A MISSION FIELD IN AFRICA

In January 1933, EMM announced that eight candidates had come forward and that either Ethiopia or Nigeria would be the probable field. At the annual meeting of the conference in April at the Paradise Meetinghouse, the examining committee recommended Elam and Elizabeth (Kauffman) Stauffer and John H. Jr. and Ruth (Histand) Mosemann. John was twenty-six and Elam was thirty-four. Both boards—EMM and the Board of Bishops—approved the choice of their pioneer missionaries.[57] The idea of an African mission was now personified. At Mellinger's Church on April 19, Elam Stauffer and John Mosemann Jr. were ordained to serve the eventual mission in Africa. The ordinations assumed the partnership of spouses, Elizabeth Stauffer and Ruth Mosemann.

Further, Orie was to accompany Stauffer on an exploratory tour of Africa.[58] Who else in the Lancaster Conference had international travel experience? Their plan was to visit mission agencies in England, Germany, and Sudan before proceeding to East Africa. Fifteen hundred people gathered at Weaverland Church—filled from basement to balcony—on December 7 to give a grand and emotional send-off. Bishop Noah Mack, S. C. Yoder, president of the MC Board of Missions, and John Mellinger offered "impressive words of farewell." With "tears of rejoicing" the large crowd stood "in the presence" of Orie Miller, the Stauffers, and the Mosemanns to sing a final hymn, "Use Me Savior."[59] Clearly, the balance in the conference had shifted in favor of progressive foreign mission work. Orie felt gratified by the affirmation, but the responsibility before him weighed heavily.

From the SS *Bremen*'s stateroom 492 out on the Atlantic Ocean, "your brethren Orie O. Miller and Elam W. Stauffer" sent a farewell message of their own to the readers of the *Missionary Messenger*: "We are off to Africa with the Gospel. Bearers of the good news are happy." About forty people had traveled to New York for a final send-off in a social hall of the hotel, and then from the pier. "Leaving under the strains of gospel songs sung by about forty Christian voices at midnight, waving handkerchiefs" until the voyagers were out of sight left a long-lingering impression. "We bid you goodbye . . . in Jesus' name."[60] This was Orie's third transatlantic voyage and the fourth journey on the "briny deep."

Contacts with a variety of mission agencies and government officials all pointed to East Africa. In London, England, the Mennonite scouts visited Alexander McLeish of the World Dominion Movement, who mentioned Ethiopia, Sudan, or Tanganyika as potential mission sites. If in Tanganyika (now Tanzania), McLeish recommended the Musoma region

on the shores of Lake Victoria. The World Dominion Movement had begun in 1923 to promote "evangelism and the founding of the Indigenous
Church as the natural agent for the continuation of the work of evangelism
and the development of all forms of Christian work on the field."[61] Orie
had been reading journals and books published by World Dominion.[62]

At the London office of the Africa Inland Mission, Orie and Elam
Stauffer met director D. M. Miller. At first aloof, the director soon lost
his cool demeanor as he listened to the seekers' passionate vision for
Africa. After writing a letter of recommendation to field director William
Maynard in Tanganyika, the three joined hands as the director prayed that
"no time and not one cent of money be wasted" in the new Mennonite
venture. In Germany, the two explorers visited Dominion offices in Berlin
and Munich. Each office gave letters of introduction to mission leaders in
East Africa.[63]

Orie observed that Germany's newly appointed chancellor, Adolf
Hitler, "seemed to be taken for granted and everywhere one notes deep
appreciation for the present good order and safety." Europe's economy
seemed to have recovered from the Great Depression, which convinced
Orie that the worst of the crisis had past. He told his business partners in
Akron that America's economy should steadily improve.[64]

To Elta he expressed his mission philosophy and his apprehension:

> I believe our missionaries are going to do good work in foreign fields
> even tho not as well educated as others if they can shake off, mentally at
> least, the traditional attitudes towards other Christian groups. One doesn't
> need to compromise in principle or simply molly coddle other folks, but
> one must give them the same rights to interpret Christianity's basics as one
> reserves for oneself. Sometimes I get shivers on just this point. "[65]

Stauffer later recalled that Orie helped him understand "how to learn
from others without despising our own rich heritage."[66] As a traveling
companion, "Elam & I get along fine," he told Elta. Stauffer "is quiet &
reserved & tries his best to be adaptable & happy & true to his vision. He
is measuring up to all & more than I had expected."[67]

Back aboard a ship, Stauffer and Miller crossed the Mediterranean Sea
to Egypt, and passed through the Suez Canal and into the Red Sea. They
docked at Port Sudan and traveled by rail to Sudan's capital, Khartoum.
There they consulted Reid Shields, director of Presbyterian missions. Their

own field, said Shields, was too large for them, so he offered to share a territory west of Khartoum. "We won't decide until we see Tanganyika," said Orie.[68]

They returned to the port and boarded a ship heading through the Gulf of Aden to the Indian Ocean. On board were missionaries representing five Catholic and Protestant churches, all free with their counsel. Guidebooks Orie had purchased in London gave the relevant statistics and history of Tanganyika. According to the 1929 census, of 6,000 foreigners in the province half were English, a third were German, and only 59 were American.

A PLACE OF WEALTH AND WONDER

East Africa had been a place of wealth and wonder. Archeological evidence from Olduvai Gorge, east of Lake Victoria on the Serengeti Plains, indicates that Tanganyika/Tanzania, Kenya, and Ethiopia may be the region where human life originated. Building on pre–World War I discoveries, Louis Leakey in 1931—two years before Miller and Stauffer reached Africa—began excavating the gorge and concluded that this region was the "Cradle of Mankind."[69]

The Bantu peoples from Nigeria and Cameroon in West Africa migrated eastward in the early centuries, bringing with them expertise in agriculture, cattle-raising, and iron metallurgy. The Swahili (coastal traders) tribal groups expanded to become city-states and regional kingdoms—some of great wealth and culture. Islamic traders discovered the richness of the coastal kingdoms around the eighth century, and brought not only goods but Arabic culture and Islam. Swahili merchants traded gold, slaves, and ivory from the interior for glass, pottery, and textiles from China, India, and Persia. In the most prominent port cities such as Mombasa, the Island of Zanzibar, and Kilwa, wealthy Swahili merchants and ruling officials constructed stone and coral buildings— impressive compared to those built of mud bricks and wood. Conversion to Islam enhanced trade with Arab merchants.[70]

European adventurers discovered East African ports in the nineteenth century, as did the Scottish pioneer missionary David Livingstone. In the late nineteenth-century "scramble for Africa," European nations claimed nearly all of Africa as colonies, euphemistically calling them "protectorates." They systematically stripped away natural resources and dominated human populations. Germany established German East Africa in 1880. European overlords drew over one million Africans into the Great War. Many more were forced into supporting roles as porters and carriers. As one of the spoils of war, the British took part of German East Africa that became Tanganyika. The League of Nations confirmed British rule in 1922. The important trading city of Dar es Salaam (Harbor of Peace) became its administrative center and the largest city of Tanganyika.[71]

FINDING THE FIELD

Nearing Mombasa, Kenya—one of the ancient cities of wealth—on January 12, 1934, Orie wrote to Elta. They were thirty-six days out from New York and had three more to go before disembarking. He and Stauffer were learning a lot about Tanganyika and Urundi (Burundi) from missionaries on board the ship. The most promising discovery was that they would arrive just in time to attend the first Protestant missionary conference of the region in Dar es Salaam. Their contacts there would surely help them discern a location for the mission "without having to leave the city." The timing could "hardly be other than providential." A Salvation Army missionary was sure Urundi was the place for them. More helpful was a young geographer, who freely shared his maps of Africa, showing roads, railroads, elevations, villages, tribes, and languages. Orie was confident that God "again would marvelously open a way." Still the responsibility of this mission was on his mind "almost every waking hour."[72]

As they traveled, Orie probed Stauffer for his ideas about launching the mission. Stauffer began by eliminating the things that he would not do. Orie stopped him and said, "I am not interested in what we cannot do. I want to know what we *can* do." Stauffer was learning. The missionary-to-be wondered how they would know if something of a serious nature happened back home. Orie's practical nature came to the fore: "No news is good news; if anything serious happened at home, they would contact us."[73]

During their stop in Mombasa, Kenya, Orie visited the fabled city of Zanzibar, off the coast of Tanganyika. Local guides worked hard to convince the obvious foreigner that he could not do without their services. Despite their best efforts, Orie "did not use any, paid none, felt bad at no time, and returned to the ship in good humor."[74]

Orie and Elam Stauffer arrived at the seaport of Dar es Salaam, Tanganyika's main port, on January 14, 1934. After checking in at the New Palace Hotel, the two prospectors visited numerous mission headquarters in the city. The twenty-some Protestants gathered for the Tanganyika Mission Council, where "a good spirit prevailed," received the Mennonites "cordially." It seemed they all directed Miller and Stauffer toward two areas of Tanganyika, one in the north and one in the south. "What swung the balance" in favor of the Musoma region in the north was a visit to the office of P. E. Mitchell, acting governor and secretary of native affairs. He had been expecting them. Bishop Chambers of the Anglican Church Missionary Society had spoken to the governor "repeatedly in our favor." In a short time Chambers, Orie told Elta, had become an "outstanding friend" and "a real father and counselor to us." Mitchell had a recommendation. Getting up from his desk, he walked to the wall and put his finger on the map right up in the Musoma area, saying, "'I would like to see you two young men go right up there to establish your work. It is a neglected area. The natives there look rather wild and savage, but you don't need to fear them; they're alright.'"[75]

The Musoma region, which had also been one of McLeish's recommendations, was seven hundred miles from Dar es Salaam on the eastern shore of Lake Victoria. Just south of Kenya, it contained a wide mixture of tribal groups and languages. Hearing that Swahili seemed to be the most common language, Orie asked Stauffer how old he was. Stauffer answered that he had turned thirty-five while in Dar es Salaam. "Well, Elam," said Orie, "at your age the muscles of your mouth have been pretty well set, so you will not get the language very well." That was all the incentive Stauffer needed. To prove Orie wrong, Stauffer would "get the language or die trying!"[76]

At Shinyanga, they met William Maynard, director of the Presbyterian mission, for whom they had a letter of introduction from the Khartoum office.[77] Maynard told them about Emil Sylwulka, an Africa Inland Mission worker in Mwanza. By telegram, Maynard asked Sylwulka to meet the Mennonites at Mwanza, where the railroad ended.

Following Maynard's instructions, the two boarded the train. As they approached the Mwanza station, Stauffer wondered how they would recognize Sylwulka. In answer, Orie pointed to a man among those gathered at the station and said, "There he is." "But, Orie, how do you know?"

the incredulous Stauffer asked. Said Orie, "I know a missionary when I see one!"[78]

It was, indeed, Emil Sylwulka. It soon became apparent that the congenial missionary liked Stauffer and was the ideal guide. Both Orie and his companion felt an immediate affinity with Sylwulka when they learned that he had been a member of the Defenseless Mennonite Church of North America—earlier known as the Egli Amish and later called the Evangelical Mennonite Church. This genial missionary was clearly an answer to their prayers and surely a key to their success. "I doubt that we could have found a man in all Africa who knows Mennonites" the way Sylwulka did, Orie wrote. Nor could they have found anyone more helpful and sympathetic to their mission. "Surely," Orie exclaimed to Elta, "the Lord has undertaken for us!"[79]

Suwulka was willing to devote the next thirty days or more to help locate a mission location. Orie and Stauffer were now so confident that the Musoma region, still unseen, was to be their mission site that they wired Elizabeth Stauffer and the Mosemanns to come at once. It was January 21, only one week after the two stepped onto the pier at Dar es Salaam.[80]

With his mission nearly accomplished, Orie "deposited" Stauffer with Sylwulka and returned to Dar es Salaam. Stauffer later joked that Orie deserted him at the end of the railroad when he and Sylwulka still had a challenging, ten-week overland journey on bicycles.[81]

SHIRATI BY LAKE VICTORIA

After a long and arduous journey, Stauffer and Sylwulka found themselves on the low, flat-topped Kuturu Hill overlooking a small trading village near the eastern shore of Lake Victoria. In the region lived 550,000 people in 402 villages, "with hardly four Christians." Chief Nyataya, who had led them to the hill, said, "Here is where I think you should build." Sylwulka agreed, "That is your field." On February 16, Stauffer, confident that this was, indeed, the place, stepped off the perimeter of the mission compound.[82] It was a place called Shirati—a name that for Lancaster Mennonites would become as familiar as Salunga.

Though Orie would not see Shirati for eleven years, he was exuberant. In a letter from Dar es Salaam, his port out of Tanganyika, he told Elta, "You cannot imagine how happy & thankful I feel!" Everyone that Orie and Stauffer encountered seemed delighted about their coming, with the possible exception of the Seventh Day Adventists at Musoma. Orie's counsel to Stauffer was to treat them right as believers, "but otherwise ignore them."

Instead of returning home directly, Orie was now crossing the Indian Ocean and the Arabian Sea to India, where his brother Ernest and his wife, Ruth, were serving as missionaries. J. A. (Jacob A.) Ressler, a Lancaster Conference native, had launched the first MC foreign mission under the Elkhart Board of Missions in 1899. In January 1934, Orie had received an urgent telegram asking him to come to Dhamtari, India, because Ernest was ill.[83] Ruth wrote, "He is making progress, though he still gets his periods of depression." Too much "noise and excitement" unsettled him. When a recent meeting of missionaries and Indian leaders at Dondi proved to be too stressful, Ruth and the doctor took Ernest into the jungle to soothe him. The doctor said Ernest would improve faster if he were removed "from mission business and contact with Indian people." Though she hesitated to inconvenience Orie, it "would help Ernest so much" if Orie could come to India.[84] Though it cost extra and delayed his return home, Orie responded to the need.

A DRAMATIC MISSIONARY SEND-OFF

Orie was also thinking of home—the new house they would build "in a year or two," and the income they would need in the future. Indulging in a bit of prosperity gospel, Orie hoped they could enjoy the money "so much the more by having been faithful when He called." As was his custom, he worked columns of numbers in pencil on hotel stationery and figured how much income he was losing. With the loss of salary and the travel to India, it was costing him $2,000–$3,000. Even so, "that is little compared to the results of not being obedient when He calls." Orie need not have worried. Though the world was wallowing in the Great Depression, his net income had more than doubled the previous year—from $8,133 in 1932 to $18,724 in 1933.[85]

From home, Elta kept Orie informed of events as they unfolded. John Mellinger invited Elta to a meeting at the Oreville "Old People's" Home, along with Elizabeth Stauffer and John and Ruth Mosemann. "Bro. Mellinger surely has all the confidence in you—he made a very nice speech," Elta wrote Orie. Mellinger said if Orie believed Stauffer and the Mosemanns should leave now, "it should be that way." Elta considered traveling to Dar es Salaam with Elizabeth and returning with Orie, but decided against it.

When the departure date for Elizabeth Stauffer and the Mosemanns was moved ahead, Elta reported its effect on Mary Zimmerman, a self-appointed mission correspondence secretary from Lancaster City: "I have the impression and I guess pretty correctly that Mary Zimmerman got very much excited." She did not think it proper that the missionaries would leave in advance of their cargo of clothing and supplies, and "insisted that everything must be right there when they get there, so they are taking a later boat."[86] Assisted by two others, Zimmerman collected and circulated letters from missionaries in various parts of the world.[87] Apparently, she also took for herself a coordinating role—with considerable influence—in the preparation and travel of the new Africa-bound missionaries.

Elta and A. N. Wolf were excited for other reasons. John Mellinger had said Orie need not wait for the missionaries to arrive in Tanganyika, but could return home. Furthermore, Elta "felt sure" that Orie would want to be home for the busy season of taking orders for the fall shoe trade. "Milo" would probably do okay, but he was new to sales and had said he could not "get around" the way Orie could. Adding some pressure, Elta reminded him that he had "obligations" at home and many were counting on him. Unless he intended to resign from the shoe companies, he should get home by May 1.[88] On the same day, Wolf also wrote, saying they were not getting so many orders since Orie was gone. "I am sure for the best interest of the business you should come not a bit later than May 1st."[89]

Again, Elta reported Mellinger's opinion that there was no need for Orie to wait for the new arrivals. "I surely do not want to hinder the work, but I thought since you had planned to be here to help with the spring orders I feel you should as long as you want to keep the work. You have done for the mission board what you promised, and you cannot help that they [Stauffer and Mosemanns] are taking so much time in getting over." Apparently, EMM was unwilling to bear the cost of Elta's peace of mind. Unhappily, she said, "I felt all the time more cables should be send [sic] back and forth [so we could] fully understand each other, but others did not think so."[90] By letter, Elta kept Orie apprised of plans for the missionary send-off.

Lois, now a student at Goshen College, wrote to Orie in Dhamtari, India: "I suppose you do know this is ministers' week. Everywhere you look you see a preacher. There are sure a lot of them here." Signed "from your bad girl, Lois."[91] She was turning out to be a free spirit.

Lois would have been shocked had she seen the number of preachers in New York City on February 21, 1934. Elta told Orie that Elizabeth Stauffer and the Mosemanns were given a spectacular send-off in New York City. A send-off, indeed! Plain-clothed Lancaster County Mennonites on Fifth Avenue were a sight to behold—even in a city as diverse as Manhattan. A special train of ten coaches delivered 400—the *Lancaster New Era* said 360—Lancaster and Dauphin County Mennonites to Manhattan's Pennsylvania Station. The somberly dressed travelers "peered about in timid bewilderment through gold-rimmed spectacles" as they transferred to buses.

At the pier, they explored the SS *Deutschland* that would take the missionaries across the Atlantic to Southampton, England, for transfer to another Hamburg-American liner to round the cape of Africa. At Fifth Avenue and Forty-Fifth Street, the "lace-capped women and buttoned-up men" entered a Horn and Hardart Automat restaurant for a light meal. Those who were leery of city food had brought their own. Four hundred voices singing "I was sinking deep in sin" elicited "stares and titters" from the regular diners. For two hours, the singing and sermons went on. Among the speakers was Anna Engle, a Brethren in Christ missionary,[92] surely the only one present with experience in the field. The Brethren in Christ were several decades ahead of Mennonites in sending and supporting foreign missionaries.

In the evening, the Lancastrians returned to the ship. In an onboard saloon, they gathered for more singing and speeches. *Time* magazine's reporter quoted a verse of the most exotic song, "Africa": "Africa, dark Africa / We have heard our Master's call / Fear not! Oh despair not! / Jesus died for all." Finally, they shook hands and kissed all around (not likely), and sang "God Be with You till We Meet Again." About midnight the *Deutschland* left the harbor with Elizabeth Stauffer and John and Ruth Mosemann, "who were sailing off to preach God's word to black men." A photo of the singing group illustrated the March 5, 1934, *Time* article; its caption: "God-Speeding Mennonites, *They were sinking deep* in Sin."[93]

The exhausted adventurers arrived back at the Lancaster station the next day at 6:45 a.m. While New Yorkers were amused by the incongruous "God-Speeding" pilgrims in the city, they themselves were impressed by Broadway's countless flashing lights and the automatic doors in the New York train station.[94]

Elta, however, was not impressed by the news coverage: "Our people meant it for good [but] the curiosity it aroused . . . in New York and the way it was written" in the city papers of New York, Philadelphia, and Lancaster "hurt me." She cautioned Orie, "Don't mention this to them [in Africa] though, but you know 400 having a service in a N.Y. cafeteria seemed strange and what is precious to us, they put in a ridiculous light."[95]

DHAMTARI, DAR ES SALAAM, AND HOME TO AKRON

From Dhamtari, India, Orie told Elta that his coming to India "just now seems providential in a number of ways," but the specifics he would leave until he returned home in May. From what others told Orie, Ernest was much better than before, but his recovery was not consistent. Orie was not sure what to make of his brother: "His is a baffling case to understand."

Aside from the mission in Shirati and Ernest in India, Orie was thinking about Miller Hess. He resolved to put the shoe business "first" and give it his "full energy" to ensure its profitability, so that the "interests of our family are conserved." He said he would devote only his "spare energy & time" to the church and its boards and committees. Orie was sure that "the Lord wants it so." But it was not likely.

He was also pleased with the Lord's "choice" in the recent bishop selection. Amos Horst "would have been my choice." Ever politically astute, Orie concluded, "I believe his presence on [the] Bishop Board will make my own future Mission Bd. Work & relationships easier & simpler."[96] But MCC was another matter. Horst was known to be among Lancaster leaders who believed MCC was a distraction from EMM and after the 1920s mission to Russia should have beeen discontinued.

Elta in Akron was talking about remodeling her kitchen, but her father advised otherwise. A new kitchen would not increase the house's value "and that's all I ever hear," she grumbled to Orie. Elta wanted to keep the place "nice" and needed more room for the boys. She reported that Lois was doing okay at Goshen College, although she was having "trouble passing chemistry." Elta had other concerns: "I think her greatest temptation now is with her clothes. She wants them just like the other girls and I hardly know what to do." But still, "all in all . . . we can be pretty happy" with Lois.[97]

While Lois was navigating the cultural milieu at Goshen, Orie was taking his brother Ernest on a tour of "important cities" in India. From Bombay, Orie wrote to Elta of his "easy life compared to the daily grind you have all of the time." Showing a touch of guilt, he promised: "Maybe I can be a better husband & helper to you in the future." Thinking of his return, he proposed that Elta take the boys to Miller relatives near Middlebury for the summer, attend Board of Missions meetings in Goshen, attend commencement exercises at Goshen, and bring Lois home. Between those events, he would work his sales territory—"that is if I have a job."[98] Company partners had still not come to peace with Orie's long absences.

Orie was back in Mombasa on March 30 for the arrival of Elizabeth Stauffer and John and Ruth Mosemann. Three days later, the four journeyed to Dar es Salaam, where Elam Stauffer awaited them. When Stauffer reported the Shirati location, Orie's first question was, "Elam, why did you choose your first station in Shirati instead of Musoma like we had agreed?" Having forgotten that conversation, Stauffer explained it as Sylwulka's recommendation. It was a strategic location: a mission at this location would block missionaries from Kenya from entering Tanganyika. "Orie was perfectly satisfied with my answer," Stauffer later remembered.[99]

For three days, the five "met in conference" to pray and to plan strategy. In answer to the inherent difficulties of communicating with EMM back in Lancaster from such a distance, Orie said, "We just have to trust each other." On April 6, the Stauffers and Mosemanns took a train to Mwanza, while Orie went to Mombasa where he boarded a steamship bound for home.[100]

APPOINTMENTS AS MCC AND EMM EXECUTIVE

The year 1935 saw another important milestone for Orie. The MCC executive committee selected him to be its executive secretary-treasurer in place of the late Levi Mumaw, who had served conscientiously in that role since its founding in 1920. Orie, the new executive, moved the MCC files from Mumaw's office at the Mennonite Publishing House in Scottdale to the Miller home in Akron. Thus, the inter-Mennonite relief agency's office was relocated to the heart of Lancaster County, a constituency wary of such cooperation.

In the same year, Orie also became secretary of Eastern Mennonite Missions, a role he maintained simultaneously with his MCC role until he retired in 1958. As he had gravitated to influential positions in church-wide boards and committees, he now at forty-three also held central roles of influence in the Lancaster Conference. As Harry Herr, a Lancaster Mennonite observer, reported to his family, the new secretary was "such a very capable young man."[101] Despite the earlier opposition from John Mosemann Sr. to Orie's peace advocacy, Orie continued his active role as secretary of the Peace Problems Committee. Then an important meeting in Newton, Kansas, intensified his peace work.

"It begins to look as if a major war is in the making," Orie wrote from Chicago on September 17, 1935. "One wonders how can it be that so little has been learned from the futility & terribleness of the last one."[102]

At least 250 other Mennonites saw it coming too. H. P. Krehbiel, editor of the inter-Mennonite *Mennonite Weekly Review*, invited Mennonites "from all the groups," along with several Quaker and Church of the Brethren speakers, to gather for a peace conference in Newton, Kansas, October 31–November 2, 1935. They considered the church's response to an eventual war. Orie later recalled that this was the time when Harold Bender emerged as an articulate spokesperson. As a member of the findings committee, Bender drafted "a one-paragraph statement . . . which gave us direction which took us right through World War II."[103]

Another outcome was a three-member committee to represent Mennonites, Brethren, and Quakers. Their task was to carry forward the concerns of the Newton conference. For Orie this proved the effectiveness of small-group meetings. For broader consultation, the committee of three invited about twenty people at a time from a variety of constituent interest groups—representatives of colleges, missionaries on furlough, publication boards, and other such groups.[104] Most significant was

Harold S. Bender. MC USA Archives–Goshen.

The new house at 1115 Main Street, Akron, Pennsylvania. John E. Sharp.

the groundwork established at the Newton meeting for the major work ahead: the united effort of the historic peace churches in the creation of Civilian Public Service as an alternative to military service.

In 1936, Orie made good on his promise to Elta to build a new house, two lots west of the house at 1125 Main Street that had been their home since 1915.[105] The new house was an attractive, two-story brick Colonial Revival structure. The substantial home, spacious enough for a growing family, was the largest house in Akron. At the west end was an open porch; on the east end was a sunroom. The attractive front entrance faced southward toward the Wolf property across the street. The impressive house and lot were twice the value of the older home.[106]

TRANSITION AT GOSHEN COLLEGE

Another presidential transition at Goshen College required Orie's attention. In January 1938, Orie and Goshen College president Sanford C. Yoder had agreed, given Yoder's declining health, that the time was right to relinquish the presidency. But then Yoder had second thoughts. "After mature reflection," he thought it unwise to install an administrative committee to manage the school in the interim. It would, he confided to Orie, concentrate too much power in the hands of a few. As it is, there are "two people within the school right now . . . who about half feel that they are President." Both "Bender and [business manager Chris] Graber . . . like to assert authority," and could walk over an interim administrator. Yoder's solution was to appoint Orie's brother Ernest, back from India, as president. Paul Mininger was another possibility, but Yoder was concerned that Mininger was too young and inexperienced. Ernest, on the other hand, *could* stand up to Bender. But if the Mennonite Board of Education was unwilling to appoint Ernest, Yoder was willing to serve still another year.[107]

Meanwhile, word of President Yoder's resignation caused a rumble across campus. A number of anxious students drove to the country home of David A. Yoder, MBE president, to voice their fear that dean Harold Bender would move up to the presidential office. They even wondered whether Bender was working behind the scenes to make it happen. "If Bender becomes president," said one of them, "I'll pack up" and go home. Students were reacting to what they perceived to be Bender's heavy-handed discipline and his intimidating demeanor. David A. Yoder, uncertain about how to handle the impending crisis, consulted Orie.[108]

As chair of the current oversight committee, Orie was the "point man," receiving and sending dozens of letters regarding the transition. S. C. Yoder wrote again to say that he would agree to an on-campus administrative team only if Orie were chair. If Mininger were to be appointed, then Orie "could help him get started and should have the right . . . to uncover anything in any of the offices you desire to go into. You should have this right anyway, whether you are on the administrative committee or not." Yoder added that, if necessary, he would continue as president for the good of the college, "for another year or till I die for that matter." Since his administrative load had been reduced, Yoder quipped, his health had "improved so much that it is almost a pleasure to live!"[109]

Patriarch Daniel Kauffman wrote to say he had been in Goshen for various meetings. Afterward "things were revolving in my mind," especially about Goshen College. He wished he could "have the privilege of spending an hour or two or three with Orrie [sic] Miller in talking over these problems," and he hoped Orie could stop in Scottdale when he had the time. Kauffman's respect for Orie was evident.

As an aside, Kauffman said he sat with Orie's father in board meetings and was especially impressed with D. D.'s "poise." With a flair for understated humor, lost on most of the church, Kauffman said that on whatever board D. D. was "destined" to serve, "I want to see him on the firing line until he is too old and feeble to fire."[110] Orie knew Kauffman was referring to the future role of S. C. Yoder and his impact on the boards in question.

In his response, Orie outlined what he believed would be the best use of Yoder's time—part-time Bible teaching at Goshen and nearly full time with the mission board, a "combination [Yoder] would love above everything else." Orie had already discussed this with a member of each board and with his father and had received "their assurance" that they would support the plan.[111]

Instead of appointing Ernest Miller president, MBE named him chair of the administrative committee. Chris Graber wrote to say that he and the local board (of directors) had hit a "snag" regarding Ernest's salary. They were not inclined to give him the "top salary" of $1,800, since he did not have the requisite two years teaching experience, which Ernest said he *did* have. The local board had agreed on $1,500. To resolve the dilemma, Ernest suggested that Graber and Orie should "fix it up." Graber wanted Orie's counsel.[112] Orie told Graber that Ernest had already written about the problem. Wisely, Orie abstained from expressing an opinion but did say that he would "see to it that Ernest makes no protest to any decision" made.[113]

In July 1939, Orie and Graber exchanged letters about the current fundraising campaign for a new library at Goshen. Orie sent a contribution of $2,000 in stocks, cash, and a loan—toward a larger sum pledged. After noting what funds could be expected, he suggested that Graber raise the balance by getting in his car to "take a week's tour" to collect from smaller donors.[114] By August, both believed they would have the necessary funds to break ground in the fall. In the meantime, Graber was negotiating with builders and suppliers. He assured Orie that he was "pulling his hair to make this thing go." As for further counsel, Graber said that, as always, he would defer to his friend's "superior judgment."[115]

GROWING CHILDREN

Fundraising was not the only thing on Graber's mind. In an undated handwritten letter, Graber wrote to Orie "as a favor," citing Lois's less-than-stellar conduct as a Goshen College student. Several times during the fall, Lois had spent weekends with her grandparents, Nettie and D. D. Miller, at the Board of Missions headquarters on Prairie Street. The problem was that she went out every night and came home late. Recently, Grandpa D. D. had checked his watch when Lois came in—it was 3:00 a.m. Furthermore, she was flouting conference rules by wearing not a bonnet but a hat with feathers. In the course of her conversation with D. D., Lois said she did not know how long she could remain a Mennonite. Graber knew of no "tilts" with college administrators, but "the weekend business had to be stopped." They had decided not to "raise a rumpus" before the Christmas holidays, but when she returned to campus, Graber was "going to wake her up."[116]

Lois survived the "waking up," but she had a complaint about her grandfather. She wrote to "Darlin Mumsie" in May 1935 to report that D. D. had brought little brother John, eight years old, to campus to attend a meeting. Instead of allowing John to visit Lois, as she expected, he was left sitting in the car "for hours." Eventually, John "yelled at my window." When Lois discovered the situation, she "held and kissed him" and then took him to the meeting room and sent him in to tell Grandpa that he, John, would be with Lois. When John didn't return, Lois looked into the room and saw John crying on D. D.'s lap. The meeting would soon be over, Grandpa said, and John needed to stay with him. "Well! I took John out to kiss him goodbye and he had me crying."

Then there was the transfer of her church membership. "I was taken into [the college] church here this morning, "Sis" wrote to "Dearest Mother" on December 8, 1935. Lois was relieved that it was "all over." She had earlier written that she could not "do all I would have to" do to be a member in good standing at the Ephrata home church. Having a church she could call her own made her feel "so much better." Then she wrote of plans to see Ronnie Beach, the son of an Episcopalian organ builder whom she had met the summer before at the Jersey shore. She had invited him to Akron for the Christmas holidays, but he refused to go, saying he did not feel welcome since he was "not of the right religious caliber." Lois begged her mother to write Ronnie a nice letter and invite him to the Miller house. "Please, if you want to make me happy, please!"

Lois's temper showed in the next letter: "Why did I not mention more religious things? Boy! You folks sure do have superb imaginations. There isn't a thing wrong. Honest! I've been going out to E. Goshen every Sun

... and Christian Workers is the same too." Then a word about Ronnie: "We have an understanding—we aren't formally engaged but someday hope to be. . . . I don't care to date other fellows except to get places and . . . to stay up socially."[117] Later Lois wrote about campus "politics": "Jim didn't study and was as dumb as I was [in German class], but Mrs. Bender likes him. She gave him a C+ and me a D. I was absolutely sick and so mad at her that I couldn't fight back. . . . Honestly the rotten politics here gets me sick."[118] Perhaps Orie found managing boards easier than raising a daughter. While Lois often addressed her letters to Elta, Orie visited her when he attended meetings in Elkhart. She seemed to look forward to his visits.

"I had another one of Grandma Miller's typical letters yesterday," Lois wrote in October. When Lois had asked whether she and Ronnie could stay with D. D. and Nettie over Thanksgiving, they said no. "Then she said that stuff about praying for me & I'd reap what I sow, etc. & ended by quoting the verse 'Honor your father & your mother' etc. I didn't get the point cause I don't know what I'm sowing & as for you & dad—I've never loved & respected you more in my life. The whole thing makes me sick."

By January 1937, Lois wrote, "Mother, now that you know that Ron & I are really serious why don't you start collecting nice sheets, towels, etc. for me? I'd appreciate it. Oh Mumsie he's a dear. I'm awfully happy & believe it or not all desire to go with anyone else even just for fun or to get places has fled. He completely satisfies me (That from me *is* something)."[119]

Lois was, indeed, happy with Ronald Oakley Beach. They married on September 7, 1937, and moved to Nutley, New Jersey. As a Mennonite leader, Orie did not think it appropriate to "give her away," but he and Elta gave the couple a new car and signed a mortgage for their home at 28 Rhoda Avenue.[120] Son Larry Beach was under the impression that the mortgage was never signed over to Lois and Ronald. Others believe that since Orie and Elta paid $7,000 for Lois's house, each of the sons was given the same amount toward a house. The family speculated that Orie "had plans for Lois as his personal secretary traveling the world to-gether." He may have thought Lois was marrying "beneath her station in life." Larry recalls that "Ron was constantly trying to prove himself to Orie."

Orie and Elta adjusted to their Episcopalian son-in-law and to the daughter who charted her own path—or as Orie once put it, "Wherever we drew the line, she was outside of it." Ronald worked with his father, Earle Beach, whose company was based in Newark, New Jersey, in designing and building amplified cathedral chimes and organs. John W. Miller recalls that he and his brothers were fascinated by Ron, who brought a different perspective to family conversations and had the latest movie cameras.[121]

DEATHS OF PARENTS

There were transitions of another kind in the family. On January 16, 1938, Orie's mother, Nettie (Jeanette) Miller died of a heart attack in their home on Prairie Street, Elkhart. She was sixty-seven. A year earlier Nettie had suffered from an attack of influenza and from that time grew steadily weaker. Her obituary noted that she was "active and much interested in sewing circle work," and was a long-serving Sunday school teacher. She was eulogized as "a kind mother, caring patiently and carefully for her family of children while her husband was engaged in evangelistic work and other Church activities."[122] Of Orie's response, there is no written record.

Of more immediate import was the death of A. N. Wolf, Elta's father, on March 31, 1939, at age seventy-one. Aside from a few fainting spells in recent months, he had appeared healthy and followed his usual routine. His death was attributed to heart disease. A. N.'s obituary noted that his own father had died young and "by hard work on the part of all, the mother kept her family together." In addition to being a founding partner of Miller Hess and its secretary-treasurer, Wolf was also a founder of the Oreville Mennonite Home near Lancaster and for thirty-some years served as its board secretary. In recent years, he had been a member of the building committee for a new meetinghouse in Ephrata.

Orie's brother Ernest preached the funeral sermon from John 14. A. N. was buried in the Wolf family cemetery at the edge of town on the site of an early Church of the Brethren meetinghouse. The following verse was attached to his obituary: "There is no death! The stars go down / To rise upon some fairer shore; / And bright in Heaven's jeweled crown / They shine for evermore."[123]

Wolf's will provided for a trust fund of $50,000 for his wife, Anna, to be managed by the Fulton National Bank of Lancaster. She was to have full access to principal and interest. Any remaining balance after her death was to go to Elta. The remainder of the estate was given in equal shares to Anna and Elta. Orie and Anna were executors. Total assets were $179,499.[124]

Orie did not receive any part of his father-in-law's estate, but his own assets were almost equal—$170, 653. In 1939, Orie's stocks and bonds were worth $117,700, and he had loaned out $6,170. His salary and allowances were $43,433. Orie's charitable contributions that year totaled $7,684, nearly 18 percent of his salary.[125]

As Orie's income multiplied, so did his church-affiliated offices. By the end of the decade, he was a member of twenty church boards and committees and served as an officer on most of them. In addition to continuing in major roles with MCC, EMM, MBE, and Goshen College, Orie had scouted for a mission site in Africa, visited his brother Ernest in India, and traveled to Mennonite colonies in Paraguay and Brazil.

Another event of note was the 1937 incorporation in Akron of MCC, giving it permanent status seventeen years after its founding. The relief organization was now poised for the major expansion that would come after World War II.

Chapter 8
Work of National Importance: 1940–1942

"War is sin . . . violence must be abandoned. . . .
We love our country . . . but true love . . .
does not mean hatred of others."

Although Orie, tuned as always to world events, saw the war coming in 1935, he could not possibly have imagined the destructive power of the approaching global apocalypse. How was it possible to have learned so little from World War I?

The world in 1940 was once again engaged in a major war. Hitler had annexed Austria, occupied Czechoslovakia, and invaded Poland, Denmark, Norway, Belgium, France, and the Netherlands. Flush with victories on the Western Front, Germany attacked the Soviet Union on the Eastern Front in 1941. Nazi Germany formed an alliance with Fascist Italy and Imperial Japan, comprising the Axis Powers. Italy had conquered Ethiopia; Japan had invaded Manchuria and China and clashed with the Soviet Union. In an effort to block Japanese expansion in Southeast Asia, president Franklin D. Roosevelt froze Japanese assets and restricted oil imports to the empire. In response, the Japanese attacked the Pacific Fleet of the United States Navy at Pearl Harbor, Hawaii, on December 7, 1941, effectively ending a long debate about American isolationism and neutrality.[1]

In February 1942, President Roosevelt in a "fireside chat" radio broadcast told Americans, "This war is a new kind of war. It is warfare in terms of every continent, every island, every sea, every air lane." He was right. At that time, twenty-six nations were at war against the Axis Powers. By the war's end, sixty-one countries were involved; only five remained nominally neutral.[2]

The worldwide conflagration that came to be called the Good War exceeded by far the unthinkable destruction of the Great War of 1914–18. A major textbook is unusually forthright in its description:

> It was so terrible in its intensity and obscene in its cruelties that it altered the image of war itself. . . . Racist propaganda flourished on both sides, and excited hatred of the enemy caused many military and civilian prisoners to be tortured and executed. Over 50 million (60 million according to other sources) deaths resulted from the worldwide war, two-thirds of them civilians. The physical destruction was incalculable. Whole cities were leveled, nations dismembered, and societies transformed.[3]

War hysteria and racism at home led to Executive Order 9066, which forced 112,000 Americans of Japanese descent from their homes and businesses into "war relocation camps." Overseas, the personnel reserves and industrial capacity of the United States were critical factors in the eventual Allied victories. American industrial output supplied the planes and bombs that leveled fifty German cities and fifty-nine Japanese cities in an unsuccessful attempt to demoralize their citizens.

In 1945, U.S. bombers dropped two thousand tons of bombs on Tokyo on March 9 and 10, incinerating one hundred thousand civilians at temperatures reaching eighteen hundred degrees Fahrenheit and leaving more than one million homeless. If the bombing of Tokyo was payback for the attack on Pearl Harbor, James Juhnke and Carol Hunter write in *The Missing Peace*, it was shockingly out of proportion: thirty civilians in Tokyo alone died for every American military death at Pearl Harbor.[4] Hiroshima and Nagasaki were reserved for the products of the Manhattan Project—the experimental atom bomb. On August 6, the *Enola Gay* dropped "Little Boy" on Hiroshima, and three days later *Bockscar* delivered "Fat Man" over Nagasaki. Combined deaths, mostly civilian, totaled two hundred thousand.[5]

The United States and the Soviet Union—a democratic republic and a totalitarian dictatorship—made strange bedfellows in the war against the Axis Powers. In the United States, military conscription and nationalization of industry belied the democratic process. Both nations emerged from the war as superpowers and soon became adversaries, competing for the hearts and minds of nations in the long Cold War that followed from 1947 to 1991. When the United States and Western nations created the North Atlantic Treaty Organization (NATO) as a hedge against Soviet aggression in Europe, the Soviet Union created its own alliance, the Warsaw Pact, as a defense against the West. Far from making peace, the war rearranged national boundaries, instilled new hostilities, and diverted trillions of dollars from global humanitarian needs to an insane nuclear weapons race that held the world on the brink of a nuclear holocaust for decades.[6]

HISTORIC PEACE CHURCHES RESPOND

World War II also had a profound effect on Mennonites and those from other peace churches. It became something of a watershed; some chose military service, while others chose the nonmilitary option of Civilian Public Service (CPS) in the United States and Alternative Service Work (ASW) in Canada. In both cases, young Mennonites left home congregations and communities and entered a complex world. Both avenues led toward assimilation and the integration of Mennonites and Brethren in Christ into North American society. For those choosing the military, it was often a doorway out of peace churches and into the mainstream. Those who served in CPS or ASW typically caught a new vision and passion for service and mission, which reshaped the church and redefined Mennonite identity. At the fore were mentors like Orie Miller and Harold Bender.

Long before the United States entered World War II, Orie and his colleagues believed the North American peace churches must do better in teaching peace than they had done during World War I. This was the impetus that had regenerated peace committees and brought seventy-nine Mennonites, Brethren, and Friends to Newton, Kansas, on October 31 to November 2, 1935.[7] Just as MCC had been revived in 1930 to meet a new crisis in Russia, so the gathered body at Newton revitalized the Continuation Committee of the Conference of Pacifist Churches of earlier days. The terminology of "pacifist churches" gave way to "historic peace churches."

In that historic Newton meeting, convener H. P. Krehbiel, president of the GC Mennonite Church, made a ringing opening statement of purpose. They were gathered as "old historic groups of disciples of Jesus to clasp hands for the promotion of Christ's peace." He rejoiced that they were witnessing an awakening: "Great numbers of Christians that heretofore were military-minded [are] now repentant of that disloyalty to Christ . . . and now give heed to the admonition to love and not to hate." Did not God preserve the "friends of peace through ages of tribulation for just such a time as this?"[8]

By the end of the first day, all felt that they did, indeed, have "a common basis for peace testimony" and could therefore plan for "united peace action." On Friday, Orie Miller was named to a committee on Cooperative Action. Serving with him were Emmett L. Harshbarger, master history teacher at Bethel College; Rufus Bowman, Church of the Brethren leader and soon to be president of Bethany Biblical Seminary; and Guy W. Solt of the American Friends Service Committee.

Four others were appointed to write a common peace statement: Harold Bender, Goshen College dean; Amos E. Kreider, professor of Bible at Bethel College, North Newton, Kansas; C. Ray Keim, Church of the Brethren teacher at Manchester College, North Manchester, Indiana; and W. E. (William) Berry, from Oskaloosa, Iowa, representing the Peace Association of Friends in America. They agreed that their passion for peacemaking was not based on secular dreams, but were of "complete unanimity" in the conviction that their "highest loyalty must be to Christ and his teaching." Differences emerged, however, in the application of that conviction. Most wanted to grant "a certain degree of liberty of conscience," but others, generally Quakers, insisted on the possibility of an "absolute refusal" to cooperate with the state.[9]

When will war come and how should they prepare? Quaker Ray Newton believed war would come within six months to three years. Nevertheless, he said they should "make a tremendous effort to keep this country neutral." On November 2, the final day of meetings, Orie's committee reported its statement on "Christian Patriotism." It forthrightly declared that "war is sin" and "violence must be abandoned." Furthermore, "We love our country," but "true love . . . does not mean hatred of others"; "only the application of . . . peace, love, justice, liberty, and international goodwill" will create "the highest welfare" for "humanity everywhere." Finally: "We feel that we are true patriots because we build on the eternal principles of right which are the only foundation of stable government in our world community."[10]

Harold Bender's peace statement committee petitioned the government "to continue the utmost efforts to keep this country out of war." It commended the state for its neutrality thus far and "respectfully suggest[ed]" that the 1928 eighteen-nation Kellogg-Briand Pact to outlaw war should continue to guide the United States and Canada in their "relations with other countries." The committee offered the statement "with a deep sense of our love for our country," but it also warned that in the event of war "we cannot cooperate in military service." The assembly approved both statements.[11]

The conference's "somewhat official" Joint Committee on Peace Action consisted of three members: Orie Miller, C. Ray Keim of the Church of the Brethren, and Robert W. Balderston of the American Friends Service Committee. Building on the ecumenical and secular peace conferences and the educational thrusts of the 1920s, the new committee was charged with "studying the fields of service in wartime compatible with our common peace testimony." They would do so by reviewing "present-day peacetime relief and reconstruction service projects." Together they would approach the United States government (as a Canadian committee was doing in Ottawa) with a plan for alternative service for conscientious objectors in the war already brewing in Europe and Southeast Asia.[12]

PRELUDE TO CIVILIAN PUBLIC SERVICE

In the next five years, a dizzying array of peace committees, some newly minted, held a myriad of meetings and conferences and sponsored publications to nurture peace convictions. Orie was in the center of activity as the secretary of the MC Peace Problems Committee; executive secretary of MCC; vice president of the Continuation Committee of Historic Peace Churches; the Washington link for the Mennonite Central Peace Committee, which became MCC Peace Section in 1942; and finally, vice president of the National Service Board for Religious Objectors (NSBRO) when it was formed in 1940.

Harold Bender was a second important actor on the peacemaking stage. He became chair of the PPC in 1936, chair of the Mennonite International Peace Committee in the same year, and secretary of the Mennonite Central Peace Committee in 1939. Bender proved to be a most articulate spokesperson for peace concerns. Bender was a better speaker and writer than Miller, but Orie was the one who made things work and had a deft mind for finances. Orie preferred to work behind the scenes and cast himself as the practical Nehemiah teamed with the prophetic Ezra, or as John Mark, the assistant to the apostle Paul.[13] In matters of history and theology, Miller deferred to Bender. In matters of budgets and finances, Bender deferred to Miller.

Paul Landis tells a story that illustrates the differences. Orie took Landis, then a young Lancaster Conference bishop, to a PPC meeting in Chicago to enlarge his protégé's horizons. In the course of the meeting, Bender and Guy Hershberger, chair and recording secretary respectively, got into a little spat about some detail they both cared about. When it became clear the two were not going quit the debate anytime soon,

> Brother Orie very gently raised his hand, and said, "Brother Chairman, I would like to make a motion." When Bender acknowledged Miller, Orie said, "I move that the chairman of the Mennonite Peace Problems Committee and the secretary of the Mennonite Peace Problems Committee retire to another room and resolve their personal peace problems so that we can get on with our work."

> Bender's quick response was "I refuse to accept that motion." Orie was not finished. He said, "We have an assistant chairman. Brother Vice Chairman, I make the motion and it's up to you to handle them." Bishop John E. Lapp of the Franconia Conference said, "I receive that motion." When the others around the table affirmed the motion, Lapp said, "The motion is carried. So we'd like you two brothers to follow through on this motion." Bender and Hershberger sheepishly left the meeting. When after some time Bender and Hershberger returned, Vice Chairman Lapp asked, "Have your personal differences been resolved?" They both said, "Yes, they have." Lapp said, "Okay, Brother Bender, you're the chair. Let's go on with our agenda."[14]

In January 1936, the PPC sponsored an important conference in Goshen attended by a significant number of MC leaders. Among the papers presented was Guy Hershberger's "Is Alternative Service Desirable and Possible?" He declared that the only path open for a nonresistant church was complete refusal to serve in the military, unless the government provided an alternative service option. He cited the precedence of Mennonites in Russia, who had organized and financed forestry and Red Cross service as an alternative to military service starting in the late nineteenth century. Hershberger's paper provided the broad outlines for what became CPS five years later.

Harold Bender, elected chair of the PPC at the same meeting, made a case for continuing the witness to government as Orie Miller and the committee had been doing since 1925. Also at this meeting, the Jacob ter Meulen Peace Manifesto of the Dutch Mennonites was endorsed and plans were made to gather signatures of North American Mennonite leaders in support of the statement. In addition, Miller and Bender were appointed to attend the conference on peace and war at Witmarsum, Friesland (Netherlands), on July 3.[15]

At the February 18, 1936, meeting of the Continuation Committee of Historic Peace Churches, Orie explained the "groupings and organizational tie-ups of the Mennonites as well as some of their attitudes on peace problems." Some MC members saw the interaction with the more liberal Quakers, Brethren, and other Mennonites as a threat to their identity as a people apart. Miller was asked more than once what kept him from being "spoiled" by the "more liberal pacifist thought." Orie said it was a matter of witness: "You must take your shoes off when you meet the other person, and you must hear him. You must listen before he can hear you. And it's only on that level of complete exposure that you can really be heard yourself. Isn't it?"[16]

The CCHPC agreed on an exchange of fraternal delegates to yearly meetings and annual conferences "that would do much to promote a feeling of fellowship among the peace churches." They also planned to send delegates to the Methodist and Congregational annual conferences, and made plans for "pooling our literary resources" and scheduling the next meeting in May. Sending foreign delegates to foreign countries "in the interest of peace" was to be on the agenda for the next meeting. Orie said South America countries should be included.[17]

In the May 16, 1936, meeting at the La Salle Hotel in Chicago, Robert Balderston, Orie Miller, Ray Keim, and Fred Winslow agreed to send delegates if possible to the Baptists, the Colored Baptists, the Church of God, the Nazarenes, and perhaps others. Orie informed the committee that he and Harold Bender would be attending the upcoming conference on peace and war in the Netherlands, and visiting the Mennonite Center in Karlsruhe, Germany, and the Friends Center in Paris. Upon his return, he would report on the "German refugee problem in France."[18]

NEW STATEMENTS ON WAR AND PEACE

In September of 1936, a "Sub-Committee on Literature" of the CCHPC met in Chicago. After a review of peace literature available in each church, they agreed that new peace education materials were needed "in the face of war crisis with the perils of an enlarging army and navy." Each church was to write a new position statement on peace and war to be circulated to the other member churches. Guy Hershberger, Rufus Bowman, and William Harvey were appointed to create a handbook of war resistance for future draftees.[19]

The PPC made two major writing assignments in the April 14, 1937, meeting. Bender, the chair, was assigned to "formulate" a resolution on war and military service to submit to the General Conference in Turner, Oregon, that summer. Guy Hershberger, who had been writing articles all along for church periodicals, was asked to write a peace study book of about 150 pages, targeting young people, age fifteen to thirty. Both Bender's position paper, "Peace, War, and Military Service" and Hershberger's book, *War, Peace, and Nonresistance*, became classic statements of Mennonite peace convictions. Later in 1951, when Bender helped craft a new statement on peace, Orie quipped, "I don't think you said anything new."[20] Hershberger's magnum opus of four hundred pages was published in 1944.[21] When the Conservative Amish Mennonite Conference asked to be linked to the PPC they were welcomed. The PPC said it was ready to offer assistance to other nonresistant churches as well. The new group appointed Shem Peachey of Springs, Pennsylvania, as their representative to the PPC.[22]

The Mennonite Church General Conference considered "Our Position on Peace, War, and Military Service" at Turner, Oregon, August 25–26, 1937. The PPC—with Orie as secretary, Harold Bender as chair since 1935, and Chris Graber an active member since 1925—presented the statement. Bender, too busy to write it earlier, had composed the statement on the cross-country train ride to the conference. After some editing by other members of the PPC, the assembly adopted "Our Position on Peace, War, and Military Service" as its official statement. It was the first MC peacetime declaration specifically on nonparticipation in war.[23]

The peace convictions expressed in the statement were long-held principles recast for a new time and context: "As followers of Christ the Prince of Peace," we are required "to renounce the use of force and violence." As citizens, "we love . . . our country and desire to work constructively for its highest welfare," but we are "constrained by the love of Christ to love the people of all lands and races." If there should again be a military draft and some form of service is required, "we venture to express the hope that . . . it may not be under the military arm of the government." The statement expressed "appreciation for the endeavors of our governments, both in the United States and Canada, to promote peace and good will among nations, and to keep from war." Further, "we desire to endorse the policy of neutrality and non-participation in disputes between other nations."[24]

Predictably, the latter statement raised the hackles of fundamentalist conservatives, who thought the church had no business telling the government what to do; rather, the church's task was simply to inform the government of its nonviolent principles and let the country do what it will.[25] But Paul Comly French, the Quaker journalist who became executive secretary of the National Service Board for Religious Objectors, believed the statement to be "the most concise and the most logical of the stated views of any church group."[26]

The 1937 Turner conference statement was widely used and endorsed by others, including the Conservative Amish Mennonite Conference and numerous Old Order Amish congregations. In 1941, GC Mennonites adopted a majority of the statement for their own. Copies were sent to Canadian and American officials. In Washington, DC, it went to the president, secretary of war, secretary of state, the chief justice, and the chairs of the Foreign and Military Affairs committees of both houses. Copies were also sent to governors of states with significant Mennonite populations.[27]

FORMATION OF THE MENNONITE CENTRAL PEACE COMMITTEE

On September 30, 1939, four weeks after Germany invaded Poland, representatives of seven Mennonite groups met in Chicago to organize a new Mennonite Central Peace Committee (MCPC). This inter-Mennonite committee's task was to draft a blueprint for action in case the United States joined the war. Though President Roosevelt continued to proclaim neutrality, the War Department was planning for "a complete mobilization of the man power and material resources" needed in the event of war. The members of the MCPC were resolved to "hold firmly to the principles of Biblical non-resistance, peace, and love" and were "committed to a way of life which involves non-participation in war in any form." They were ready "to render a service of love to the needy in war time as well as in peace time."[28]

The "Plan of Action for Mennonites in Case of War" had five points: (1) Individuals are to register when required and declare conscientious objector convictions; (2) if called for service, the draftee is to make a statement of conscience; (3) the church pledges to create acceptable forms of alternative service; (4) that service is to be under civilian control; and (5) concrete proposals are to be given the president very soon so he can assign COs to alternative service when others are inducted into the military.[29]

The writers of the action plan imagined such service projects as relief for war sufferers and refugees; reconstruction; resettlement of refugees; conservation or forestry work; farmwork; medical, nursing, and health-care for women as well as men. The plan was not born of rebellion or dis-loyalty. Conscientious objection was the very best kind of patriotism that expressed love and loyalty for the country, and the historic peace churches were willing to make sacrifices for the spiritual and material well-being of the country. The plan challenged the right of a nation to call its people to military service, while proposing a higher expression of service that would benefit all people.[30] As an afterthought, it occurred to Harold Bender that he and Orie as laymen were forging ahead of ordained leaders, who had the power to derail the plans. So in October, the MCPC presented the plans to ministers, who approved it without dissent.[31]

NEGOTIATING WITH WASHINGTON

The German invasion of Poland on September 1, 1939, added a sense of urgency to the work of the historic peace churches. The CCHPC met in Goshen two weeks later on September 17. The first agenda item was a discussion about whether to attempt a second "interview" with President Roosevelt. Two years earlier, the PPC had met with the president to in-form him of their position on peace and war, and to present their hope for nonmilitary alternative service.[32] Regarding a second visit, Orie coun-seled, characteristically, that if they did, they should make sure to have a "concrete, definite proposal."

All agreed that the CCHPC should develop a civilian service organiza-tion to present to the president. In the case of a draft, Orie "favored obey-ing the government as far as possible" and avoiding "any appearance of dictating to the government what they should do." They wanted Roosevelt to know of the difficulties COs experienced in the last war and agreed that waiting until war came would be too late to "accomplish much with the president."

On the question of an alternative service program, Harold Bender wanted no connection to the military. When Brethren field secretary Dan West said that doctors and nurses should be engaged in humanitarian aid, Orie wondered why medical personnel were not already offering humanitarian service. He "urged the use of war incomes for relief" work and reported that three Mennonite relief workers were currently in Spain as a result of the Spanish Civil War.[33]

The CCHPC agreed to visit President Roosevelt again, to explore relief work in Europe, and to develop a common position paper on conscription. Most were ready to adopt the MCPC's "Plan of Action," but the Quakers pushed for the inclusion of an absolutist stance of noncooperation and refusal to register. They believed the Mennonite plan to be too accommodating. Mennonites, knowing that an absolutist option would not play well in their circles, refused to alter the statement. Eventually they worked out a compromise; along with the current statement of position they would add a "confidential memo" that recognized the validity of the absolutist position.[34]

On January 10, 1940, three delegates went to the White House: Rufus Jones, P. C. Hiebert, and Harold Bender. Jones, speaking for the group and from memory, outlined the essence of the statement. Roosevelt was charming and thought they should present their statement to the U.S. attorney general. The delegation left believing they had made a good impression on the president. Hiebert was convinced they had warded off "an almost incalculable amount of suffering and heartache." But in fact, the president didn't like the plan, nor did he like COs.[35]

Meeting in Chicago on February 17, 1940, the CCHPC debriefed the January 10 meeting with government officials in Washington. The absolutist position remained a point of discussion: Balderston argued that COs on all grounds should be recognized, and that they would have to "face the problem of at least a few absolutists in each group." The committee agreed to meet in special session during an upcoming meeting of the Federal Council of Churches (FCC) in Philadelphia. Bender and two others to be appointed were to report to churches on the conversations in Washington and to consider an additional meeting with U.S. attorney general Robert H. Jackson.[36]

The conversation continued in a meeting of the MCPC executive committee on June 9, 1940. Orie reported on "an important contact" that he, Dan West, and Clarence Pickett, executive secretary of the American Friends Service Committee, had with solicitor general Francis Biddle regarding the presidential petition. There was no doubt that the United States was moving "definitely toward preparation" to join the "European War." Biddle requested information from each peace church group on "manpower," information on Britain's experience with COs, and what the historic peace churches were willing to do in a time of war (which had already been addressed). In addition, he asked for a "textual draft of proposals regarding the COs to be incorporated in the new draft law." Apparently all of this was a diversionary tactic, since Biddle had absolutely nothing to do with the pending draft legislation.[37]

Orie reported that Quaker lawyer Harold Evans of Philadelphia would draft a text spelling out a CO option to be inserted into any future draft law. The committee "agreed that since Orie Miller is available to aid the MCPC in keeping in touch with Washington authorities . . . and is favorably situated for speedy and economical operations, he be asked to continue to represent and serve the MCPC in these contacts."[38] That summer Orie and H. A. Fast were in Washington "every couple of weeks" consulting the Quakers on the text and progress of the plan that became the Civilian Public Service.[39]

THE WORLD AT WAR AGAIN

In May 1940, the newly appointed and desperate British prime minister Churchill appealed to President Roosevelt for help. In order to survive the onslaught of Nazi Germany, the democratic societies of Europe needed the support of the world's greatest financial and industrial nation. Coming to the aid of England seemed unlikely for Roosevelt, who faced three obstacles: finding a way around the prohibitions of the Neutrality Act, reshaping public opinion, and rebuilding the armed forces through a peacetime military draft. The Neutrality Acts of 1935 and 1937 prohibited export of arms, material, and financial aid. The majority of Americans—83 percent according to one poll—were in no mood for an intervention that could pull them into another European quagmire. In addition, the secular postwar peace movement, in which Orie's PPC participated, was very strong and vocal.[40]

In 1939, a much-modified Neutrality Act had dropped the restrictions against assisting "belligerent" nations, and simply banned the country from "active interference" in battlefields. The financial sector favored the lucrative "cash and carry" arms deals to help former allies—and to pull the economy out of the persisting Depression. Millions of Americans were still out of work.

Events in Europe marched on. In May 1940, Germany invaded France. If France fell, only Britain would remain to stand against Nazi aggression. Without alerting the American public, Roosevelt responded to Churchill's plea and ordered "vital military equipment" to be sent to England, with the promise of more aid to come.[41] The president also ordered a massive retooling of industry to produce arms, and waited for American minds to change. The War Department recruited a new breed of talent to manage a monstrous growth of the arms industry, and new war contracts were awarded totaling more than ten million dollars.[42] Congress, meanwhile, appropriated $2.5 billion to rebuild the military.[43]

Many Americans approved of spending money to reconstruct a strong military defense, but sending sons, brothers, and husbands to fight on another continent was quite another matter. Facing an election in November and understanding the volatility of military conscription, Roosevelt exercised his usual political craft: innuendo, apparent indecision, half-truths, hints, and nudges from the sidelines until consensus formed. When major papers editorialized in favor of intervention, Roosevelt looked on, secretly pleased. By the time the Germans entered Paris in mid-June, a majority of Americans favored a draft, but opposition from students, Marxists, and pacifist groups was still strong.[44] Forced military conscription seemed more like the ploy of Fascist and National Socialist regimes than that of a democracy.

On June 20, the day the Germans marched into Paris, Grenville Clark, an influential New York attorney representing the Military Training Camp Association, managed to get draft legislation introduced to Congress. The debate now shifted from streets, campuses, and pulpits to Capitol Hill. The Burke-Wadsworth bill called for conscription of one million men for a period of one year, and the registration of all sixteen million young men between twenty-one and thirty-five.

Like the legislation of World War I, the bill assumed only historic peace church members would be conscientious objectors and that they would serve as noncombatants in the military. Fearing COs would be sent to boot camps as they were in the last world war, the historic peace churches organization stepped up its work. Throughout the summer, CCHPC representatives testified to House and Senate committees, asking for broader definitions of conscientious objection and for a civilian alternative service to be managed by nonmilitary personnel.[45]

PAUL COMLY FRENCH

Orie always said that Mennonites led the way in the planning for alternative service, but the Quakers made the most difference in Washington. In July, Quaker journalist Paul Comly French went to Washington to lobby for peace church concerns. French had been a reporter for the *Philadelphia Record* and the *New York Evening Post*. Joe Weaver, a Mennonite who worked in the NSBRO office in Washington, later said he admired French because he was dynamic, fearless, persistent, and resourceful. He believed French was "THE man for THE place at THAT time."[46]

Orie respected French's abilities too. Part of his genius, Orie thought, was his ability to anticipate a problem and its solution."[47] M. R. (Robert) Zigler, Church of the Brethren representative on the CCHPC, said French was "one of the fairest men I have ever met. He was a Quaker, but somehow he understood Brethren."[48]

French and E. Raymond Wilson, Quaker peace lobbyist, contacted a majority of senators and over half of the members of the House. They were at home in the halls of power and knew how to make things happen. Clarence Pickett knew the First Couple and had the ear of Eleanor Roosevelt.[49] The American Quakers learned from the experience of their British counterparts, who had managed to include alternative service before Britain went to war. P. C. Hiebert spent August contacting legislators and reported to Orie that he had not heard any opposition to his concerns, but in fact there was almost no support among legislators for an alternative service clause.

FIRST PEACETIME DRAFT

With an eye toward the November 1940 election, Roosevelt hedged his bets and appeared lukewarm toward the Burke-Wadsworth bill that was introduced in June. But when his Republican rival for the White House, Wendell Willkie, came out in favor of the draft, Roosevelt believed he had nothing to lose, so in August he used his bully pulpit to urge Congress to pass the bill. Congress did, but it was not an overwhelming win. The House voted 266 to 245 in favor and the Senate passed it 58 to 31.[50] The bill confined the training to twelve months and limited service to the United States and its territories.[51]

Orie reported the final form of the draft law to the members of the MCPC on September 14, the day Congress passed the bill. The committee appointed H. A. Fast to represent the concerns of the committee to the proper agencies in Washington "during the preparation of the administrative regulations covering the operations of the draft law." Fast was to handle the administration of conscription law, registration, classification, and appeal process. The committee further agreed that MCC should be responsible for service projects for Mennonite COs, and that MCC and the MCPC should "work out a division of labor between the two committees."[52]

Two days later President Roosevelt signed the Selective Training and Service Act, authorizing the nation's first peacetime draft. Despite the careful and persistent advance work of peace church delegates, there was no acceptable plan for conscientious objectors. Rather than admitting defeat, the alarmed peace organizations immediately went back to work. They needed to educate the bill's sponsors and testify in hearings of the Military Affairs committees of both houses of Congress. During this time, Orie became more active in the lobbying efforts.[53]

Sixty-five peace church leaders gathered for the annual meeting of the MCPC in Chicago on October 4 and 5, 1940. They heard a report from H. A. Fast, the committee's representative to Washington. Orie presented recommendations from a Washington meeting of Mennonites, Brethren, and Friends, and led the discussion on alternative service. Those meeting in Chicago agreed unanimously "in favor of a church-directed service project for our draftees" and that MCC should manage such a service project for Mennonites. They again affirmed their intention to cooperate with other peace churches. They wrestled with such questions as whether draftees should be paid, and whether they should accept government subsidies if any were to be offered. They left the questions open, but emphasized that "the spirit of sacrifice should be urged, both upon the churches and the draftees."[54]

In the next day's session of the Chicago meeting, the leaders appointed the three executive committee members of the MCPC—P. C. Hiebert, E. L. Harshbarger, and Harold Bender—to represent Mennonites on a National Council for Religious Conscientious Objectors to be organized in Washington. They also appointed Orie to represent MC interests on the council's executive committee.

The National Council for Religious Conscientious Objectors was designed to "provide for continuing personal relationships" with federal officials, including the Selective Service Board, the army, the Department of Justice, and agencies that might be appointed to direct the "civilian work of national importance." A general committee was to represent other religious organizations, in addition to the historic peace churches. Secular groups would become members of a general council, and it was to be "thoroughly flexible in its procedure and should proceed only on behalf of the groups within which there was essential agreement."[55] An executive committee of seven members would act for the general council between meetings. The peace churches should "proceed at once with the work in Washington" and organize the national board. They further recommended that Paul Comly French be appointed executive secretary of the general council. He was to set up an office in Washington and invite other religious groups to participate. A joint meeting of historic peace churches on the following Saturday accepted these recommendations.[56]

Eleven days later, on October 16, registration for the draft began.

Chair M. R. Zigler presided over the first meeting of the National Council for Religious Conscientious Objectors in Washington on October 22, 1940. Orie Miller was made vice chair, and Paul J. Furnas of the American Friends Service Committee was named treasurer and recording secretary. Things were developing so fast one could hardly keep track of them, said Zigler: "It was a real drama of real living in crisis."[57] Joining the three historic peace churches on the executive committee of seven were representatives of the Fellowship of Reconciliation, the Methodist Commission on World Peace, and the Disciples of Christ.[58]

Paul Comly French presented a proposal for the administration of "Work of National Importance," to be placed under civilian control as provided under Section 5(g) of the National Training and Service Act

of 1940. According to French's proposal, COs should be referred to the
NCRCO for assignments, and the NCRCO would provide lists of acceptable work to local draft boards for draftees to select. General administration was to be handled by the NCRCO, which would assign draftees to
approved service projects, and serve as the liaison between COs and the
Selective Service Board. Orie then presented the policies and procedures
that would govern Mennonite-controlled alternative service. Minutes
from the meeting noted "a general unity on the basic plan of action,
though the Quakers still wanted recognition of absolutists."[59]

On November 26, 1940, the National Council for Religious
Conscientious Objectors merged with the Civilian Service Board to form
the National Service Board for Religious Objectors. To accommodate
more constituent groups, the board formed the Consultative Council on
April 16, 1941, which eventually included thirty-nine groups, primar-
ily church denominations. In 1942, Walter van Kirk, representing the
Department of Internal Justice and Goodwill of the Federal Council of
Churches of Christ in America, joined the board.[60]

THE FACE OF THE GOVERNMENT

The NSBRO consulted with the successive directors of the Selective
Service administration, Lewis B. Hershey and Clarence Dykstra, as they
constructed the program that became Civilian Public Service. Dykstra,
president of the University of Washington and a respected political sci-
entist, seemed a better fit in some opinions than did a career military
brigadier general. Of Dykstra's appointment, *Time* magazine said, "It
was the addition of one more big name to President Roosevelt's impressive defense corps . . . to keep the army from civilian draftees until actually inducted into service."[61] The peace churches found Dykstra to be
"understanding."[62]

Dykstra resigned in April 1941. Not until August did Roosevelt appoint Hershey director. The office was considered a plum post with a
salary of $10,000. Hershey, who became a major general in 1942, served
in this office until his "Hershey Directive" made him so unpopular during
the antiwar protests of the Vietnam Era that President Nixon removed
him in 1970. This heavy-handed directive gave Hershey the authority to
reclassify anyone who demonstrated against military recruiters. With a
snap of his fingers, he could send them into active military duty.[63]

Brigadier General Lewis B. Hershey (*center*) listens to Amish bishop David Z. Fisher on Fisher's farm in Paradise Township, Lancaster County, Pennsylvania, ca. 1941. Two Old Order Mennonites listen in. MCC.

Despite the fact that General Hershey was, in Perry Bush's words, "a red-headed, agnostic military bureaucrat," the Mennonite name helped win the confidence of at least the Mennonites. More importantly, Hershey went to bat for COs against the attacks of such groups as the American Legion and a hostile Congress.[64] Joe Weaver from Harper, Kansas, who later worked for the NSBRO, said that Hershey handled the CO problems "adroitly." Without General Hershey's support, "we would have never gone through the war as intact as we were as a peace organization."[65] Hershey related well to the peace churches, seemingly with the agility of a chameleon; he could find common ground with most anyone. The general could listen sympathetically to CO concerns, but he could swear "like a sailor" in other settings.

For Orie, Hershey was the face of the government. "The government as far as we were concerned was General Hershey. We couldn't go past him or around him. We wouldn't try to either."[66] Orie also considered the general a friend, and still into the 1970s, the two exchanged Christmas greetings. When the general was planning a trip to Europe, he asked Orie about researching his own Swiss Mennonite roots. Hershey believed his grandfather had once been a Mennonite.[67] On occasion, Hershey took pleasure in calling himself the "Mennonite General."

Since Hershey's main job was to provide soldiers for the military, he delegated the oversight of CPS to Colonel Louis Kosch, chief of the Camp Operations Division of Selective Service.[68] Kosch's grandfather and all but five of his siblings had immigrated to the United States to escape serving in the Prussian Army. When Kosch started school, he spoke only German in a classroom of Irish students and was harassed for it. In theory, at least, Kosch understood the minority position of COs.[69]

MCC and the parallel Brethren Service Committee (BSC) and the American Friends Service Committee (AFSC) were authorized to design and administer CPS camps. For Mennonites, the Mennonite Central Peace

Committee clarified the theology and practice of nonviolence, and MCC, with its twenty years of experience in service and relief projects, would operate CPS.[70] Orie's forte at making things work, putting wheels under a new idea, and organizing structures to get the job done made him ideal for serving on both committees. Others were more visible in Washington, but the steady, disciplined hand behind these activities was Orie Miller's. CPS, however, was not yet a reality.

Since no one in government was giving any serious thought to civilian service, Hershey asked Paul Comly French if the peace churches were willing to take responsibility

Lifelong friends: M. R. Zigler (left) and Orie O. Miller in Paris, France, 1945. MCC.

for all COs: "You fellows . . . make up your minds as to what you want to do and how it ought to be done and then we are in a position to talk intelligently about it." The MCPC had decided that Mennonites, through MCC, would accept responsibility for the administration, discipline, and education of Mennonite COs, and that the government should furnish housing, subsistence, equipment, and technical direction.[71]

Winning the trust of the Congress, the president, and even the military took time and effort, M. R. Zigler remembered. "But the government did learn to trust us and they gave a great deal of freedom." Zigler said later that he found it easier to "talk to men of the government about conscientious objectors than [to] . . . the religionists of the day."

AN EXPERIMENT IN DEMOCRACY

On November 13, 1940, Orie wrote, "Within the past hour in telephone conversation with Paul French, he informed [me] that in conference with Dykstra and Hershey yesterday these two individuals have approved in full the plans for alternative service . . . under French's leadership and as a result of his contacts in Washington and with several departments."[72]

Two weeks later, on November 29, Director Dykstra presented the proposed plan for Civilian Public Service to Roosevelt. The president "expressed instant and aggressive opposition." Then he grumbled that COs should be drilled by army officers; civilian control would be too easy. Dykstra and French got one of the president's aides involved, who helped the president see the merits of the program. Dykstra reminded Roosevelt that in the last world war, sending COs to military camps created more problems than the small number of objectors would suggest. Reluctantly, the president approved the plan by Executive Order 8675 on December 19, 1940.[73] General Hershey called CPS an "experiment in democracy to find out whether our democracy is big enough to preserve minority rights in a time of national emergency."[74]

The next challenge was figuring out how to finance the newly formed CPS. Director Dykstra and Major Hershey met with the NSBRO to report Roosevelt's unfriendly attitude and the problem of funding. Government funding would require congressional hearings, which would bring attention and public hostility that could endanger the service program. Even if such support were to be developed, it would apply only to government-run camps. Furthermore, the peace churches wanted to avoid Washington control of camps.

"It all came to a head," Orie remembered, "when Hershey apparently developed a conviction himself. He said, 'I would advise you folks not to sell out what you have for a mess of pottage. If you insist on government supported camps we can get them, but if I have any advice to give you I would advise you not to ask for it.'"[75]

As a result, the historic peace churches took on the massive financial obligation for CPS. The "normally reserved" Orie Miller, to use Al Keim's appropriate characterization, spoke for his people: Mennonites "would gladly pay their share of the bill. They would do it even though every Mennonite farmer had to mortgage his farm."[76] While it may have been "a rash decision for such normally cautious people," it was the way to avoid government control and to demonstrate the depth of their sincerity. Hershey and Dykstra liked it, since it would not appear that they were making it too easy for the COs.[77]

It was an unusual arrangement. Government agencies made available Civilian Conservation camps "that were going out of business,"[78] along with furnishings, transportation, and supervision of work projects.

The supporting churches paid for everything else. This cooperation did not provide clear answers to critical questions asked later about whether the churches were serving as government agents. While the peace churches were ambivalent about the arrangement, the Selective Service was pleased with it. CPS kept the controversial COs out of sight; the churches were paying for it; and, unlike in World War I, the military was saved the hassle of dealing with men who refused to fight.[79] Thirty years later, Joe Weaver believed keeping a low profile was "sound judgment."[80]

Editorial cartoon about conscientious objectors: "Peace Loving–It's Wonderful!" *Philadelphia Inquirer* (June 28, 1941).

The fact that the churches were paying the bill and the COs were not getting paid was good public relations. It helped bring the critics "down a notch or so," said Colonel Kosch. Kosch and Hershey could report that the COs "don't even get their feed from the government, they don't get their clothing from the government, they don't get anything out of your tax money. And still they are going out and doing these things for you."[81] Such a defense given by Kosch and Hershey, both military commanders, helped tone down public criticism.[82]

When the United States declared war on Japan on December 8, 1941, and on Germany three days later, CPS camps were already in operation. The first camp opened on May 15, 1941, at Patapsco Park, near Baltimore, Maryland, under Quaker administration. The first MCC-administered camp for Mennonites and Brethren in Christ

Civilian Public Service workers at Camp 29, Hagerstown, Maryland. MCC.

opened a week later at Grottoes, Virginia, followed by the Church of the
Brethren camp at Largo, Indiana. By July 1942, a total of 3,738 men were
serving in CPS. By April 1947, when the program closed, 12,000 men
and a few women had served in 152 places. Of that total, 5,830 served
in MCC-operated camps. In six years, CPSers invested over eight million
"man-days" in the welfare of the country.[83]

EQUANIMITY UNDER FIRE

While CPS was a unique church-state experiment and represented a great
effort on the part of the peace churches, not everyone was happy with the
result. Mennonite conservatives complained of the influence of liberals in
their camps. For others, CPS blurred the distinction between church and
state, or as some put it, CPS created "an unholy alliance" between the
two. In 1941, complaints from the Virginia Conference executive committee sparked an MC Investigative Committee, headed by Orie's friend
A. J. Metzler of Scottdale, Pennsylvania. Its task was to investigate all
charges of liberalism and "mismanagement" of the Mennonite camps.

Among the complaints were that a few laymen, Orie Miller and
Harold Bender in particular, had far too much influence. Sanford Shetler
of Johnstown, Pennsylvania, secretary of the MC General Conference and
member of the Investigative Committee, griped that some on the committee believed Miller and Bender were "brilliant." Someone else quipped,
"If they are so bright, let's just ordain them." That prompted some smiles.
It would solve part of the problem—accountability to church authorities—but on the other hand, it would give them even more influence.[84]
Another fear was that the intertwined conglomeration of relief work,
peace advocacy, MCC, and CPS, hardly accountable now, would become
permanent fixtures after the war.[85]

March 17, 1942, was a day like no other for Orie. He and Amos Horst
were in Harrisonburg, Virginia, at the call of the Virginia Conference
executive committee. Not content to leave the investigating to the denominational committee, Virginians were eager for their own face-to-face
encounter with Orie Miller. Miller and Horst represented the PPC, and of
course, Orie also represented MCC, MCPC, and NSBRO. John Mosemann
Jr., one of the earliest EMM missionaries to Shirati, Tanganyika, who had
returned home in 1939, attended the meeting as the director of the CPS
Camp in Grottoes, Virginia.

Editorial cartoon: "What Communion Hath Light with Darkness?" *Sword and Trumpet* (March 1944).

Seventeen Virginians had questions and doubts about CPS, PPC, MCC, and NSBRO. The inquisitors, armed with minutes from meetings of all four organizations, probed for inconsistencies and evidence of liberalism. Throughout the day, Orie was careful to keep the functions and lines of accountability of the various boards and agencies clear. The Virginians sometimes confused them.[86] The Virginians had brought two stenographers to record every word for future scrutiny. Their transcript of 117 pages is now lodged in the Ernest G. Gehman Collection in the Archives of Eastern Mennonite University.

The concerns of the Virginia Conference included unholy unions with liberal Mennonites, Brethren, and Quakers, which threatened the MC doctrine of nonconformity; CPS camps being "invaded by subversive agents"; the "needless and unchristian waste of money" on the NSBRO; Mennonite boys in CPS camps being misled by leaders of "communistic and socialist" organizations such as the Fellowship of Reconciliation and the Federal Council of Churches; peace churches telling the government what to do; mistrust of Orie Miller and other the leaders of MCC, CPS, and the NSBRO; lack of accountability of such agencies to conference and denominational authority; doubt that such organizations were necessary; unchristian conduct of men in CPS camps; and Mennonites bearing the burden of paying for the support of non-Mennonite COs.

Near the end of the meeting, George Brunk voiced the Virginians' "very grave concern for our distinctive nonresistant testimony." In Orie's final statement, he addressed the criticism that the traditional MC stance of biblical nonresistance was being overtaken by secular pacifism:

> Since we are giving our convictions, I would like to give mine on one point. At the present time I have no evidence that pacifism has made many inroads on us at all. The influence has been the other way, that we have had an influence out. . . . My wife said to me, "Now answer the questions as fully as you can and don't say what you aren't asked." But I have my fears about this too. I am just a layman and a very ordinary one at that and I have heard Brother Stauffer speak about the twin positions for which we stand. One we call nonresistance and the other we call nonconformity to the world. We apply it in various ways from east to west in our church.

> I have detected no evidence [of liberal pacifism] among our 1,000 Mennonite boys. But [non-Mennonites] coming to camp knowing nothing but pacifism are getting their eyes opened. They are beginning to see a distinction [between pacifism and nonresistance] they never saw before . . . but the MCC can't do it alone. . . . It seems to me it gives us opportunity like we never had before. . . . The greatest danger is not in losing our nonresistance, but how to keep before [others] in camp the sense of importance as to what we hold as Mennonite groups.

The meeting ended with the Virginians disagreeing among themselves about whether nonresistance and pacifism had been linked or distinguished in World War I.

CONTINUED ATTEMPTS TO DISCREDIT ORIE MILLER AND OTHERS

True to form, Orie never complained of unfair charges, nor did he speak disparagingly of his Virginia interrogators. Robert Kreider, on staff at the MCC Akron office and responsible for CPS hospital units, was aware that MCC and CPS were "under surveillance" from fundamentalists such as "the *Sword and Trumpet* people," who were well-represented in the Virginia meeting. Orie's equanimity under fire increased Kreider's already high respect for him.[87]

Ruth Krady (Lehman), a secretary at MCC headquarters, recalled being summoned to take dictation from both Harold Bender and Orie. The "great minds at work" dictated several telegrams and overseas cables, and then mentioned MCC's critics John Kurtz and Ernest Gehman. Daughter Lois, who happened to be present, asked why Orie paid any attention to such people. Orie replied, "Lois, we never go ahead alone [without the church]. We need the cooperation of everyone."[88]

Ernest Gehman, German teacher at Eastern Mennonite College (EMC), and self-appointed guardian of tradition, continued his efforts to discredit Orie. The most disparaging characterizations of Orie appear in private correspondence after the Virginia meeting. Writing to Sanford Shetler, Gehman gloated over what he believed was the success of the "big meeting" with Orie.

Suffice it to say the meeting did not turn out in favor of the status quo. Our contentions were proved correct in almost every detail. . . . Orie *admitted* the danger and viciousness of the Fellowship of Reconciliation; *admitted* facts proving that the MCC is almost without duly constituted authority—originating in a self-appointed handful of men, who got together years ago to answer some questions for a European Mennonite historical student [an obvious misunderstanding of the nature of the Russian Mennonite *Studienkommission*!]; *admitted* . . . an unequal yoke in his own shoe factory; *admitted* to having helped regulations and decisions in the NSBRO that in principle are contrary to Mennonite . . . standards and decisions, but justified [it] on the basis that he did it for other groups, knowing that our group would not work accordingly anyway; *admitted* that he and Harold [Bender] and [Paul Comly] French . . . visited among congressmen and senators to solicit their votes and support—a thing which many politicians would condemn as lobbying; *stated* that he makes all camp-official appointments . . . [and] *admitted* to relations with the FOR.[89]

Gehman's commentary to Shetler continued: "These and other similar revelations from the idolized Orie, the most influential man in Lancaster and General Conferences, and not an ordained man at all—these revelations were quite a body blow to the earlier contentions of his local admirers." Gehman further reported a growing inclination among Virginians to sever ties with the rest of the Mennonite Church in order to "repudiate and tear away from the NSBRO and MCC."

In a later letter to Shetler, Gehman asked for "any and all information you can give me . . . to make plain to Bro. Stauffer and others that again Orie has been leading them around by the nose. You remember that Bishop Geo. R. Brunk once said that it was about as easy for a conservative . . . to catch a modernist as it is for a shepherd dog to catch a weasel in a woodpile."[90]

Gehman's correspondence after the March meeting in Virginia was voluminous. To C. Z. Martin of Mountville, Pennsylvania, he wrote:

> Now if it can be definitely established that Orie has messed us up with communism and defends the situation, then this Mennonite Church of ours is headed for trouble and it is time that some of us get busy and roll up our sleeves and start to straighten out this matter. I think the right place to start will be to remove the idolized Orie from the throne onto which he has climbed, and from which he is steadily leading the church into liberalism and worldliness.[91]

Sanford Shetler, who in addition to being a member of the Investigative Committee was also director of the Sideling Hill CPS camp in Pennsylvania, said that he had heard "from the other side" that the Virginia charges were "too radical" and that Gehman was forced to apologize. When Gehman told Shetler that Orie had admitted the danger of the interfaith FOR, unaccountable to the Mennonite Church, Shetler reported that Orie had sent him copies of his correspondence with "Bro." A. J. Muste, "which does not indicate such feeling whatsoever." Shetler said he had barred the FOR from the Sidling Hill CPS Camp, and "raised the ire of the MCC." After Orie and CPS director H. A. Fast attempted to "set [Shetler] right in his thinking," Shetler wrote a long letter to inform Orie, "The FOR will either *stay out* of Sideling Hill or *I* am *getting out* and there is no mistake about that!"[92]

Shetler's assessment of the state of church affairs was that Miller and Bender,

> with the blessing of a few modest bishops laid the foundation for the present program, while the majority were [sic] sitting around twiddling thumbs, over-confident that all was right and well done. Then when conscription came, wide-eyed and open mouthed, they accepted at face value the outcome of their deliberations. And now, sad to say, they have taken us almost past the point of retreat. . . . I am no longer willing to accept the major premise

of the committee which is repeated parrot-like by all idol worshipers *that this was the only way out; we had to hook up with all the peace groups and war-resisters.*[93]

George Brunk wanted to make sure the denominational CPS Investigative Committee had all of Gehman's "dope." He complained of the secrecy of the committee, using the unfortunate analogy of the GPU, an early form of the Soviet secret service.[94] In June, Brunk wrote Gehman: "I suppose Orie went away from the March 17 meeting feeling like he could have answered more than we brought up . . . some of these fellows who were trying to obstruct your exposé [on French] must now be at least partly convinced that there was a coon in the tree when you barked treed."[95]

After reading the 117-page transcript of the Virginia meeting, Shetler scolded Gehman for missing opportunities to make Orie "warm."

I do not believe you realized how nearly floored he was at a few instances. He must have almost held his breath at these points! But instead of staying there, the moderator led on to the next question and the cat had made his escape from the bag. . . . My feeling is that most of your listeners left the meeting feeling that Orie had made a good acquittal of himself. . . . His reply on pages 71 and 72 are very, very weak.

Shetler continued,

When Orie said, I am open for more light on page 75 . . . the meeting should have come to a dead stop. If he is . . . so ignorant, it is high time to appoint another in his place. This, I can tell you is a case of feigned ignorance. . . . Attributing his own failures to his immaturity during the early days of the Peace Committee may be Dale Carnegie but it doesn't answer the point. General Conference is large enough that there should be no need of putting immature men in such important positions. The Mennonite church should have been more awake during the summer of 1940. We trusted too much in a few men. Now we are paying for it.[96]

Orie Miller was included on a list of NSBRO members whose activities were "reckoned as subversive by patriotic groups," which Gehman sent to John L. Horst of Scottdale, Pennsylvania, on August 8, 1942. Gehman wanted Horst, a member of the denominational Investigative Committee, to know the truth about these dangerous individuals.

Gehman paraphrased a speech given by Brethren leader Dan West, "a socialist-minded, young Dunkard preacher." In telling the CPS story, West said, "the CO problem seemed almost impossible to us, until Orie Miller, speaking for the Mennonites, said, 'We have a common problem. We'll work with you.' Then the clouds immediately began to roll away." Gehman concluded, "Right there we were sold down the river."[97]

Gehman also gathered from a FOR newsletter the story that when FOR and other radical war-resisters in a meeting in Chicago heard that Mennonites and other peace churches were proceeding to negotiate a plan for objectors, "the crowd made grand whoopee for a while." Gehman's editorial comment: "We're being taken for a ride and don't know it."

Further grist for Gehman's mill was Paul Comly French's account at a CPS conference of the Burke-Wadsworth conscription bill and "the efforts of the historic peace churches to combat conscription." French had "lobbied" for the inclusion of a civilian service option. Gehman's interpretation followed: "Here we are authentically informed that we participated in a movement to obstruct a proper-functioning of the United States government. Then when that failed, as it should have, our representative (accused of a communist record) admittedly lobbied for favorable legislation, although we were assured . . . that he does not do that and never did!" Gehman concluded with a new twist to an old adage: "What a tangled web we weave, when the paths of God we leave!"[98]

STRANGE BEDFELLOWS

Since 1941, Ernest Gehman had been corresponding with an unlikely ally in Lancaster, Mont. H. Smith, a self-appointed watchdog of things he considered un-American. On file are twenty-one exchanges. Smith, a county employee with no apparent links to Mennonites, was intent on exposing Paul Comly French as a communist and more. He was happy to paint Orie with the same brush. Gehman was only too eager to join Smith's vitriolic campaign.

Smith heaped praise on Gehman: "You are the first man among the plain sects that has had the moral courage to let me know that you wish to investigate the charges that I have made against that revolutionary, subversive communist named Paul Comly French—the others the Mennonites, Quaker and United Brethren [sic] have soft pedaled and hush hushed the matter, but the exposure goes on just the same."[99]

Despite Ernest Gehman's criticism of Orie's Washington "lobby-ing," Gehman himself turned to the government for evidence to use against Orie. On July 9, 1941, Gehman inquired of the FBI whether the Fellowship of Reconciliation or the Federal Council of Churches had any communist or socialist "leanings or connections." On the same day, he wrote to Virginia senator Harry F. Byrd Jr. to ask whether the government saw any difference between pacifists and COs who base their convictions on the Bible. And did the government distinguish between historic peace churches and FOR or NSBRO? Again on the same day, Gehman wrote a congenial letter to Donovan Smucker of FOR, saying he was "interested in the work and able leadership" of FOR. He wanted to know, "Who are the Mennonite members of the FOR?"[100]

Smith sent Gehman copies of his letters to government officials, such as a December 21, 1941, letter to the War Department General Staff, Military Intelligence, Division G-2 in Washington, DC. Smith identified himself as "a man who has proudly worn the uniform of the US Army, and as a man whose only son has within the last several weeks become eligible for Selective Service from which he will not shirk." After two pages of "evidence," Smith wrote, "I charge Paul Comly French with treason."[101]

Smith also reported to Gehman a meeting in his own Lancaster home with Orie Miller and Quaker Paul Furnas "on or about" December 12, 1941. As evidence against Paul Comly French, he presented issues of the *Forerunner,* the newsletter of the Federal Writers' Project. French had been the Pennsylvania director for three years. "I showed [Miller and Furnas] the printed filth, sacrilege, blasphemy, revolting sexual situations, and communistic suggestion of forcible seizure of private property which emanated from the poisoned pen of Paul Comly French himself. . . . I was amazed at the attitude of Orie Miller, he actually defended French." But when Miller and Furnas asked Smith if he wanted to take his concerns directly to French, he was unwilling to do so, saying, "Gentlemen, this is NOT a blackmail plot, I can have nothing to say to French; I am not blackmailing him, I am exposing him." Then he promised that "the big blast against him is yet to come."[102]

Smith's diatribe against FOR continued: "A. J. Muste, the secretary of the radical FOR, has been arrested for leading strikes and encouraging the overthrow of the American government. An undiscerning Mennonite [Orie Miller] often present at NSBRO meetings describes him as 'a very competent man and his council [*sic*] is appreciated.'" Despite Orie's explanation of his relationship with the organization, Gehman reported in a missive to the Virginia Conference leaders that Orie had been a member of FOR "for many years." He said Orie's membership on the "socialistic National Committee against Militarism in Education" implicated him—again, despite Orie's explanation in the March meeting in Virginia. Since most of the members of the National Service Board were pacifists, "the candle of our scriptural nonresistance is being smothered under the bushel of worldly pacifism."[103]

Gehman also quoted extensively from the investigative reports of the House Committee on Un-American Activities, chaired by Martin Dies Jr., a Texas Democrat. The Dies Committee investigated alleged subversive activities of citizens and organizations suspected of having Fascist and communist loyalties. Gehman approved of the Dies Committee's definition of pacifism, which equated it with communism, socialism, and anarchism, all of which "are contrary to the American traditions and form of government and that they are therefore un-American." According to the Dies Report to Congress, the Mennonite Church and the Goshen College Peace Society were named as pacifist organizations.[104]

Smith and Gehman discussed plans for a mailing to 650 Mennonite bishops and ministers to warn them about French's subversive, "communistic and fascist" agenda. Gehman supplied the names and addresses and intended to share the printing and mailing cost. Smith promised he would not reveal Gehman's complicity. Smith also sent letters to the governors of the sixteen states where CPS camps were located and to numerous branches of the federal government.

Gehman wrote to Smith on May 18, 1942, "Your information on Orie Miller corroborates fears and suspicions that a number of us had for some years. Anything further that you know regarding him will help to clarify the situation for us when the time for action comes."[105] Gehman requested that Smith write to J. L. Stauffer about his knowledge of French. Stauffer passed a copy to John R. Mumaw, who wrote in alarm to Harold Bender. In no uncertain terms, Bender told Mumaw that the PPC knew of Smith, and that no Mennonite should have any contact with him, because he was "a man who is not of like faith with us, and who evidently is of a peculiar mind, and uses intemperate language in his communications." Many of Smith's claims, Bender declared, were "patently false."[106]

Gehman's inquiry to the FBI on July 9 regarding communist or social-ist activity by FOR did not produce the desired results. J. Edgar Hoover, FBI director, answered, "Without the authority of the Attorney General, no confidential FBI files can be released."[107]

IN RETROSPECT

The accusations of Mennonites like Ernest Gehman and Sanford Shetler were unfortunate. To impugn the motives of brothers in the faith and to characterize ordained leaders as thumb-twiddling, undiscerning, and idolatrous, blindly following a communistic, "idolized" Orie is appalling. Such was the vitriolic language of some fundamentalists who believed they were waging a war against modernism, liberalism, and the erosion of traditional practices and convictions.

Their concerns, however, were reasonable and prophetic. The experi-ences of men and women in CPS did change the Mennonite Church, as it did all Mennonites. The exposure of participants to one another and to a world in need eroded traditional boundaries of separation, noncon-formity, and identity. It led young men and women to rethink traditional nonresistance and generated a move toward active peacemaking with a concern for social justice.

As MC conservatives and fundamentalists alike feared, young men in CPS discovered common convictions across denominational boundaries. The program served as a doorway to a much larger and more complex world—and to an accelerated American acculturation. Despite its short-comings, the CPS program helped to shape the future of the participating churches. More than an escape from military service, the experience of CPS brought new vitality into church life, reawakened the call to service, and enlarged its witness.

As historian Paul Toews has put it, the experience "helped link or-thodoxy to social compassion." Grounded in a theologically conserva-tive base, Mennonites launched an amazing array of ministries, outlets for "servant activism." These forms of engagement also produced in Mennonites "new self-confidence and sense of self-worth."[108]

The Virginia critics were also disgruntled by their observation that too much power resided in the hands of a few leaders at the top of the eccle-siastic pyramid. A decade later, an intellectual think tank in Europe called the "Concern" group voiced similar concerns. Orie Miller, along with

Harold Bender, was the target of both sets of critics. There is no doubt that Miller and Bender carried an unusual amount of influence, partly because of their membership on multiple church boards and committees. Their influence also came from their personal strengths. In the case of Bender, it was his articulation of Anabaptist and Mennonite values and beliefs. For Orie Miller, it was his far-ranging vision, his gift of administration, and his ability to spot potential leadership and delegate authority.

Chapter 9
Sheeplike Living in a Wolves' World: 1942–1949

*"When the church asks you to serve,
let your answer be yes, unless there
is a good reason to say no."*

"I was glad to read the article in *Time* magazine," John W. Miller wrote happily to his mother on February 10, 1947, the day a feature article on MCC and its executive officer appeared. "Almost everywhere I go someone quips to me about my 'greying and bespectacled' father!"[1]

The article, titled "Plain People," begins with a quote from Conrad Grebel: "True believing Christians are as sheep in the midst of wolves." After a broad sweep of Anabaptist martyrdom history, and under the subtitle "Wolves' World," comes a survey of current Amish and Mennonites. The requisite photo shows two plain-suited men exchanging a "Mennonite 'Holy Kiss.'" Then on to the main point of the article. Akron, Pennsylvania, a "tiny town" of 877, is identified as "the center" of the United States for most Mennonites. There lives the "greying, spectacled Orie O. Miller," the chief administrator of MCC.

Working out of "five white houses," the staff of "fifty-odd men and women administer a foreign corps of 260 workers in 16 countries." Their work includes relief operations and caring for "conscientious objectors in all parts of the world." Some of the men wear "snuff-colored" suits and some women the traditional white 'prayer caps,' but "all work for mere subsistence wages." Though MCC headquarters are in a small town, the organization's expenditures are large. In the previous year, MCC spent $3 million, an average of $15 per constituent member. In the current year, MCC expected to spend $2.5 million to resettle refugees. The article concludes by returning to the theme of the opening lines: "Mennonites have come to regard such assessments [expenditures] as one inescapable price of sheeplike living in a wolves' world."[2]

FAMILY MATTERS

In 1942, Albert Wolf Miller, Orie and Elta's oldest son, was a student at Goshen College, and second son Daniel Wolf Miller was at Eastern Mennonite High School (EMHS) in Harrisonburg, Virginia. Albert kept his parents posted on the Middlebury Millers. He wrote of a tragedy in April: "I suppose you have heard by this time that Grandpa's house at Chanceys [*sic*] practically burned down. I haven't seen it yet and I don't know how it started. They were eating in the kitchen when smoke started coming through the doors from grandpa's room. I think the summer and the winter kitchens are still standing. They are living at Arts now, I think." That Saturday, Albert rode his bicycle the twelve miles to Brookside Farm to see the burned house. D. D. was salvaging bricks from the remains, but said he was glad for a rest now that Albert had arrived. Carpenters were beginning that day to rebuild the house, smaller than before.[3]

Orie's sister Alice had married Chauncey Oesch, and they were farming the Brookside Farm across the road from the Forks Mennonite meetinghouse. Sister Clara and her husband, Art Augsburger, were farming Cloverdale, the Miller family farm. D. D., now a widower and retired, was living with his daughters—sometimes with Alice and sometimes with Clara. Unfortunately, the house fire at Brookside destroyed all of D. D.'s books, sermons, letters, and records.

Albert also reported that he was eager to hear the college women's speech contest "because at least two of my old girl friends are in it and also the two Graber girls. They are very ambitious." Acknowledging his own lack of motivation, he surmised, "I guess I could use a little of that." The girls were daughters of Orie's friend, Chris and Mina Graber.[4]

In May, Albert commented on a donation Orie and Elta made to Goshen College to buy new dormitory floor covering. "The linoleum was put in the past weekend and everyone comments on how it improves the place." Then a comment about the money: "It seems you really know how to spend money . . . in spite of all I've said about your spending at times."[5]

Albert was doing well at Goshen. He reported that his academic pursuits were giving him "a great deal of satisfaction." For a course on "War and Peace," presumably taught by Guy Hershberger, Albert was reading G. H. C. Macgregor's *The New Testament Basis of Pacifism*, a book he had started on

Orie O. and Elta (Wolf) Miller, twenty-fifth anniversary portrait, 1940. Edward L. Miller.

his own. He was also working on a seminar paper on John Funk, the influential Mennonite publisher in Elkhart. He was reading *Story of the Mennonites* by C. Henry Smith and doing research in the archives in the basement of Memorial Library, for which Orie had helped raise money. It was inspiring work: "It awes me to think of the privilege that I have of finding out knowledge for myself. I like to daydream that this piece of work will make me famous."

His time away from home was giving him a new appreciation for his mother: "I owe so much more to you than I do to anybody else and often feel that I never let you know that I feel it." He was also gaining a sense of his inherited legacy: "I try not to forget that all heritage and background is useful for emulation but that each generation's battles must be fought anew."[6]

Orie, in a letter to Elta, wrote of the intense scrutiny by two Civilian Public Service investigating committees: "We had a good day yesterday & my problems cleared up again; the MCC seems to have 100% confidence in me & my efforts & that helps."[7] Apparently, the children were aware of the "problem." Albert wrote, "I hope Daddy is around by now and feeling [more] chipper than ever." Then the inevitable comparison, the dilemma of children of famous parents: "I wonder if I will ever be as indispensable to so many people as he is." For the time being, Albert settled for a post as editor in chief of the Goshen College student newspaper, *The Record.*[8]

In 1943, Lois was living in Washington, DC, with her husband, Ron Beach. Dan was now with Albert at Goshen College, enrolled in the Bachelor of Theology program, while John was at Eastern Mennonite High School, planning for a career as a medical missionary. Youngest son Bob was living at home in Akron.

From Coffman Hall at Goshen College, Dan wrote home in glowing terms of Albert's success as editor of the student newspaper: "Did you like this week's *Record*? I think it was pretty good. Prof. [Paul] Erb praised Albert's editorial something terrific in Intro to Lit class this morning. He said that he feels proud and encouraged that the college is training such good thinkers as Albert." It was a high compliment from the future editor of the *Gospel Herald.*[9]

That summer Albert married Esther Lehman from Columbiana, Ohio, and was called into service by the draft board. He chose CPS, for which his father and others had worked so intensely, and was assigned to Grottoes, Virginia. Esther went with him. From Grottoes, Albert reported a strange encounter with Orie's critic at a Christmas program at Eastern Mennonite College: "So many EMC professors wondered how I like the life over here, but some of their attitudes chilled me a bit. Especially E. G. Gehman gave me a cold once-over; perhaps I just thought this because I hear that he is not so hot on CPS camps."[10] And perhaps because Albert was Orie Miller's son.

CALLING OTHERS TO SERVICE

Civilian Public Service opened a new world for the 4,665 Mennonites and Brethren in Christ who chose alternative service. They constituted 46 percent of draft-age Mennonite and Brethren in Christ men. Nearly 54 percent chose military service as combatants or noncombatants. That more young men chose military service over alternative service was, of course, troubling to church leaders.[11] Though CPS numbers were small, CPSers gave significant service in the war years, far more than their numbers would suggest.

CPS was also an ideal recruiting field for Orie, who had an "uncanny" gift for "spotting talent."[12] He could observe CPSers' conduct, assess their abilities, and measure their commitment to the church and to Christian service. There he found administrators for MCC, relief workers for post-war reconstruction in Europe, mission workers for Africa and South America, and employees for Miller, Hess & Company. Harry Martens spoke for many when he said, "I've never figured out why, but every time God calls me, it comes through the voice of Orie Miller."[13]

Orie encouraged Mennonite pastors and leaders to visit the young men in the camps. He also welcomed the talent of C. N. Hostetter Jr., Brethren in Christ leader and president of Messiah College in Grantham, Pennsylvania. The Brethren in Christ were spiritual cousins who emerged as a renewal movement in Lancaster County, Pennsylvania, after the War of the Revolution. While anchored in Anabaptism, they were inspired by the passionate preaching of evangelists of the Great Awakening. They combined Anabaptist discipleship with pietism that emphasized heartfelt conversion and holy living.

A shared concern for nonresistance had brought the Brethren in Christ and Mennonites together at the beginning of World War II, in forming the Continuation Committee of Historic Peace Churches. The relationship was reinforced when Orie drew Hostetter into MCC's orbit. After Hostetter conducted a series of Bible study and prayer meetings at Goshen College in January 1941, president Ernest E. Miller reported to Orie that Hostetter had been especially effective. Orie then invited C. N. to provide the same kind of spiritual ministry to CPSers.[14] Hostetter, in turn, gave Orie a standing invitation to speak at Messiah College.

Hostetter's teaching ability, pastoral presence, and relational skills made him a welcome face in camps from the East Coast to Colorado. He also taught at CPS summer training sessions on college campuses and spoke in Mennonite churches and conferences. Hostetter's effective ministry and the mutual respect between the two leaders further strengthened the relationship between Mennonites and Brethren in Christ. The Brethren in Christ became full members of MCC in 1942.[15]

Hostetter participated in the 1948 Mennonite World Conference and served on an MCC study committee to evaluate MCC's role in Europe. Also in 1948, he became the Brethren in Christ representative of MCC and immediately began representing MCC concerns before government officials in Washington. In 1951, Orie urged MCC to add a seat to its executive committee and invited Hostetter into MCC's inner circle. When P. C. Hiebert, chair of MCC since its beginning in 1920, retired in 1953, the able C. N. Hostetter became the new chair of the executive committee. Hostetter's biographer, E. Morris Sider, noted Orie's "skillful yet brotherly hand" in planning for Hostetter's leadership office.[16]

Unlike Hostetter, Orie was not a dynamic speaker—some thought he was dull and bland—but his broad experience and wide knowledge of the world inspired people. He often brought the latest news from Washington, DC, Rhodesia (now Zimbabwe), Indonesia, Germany, or Paraguay. Robert S. Kreider, assigned to CPS Camp No. 5 at Templeton Gap near Colorado Springs, Colorado, observed Orie's visit in September of 1941. After Orie spoke to the men about the work of MCC, ten men volunteered on the spot to serve in South America. "Orie made a hit with the fellows," Kreider wrote in his journal. It was the content rather than the delivery of the speech that inspired them.

Kreider, though, was less impressed. The budding CPS leader at twenty-two engaged the veteran churchman in a genial debate. While Orie advocated the efficiency of centralized management of farms and industries, citing his own control of two Akron farms and the Miller Hess shoe company, Kreider thought efficiency and "benevolent paternalism" were not the best measures of success. When Kreider was hesitant to accept an appointment as assistant director and educational director of the Templeton Gap Camp, Orie shared one of his guiding principles: "When the church asks you to serve, let your answer be yes unless there is a good reason to say no." [17] Kreider accepted the new role.

As assistant director from 1941 to 1942, Kreider was often in charge of camp operations when director Albert Gaeddert was gone. With his new assignment also came duties as educational director. CPS affirmed Kreider's "yen to create and administer" and permitted him "full freedom in developing the camp education program."[18] Kreider adopted Orie's "principle of life" as his own, and said yes to the church's call many times throughout his long and effective life of service."[19]

At the same time, Ray Schlichting from Weatherford, Oklahoma, was picked for a leadership role as business manager, also at Templeton Gap. He recalled a daylong meeting of the CPS and MCC leaders at the camp to discuss the appointment of leaders. Orie advocated selecting young, drafted men already in camp, while Harold Bender and P. C. Hiebert were skeptical that men so young could be trusted in responsible positions.

Orie, in his quiet, persistent manner, had his way and appointed both Kreider and Schlichting to their administrative posts.[20]

After their terms with CPS, both Kreider and Schlichting were invited to work at the MCC headquarters in Akron—Schlichting as field auditor and Kreider as secretary for education. In time, Schlichting carried heavy administrative responsibilities as chief accountant and controller of MCC operations. Kreider represented the work of MCC in Mennonite pulpits in eastern Pennsylvania and developed leadership-training curricula for courses taught in Akron and Washington, DC.[21]

"Happy as a lark" was Kreider's depiction of Orie when he returned to Akron on March 10, 1943. Orie brought news of support in Washington for a CPS relief unit in China. Many in CPS were eager to work overseas, and the NSBRO was preparing to initiate a reserve college training program to prepare volunteers for overseas relief work. When Henry Fast, director of Mennonite CPS, invited Kreider to be among the first to go to China, Kreider was eager to go despite potential dangers and hardships. As Kreider drove Orie to the Lancaster train station, Orie confirmed that he would indeed be among the first to go to China. His administrative abilities had led to the appointment to serve under the American Friends Service Committee. For Kreider, it was a "great honor" to be chosen for such an assignment as well as a welcome "escape from the routines."[22]

After intense preparation and a few language lessons, Kreider and his seven colleagues—among the seventy appointed for service in China—departed by ship from New York Harbor on June 18, 1943.[23] Two months later, in the seaport city of Durban, South Africa, the team learned by cable the disquieting news that their China assignment, so eagerly anticipated, had been aborted by an act of Congress.[24] An amendment to the Military Establishment Appropriation Act prohibited the Selective Service from appropriating any funds for "the service of such conscientious objectors outside the United States, its territories and possessions."[25] Consequently, on December 19 Kreider was back to the old routines in Akron, assigned to assist J. N. Byler in the administration of the MCC-CPS Hospital Section.[26] In a few months, at age twenty-five, Kreider replaced Byler as director and plunged into the daunting administrative work. Service in mental hospitals was one of the most significant forms of CPS work, with perhaps the longest-lasting legacy.

THE FORMATION OF MCC CANADA

In 1943, Orie initiated the idea of establishing an MCC office in Canada. He arranged for a meeting in Winnipeg, Manitoba, of representatives from four active relief organizations—the Non-Resistant Relief Organization, the Conference of Historic Peace Churches, the Mennonite Central Relief Committee, and the Canadian Mennonite Relief Committee (CMRC)—and MCC's executive committee on April 2 and 3. His goal was to share information of MCC's activities and plans for a program to train volunteers for postwar reconstruction in Europe. The executive committee also invited counsel on MCC's work and suggested that a Canadian commissioner be appointed to meet with the executive committee. At a subsequent meeting in December, Orie proposed the establishment of an MCC office in Canada. Representatives approved the idea and in January 1944 an office was opened in Kitchener, Ontario. The office would coordinate clothing collection, give information to Canadian churches in both English and German, receive Canadian funds, serve as a liaison to Ottawa, and approve relief workers. C. J. Rempel, a Mennonite Brethren, became office manager.[27]

In 1948, MCC opened a short-lived second office in Winnipeg, Manitoba. Then MCC invited Canadian Mennonite relief organizations to appoint members to its executive committee. With the addition of C. F. Klassen, J. G. Toews, Oscar Burkholder, and J. B. Martin, MCC became international in scope. There were many challenges in working with diverse agencies in addition to the Conference of Historic Peace Churches.

The most contentious issue concerned the support of Mennonites in Paraguay. The issue surfaced between MCC and the Canadian Mennonite Relief Committee. While MCC's assistance in resettling and supporting Russian Mennonite refugees was monumental, members of the CMRC were unhappy that some of the assistance was given as a loan instead of a donation. The disapproval sharpened when MCC began allocating some of its funds beyond the Mennonite family to other regions of the world. Was not their first obligation to those within the household of faith?[28]

Tensions came to a breaking point in 1951, when only $12,000 of MCC's budget of $180,000 was earmarked for Paraguay. When MCC refused to waver, the CMRC cut its funding to MCC in half and diverted that amount to Paraguay. In addition, eastern Canadians objected to MCC's plan to establish a second office in a western province. In the opinion of some, MCC was meddling in conference affairs and becoming "a super-conference."[29]

Nevertheless, that experience eventually led to the formation of Mennonite Central Committee Canada. As historian Esther Epp-Tiessen has observed, "By supporting the US-based agency, [Canadian Mennonite relief agencies] found a common purpose beyond their own borders which they sometimes had difficulty finding on their own."[30] Discussions began in the 1950s that resulted in the formation of the new organization in December 1963, which for the first time represented all the Mennonites in Canada. Delegates of the Canadian Mennonite Council, meeting in Winnipeg, December 12–14, 1963, approved the plan and adopted the name MCC (Canada). Immediately, leaders sent a telegram to Akron asking for permission to use MCC's name. Curiously, Akron did not receive the dispatch, so the Canadian organizers read the silence as approval. When MCC officers learned of the name, they were surprised but did not object.[31] While over the coming years MCC Canada would have to work out its relationship to the Akron office, it was, indeed, an important development. It set the trajectory for a realignment of MCC along the forty-ninth parallel in 2010.

TRANSFORMING THE "BEDLAM" OF MENTAL HOSPITALS

"Most U.S. [mental] hospitals are a shame and a disgrace," declared *Life* magazine in 1946. Titled "Bedlam 1946," the article featured the deplorable, filthy, subhuman conditions of state hospitals. "Conchies," as COs were derisively called, changed all that. The overwhelming staff needs in hospitals and the growing desire of CPSers to do more significant work eventually trumped General Hershey's strategy of keeping COs out of sight. Before hospital units were opened to CPSers, Robert Kreider noted in his journal in December 1942, there were already 726 men who had volunteered for hospital work.[32]

At Byberry, the Philadelphia State Hospital, only two hundred of the previous year's one thousand staff remained in 1942. Hospitals could not compete with high wartime industrial wages. The aging facilities, built for 2,500 patients, now contained 6,000. Ten CPSers volunteered to take on the incontinent-patient ward, the worst place in the entire hospital.[33] Farm animals at home fared better than the ward's 350 patients, who were kept "with almost no care, naked, filthy and ill-fed."[34] All were in

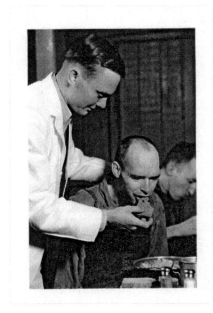

Humanizing hospital care in CPS Camp 51,
Western State Hospital, Fort Steilacoom,
Washington. MCC.

one large room with a floor of concrete and no furniture. The men, most naked, wandered aimlessly or huddled on the floor and against the dirty walls. Compassion, patience, and persistence transformed the ward. The COs refused to control patients with violence, dramatically improved patient care and sanitation, established regular routines—and painted the entire building.[35]

Concerned about the fate of patient care when the CPS program ended in 1946, Quaker CPSer Charlie Lord secretly captured the deplorable scenes with his small Agfa camera. Over the course of several months, Lord shot three rolls of 36-exposure film. Eleanor Roosevelt, then a widow, was among the first to see the grainy black-and-white photos in September 1945. Shocked, she at first refused to believe conditions were that horrendous.[36]

Then Lord's photos appeared in the May 6, 1946, issue of *Life* magazine. The images reminded readers of Nazi concentration camps and "created a kind of mass uproar, nationally," said Steven Taylor, professor of disabilities at Syracuse University and author of *Acts of Conscience: World War II, Mental Institutions and Religious Objectors.* "People could not believe that this was the way we treated people with mental illness and intellectual disabilities in our society." According to Taylor, the exposé "punctured a national sense of American superiority."[37]

CPS men who studied medicine and psychiatry after their discharge founded the National Mental Health Foundation and revolutionized mental health care in the United States. Eleanor Roosevelt, as the foundation's sponsor, actively promoted the reform. Kreider's final task before his release from CPS—and before his marriage to Lois Sommer on December 30, 1945—was to report on his extensive study of mental health needs among Mennonites.[38] Fifteen hundred COs had served in twenty-three state hospitals and five schools for the mentally handicapped. In addition, several hundred women, friends, and spouses of CPSers were employed in the same settings. Kreider's two publications, one an edited collection of articles and the other an article in the *Anniversary Review* of the Harrisburg, Pennsylvania, CPS unit in 1945, led Orie Miller to claim that mental health was a need that MCC could and should take on. Kreider's "Special Hospital Study Report" bore fruit.[39]

Mennonite ministry to the mentally ill had precedents in Russia and Canada. The earliest known institution was Bethania Hospital, founded in 1910 near Alt-Kronsweide in Chortitza Colony, South Russia.[40] One of Bethania's workers, Henry Wiebe, carried his compassion for the mentally ill and mentally challenged to Canada when he left Russia. In 1932, he and his wife, Maria, transformed their brick farmhouse in Vineland, Ontario, into a home for the mentally ill. The home became a ministry of the Canadian Conference of Mennonite Brethren Churches.[41]

At its annual meeting on January 3, 1947, MCC committed its resources to establishing mental health centers in three regions of the United States: Brook Lane Farm in Hagerstown, Maryland, in 1949; Kings View in Reedley, California, in 1951; and Prairie View Hospital in Newton, Kansas, in 1954.[42] Orie Miller added mental health services to his administrative duties. His recruitment of Myron Ebersole to be the first administrator of Prairie View was typical. During an administrative visit to the Middle East in 1952, Orie was viewing relief work with Ebersole, a volunteer on assignment. While traveling from Jerusalem to Jericho, Orie asked Ebersole about his plans for the future. When Ebersole expressed interest in training for mental health, Orie encouraged him to pursue his educational interest and then engaged him to be the first director of Prairie View, beginning in March 1954.[43]

MCC managed the institutions from Akron. Elmer M. Ediger and Delmar Stahly, the first two directors of Mennonite Mental Health Services (MMHS), incorporated in 1952, were responsible for hospital operations and reported to Orie.[44] But management from a distance proved untenable. A 1957 study committee concluded that the program had grown too large, too diverse, and too complex to manage from Akron, and recommended a decentralization of control. While administrators reported to local boards, Orie remained treasurer and served on the MMHS board as ex officio member.[45]

Orie and H. A. Fast, who had been deeply involved from the beginning, resigned from the Mental Health Services board in 1966.[46] In further developments, Oaklawn Psychiatric Center was established in Elkhart, Indiana, in 1963; Kern View Hospital, Bakersfield, California, affiliated with the MMHS board in 1967; Eden Mental Health Centre, Winkler, Manitoba, in 1968; and Philhaven Hospital, Mount Gretna, Pennsylvania, joined the MMHS network in 1972.

Elmer M. Ediger, a pioneer in the Mennonite mental health care movement, and executive director of Prairie View from 1957 to 1983, reflected that Mennonite institutions "have sought to use the best of the church and the best of psychiatry to meet human needs that continue to baffle both church and the world."[47]

AN INFORMAL ADMINISTRATIVE STRATEGY

While Orie was often affirming of the work and ideas of his protégés, he didn't like every idea they came up with. Out of the many "bull sessions" of MCC-CPS workers living in the "Monastery," a former Wolf carriage house converted into staff housing, an idea emerged in late 1945 about relocating MCC headquarters to a more central location such as Newton, Kansas, or Goshen or Nappanee, Indiana. Long-term MCC service appealed to these "westerners," but they did not relish raising families among the "plain" people of Lancaster County. In November, the Monastery group delegated Ray Schlichting to speak to Orie about such a relocation. Ray remembered Orie dismissing it in one sentence: "It may be a good idea, but I wouldn't be any part of that." That was the end of it.[48]

Schlichting had other conversations with Orie that fell flat. He was disgruntled with what he perceived as a "haphazard, topsy-turvy operation" of MCC, characterized by a lack of clear job descriptions, slipshod lines of accountability, informal compensation schedules, and no centralized accounting system. Schlichting drew up organizational flowcharts and systems to streamline operations. Schlichting remembered Orie was not impressed, saying, "'We don't need it.' He was not really adamant, but he liked his ways better than mine," Schlichting recalled.[49] When he recommended getting rid of "dead wood"—staff members Ray believed to be ineffective—Orie responded, "We take who the Lord sends us." Rather than replacing an inept volunteer, Orie preferred to move such a person laterally into another assignment for which the person would be better suited. When one volunteer complained about being transferred to a new post, Orie said, "You said the Lord was sending you. All we do is buy the plane ticket."[50]

In response to continued concerns about work patterns at Akron, Orie consented to an open forum where staffers could air their suggestions. Nearly everyone came. "There was a good exchange of ideas," but Orie turned every one of them down. He saw no need for change. At the end of the forum, Schlichting heard Elta, who had come to hear the discussion, exclaim, "Orie, I thought these were nice boys! I thought these were *all* nice boys!" In her mind, it seemed, no one who disagreed with Orie could be "nice."[51]

Though he himself was the master of discipline and efficiency, Orie did not build carefully scripted, modern organizational systems. His style of management was informal and fluid, folksy and communal, relational and charismatic—all built on trust. He provided vision, established policies, offered general supervision, sketched broad outlines of delegated responsibility, and granted appropriate authority and freedom. Granting a large measure of freedom to his protégés was especially evident during postwar relief and reconstruction in Europe. Orie also knew how to work the system, as in the case of founding Mennonite Mutual Aid (MMA).

FORMATION OF MENNONITE MUTUAL AID

On October 16, 1943, Guy Hershberger, Harold Bender, Chris Graber, and Orie—fertile minds all—sat at the kitchen table in the Millers' Akron home. They were inventing a new organization to manage financial assets, to assist families in need because of loss of property and life, and to help CPSers reintegrate into civilian life after the war. As Hershberger remembered it, Orie, pencil in hand, scratched out a name for the new organization: Mennonite Mutual Aid (now Everence).[52]

They were institutionalizing a long-held practice of bearing one another's burdens, to use the imagery of Galatians 6. Hershberger had been calling for such an agency that would "mark the kind of human, social relationships that the church was called to demonstrate, as a witness."[53] They agreed that the Industrial Relations Committee would recommend to the MC General Conference the formation of the new agency.

According to traditional Mennonite teaching, the purchase of commercial insurance indicated a lack of confidence in God's providence and in the congregation's ability to care for those in need. The church's practice of mutual aid was the safety net for its members in need. D. D. Miller, Orie's father, had formulated this teaching in a chapter in Daniel Kauffman's *Bible Doctrines*, published in 1914, and its restatement in the 1928 *Doctrines of the Bible*. When property insurance was sanctioned by the church as the result of a 1935 study, this did not include life insurance.[54] How could one place a monetary value on a human life? According to *Doctrines of the Bible*, not only was life insurance unbiblical, it was not necessary. It was also a poor financial investment; it enriched a few at the expense of the poor; it was a dishonorable way of attaining wealth; and it placed additional burdens on the poor when buying policies. It was also unfair, since those who needed it the most were often refused coverage.[55]

The most important meeting of the summer of 1944 was a special session of the General Conference in Goshen. The main agenda item was the threat of impending division over the discipline of the Illinois Conference, whose leaders were reluctant to enforce the norms of nonconformity. This was the showdown that Sanford Shelter, colleague of Ernest Gehman in discrediting Orie, had said he would welcome. Instead of dividing the church once again, the tensions were overcome and the structural unity of the church remained intact.

The mutual aid committee had also managed to gain a place on the agenda. In advance, Orie met with the executive committee and the Inter-Board Committee[56] and presented proposals about how to bring the MMA plan to the floor for a vote. Orie understood church politics. His strategy would be to let the discussion on the conference floor determine whether the proposal should be brought to a vote. Only if the discussion on the floor was positive should it be presented for a decision. A delay would be less damaging than a negative vote.

During the special session in Goshen, Orie introduced the concept for Mennonite Mutual Aid and then laid out the proposed plan in his even-handed, nonanxious manner. Hershberger had meanwhile spoken with an Iowa bishop, Simon Gingerich, whom he knew well. After ascertaining that the bishop was in favor of the concept, Hershberger asked if Gingerich would be willing to tell the assembly the reasons for his support, and then make a motion to adopt the resolution. Gingerich made the motion on the resolution and it carried, 70 to 21, a solid mandate.[57] The denominational body authorized the new agency with the caveat

First Mennonite Mutual Aid board, September 1950 (*from left*: Harry Diener, John I. Yoder, Simon Gingerich, Orie O. Miller, Aaron Herr [staff], C. L. Graber [*standing*], Guy F. Hershberger). MC USA Archives–Goshen.

that at least six district conferences endorse the plan. By September, five conferences had signed on: Ohio and Eastern, Indiana-Michigan, Illinois, Missouri-Kansas, and Iowa-Nebraska.[58]

In March 1945, Orie asked Allen Erb, chair of the MMA committee and moderator of the MC General Conference, for permission to call a special meeting of the General Conference executive committee to meet with the MMA committee to plan how to gain the approval of at least one more conference. Erb "heartily endorsed" the idea and agreed to ask the executive committee to meet with the MMA committee on May 31. Then he repeated an earlier understanding that Orie was to take charge: "From this point on you as Mennonite Mutual Aid Executive Secretary are to take the lead. I as chairman of the committee want to be available for counsel and help as you may suggest."[59]

When Erb forgot the time and place to which he had earlier agreed, Orie wrote to remind him. It was now May 9, three weeks before the proposed meeting. Orie reviewed the agenda and ordered, "If you have not notified your Executive Committee members of this [meeting], you should do so at once." When Erb wrote to say he would not arrive in Goshen until noon, Orie returned a telegram urging Erb to "do everything possible" to arrive earlier. Orie could not overrule the train schedules; Erb could not arrive before noon.[60]

Still one conference short of the required six, the MMA committee decided to move ahead. Since some conferences were essentially in favor but needed more study time, and since they would surely sign on, the General Conference gave the MMA committee the green light. The time was urgent, after all; earlier that month Germany had surrendered and when Japan surrendered, the war would be over and returning CPSers would need reintegration loans that MMA intended to provide. They needed to move forward. And they did.

Orie put his money where his mouth was. In June, he sent Chris Graber a check for $5,000 to be divided in three parts: to buy shares in the MMA corporation as an investment; his donation; and a donation to be credited to another's account. In November, Orie sent another donation of $2,000, for which he wanted prompt receipts.

On July 19, 1945, Mennonite Mutual Aid, Inc. was granted a charter by the State of Indiana. MMA was now a legal entity. In the meantime, the Dakota-Montana and the Pacific Coast conferences had endorsed the plan. When the General Conference had given MMA promoters permission to move ahead on May 31, they were still one conference short of the required six. By July 19, they had the support of seven conferences. They had cut it close.

On October 25, the MMA committee became the MMA Board of Directors. During the winter of 1945–46, the new agency took up rented space at 1202 South Eighth Street, Goshen—their home for thirteen years—with Chris Graber as manager.[61] Orie Miller remained its president until he turned seventy in 1962.

AT GOSHEN AND EASTERN MENNONITE

In 1944, Dan was doing well academically at Goshen College, getting no grades lower than a B. He was doing well socially too. He had been elected president of the Young People's Christian Association, the most active student organization on campus. Students and faculty alike, he said, "were so kind" to him. "Everybody yells, 'Hi, Prexy' and most of the old boys extended their best wishes, so I feel I have the students behind me." Conscientious as his father, Dan wrote, "I really want to do the best I can."[62] Laundry service in Goshen was another matter. It was so poor, Dan decided to send his shirts home to Elta to be cleaned and pressed.[63]

John, a student at Eastern Mennonite High School, was learning about local politics. He expected to be the president of his class and had hoped he could write home about it, "for I knew it would make you and Dad happy." It was not to be. John was removed from the slate of candidates for class president for wearing a necktie. Plain coats, he learned, were required of class presidents. "It left me rather bitter at first, but I can see their point and feel happy about it now." John had plenty to keep him busy. He was the editor of the student newspaper, the *Weather Vane*, president of the literary society, and vice president of the Avian bird society. His inaugural speech as president of the literary society came off "very well." He enclosed a copy of the *Weather Vane* and promised to send one home each week so Elta and Orie will "know a little of what goes on down here."[64]

Dan followed the example of his two older siblings and kept in contact with Grandfather D. D. near Middlebury. D. D. had been ailing, but when Dan visited, "it seemed like old times to have grandpa sitting at the table with us—dressed and peppy. He told stories about his school teaching days, discussed the *Apocrypha* with me, and was really on the beam."[65]

Dan was also keeping an eye on his younger brother at EMHS. In January 1945, Dan wrote that not only had John been the first high school student "ever" to enter the peace oratorical contest, he also won first place! "It was quite a sensation then for him to win over all the college contestants." The proud older brother predicted that "John will take over everything when he comes out to Goshen." Dan was enjoying achievements of his own. After a joint literary program in which he apparently had a leading role, "before I know what was happening the Avian literary president put a big box of beautiful roses in my arms and gave a little speech and I in turn was speechless and very much surprised and somewhat embarrassed."[66]

From Harrisonburg in July 1945, John sent a note that would make any parent happy: "I was rethinking anew this evening how much you and dad have meant to us. I thrill over and over again in what a wonderful family I am a part. I suppose I can never appreciate fully but I do realize a greater responsibility because of it."[67]

FAMILY TRANSITIONS

The year 1945 was full of transitions for the Miller family. In August, Lois and Ron Beach, now with two children, Ronnie and Tina, moved to Montclair, New Jersey, for a change of jobs. In September, Bobby (Robert) enrolled at EMHS. Now Orie and Elta—mostly Elta—were empty nesters in the big brick house on Main Street. In September, John wrote of Edward's birth to Albert and Esther: "Say—an Edward in the family. Albert wrote that he is about the most beautiful baby he ever saw. Boy, I can hardly imagine Al being a papa." The erudite student newspaper editor concluded, "Now ain't that realy [sic] something."[68] With Edward's birth, Orie and Elta had three grandchildren.

In 1947, John, now a student at Goshen College, wrote to Elta: "I thought for a while last week that I was too dumb to be a doctor and would consequently have to be a preacher (don't let Dan see that) but I still see faint possibilities of medical future and so am still pursueing [sic] the course with all diligence. . . . I had three dates with Louise since last I saw home. . . . I don't know if I'm in love or not—but I still wish you and dad would wife me up 'cause it's such a difficult task."[69]

EMPOWERED FOR POSTWAR RELIEF AND REFUGEE WORK

If the MCC workers in postwar Europe were "sheep," as suggested by the *Time* article on MCC, they were bold ones in a world torn apart by "wolves" of war. The workers were young and idealistic and did not know what they could not do. They negotiated with military officials and heads of state, because that's what it took to get the job done. The accomplishments of Cal Redekop, Paul Peachey, Freda Pellman, and Robert Kreider (transferred from Akron) illustrate the point.

At age twenty-five, Cal Redekop "was given [an] amazingly free rein . . . in Europe." He first worked in the Espelkamp voluntary service program in Germany, "assisting." After three months, he became director of Mennonite Voluntary Service Program, which he helped to create, with an office in Frankfurt. His work "involved organizing work camps for all of Europe . . . sponsored by the four Mennonite national conferences of Switzerland, France, Holland, and Germany, to form the *Mennonitischer Freiwilligendienst*. Orie "never questioned me about that. He trusted his subordinates very much. He would come to Frankfurt and he had read his stuff. When he came with his briefcase, he was totally informed."[70]

Yet there was accountability, and expectations were high. In the Pax program, which Redekop also helped conceive, "a couple of times I went a bit too fast or presumed too much, and at a certain point I got a letter from Orie saying in relatively unambiguous terms that 'It's probably pretty important that you first consult with us . . . before you commit us to anything.'"[71]

Paul Peachey went to Europe in early 1946. After eight months at the MCC Center in Brussels, he and his wife, Ellen, were transferred to the French zone of Germany, where they "had a real classical experience" with large-scale feedings. In Belsen, a city of 37,000 people, they "fed all of the school children, had specialized programs, distribution for the elderly, and so on." It was "just an amazing experience." Peachey was greatly impressed by "the way in which MCC, Harold Bender, and Orie . . . took people like me, young and inexperienced." They arrived "ignorant, uninformed . . . yet we were entrusted to enter into dialogue with the people in charge in cities in governmental positions, and [to] work things out."[72]

Not all MCC workers were young men. After two years working for Menno Travel Service (MTS) in the Akron home office, Freda Pellman transferred to the Amsterdam office. "Orie thought that I would have what was needed there at that time." So, "all of a sudden, this young girl who had never been very far from home . . . in Richfield, Pennsylvania, was offered a job in Amsterdam." At twenty-two she was below the required age of twenty-four for relief workers. But Orie said, "Oh, that's going to be okay. We know her. She's been here; she's going to be okay there, even though she's not quite old enough."[73] Policies were useful, but not ironclad.

And what of a personnel committee? "I think Orie *was* the personnel committee," Freda reflected. "Yes," added Cal Redekop (he and Freda Pellman later married), "he was king because . . . the empire was pretty small. So he knew where every worker was going. Later as MCC grew, this policy didn't work as well. I think it began to get out of hand."[74]

Robert S. Kreider comitted himself to going the "second mile" beyond CPS in overseas relief work. He was dispatched to the American Zone of occupied Germany to serve with the Council of Relief Agencies Licensed for Operation in Germany (CRALOG). President Harry Truman, who replaced Roosevelt in April 1945, had just authorized the council. The first order of business was to negotiate with the American Military Government in Berlin how a nonmilitary relief organization was to function. After weeks of "courteous but tenuous" conversations, the interfaith CRALOG team had a "full-dress rehearsal with the big boys: two generals, two colonels, and a major." They achieved their objective.[75] Kreider was appointed director of MCC relief operations in all of Germany.[76]

Soon needs beyond his assigned duties captured Kreider's attention and heart. In Berlin, he "stumbled onto" more than two hundred Russian Mennonite refugees. How could he help? Kreider found his way to the office of an American officer responsible for refugees in Berlin's American Sector. Implausibly, Major Thompson was from Pennsylvania, had Mennonites as neighbors, and even spoke Pennsylvania German. Best of all, he wanted to help rescue the Mennonite refugees, first by preventing the Russians from grabbing them. He could do more than that if he was assured that some country somewhere would accept the refugees as settlers. Kreider had what he needed: a letter from Orie Miller, detailing MCC's mission to assist Mennonite exiles. In addition, Orie had sent proof that Paraguay would accept Mennonite refugees as it had in 1929–30: a copy of the privileges the Paraguayan government had granted Mennonites from Canada in 1921. The *Privilegium* was still operative. That was exactly what Thompson needed.[77]

A telegram from Orie Miller arrived, confirming that Paraguay was ready to accept "any and all" Mennonite refugees. A second telegram told Kreider that MCC would bear all the expenses of transporting and resettling the refugees. Orie urged Kreider to make "refugee concerns" his top priority. Kreider immediately launched into a week of intense negotiations.

Kreider called the top military commander, Major General Barker, commanding general of the Berlin District. He was open to a conversation.[78] Kreider asked that Peter Dyck be brought in to manage refugee care and movement. Kreider liked Peter's "aggressiveness . . . confidence, and creativity." He was surely "one of the top workers we have in this game." Kreider continued his efforts from Berlin, then from Wiesbaden and Stuttgart. He introduced Dyck to the challenges at hand and wrote Colonel Stinson, who had replaced Major Thompson, to confirm their agreement to receive food from Holland.[79]

On June 4, 1946, Kreider wrote: "I was flooded with a sense that during this past month I had been placed on the edge of one of the great moments in Anabaptist-Mennonite history—a great moment electric with fear, suspense, hope, assurance."[80] He was indeed an actor in a great moment in history.

"It was a lot of *chutzpah* there," Kreider later reflected. "There's a certain empowerment that came with being youthful administrators in CPS and having a good deal of confidence that you could do things. . . . In that whole European experience, we were out there on the front line and we were coming up with ideas and Akron would affirm and approve them, and then we'd come up with another idea and they would approve it." On "all those occasions I felt the backing of Orie Miller."[81]

OPERATION MENNONITE

Peter Dyck, relief worker in London, and C. F. Klassen, MCC commissioner for Europe, picked up the negotiations for getting the refugees out of Berlin. Orie Miller's guarantee of Paraguay as their destination and MCC as the financial backer, and the American military's permission signed in Frankfurt, were three major hurdles crossed. Finding a ship was the next challenge. Miller gave the "okay" and Klassen signed a contract with the Holland America Line for an old ship, the *Volendam,* at a cost of $375,000.[82]

Back in Akron, Orie Miller and Bill Snyder were engaged in diplomacy with Washington. Snyder, a Bluffton (Ohio) College graduate with a degree in business administration and a former CPSer, did most of the legwork. Snyder's work as a liaison with Washington and New York in the movement of these refugees earned Orie's trust. In 1950, he became the assistant executive secretary of MCC, a precursor to his appointment seven years later as Orie's successor in the top office.

The large amount of money required to engage the *Volendam* naturally caused Snyder some anxiety. Orie, however, "made up for what I might have lacked in nerve," Snyder later recalled. "Orie didn't blanch at all. . . . He was a very steadying hand." When asked where MCC could find that kind of money, Orie had two answers: "Well, the cattle on a thousand hills are His," and "When we ask churches for money, they will give."[83]

Orie wrote to all constituent groups for the money. "He had a certain gift in convincing Mennonite leaders of the [value] of certain programs," Snyder remembered. Orie was known everywhere across the church, in Canada as well as in the United States, because of his own relief work in Russia in 1920. Because of that experience, "there was a certain aura about him." Snyder had watched Orie face "very, very difficult problems . . . and Orie would almost charm the birds out of the trees in explaining how to face these problems." He was a top-notch diplomat.[84]

Ray Schlichting, MCC's assistant treasurer, was responsible to handle the money for the *Volendam* and to get 50 percent of the money to the shipping office in New York City on time. Schlichting recalled "a lot of scrambling" in the Akron office to "get that much money together." Orie "was certainly there, giving everybody the go-ahead." Schlichting, his assistants, and anyone in the office "who was in the loop" pitched in.[85]

It all came down to the wire. "That last day of making the first down payment was one hectic day around MCC! I think we were down to the last $15,000 on that last day." Finally, the last check came in. Schlichting rushed to the local one-man bank, Akron National, where Mr. Hall was president, cashier, and treasurer. Ray gave him the accumulated checks and Hall wrote a cashier's check for $184,000. With the check in his pocket, Ray quickly caught a train to New York City. Minutes before the Holland America Line office closed, Schlichting handed over the required check. The agent called the Rotterdam office and authorized the *Volendam* captain to proceed. "And then, of course, we raised the other half." More than sixty years later, Schlichting marveled, "Those were the kinds of pressure points we dealt with. I just don't know how a twenty-six-year-old could do that."[86]

Twentysomethings were doing amazing things on both sides of the Atlantic. In an abrupt about-face, the American military in Germany reneged on its promise to transport refugees from Berlin through the Russian Zone. Peter Dyck went to the top of the chain of command, General Lucius Clay, who had reversed the decision. As Kreider had observed, Peter Dyck was aggressive and tenacious, well-suited for the task. Time was of the essence, since the contract for the *Volendam* specified a penalty of $15,000 for each day of delay.

At that moment, the *Volendam* was waiting at the northern port of Bremerhaven with three hundred refugees who had boarded in Rotterdam. One thousand other émigrés were traveling by train from Munich to the port. In Berlin were more Soviet Mennonites, now totaling twelve hundred. On the day the ship was to leave, the Berlin refugees were still stranded.

SS *Volendam*. MCC.

There were calls to Washington, a meeting of General Clay and Marshal Sokolovsky, his Russian counterpart, and a meeting with American ambassador Robert Murphy. With those efforts, and the prayers of hopeful refugees in Berlin, permission to travel through the Russian Zone was finally granted. It seemed a miracle. For Peter Dyck, now with the people waiting on the *Volendam*, it was "a once-in-a-lifetime moment when time stood still and God was among us."[87] In Berlin, a "jubilant" Colonel Stinson told Elfrieda Dyck that "Operation Mennonite" was going forward! It had to be quiet and fast.[88]

Robert Kreider was on hand at Berlin's Lichterfelde West railway station to help get the people into the boxcars. When all had boarded, the train moved slowly westward into the Russian Zone. On Friday, January 31, 1947, when the freight train left the Russian Zone and crossed into the safety of the British Zone, a thousand voices erupted in song: "*Nun danket alle Gott*," "Now thank we all our God." Peter and Elfrieda Dyck saw in it a parallel to the biblical story of the escaping Hebrews crossing the Red Sea. At 2:30 a.m., the train arrived in Bremerhaven, where an additional thirteen hundred émigrés waited with the MCC workers C. F. Klassen, C. J. Dyck, Marie Brunk, and Magdalen Friesen.

The *Volendam* steamed out of the harbor at four o'clock in the afternoon on Saturday, February 1, 1947. Its cargo: 2,303 Russian Mennonite refugees, escorted by Peter and Elfrieda Dyck, on their way to South America. They had escaped Soviet "Egypt" and were steaming toward a South American "Canaan."

The dramatic deliverance had been thrilling, heart wrenching, and miraculous. But their pilgrimage to a new and forbidding tropical home would require more miracles. General Lucius Clay later wrote to Peter Dyck: "Your letter [about the refugees' arrival in Buenos Aires] . . . made me very happy, not because I was able in a small way to help the Mennonite refugees leave Berlin, but to know they have found a home. They are fine people and deserve the opportunity to live as free men [and women]."[89]

ECUMENICAL AND INTERNATIONAL ACTIVITIES

CPS, NSBRO, and MMA were not the only things occupying Orie's time, nor were they his only ecumenical activities. Beginning in 1940, Orie served on the board of the Biblical Seminary in New York (known after 1965 as the New York Theological Seminary), which was founded in 1900 and located at 325 East Forty-Ninth Street in New York City. That a significant number of Mennonite students enrolled there led to Orie's appointment. When he became chair of the board, he had weekly, sometimes daily, phone conversations with the seminary president. During his time of service on the board, as many as twenty-two Mennonites studied there, including sons Daniel and John. Orie later remarked on the irony of his serving on this seminary's board while Goshen Biblical Seminary (GBS) was germinating.

There were times of intense conflict at the Biblical Seminary in New York, and Orie recalled that theological issues nearly caused a split. When a board such as this was divided, his practice was to abstain from voting. He chided Paul Landis, then a young bishop who at a recent meeting of the Lancaster Conference Board of Bishops voted for change: "You don't vote for change if it's divisive." When on occasion Orie could have had the "swing vote," he refused to exercise that option. He did the same on the board of the American Leprosy Mission (ALM) when "things were falling apart." Since Orie did not cast a vote in such instances, both sides confided in him. Landis observed that Orie "was a peacemaker with his bureaucratic skills."[90] At Orie's death, former ALM president Oliver M. Hasselblad paid tribute to Orie's contribution as chair of the ALM Board of Directors: "He set the organization on firm new directions. At times a hard taskmaster for whom to work, his disciplines were always in love and kindness." He said further that Orie represented ALM at the founding of All Africa Leprosy Rehabilitation and Training Center (ALERT), and recruited a Mennonite missionary from Ethiopia to be the first business manager.[91]

Orie's ecumenical interests were deep-seated. "One could tell that Orie was, in terms of the Mennonite world and beyond . . . ecumenical," remembers Robert Kreider.

> He reached out, he was inclusive. The curious thing, I think, is that in this big phenomenon of CPS and the life of the church, all four of the general directors of MCC-CPS were General Conference persons, and they all came from Kansas, and they were all graduates of Bethel College. They were Henry Fast, Eldred Gaeddert, Erwin Goering, and Elmer Ediger. Now that's Orie Miller. That's not Harold Bender. Bender was an exclusivist. It was Orie Miller, the businessman, who was moving out into a larger world. It was Orie Miller who kept up connections with the Quakers, believed by some to be liberal and dangerous. Relating to other traditions was part of Orie's world mission.[92]

Peter Wiebe, longtime pastor and member of various boards with Orie, agrees. "Orie Miller *was* inclusive. He could bridge the gaps. He knew more than any other leader we worked with how to get things done abroad. He had a broader view. He was an internationalist." Wiebe first met Orie when Harold Bender invited him, at the young age of twenty-five, to serve on the PPC. When they were planning to go, for example, to Washington, DC, to testify before a congressional committee, Orie would often say, "Let's take Peter along; it would do him good."[93]

Perhaps Orie's most significant contact beyond his peace activities was Willem T. Visser t' Hooft, general secretary of the newly organized World Council of Churches (WCC). During the war, Orie wanted to know the council's plans for postwar reconstruction. Visser t' Hooft told Orie that he had made no such plans; he and the World Council were preoccupied with getting refugees out of Nazi Germany.[94] Orie thought the WCC could also do reconstruction.

HOSTING MENNONITE WORLD CONFERENCE

"As we have therefore opportunity, let us do good unto all men, especially unto them who are of the household of faith" (Galatians 6:10 KJV). With these words, Orie introduced his address on "Basic Principles Underlying the Services of the Mennonite Central Committee" to the Fourth Mennonite World Conference in Goshen, Indiana, on August 4, 1948. This biblical text, he continued, "enunciates clearly the basic brotherhood conviction that led to the birth of the MCC in 1920." Supplementing the "Scriptural word is . . . the Mennonite interpretation of faith and life, which leads logically to . . . response to today's physical distress and suffering."

The Christian relief worker occasionally "can rejoice and marvel as the disciples did when five loaves and two fishes passing through Christ's hands satisfyingly fed a multitude." The worker "senses a spiritual mathematics operation beyond the normal human computations. He senses a symbolic witness value in his work, which is, in the main, unmeasurable."

Serving humanity, Orie declared, "without class, race, religious belief, and friend or foe distinction is also required in today's needy world to make Christian nonresistance intelligible." Furthermore, "Simple obedience to the commands of God requires it." In his famously complex syntax, he continued: "God-given, man-to-man, neighbor-to-neighbor, one-world-in-and-for-Christ sensitivity to man's plight and need, demands such a channel of sharing . . . to the extent that we thus suffer with suffering humanity can we be welded into a fellowship of holy purpose, honoring our Christ in whose name we profess to do it." Relief work, Miller concluded, "is one of the nuclei of the whole structure of Mennonite faith. This must fructify into a program of sacrificial service based on faith."[95]

The Fourth Mennonite World Conference met in Goshen, Indiana, and North Newton, Kansas. Three rather informal assemblies of fellowship in Europe had preceded it. The First Mennonite World Conference, marking the four hundredth anniversary of the birth of the Anabaptist movement, was organized by Christian Neff of the Weierhof in Germany—the "father" of Mennonite World Conference—and held in Basel and Zürich, Switzerland, in 1925. The second assembly, conducted five years later in Danzig, Poland, focused on Russian Mennonite refugees who were settling in Paraguay, Brazil, and Canada. David Toews and Harold Bender represented North American Mennonites.

The third assembly, Orie's first, gathered in Amsterdam and Elspeet, the Netherlands, in 1936 to mark the four hundredth anniversary of Menno Simon's conversion to Anabaptism. Orie, Elta, and daughter Lois, about to graduate from Goshen College, were among the seven North Americans who attended the Amsterdam conference. Orie and Harold Bender were the only American MC attendees at the conference. While not official delegates, they both spoke: Orie on Mennonite missions and Bender on the Mennonites of the United States.[96]

Miller and Bender published a report of the 1936 conference in a variety of papers, including the *Mennonite Quarterly Review* and the *Gospel Herald*. With the disapproving MC audience in mind, the authors were careful to note the assembly's "entirely unofficial character" where no business was conducted, except for two resolutions on relief work. The "entirely unofficial" assembly could not plan for another conference, but some hoped for another global assembly in five or six years, perhaps in North America. Of course, "one should not expect too much" from a meeting like this one, but still it was a unique opportunity for "mutual and fruitful contact between Mennonites of various lands."[97]

For the benefit of their wary MC readers, Miller and Bender continued: "Those of us who hold to a full-Gospel faith cannot help but be grieved" to acknowledge some parts of "world Mennonitism where the simple Bible faith . . . has been abandoned." Nevertheless, amidst the cautious language came a ringing endorsement: "What a marvelous and blessed thing it would be to have a World Mennonitism united in faith and practice and work. Such a unity would without doubt strengthen the Mennonite Church everywhere."[98]

Influential *Gospel Herald* editor Daniel Kauffman warned that the doctrines that separated the Mennonite Church from other Mennonite denominations "makes it idle to dream of a federation and . . . amalgamation."[99] As could be expected, Lancaster bishop John H. Mosemann Sr. also reacted negatively. He denounced a possible fourth global assembly and expounded on the gap between MC doctrine and theology and that of other Mennonites. Finally, he asked, "Would not a world conference of Mennonites be sorely displeasing to the Lord in the light of the fact that some of them are practically unbelievers?"[100]

With Virginia conservative J. L. Stauffer as moderator of the MC General Conference, it was no surprise that the Mennonite Church, the largest Mennonite group, went on record in 1946 as opposing official participation in a global assembly. Orie's powers of persistent persuasion failed to move Stauffer. However, the ever-practical Orie Miller found another way to make it happen, writing to Harold Bender in Europe: "Since you and I are on the executive committee of MCC, we'll represent the MC Mennonites." Miller and Bender sent P. C. Hiebert on a goodwill tour of churches in key Mennonite communities to promote Mennonite World Conference. Hiebert found broad support, but did not win over J. L. Stauffer in Harrisonburg, Virginia.[101]

With only ten months of lead time, MCC took on the responsibility for planning the 1948 World Conference. The executive committee appointed a six-member Committee of Guidance and Counsel, with P. C. Hiebert as chair and H. A. Fast as vice chair. The four additional members, two bishops and two ministers, included J. L. Stauffer! Hiebert was also made chair of a "conference staff of officers " that included H. A. Fast, vice chair; Raymond C. Schlichting, secretary-treasurer; Ernest E. Miller, technical chair at Goshen; and Lester Hostetler, technical chair at North Newton.[102] Harold Bender and C. F. Klassen served as MCC commissioners in Europe, promoting Mennonite World Conference and issuing official invitations.[103] The MCC-sponsored Fourth Mennonite World Conference would be conducted in two locations: August 3–5 in Goshen, Indiana, and August 7–10 in North Newton, Kansas.

Bill Snyder, Orie's successor as MCC executive secretary, recalled the conference as "an Orie Miller thing," but assistant treasurer Ray Schlichting was drawn into the "center of it."[104] At the January 1947 Chicago meeting of the MCC executive committee, when the decision was made to manage the global assembly, Orie was reluctant to commit the necessary resources. Finally, "right in the meeting, Orie finally said, 'We can't handle it unless Ray Schlichting is willing to stay for another two years and do all of the logistical work; just simply take charge of . . . program planning and transportation and housing.'" Schlichting had already extended his term of service with MCC for two years, with a planned termination date of December 1947. "What could I say? I had been pressured by Orie to extend my stay, but it was pending and to say no would simply be the goat, so I said okay." Planning the World Conference was a monumental task, but Schlichting said, "I had two of the best, most capable clerical people in the office assigned to me, and then we just simply worked it."[105]

As to the two locations, "the planners couldn't decide . . . whether it should be in the Indiana area or the Kansas area." Goshen was the MC mecca, and North Newton, the GC epicenter. "It was not our finest hour," Bill Snyder remembered, "but it was the only way it could be held. It mattered to some GC and MC leaders," and it mattered to Bender and Ed G. Kaufman, Bethel College president. They faced the differences openly and straightforwardly. They finally decided it was "better to have it in two places than not at all. But it was telling the world that we were a divided house here."[106]

Planning for a conference in two locations eight hundred miles apart was something of a logistical nightmare. It included arranging for train transportation from Goshen to Newton for thirty-seven foreign guests. A greater challenge was arranging for them to visit churches. "Well, that's fine and good; that sounds . . . logically reasonable and appropriate, but they 'absolutely' wanted to see such tourist sites as the Grand Canyon, the Redwood National Park, and more. Well, we just had to compromise on a lot of that. We did get them around to some places."[107]

Nevertheless, "any tension between American Mennonite groups could hardly compare to the tensions felt among representatives from the war-torn countries of Europe," according to John A. Lapp and Ed van Straten. Dutch and German Mennonites were not immune to the hostilities of wartime Europe, where the Dutch suffered under Nazi occupation. Tensions erupted between the Dutch and German delegates traveling aboard the same ship on the transatlantic journey.[108]

In public MWC sessions, several German delegates spoke of the collective German guilt for the atrocities of the war just three years earlier. Addressing "my Dutch and French brothers and sisters," Krefeld pastor Dirk Cattepoel admitted that "terrible things have happened to your people through representatives of mine," and expressed understanding that "from the human angle forgiveness seems impossible." Nevertheless, he appealed to their spiritual bond: "And yet, for Christ's sake I ask you: Forgive us! And grant us—in the name of Christ—a new beginning of Christian brotherliness!"[109]

Planners and speakers at the Fourth Mennonite World Conference, Bethel College, North Newton, Kansas. MCC.

Speaking to the point, H. A. Fast, assistant moderator, closed the conference by admonishing everyone present to grant the forgiveness for which the German delegates had pled, and to accept them "into the full fellowship, love, and trust of the Mennonite brotherhood." They should not return home without the assurance "that we have heard and that whatever there is to be forgiven is forgiven." After all, none of "our hands are clean, nor our hearts pure, nor our service perfect."[110]

At the final business session, the delegates had broken new ground by authorizing a "continuation committee" to plan for a future world assembly in 1952 or 1953, perhaps to be hosted by Swiss and French Mennonites. Symbolizing the new attitude of MC leadership toward Mennonite World Conference, a smiling Paul Erb, editor of the *Gospel Herald*, appeared with the speakers at Goshen. In marked contrast to the dire warnings of previous editor, Daniel Kauffman, Erb lauded the 1948 conference as "an event of outstanding interest and importance."[111]

A photo of the 1948 conferees, taken on the steps of Bethel College's Memorial Hall, shows the six planners of the conference standing in the front row. Plain-suited Orie Miller and Harold Bender appear with J. J. Thiessen and C. F. Klassen, Canadian GC representatives; H. A. Fast, Kansan GC member; and P. C. Hiebert, Kansan MB member. Just as the "*Sword and Trumpet* people" feared and predicted in 1942, the isolation of MC Mennonites was eroding and inter-Mennonite cooperation, which Orie Miller so well symbolized and advocated, was on the rise.

ENGAGING THE WORLD

Orie's conflict with the Virginia conservatives and fundamentalists in 1942 had represented a watershed in MC life. Both sides were concerned about identity and witness. The Virginians and others across the church concerned about safeguarding traditional patterns of faith looked askance at the way Orie crossed boundaries to form ecumenical alliances to engage "the world." Traditionalists felt overpowered and outmaneuvered. Ira Johns of Goshen complained, "Whenever you put liberals and conservatives together on a committee like this [Mennonite] Central Committee, the liberals are sure to take control."[112] Sanford Shetler of Johnstown, Pennsylvania, thought drastic action was required: "Unless some definite changes are noted very shortly, then the time is here to use a different method of attack. . . . If it ever comes to a split, I am in favor, if that is what it will take to preserve the faith."[113]

For Orie and his colleagues, the inter-Mennonite and ecumenical organizing gave them strength to carry out important work such as organizing postwar relief, establishing mental health institutions, MMA, and MCC (Canada). Rather than a sellout to liberals, it was an intense effort to preserve the core value of nonviolence and to perform a worthy service for country and humanity. In creating CPS, they seized the opportunity to organize a system, however imperfect, that would avoid the bumbling humiliation of COs during World War I. It was an attempt to demonstrate "true patriotism" through the means of another core component of Mennonite witness—service. The conservatives were right; the world was changing and so was the church. The young men and women who served in CPS caught a vision for engaging the world that led them into far-flung ministries of relief, service, and mission around the globe.

Chapter 10
To the Ends of the Earth: 1950–1959

"But don't forget—it is His church—He is building her. Our responsibility is to seek to see His building and our place as Body members and in that find the fullness and eternal living assured."

When Cal Redekop met twenty young American farm boys at the harbor in Antwerp, the Netherlands, on April 6, 1951, it was the beginning of yet another MCC mission of international goodwill. With a "vast amount of vigor, vitality, and energy," these twenty—and 1,160 others who followed them—enacted "a remarkably idealistic, naïve, flexible, experimental, and ingenious jerry-built dream" called Pax. There was little romance, though, in the ditches they dug, the rubble they shoveled, the cement they mixed, and the concrete blocks that they laid up. With shovels, picks, hammers, and good intentions, they were waging peace in a world torn apart by guns, bombs, and evil designs.[1]

The Pax (Latin for "peace") program was inspired by postwar MCC relief work and sparked by a conversation in Frankfurt, Germany, between Paul Peachey, director of special projects in Germany, and Cal Redekop, director of Voluntary Service. These two young MCC workers dreamed of bringing young North Americans to Europe to build refugee housing, nurture international networks of understanding, and enlarge their worldviews.[2]

Peachey and Redekop communicated their dream by letter to Orie Miller at MCC headquarters, Peachey in late August 1950 and Redekop in late November. Orie liked the concept, and only four months later, the first Pax unit was at work in Germany. "This was incredible! Unbelievable!" Redekop recalled sixty years later.[3]

Orie went to the MCC board and said, "We are going to call this thing Pax."[4] On March 15, 1951, MCC catapulted the recommendation into a program. This "amazing feat" demonstrated how quickly a top-down, centralized bureaucracy with a few powerful leaders—which both Peachey and Redekop would severely criticize two years later—could act. When Orie Miller liked an idea, he could make it happen.

The Pax program was the Mennonite response to a new war, this time with North Korea. On June 25, 1950, North Korea invaded South Korea, and in December, U.S. president Truman declared a national emergency. The Selective Service Act of 1948 had supplied a new infusion of troops, and the Pax program provided an alternative service opportunity for drafted conscientious objectors.[5]

Pax crews came from North America, money came from the government, and leadership came from Redekop. MCC sent Chris Graber, the entrepreneurial Goshen College business manager, to negotiate the release of funds. Graber met with German and Allied High Commission officials and "got the United States Government to release blocked German funds held in Swiss banks." The released money became "a revolving loan fund" used to build housing in Germany for "Danzigers"—refugees from Danzig (now Gdańsk), Poland. Director Redekop continued to negotiate with commission officials in Frankfurt, across the street from the MCC center, for what was needed.[6] By the time the first "Pax boys" arrived in April 1951, authorization had been given to begin building. For Redekop, sixty years later, the rapid launch of Pax was still "an incredibly unbelievable story."[7]

What started in Germany with twenty young farm boys from the United States spread across the globe to include 1,180 men and women in more than forty countries. Among them were 110 Canadians, who served without the nudge of military conscription.[8] Projects expanded into agricultural and community development in Greece and Crete, education in Zaire and Nepal, road building in Peru, medical assistance in Vietnam and Burundi, and refugee resettlement in Israel and Bolivia.[9]

Pax workers, Vienna, Austria, ca. 1959. MCC.

Pax volunteers also participated in the monumental task of building the Trans-Chaco Highway in partnership with the Paraguayan government. The 250-mile highway linked the colonies to Asunción, Paraguay's capital city. It was MCC's largest project of the twentieth century, involving about fifty Pax men who operated more than forty pieces of heavy equipment between 1957 and 1962. The highway to Asunción markets became a major factor in the financial success of the colonies.[10]

Harry Harder, Trans-Chaco Highway MCC project leader (*left*), and Verdel Rider, representative of the Caterpillar company. Koloniehaus Museum.

"Pax girls" often took on traditional roles that "Pax boys" could not—or would not—do: engage in "women's talk" with village women, teach classes of five-year-olds, serve as matrons, teach sewing skills, swap recipes, cook unit meals, practice nursing, and more. Doris Gingerich from Oregon, for example, did office work in Espelkamp, Germany; Lois Martin from Pennsylvania served as unit matron in Greece; and Lydia Schlabach from Illinois worked as a nurse in Korea.[11]

Refugee houses in Europe, the work for which Pax is best known, stand as physical monuments to the idealistic yet pragmatic witness of the men and women in Pax. Less visible, but more significant, were the transatlantic relationships forged and the dramatic shifts in worldview. The beautiful but limited skylines of Pennsylvania mountains and the wider horizons of the prairies of Kansas and Saskatchewan expanded for many to embrace the global village. Family and church circles stretched to embrace cultural, social, and linguistic diversity.

During his days of involvement in Pax, Cal Redekop learned how to lead by watching Orie Miller. "Every time Orie wrote a letter, it would not only be informative, it also stated policy. He would say, 'It is MCC's policy to do this—.'" Redekop adopted this and other features of Orie's administrative style. When Orie wrote letters, he sent multiple copies to administrators on "about four different levels of authority," keeping everyone involved in the loop of communication. Redekop observed Orie as "a man of order, a man of structure," and more than that, "a man of decency. I never sensed any place where I was used for somebody else's benefit."

Both Freda Pellman and Cal Redekop, along with many others, found Miller to be "respectful, calm, and a bit stern. He didn't chew the fat, tell stories, or . . . take off his shoes. We never saw him in that mode. We always saw him in a very, very formal business-like mode."[12]

On occasion, a light, humorous moment would seep through Orie's controlled, all-business veneer. For nearly sixty years, Cal Redekop has delighted in telling the story of just such a moment. Orie came to inspect the first Pax project in Espelkamp, Germany. During a long lunch with H. A. Fast, European MCC director, Orie, and about twenty Paxers, Redekop and Peachey reported on the project's progress and challenges. After lunch,

> one of the Pax fellows said as they were walking out, "Say, Mr. Orie Miller, could we have a picture of you?" Well, that sounded okay. They all lined up with Orie. A couple of the fellows took pictures, and then this fellow named "Blacky" Yoder . . . got close up to Orie, and I wondered what was he getting up so close for. Blacky lined his camera up with Orie straight on, and pushed the trigger—and out squirted this flash of water that hit Orie straight in the eye! Everybody was absolutely petrified.

> I will never forget: Orie . . . grimaced a bit, and then you could see a change come over him, and he discovered what this was and he started laughing. And he laughed and laughed and laughed. He could hardly contain himself. This was an unbelievable moment! Henry Fast and Paul Peachey started laughing after Orie laughed, and of course we all busted out laughing. For the Pax guys, this was the top of the week, if not the year!

Another story has taken center stage in MCC lore, a story repeated often around the world. Karen Beechy is credited as its source, with salient facts recalled by John Lapp and Robert Kreider. Cal Redekop spins the story in modified form:

Orie (*middle*), shown here with Paul Kraybill (*left*) and Amos Horst, was known for his hearty laugh. John L. Ruth papers, LMHS.

Orie, in 1948, was sitting at the table of Atlee and Winifred Beechy, hosts at the MCC center in Basel. [Other sources place the event in Amsterdam or London.] There were about twelve or so people at the table. When the hostess had served tea and . . . some kind of cookie, she had counted out—this was during reconstruction and things were tight—so she had counted out exactly the right number of cookies. When they passed them around, Orie was somewhere in the middle; he said thanks to the person before him, and took two cookies and passed the plate on. The last person didn't get one. And nobody said a word. And the ceremony continued. And of course, after Orie left, the whole staff just had a rip-snorting time, laughing and saying, "Go ahead, take two." Okay, then after that . . . anytime an MCC Center anywhere would serve cookies, someone would say, "Take two, Orie does!"[13]

FROM MEDICINE TO OLD TESTAMENT STUDIES

After graduating from Goshen College, John W. Miller and his wife, Louise (Heatwole), were intending to study medicine. Both planned careers as medical missionaries "somewhere in the world." Both had been accepted—she to study nursing at University of Pennsylvania Hospital, and John in a Philadelphia medical school. In 1948, at the end of a summer pre-med internship in New York City, Harold Bender and Uncle Ernest Miller, Goshen College president, came calling.

Bender and Ernest asked John to consider redirecting his vocational training toward Old Testament studies. After his training he would teach at the developing Goshen Biblical Seminary. Only two weeks before medical school was to begin, Bender and Ernest expected an answer. They asked John to meet them during a short layover at the Lancaster Pennsylvania Railroad Station. With his mind in turmoil, John rode with Louise, Orie, and Elta the eleven miles from Akron to Lancaster.

"I couldn't make up my mind," John recalled. The connecting train was due soon, and Bender and Ernest wanted an answer before they left. So John said he would "walk around the block and then give my answer." He walked and prayed but "still couldn't make up my mind." But when he came back to the station, he said yes to the Bender-Miller redirection. Difficult? Absolutely. Regrets? No. Like his father, when John made a decision he "never looked back." Did Louise and Orie influence his decision? Both were "perfectly neutral about it. They left it up to me entirely."[14]

Instead of medical school in Philadelphia, John enrolled in Old Testament studies at the Biblical Seminary in New York, as both Bender and Orie recommended. Bender, however, wanted John to do his second year at Princeton. John would have preferred Edinburgh, but Harold Bender was "hovering over me, concerned that I come out right at the end, and that I would be able to conform to his expectations."[15]

Not shy about challenging Bender's theology, John began crossing swords with him. Bender was concerned about John's developing liberalism, and John was increasingly critical of Bender's old-fashioned view of theology and the Bible. If not stubborn, John was tenacious. After two years at Princeton, he earned a master's degree in literature from New York University to fill out what he missed by taking the pre-med course at Goshen in three years. Then Bender recommended a "safe" German Old Testament theologian, Walther Eichrodt at the University of Basel in Switzerland. John wrote his dissertation under Eichrodt—in German, since Eichrodt did not speak English—comparing Ezekiel and Jeremiah theologically and linguistically. To this day John doesn't know how he managed to write it in German. Orie supported John and Louise financially: "He had us on an imprest fund; he gave us a certain amount of money and we could replenish that money when we accounted for what

272 MY CALLING TO FULFILL

we had spent." Fortunately, Louise was as careful with money as Orie was, and Orie never questioned what they spent.[16]

The differences between Bender and John grew during the three years John taught at Goshen. John's vision for intentional community led to the founding of Reba Place in Evanston, Illinois, in 1957, and threatened traditional definitions of church and community.

Reba Place's first newsletter, in June 1958, informed readers that their intentional community at 727 Reba Place, Evanston, was a "church-centered Christian community in the urban environment." There were nine people "linked together in life and work for Christ." Daily they were reading Clarence Jordan's *Sermon on the Mount* study. They hoped their life in community and their social ministries would "testify to the power of Christ to shatter the deceptively lonely community of greed which urban man has built and to unite him in a family of love."[17]

In what turned out to be a last-ditch effort to breach their misunderstanding, on December 9, 1959, Harold Bender and Paul Mininger met with John, Louise, and the Reba Place Fellowship. Mininger had sent nine questions that would form the basis of their conversation, and Reba Place Fellowship had carefully written a response to each. The issues included the nature of membership in the fellowship, the basis for membership and accountability, discipline, and leadership. Bender and Mininger feared a nebulous membership and a dangerous leadership pattern that could result in "secretive domination . . . by a strong personality." The Reba Place responses somewhat "allayed" their fears. They agreed that the church was to guide ethical decision making, but the Goshen men could not agree that the church should take up "personal matters" such as choice of home, job, use of money, or role in the church—all of which were "subject to grave dangers of group control."[18]

The fellowship was concerned about not only militarism but also materialism and "mammonistic" spirit toward possessions and wealth. The fellowship based its community life on the discernment pattern of Matthew 18 but knew of no "scriptures that would draw the distinction between ethical matters and personal matters which Bender and Mininger suggest." The fellowship was "dismayed" that there was no agreement on the matters of "discipline" and "puzzled" about Bender and Mininger's insistence that part of the fellowship be excluded from the discussion. John thought it a ploy to isolate and influence.[19]

Four generations of Millers (*from left*: Orie, D. D., John, and Christopher Miller). John W. Miller.

The discussion "didn't change anything." Bender and Mininger "had already replaced me at the seminary," John remembered, "but we went through the ritual of discussing the issues that they were raising. After that I had no personal contact with Bender again."[20] John W. Miller, the Concern group, and Reba Place had become "more Catholic than the Pope," that is, more Anabaptist than their teacher and mentor Harold Bender. Bender died almost three years later in 1962.

GOSHEN BIBLICAL SEMINARY

The board of the seminary for which John was trained to teach was sketching plans for new facilities. The founding of the General Conference Mennonite Biblical Seminary (MBS) in 1946 had motivated Harold Bender to propose an MC version, to be called Goshen Biblical Seminary. The Mennonite Board of Education had deferred earlier building plans to give preference to more pressing needs on the Goshen campus. Now, in 1948, the board was ready to give the seminary project priority. A new committee, the Joint Church Building Committee was formed. As a member of this committee, Orie requested from Nelson Kauffman, MBE president, all minutes and actions of the earlier committee as background to the current committee's work. In November 1950, the joint committee proposed a "gable-type structure" that would meet the needs of both College Mennonite Church and the new seminary. It was to include a chapel, offices, seminary classrooms, and Sunday school classrooms.[21]

Orie and Elta pledged $42,500 each for a lead gift of $85,000, with the condition that the college and seminary raise an endowment of $45,000 for the building's maintenance. Their gift was to honor the memory of their parents, D. D. and Nettie Miller and A. N. and Anna Wolf. In November 1951, Orie's brother, Goshen College president Ernest Miller, asked for clarification on the donors' expectations. He had perceived reluctance on Elta's part: "Although Elta has come along with you on this project, yet I know that she is not altogether happy over the undertaking."[22]

As he was inclined to do, Orie spoke for them both: "Elta and I . . . are in complete agreement in our desire and readiness to make this contribution as outlined." Orie's further response reflected his multiple, overlapping roles, and his typical clarity about which hat he was wearing. He was writing as (a) prospective principal donor, (b) member of the seminary planning committee, and (c) member of the executive committee of the MBE. As a donor, his reaction to building a chapel apart from the classrooms and offices was "decidedly negative." Their pledge was intended for "one distinct, particular [and inclusive] building facility." In roles a and b, Orie favored using architect Orus Eash, who had designed other college buildings, but if the rest of the planning committee had reason to use a Chicago firm, Orie would concur. As to whether the seminary should be managed as a separate entity, Orie, in role c, said both the college and the seminary should absolutely be controlled by one administration.[23]

Nelson Kauffman reported to Orie that Bender wanted to push the proposed plans forward without waiting for president Ernest Miller, then in Europe. It was, Kauffman assured Orie, simply a matter of practicality and not an attempt to exclude Ernest.[24]

PRESIDENTIAL TRANSITION: ERNEST MILLER TO PAUL MININGER

At Goshen the relationship between the dean and president was, as Orie described it, "disintegrating." Orie's handwritten notes, apparently a draft for consideration by the board's executive committee, laid out the problem:

1. We appreciate both Harold [Bender] and Ernest in their present assignments and their ready full commitment of gifts and energy to school and church.

2. We have no present sufficient reason to suggest either resigning from his assignment.

3. We deeply regret their inability to integrate their energies as well as could be reasonably expected to the common goals, and believe unless remedied will have a deteriorating effect on the institution's service and witness.

4. We believe the seminary Deanship will increasingly require the Dean's full energy and attention, and would like to see the brethren agree on this outline.

5. If Harold's outside responsibilities cannot or should not be reduced, the Exec. Com. would be ready to consider Paul Mininger [assistant professor of Bible], for seminary Deanship, provided he felt called to same.[25]

Meanwhile, Bender was making plans for Ernest. Recently, while in Akron, Bender gathered from Bill (William T.) Snyder, director of MCC Mennonite Aid Section, that someone of a "higher overall ability" than any present staff was needed for a "Henry Fast job of the new draft set-up." Bender had a suggestion: Ernest Miller. "We should use people," Bender wrote, "for what they are best able to do." Ernest would be ideal.

Clearly, Bender thought Ernest did not have the requisite presidential gifts. "In the change you have in mind for the presidency," Bender advised Orie, it is also necessary to find a good alternative post for the retiring president, who could hardly continue on the staff here. . . . It is also necessary to most carefully consider the developing situation at Goshen. You spoke once of signs of disintegration. The signs are increasing. If things go too far before the change is made, it will be most difficult for any new man to swing the tiller over and change the course and recover lost ground. Somebody may get killed off in the struggle. It would not be fair to ask a man to come in, who might not be too popular in any case, and ask him to take on such a difficult assignment, when it might have been made much easier by an earlier shift.[26]

Orie received a copy of a letter Nelson Kauffman had written to Ernest Miller, dated February 22, 1952—and curiously also dated January 30. The purpose of the letter was to "review . . . past decisions of the executive committee regarding a change in the administration of Goshen College." Kauffman referred to a "confidential minute" from an earlier meeting, where "we agreed that we look forward to a change in the Goshen College administration in about three years." Kauffman quoted another confidential minute in a meeting that followed, showing "the thinking [that] this change should be made [now]. . . . The time has arrived."[27]

Then to Ernest, Kauffman proposed a discussion about the proposed transition. "We want to be as helpful to you as possible in the transition," Kauffman wrote in a patronizing tone, "and we trust you will give us the same consideration." Kauffman continued: "These experiences come to all of us, and we want by the Grace of God to work together as brethren in the spirit of love and true humility. . . . I would like to have your suggestion regarding your successor."[28] Ernest failed to sense any "spirit of love" or any "true humility."

Nor did Ernest's wife, Ruth, detect any such charitable attitude. In early March, Ruth wrote to Orie about Kauffman's letter, which they received in "agony of spirit." She reported that when Kauffman arrived on campus to discuss matters with Ernest, Ernest refused, saying he would talk only to the entire committee. "What both of us are groaning in spirit and truly asking is—why not leave us alone and *let Ernest work in peace?* . . . He has so many sleepless nights and the fear of his India experience comes back to me. It all seems so senseless to me . . . he is doing a good job."

She wrote further that a friend recently reported that Kauffman had said,

"Oh he [Ernest] is a wonderful administrator, but he does not do things in the church, he is not spiritual." May God someday be kind to those who think themselves so spiritual! If it were not for some of these top administrators in church politics, he would be on some of the church committees. . . . How I wish H. S. [Bender] and [Paul] Mininger would work on their seminary as hard as they work on a college successor. . . . Now Orie, how would you feel if someone would say to you (or more so behind your back, say), now you must retire, we want to put another chap in your place in the shoe factory and also in the MCC?[29]

In a postscript, Ruth added that Ernest had not seen this letter.

By the fall of 1952, word was getting around about Ernest's dismissal. Alumnus Jacob C. Meyer from Sterling, Ohio, believed it to be unnecessary, even counterproductive. If indeed the ouster was coming, who would replace Ernest? Dean Carl Kreider seemed a logical choice, but Meyer's counsel was clear: "I hope we do not make a second rate president out of an excellent Dean."[30]

In the spring of 1953, Orie reached the conclusion that Bender was no longer "safe in leadership," nor was Ernest able to continue as president. Both men were "ethically right and sincere," Orie believed, "but handicapped in giving their essential further contribution thru frustration." It was now up to the executive committee to "resolve the causes" and to find new capable and trustworthy leaders.[31]

Once again, Orie was a central figure in a presidential transition at Goshen. Ernest was writing to Orie, Ruth was writing to Orie, board members were writing to Orie, alumni were writing to Orie, and faculty members were writing to Orie.

Lois Winey, assistant professor of business, wrote to say she was "deeply concerned" that Orie had not been present for the interviews with faculty. How could he have a true sense of their feelings? Winey thought it unlikely that Orie understood "the possible degree of opposition and resultant complications if Paul Mininger" were to be chosen as president. Orie and the board should "consider carefully" the probable "tragedy and dissension" such a recommendation would cause.[32] Harold Bender agreed with Winey that Orie should have been present for all of the faculty interviews. "It was not good at all," Bender chided, "for you to leave." Bender urged quick action before the dissension among the faculty spread to students and community. In a postscript, as he often did, Bender ordered the letter "to be discarded."[33] Orie filed it.

Acting dean Karl Massinari wrote in support of Mininger's candidacy but thought the board should know the "explosive type of reactions which one expects from extremists." There were others whose "opinions ranged from disappointment to outright objection to Paul Mininger."[34] Faculty member Sam Yoder asked to see Orie in Akron. After a phone conversation, Orie wrote wisely, saying if Yoder were to come to Akron, there should be a "witness" present. "The whole situation seems confused and tense enough without having any one of us work at it completely alone."[35] The confusion and tension resulted, in part, from the board's lack of agreement about a timetable for the transition.

The presidential transition was even a topic of conversation in East Asia. The globe-trotting Orie Miller stopped in Tokyo to discuss Ernest's successor with dean Carl Kreider. Kreider was on a three-year leave in Japan, teaching at the International Christian University in Tokyo. Was Kreider willing to serve as president? Kreider believed his training and experience had equipped him to serve as dean and not as president. He felt neither calling nor aspiration for that office. Nor was he ready to leave. He was very happy in Tokyo, believing he was making a significant contribution to the university "at an unusually critical period of the university's history." He assured Orie that his long-term commitment was to Goshen College.

When Kreider inquired about Ernest's health, Orie said it would not be wise for Ernest to continue as president until 1955. When pressed further, Orie backed off, saying that his familial relationship with Ernest would put him in a "difficult place" if he were to "resort to special pleading for his cause."

Kreider was not about to let Orie off the hook. In addition to being Ernest's brother, Orie was also the "senior member" of MBE's executive committee "with thirty years' experience." Therefore, Orie was "bound . . . not to do the thing which may save you (and Ernest) from embarrassment, but the thing which many influential people in the church expect from your mature judgment."[36]

As for Paul Mininger, Kreider said he had educational and church-wide credentials but was "handicapped" by his relative lack of experience in business administration. If Mininger were to be chosen, however,

Kreider would do his best as dean to provide strong "educational leadership." Responding to Orie's query about how Mininger could prepare for the presidency, Kreider offered detailed and useful suggestions. As for how Ernest could serve the college after leaving the presidency, Kreider thought Ernest could help build "a strong, vigorous top-standard missions department," as Orie had proposed. Kreider hoped Ernest could teach, since he was "an uncommonly successful teacher in general psychology." He thought Ernest would also be qualified to serve as chair of the education department.[37]

A *Gospel Herald* editorial of October 27, 1953, announced the choice of Paul Mininger as president-elect. The next day Orie sent a copy to Carl Kreider in Tokyo, acknowledging a change in the timetable. Orie and some others had been "deeply convinced that a slower (probably more considered) transition would have been better." Nevertheless, "we want to accept this directive in good spirit" and do everything possible to support the president-elect. "In light of strength and health circumstances," MBE encouraged Ernest to reduce his workload and to take a month away from campus, perhaps in Florida.[38]

When Nelson Kauffman wrote again to Ernest, he said he hoped Orie could help Ruth understand the actions of the MBE in removing Ernest from office.[39] The committee's memo of understanding promised Ernest economic security until retirement age, and thereafter, a "retirement allowance." It also mandated a two-year leave beginning September 1, 1954.[40]

BUILDING PLANS AND CONVERSATIONS ABOUT GBS-MBS COOPERATION

The presidential transition and other building projects slowed the planning for seminary facilities. In addition, there was a major new development. In 1954, the GC-supported Mennonite Biblical Seminary in Chicago initiated conversations with Goshen Biblical Seminary about cooperation. Those talks were promising enough to cause MBS in 1958 to relocate to a new campus on the south side of Elkhart, Indiana—with the dream of inter-Mennonite cooperation.

The GBS building plans faltered when their primary promoter, dean Harold Bender, proposed enlarging the building. This alteration increased the cost, making Orie and Elta's gift a smaller percentage of the whole. Goshen's new president, Paul Mininger, ordered Bender to reduce the cost to $97,000, causing him to grumble that it was once again "Orie Miller's building."[41]

The plans for an MBS-GBS affiliation suffered a momentary setback when opinions clashed about where the facilities would be located. Bender did not want to leave Goshen. As a result, the cooperation was minimal in the first years. The Goshen facility, which included classrooms, offices, a chapel, a historical library and archives, was finished in 1959 and dedicated June 4, 1960. Its life as a seminary was a short nine years. In these years, students shuttled between the Goshen and Elkhart campuses. In 1969, GBS separated organizationally from Goshen College and operations moved to the Elkhart campus as Associated Mennonite Biblical Seminaries. In 1994, this inter-Mennonite seminary incorporated as one institution, and in August 2012, it was renamed Anabaptist Mennonite Biblical Seminary.[42]

Although Orie was an advocate of cooperation, the short life of the GBS facilities was a great disappointment. He and Elta had given $85,000, the majority of the total cost. Their gift honored the memory of their parents, but for less than a decade. Orie was also disappointed that the seminaries had not developed a School of Missions graduate program as he hoped. His dream for such a program at the Biblical Seminary in New York also failed.[43]

THE AMSTERDAM SEVEN

While Orie was managing the presidential transition at Goshen with its resultant controversies, overseeing reconstruction in postwar Europe, and expanding the work of Eastern Mennonite Missions in Africa, a crisis of a different nature was unfolding in Europe.

John Miller reported to his parents an "extremely interesting" conference of American Mennonites in Amsterdam, April 14–25, 1952.[44] The two-week conference had been carefully scripted by Irvin Horst in the Netherlands. Activities included lectures by four leading Dutch and German church leaders and papers by seven MCC workers: Irvin Horst, John W. Miller, Paul Peachey, Calvin Redekop, David A. Shank, Orley Swartzentruber, and John Howard Yoder.[45]

Three were relief workers: Horst, MCC director in the Netherlands; Redekop, director of MCC's Pax and Mennonite Voluntary Service Programs; and Yoder in France, also studying at the University of Basel.

Shank in Brussels, Belgium, and Swartzentruber in Paris, France, were missionaries under the MC Mennonite Board of Missions. Three were graduate students: Miller in Basel; Peachey, former MCC director in Germany, now studying the sociology of Swiss Anabaptists at the University of Zürich; and Yoder.[46] All seven were affiliated with the Mennonite Church, and all but Redekop were raised in Amish or "old" Mennonite homes.

It was a formidable collection of intellectual prowess and passionate commitment to Anabaptist-Mennonite ideals of service and peace. And it was the beginning of the so-called Concern movement, which Royden Loewen and Steven M. Nolt have identified as one of three significant "neo-Anabaptist" renewal movements of the twentieth century.[47]

The young men, who served under the directives of the "venerable Orie O. Miller" and studied under the scholarly Harold Bender, "embraced and reaffirmed the values that had brought them to Europe."[48] But they had become increasingly unhappy about what they perceived as top-down decision making from Akron without consulting workers in the field or European Mennonites.

In their close contact with European Mennonites, MCC volunteers discovered they were perceived as "condescending" to local Mennonites—especially to German Mennonites for their Nazi collaboration. For Cal Redekop, it was his relationship to local pastor Abraham Braun that shaped his awareness of "some of the strictures that MCC was placing on us ideologically . . . and on the behavioral, ideological level."[49] There was far too little respect and mutuality between the servers and the served. There were also theological issues. Harold Bender told Paul Peachey that Mennonite World Conference could not celebrate communion because Dutch Mennonites did "not believe in the deity and saviorhood of our Lord Jesus Christ."[50]

When the Amsterdam conference ended, the young men wrote to Akron, asking for a meeting with the MCC executive committee to air their concerns. Orie, in turn, invited them to a meeting at the MCC Center in Basel, Switzerland. On August 7, 1952, Paul Peachey, John Howard Yoder, and Cal Redekop appeared in Basel. Irvin Horst, who could not be present, had sent a written statement. The executive committee members present were P. C. Hiebert and C. F. Klassen (Mennonite Brethren), H. A. Fast and J. J. Thiessen (from the General Conference), and Harold S. Bender and Orie O. Miller (representing the Mennonite Church). Only

C. N. Hostetter, president of Messiah College and future chair of MCC, was absent. The director of MCC relief operations for Europe, J. N. Byler, was also at the meeting.[51]

The Amsterdam conferees expressed their gratitude for the way their MCC elders had called them to do significant work and for placing their trust in such young "upstarts." Paul Peachey was "deeply grateful" for the years of service so "decisive in our lives." MCC leadership has "influenced us profoundly [and] we have gained a deep respect for your vision, faith and courage in the great things MCC has accomplished."[52] Cal Redekop also acknowledged his indebtedness to MCC for the vision of service and witness it had imparted to him. He hesitated to speak because of his "immaturity, inexperience, and shortcomings," but his high expectations of an "older generation" and his deep concern for MCC's witness compelled him to speak.[53]

The Amsterdam seven objected to the centralized authority of MCC executives. Such top-heavy structures did not reflect the values of Anabaptism nor of the New Testament. John Howard Yoder thought the leaders were preoccupied with structures and policies, to the exclusion of clearly defined goals. Redekop said even church organizations can be self-serving when budgets and strategies overshadow their "spiritual or Christian" foundation. In their concern for the maintenance of organizations, "a few individuals at the top can lose sight of the church they represent."[54] Irvin Horst called it a movement toward "ultra-organizationalism." We cannot "run our churches and agencies in the same fashion as we operate our businesses and factories. Too much centralization permits two or three people to dominate," and far too often, they ignore or disregard "weaker or less competent" brothers and sisters.[55]

Redekop recognized that some organization in the church was necessary, but too much of it "restricts the spirit's freedom." Peachey said, "Without fail, 'excessive centralization' results in covert 'diplomatic expediencies.' . . . Faith and brotherhood cannot be re-allocated as one does . . . material aid shipments." He and his colleagues had worked long and hard "to lay foundations for spiritual rebuilding among our European brethren, only to have decisions from above" destroy "at a stroke" the goodwill they were building. Redekop agreed, saying "directives from afar without consultation often resulted in unwise decisions, destroyed relationships, and demoralized workers." European Mennonites knew "surprisingly much about organizational politics," Peachey added, because, after all, "MCC lives in a glass house."[56]

Horst, working in Amsterdam, was even more pointed in declaring that too many Mennonites had certain "deep-seated prejudices and hatred" for the Dutch Mennonites. He was particularly upset over Bender's disregard for the Dutch. Horst warned that if they continued to "talk down to them . . . we will not get to first base in winning their confidence." Horst decried the regression in the inter-Mennonite unity that CPS had forged and was deeply disappointed to witness "a revival of old suspicions and rivalries."[57]

In sum, Redekop clarified their expectations: "We are not requesting revolution. We are requesting openness. . . . The young workers want to give wholehearted allegiance to the church. We are willing to harness ourselves to the wheel. . . . We sincerely implore [your] communion and guidance; you have [gone before us and] blazed a wide trail in which we can tread."[58]

The young men were finished.

ORIE'S RESPONSE

A long period of silence followed the grueling session. As Redekop recalled, Orie finally said, "Well, if that's the way these men think, then I am going to go home and resign." The executive secretary "cried and cried." Orie's tears shocked the young critics. "We felt terrible!" Redekop remembered. After a minute or two, Orie regained his composure and led a vigorous and collegial discussion. Orie concluded their conversation with the grace of an elder statesman: "Thank you boys. We will take this into advisement."[59]

The minutes of the meeting reflected nothing of the "grueling" nature of the encounter. Rather, the words were polite and gracious. The executive committee heard "with sincere appreciation the statements and concerns and counsel . . . and hope to profit from them." Their own concerns were similar to those of the critics and they acknowledged that they had "at times failed in carrying through as intended." They reaffirmed their resolve to "do and operate as effectively as possible in the future on all the points which we jointly considered in the morning discussion."[60]

Orie was surely addressing this skirmish in a later conference address in Hesston, Kansas:

For several decades the church has been actively administering a commend-
able program of Christian activity and service. Yet along the road over which
we have traveled are the scars and debris of strife, misunderstanding, jeal-
ousy, and competition. Because the cause is Christian, we have continued in
spite of these regrettable incidents.[61]

The context for the charges of the Amsterdam seven at Basel was larger
than the MCC operations in Europe. The discontent was rooted in the
heavy-handed leadership of a few bishops, who had narrowed the acceptable range of faith and practice in places like the Indiana-Michigan
Conference during the 1920s. Orie had had an up-close view of the wrestling of the powerful in the turmoil that led to the temporary closing of
Goshen College in 1923.

Though most ministers charged with bishop oversight were pastoral
and judicious in their exercise of authority, the reputation of the few cast
a shadow over the decades to come. The Amsterdam seven coalesced
into the Concern group and continued their critique of the church establishment and its limited application of Bender's "Anabaptist Vision."
They were the forerunners of the 1960s activists, who called for a more
egalitarian, congregational polity often branded as the "priesthood of all
believers."

The challenge for Orie in the administration of MCC's rapidly expanding world ministry was how to manage an organization for maximum efficiency and effectiveness—and how to direct the energies of the idealistic
young generation he and others had recruited to do MCC's work. As for
Orie's threat to resign, the executive committee asked him to reconsider.
He continued as MCC's chief executive.

Albert Meyer, in France, had reason to think Orie's continued service
was a mistake, that his best years were past. When Al and Mary Ellen
(Yoder) Meyer were preparing for their assignment, they had interviews
with J. N. Byler and with Orie. They didn't learn much, but "Orie wanted
to know—we have joked about it all our married life—if Mary Ellen was
going to Europe as a worker or as an appendage!"[62] MCC was like that,
often informal. Meyer would never forget Orie's strategy for choosing
new fields of service:

Miller had a globe in front of him, and he put one finger on Japan . . . and
he put a finger on India and said, "I think we ought to place someone in

Indonesia." That would have been his thumb, or the third finger. Well, need them for what? Why Indonesia? Just because that's where the fingers fell or what? No, I'm sure there was more to it than that, but it showed me the strength and weakness of that personnel policy that located people and gave them freedom.

Now, when someone is placed in Indonesia with no more of a job description than that, it may be liberating, as it was for us. You make your own job. You do what's needed. You start the Puidoux Theological Conferences [in France], even though that was not in your job description. But for some people, it's been disorienting and difficult. They needed a little more structure.[63]

Mary Ellen, a sister to John Howard Yoder, was indeed more than an appendage. Equipped with a nursing degree, she cared for a group of children at the children's home in Valdoie. Albert Meyer was director of the Valdoie home, MCC director for France, and MCC representative on the Continuation Committee of the Historic Peace Churches in Europe. When Orie visited, Meyer recalled, he sometimes made "snap" decisions, which might have worked well in the chaos of postwar relief, "but it was hardly the way to maintain fraternal relationships." Meyer's concern echoed that of the Amsterdam seven in Basel.

Later, Meyer tangled with Orie over one of those snap decisions. Meyer considered the proposed relocation of MCC volunteers Jonie and Mary Klassen an unwise move:

One trip Orie came and before he came, he had asked J. D. Graber [Mennonite Board of Missions executive], "Should I have a look at your fields and your workers also?" And Graber, generous and trusting as always said, "Well, sure. You can look at the mission board people."

Then Orie came with the idea that Mary and Jonie and their little baby should relocate to Algeria in the old earthquake zone. Now as I recall, the volunteers who were preparing to go to Algeria . . . were living in tents. They had . . . a mile to go for water, which they had to carry—the last place you'd think a newborn baby should be stationed. But Orie told Mary and Jonie that he thought it was the call of the Lord that they ought to go to Algeria . . . under the [Elkhart] Mission Board.

Of course, they had some hesitation because of the rigors of that kind of life and the distance from medical facilities and everything else. So Orie came down to me in Valdoie and asked me to call together all the French Mennonite leaders—was it on twenty-four or forty-eight hours' notice?—to tell them that Mary and Jonie, who had been promised to them for a year or two yet, were going to Algeria.

I said, "I will not call these leaders. . . . That's an insult. It is breaking our promise." At one of the previous conferences, somebody had said from the floor, as I recall, "We don't want to be like the MCC that doesn't keep their word." I had heard that, and I said, "I'll resign from MCC before that." Well, Orie went on to John Howard Yoder, who was studying in Basel, and told him that the Lord was calling the Klassens. John was responsible to J. D. Graber for Algeria, so this was the mission board. Yoder said, "No way. . . . I will not be party to this." So Orie went back up to Mary and Jonie and told them that Al Meyer and John Yoder are standing in the way of the call of the Lord. So Orie went home not very happy. See, he had approved the report where I made the commitments for Jonie & Mary to work in France [in the first place]. There was no question about what we were committed to, but he was going to break it singlehandedly and report it to the others and go home, just like that.[64]

A year later, Meyer saw another side of Orie. Miller drove nearly forty miles out of his way to ask Meyer's counsel regarding MCC's relationship to German Mennonites. Orie regarded Meyer's counsel as wisdom and acted on it. Orie rarely, if ever, held a grudge. Meyer saw Orie's search for counsel as "a mark of greatness." The personal relationship between the two was "always good. Orie's weakness was in building fraternal relationships."[65]

That weakness may have been evident during a troubleshooting appearance in Puerto Rico in the mid-1940s. The voluntary service workers on the island were attempting to develop a Christian community that embraced hospital and school personnel, but it was not going well. After observing the dysfunctional dynamics of the group, Orie made his pronouncement: "You're all acting like children. If you can't talk to each other as adults, I'm going home." Carl M. Lehman, a twenty-something VSer, faced the elder church statesman with a bold declaration of his own: "Maybe you should!" Orie did go home and eventually, the group resolved its own conflict.[66]

MENNONITE ECONOMIC DEVELOPMENT ASSOCIATES

Orie gave J. Winfield Fretz, Mennonite sociologist, teaching at Bethel College in North Newton, Kansas, the task of assessing needs among the Mennonites of Paraguay. As a result, in 1952 and 1953, two "Flying Missions" of farmers, physicians, and business leaders led by Dr. Herbert Schmidt further evaluated needs and opportunities in Paraguay. When they returned, they brought their concerns to Orie Miller and Bill Snyder. The main problem was the lack of capital for equipment or entrepreneurial ventures. Church agencies operated on contributed dollars designated for particular needs. So where to find the capital? The Mennonites of Paraguay had no access to private or public lending institutions, except for banks that gave short-term loans at exorbitant interest rates.

Orie, ever resourceful and creative, brought business leaders together at the Atlantic Hotel in Chicago on December 10, 1953. The group included Mennonite entrepreneurs from across the United States as well as several from Canada.[67] Their solution was the Mennonite Economic Development Associates (MEDA), which would operate under the MCC umbrella. Orie laid out the "original formula" that the charter members promptly adopted. The ingenious solution offered compassionate business leaders an opportunity to make investments that would provide the needed capital for the Mennonite colonies in Paraguay. It entailed risk, but entrepreneurs were risk-takers. It was a way to extend their managerial expertise to mission and service projects. MEDA was legally incorporated in Archbold, Ohio, on July 26, 1954.[68]

From its first successful project, the Sarona Dairy Farm in partnership with Fernheim Colony farmers in 1954, MEDA went on to fund other projects in Paraguay and expand to mission sites in Africa, Asia, and Latin America. Between 1953 and 1968, MEDA launched and managed thirty-three projects in six countries.

Orie Miller's imprint was clear. One early MEDA leader described the sometimes random nature of the program's growth:

> Orie would travel the world wearing one Mennonite hat or another, and he'd carry a big wad of bills. He had a big heart, and if he saw a tailor struggling with a decrepit sewing machine, he'd peel off a few hundreds and give it to the guy to buy a new sewing machine. Then he'd drop by the MEDA office

when he returned and say, "By the way, I loaned some money to so-and-so. I don't have time to collect it, so let's write it up as a MEDA loan."[69]

Not all projects were successful, and increasingly MEDA faced the challenges of new cultures and new assumptions. In 1969, when the number of projects and the complexity of the work required a full-time manager, Lloyd Fisher, an Oregon farmer and Church World Service worker, became MEDA's first executive director. In the next decade, membership grew to 368. In 1977, the year of Orie's death, MEDA started a revolving loan fund in Paraguay that eventually provided agricultural credit for nine hundred farmers. By the end of 1978, MEDA members had invested $788,680 in more than twenty-five countries on five continents.[70]

MAKING THINGS HAPPEN

While Orie was involved in MCC postwar relief work in Europe, development of seminaries, presidential transitions at Goshen College, the establishment of MEDA, and the challenge of the Concern group, he was also expanding the ministries of Eastern Mennonite Missions and recruiting personnel. The following stories illustrate his manner of calling missionaries and his interaction with them in the field.

In 1950, Frances Bontrager (later married to Lawrence Greaser) walked to the Ninth Street Mennonite Church in Saginaw, Michigan, to hear Orie Miller speak. He had just returned from Ethiopia and spoke of the great need there for nurses. "By the time he was finished speaking, I knew that was where I was supposed to go." Looking for confirmation of this call, the next day Frances noted a *National Geographic* map of Africa at the hospital where she worked as a nurse. As she studied the map, she was drawn to Ethiopia and the cities of Addis Ababa and Nazareth. She believed this was the confirmation she needed.

EMM further confirmed her call to Ethiopia. Back home after a term of service, she was eager to return to Ethiopia. By letter, Orie confirmed her second term of service and asked her to appear before the EMM board for reappointment. She traveled to Mellinger Church in Lancaster, Pennsylvania, to meet the board. But instead of a reappointment to Ethiopia, the EMM board wanted to send her to British Honduras (now Belize). Another more experienced worker would be assigned to Ethiopia. Frances felt no call to Central America and so struggled with this sudden turn of events. When she could not give an affirmative response, the board members ended the interview and returned to their meeting.

After some time, Orie left the meeting and approached Frances for her answer. Realizing she was still undecided, Orie "became a little perturbed and he took me home with him overnight and talked to me late into the night." She slept that night in a nightgown borrowed from Elta, in the guest room of the "very lovely . . . elegantly furnished" Miller home. Early in the morning, Frances went on a long walk and then "sat down under a culvert and cried and prayed." When she returned, Orie pressed for an answer. Frances answered, "I said a thousand times I would go and a thousand-one times that I wouldn't."

Orie "was very upset." When asked how she could reject God's call, Frances had the boldness to say, "But Orie, you're not God!" When Orie recovered, he asked Frances what she would rather do. She wanted to earn a BS degree in nursing and return to Ethiopia. Orie said, "Well, if you want to go to school, I'll have you there by Monday." Orie called president John R. Mumaw at Eastern Mennonite College and made it happen. When Frances arrived on Monday, the president was waiting for her on the campus lawn. Everything had been arranged.[71] Such was the power of leaders who knew and trusted each other in the communal Mennonite matrix.

Lawrence Greaser remembered how Orie also made things happen in Puerto Rico. Greaser served in CPS in Terry, Montana; in the Relief Training Corp in Ypsilanti, Michigan; and then in an MCC-sponsored voluntary service unit in La Plata, Puerto Rico. As head of maintenance at the La Plata hospital, Lawrence's duties included the "care of all of our old broken-down cars." When Orie was flying into San Juan for an administrative visit, Lawrence gave the best car to Harry Martens, unit director, who met Orie at the airport. As Martens and Miller were driving "up the mountain roads, the band around the gas tank rusted out and the gas tank fell out on the ground. Orie said, 'You need a new car.' He ordered it and within a week we had a new car!"[72] Such is the power of benevolent wealth.

A similar story comes from John Hostetler, longtime MCC Material Resources director, who was business manager for MCC in Europe in the 1950s. Contributions to MCC had fallen off after the period of postwar reconstruction. Monthly funding was reduced by 25 percent more than

once. Jesse Kauffman, director of the European program, complained to
Orie during an administrative visit in 1957 that he had no car and no budget to buy one. "Orie sat down and right there on the spot, Orie pulled out
his checkbook and wrote a personal check for $700." Hostetler was also
impressed by Orie's thrift and economy in clothing. When he traveled he
wore one suit, usually gray and neatly pressed, so doing his laundry at the
MCC headquarters in Basel or Frankfurt was a simple matter. Shopping
was also easy and efficient. He told Urbane Peachey, "I go shopping once
a year. I project ahead, get what I need, and then I'm through."[73]

Orie also impressed Donald R. Jacobs, from Johnstown, Pennsylvania.
In 1953, during the Korean War, Jacobs signed up for an MCC Pax assign-
ment in Europe, but Orie had other plans. Jacobs does not "recall the day
or the situation or the time" when things shifted toward Tanganyika (later
Tanzania), "but Orie, you know how Orie, made plans for everybody. . . .
I was one of his boys . . . so Anna Ruth and I ended up in Tanganyika."

From that vantage point, Don observed Orie. "I never saw a Mennonite
move around like Orie Miller did. I mean, it seemed like he fit in everywhere. He seemed to be so at home in the world. He encouraged us and
he was very good for us." There were good leaders in the Johnstown community where Jacobs was raised "but nobody near like Orie Miller. . . .
Orie . . . became almost an icon for me, a way to be a Mennonite deeply
engaged in the world."

Orie had a vision for the work in Tanzania and he expected the missionaries' work to fit the vision. When Jacobs became involved in planning
for an ecumenical training and conference center in Dodoma, a project of
the Christian Council of Tanzania, it didn't fit the vision. Orie wrote a
very strong letter to the council: "Please now, I understand your issue,
but please, we have other plans." Training Mennonite teachers and leaders was Orie's highest priority, and he wanted Jacobs to lead the faltering
Mennonite Bible School. "He didn't back off; he didn't waver."

At the end of six years, in 1960, Orie asked whether Don and Anna
Ruth had a long-term commitment to missions. When the answer was
affirmative, Orie said, "Okay, now, do any doctorate you want to do."
When Don chose anthropology, Orie was supportive and, as a member
of the board, helped to arrange a program of study at Biblical Seminary
in New York that led to a PhD from New York University. Clearly, Orie

valued education but degrees did not impress him. When Jacobs had earned his degree, Orie's cryptic response was, "Don, you got it, now forget it."[74]

Paul and Ann (Keener) Gingrich recall Orie's tap on the shoulder when Paul, from Landisville, Pennsylvania, was a student at Eastern Mennonite College. On June 8, 1953, Orie was speaking to a student prayer meeting at Eastern Mennonite. Orie noted Paul's poise and sincerity as leader of the meeting. When the praying and singing ended, Orie placed his hand on Paul's shoulder and asked whether he and Ann would be willing to go to Ethiopia as missionaries. Nearly sixty years later, the memory still sends a chill down Paul's back. It was exactly what they wanted to do. It was where Ann's parents, Clayton and Martha Keener, were serving as missionaries. Paul ran home to tell Ann. This was the call they had been waiting for. "This was the call of God!" A week later, a letter from Orie confirmed the call to Ethiopia as a "Teacher Evangelist" couple.[75]

Paul and Ann served in Ethiopia from 1953 to 1969. On Orie's administrative visits, they found him full of knowledge, yet "very open." After listening, he would typically end the conversation with his thinking. "It was usually good stuff." Often it was one word, such as "indigenous" or "partnership." Missionaries were "partners in the gospel." He was always thinking about the future. Missions, he believed, should become self-governing. His counsel to the Gingrichs: "Work yourselves out of a job in fifteen years." By then, he predicted, the Ethiopians should be doing the work. Without pretension, he told about the places he had recently visited. He was full of information.

Orie was not an anthropologist or linguist. He told the Gingrichs he had been to Tanganyika many times but had learned only one word, *jambo*—Swahili for hello. One word, and he was not pronouncing it correctly! He knew it and laughed at himself. Although not "culturally savvy," Orie was grounded and well-read. As he told many others, it was his practice to "hold the Bible in one hand and a newspaper in the other." In his "talks," he typically referenced both.[76]

With his flair for storytelling, Paul enjoyed telling Orie's joke. He only had one:

> Two men met in an airport; let's say they met in Cairo. And they were so happy to see each other. One said to the other, "I saw you here last week."

And the other guy said, "No, I wasn't here last week. I was in [some other fantastic place]." And the first guy said, "Oh, come to think of it, I wasn't here either. It must have been two other guys." And then he would laugh his hoarse, hearty laugh.

The Gingrichs once told Orie a joke they heard from fellow missionary P. T. Yoder: "We're slow, but we do poor work." Orie did "a double take, and then started that hearty laugh . . . and just shook. It was such fun to watch him laugh!"

Another exchange with Orie caused pain. In 1959, the Gingrichs were at home on furlough, expecting to be reappointed to a second term of service in Ethiopia, but things had become complicated. A February delegation of conference leaders were shocked to see the missionaries wearing business suits and neckties instead of the prescribed plain coats. Chester Wenger had notified them in advance, but only Orie had read the letter. It was reported that the delegates retreated to a hotel room and "bawled." Soon after, the Gingrichs became the targets in a bishop board "disciplinary hearing." They met at EMM headquarters in Salunga, Pennsylvania, on April 15, Ann's birthday—"the worst birthday of her life."

Typically, Orie deferred to the bishop board and to bishop Amos Horst in these matters. It was their task to monitor and maintain conformity to the standards of the Lancaster Conference. But in this case, Orie spoke for the bishop board. He pressed Paul to promise to wear the plain coat on the mission field. Paul and Ann were shocked by his persistence. Then Paul had the temerity to ask how Orie, who wore a long tie under his plain coat, could object to Paul's wearing of a long tie. "But that was not a smart thing to say!"

Eventually, Paul and Ann were reassigned to Ethiopia, though they were not sure how they were approved. Paul promised not to wear a necktie but did not promise to wear the plain coat. Orie later mistakenly accused Paul of breaking his promise. For Paul, the issue was a matter of contextualization. What worked in Salunga may not be appropriate for Addis Ababa. The missionaries explained that a plain coat in Ethiopia identified them with Catholic priests of the Italian occupation, a decidedly negative image. Furthermore, the wearing of any kind of coat in the tropical heat of Ethiopia was impractical. Orie chided Paul once for laying aside his plain coat, but then appointed him to the responsible

Paul Kraybill (left), Orie Miller, and Elsie Cressman in Tanganyika (later Tanzania), 1959. EMM.

post as head of mission finances. Change was coming. Four years later, when Orie's successor at EMM, Paul Kraybill, laid aside his plain coat, Gingrich helped him choose business suits in Addis Ababa.[77]

AKRON NEWS AND "ESSENTIAL PRODUCTION FIGURES"
At home in Akron, Albert Wolf Miller had become the dispenser of family, business, and community news. In February 1950, Albert wrote to Orie and Elta in Uruguay, where they were visiting son Dan and his wife, Eunice, after yet another visit to the Mennonite colonies in Paraguay. Albert, who had joined the family shoe business in 1946 after his release from CPS, had just returned from a sales trip, which was not, he said, very productive since most stores were well-stocked. Albert reported having "just had a lesson on the futility of worrying." Commodity, stock prices, and speculative stocks, in which he was investing, "broke badly." He had ordered Walter, their farm manager, to sell steers just as prices dropped. Wheat also "broke" to the lowest point in several years.[78]

Daniel Wolf and Eunice (Litwiller) Miller were missionaries in Montevideo, Uruguay, where he was also a seminary teacher. In a letter to Elta in October 1952, the two marveled over Elta's social calendar. They replayed what Elta had reported; in two week's time, Elta had entertained

Ronald and Lois Beach and family; Ruth and Rhoda Ressler and a friend; the Linds; Carolyn Plank and Fannie Miller; Edwin and Irene Weaver; all of the cousins; Ruth and Ray Horst; a group of "committee couples"; and Weyburn and Thelma Groff. And somewhere between guests, Elta found time to travel to New York and Montclair! Dan and Eunice were hoping Orie and Elta would find time to spend Christmas in Argentina. Dan also thanked Elta for the "cute" birthday card and the money for Gregory.[79]

In late January 1951, Albert reported on a surprise housewarming for Abe Hallman, newly hired manager of Miller Hess, hosted by the Monterey congregation. Monterey was a newly organized congregation that chose to affiliate with the Ohio and Eastern Conference as a way of escaping the restrictive standards in Lancaster Conference. In the shoe world, Warren Leatherman was breaking sales records again at "Warren Shoes" in Lancaster. Albert was to present a "topic" for the Young People's Meeting on "The Practice of Brotherhood in Mennonite History." He was using as a source the *Proceedings* of the 1948 Mennonite World Conference, which included Orie's address on the relief work of MCC.[80]

Albert's letter was typed on company letterhead. The form of the company name had changed subtly from "Miller Hess" to "Miller, Hess & Company." The letterhead promoted their specialty: "Growing Girls' and Misses' Littleway Shoes" all with "Goodyear" stitching. Clarence W. Hess was still listed as president; W. E. Brubaker was vice president; Abe P. Hallman, secretary; and Orie was treasurer. Additional partners were J. H. Reitz and Hess's sons-in-law, H. W. Mason and H. K. Blough.

And then from Albert, the inevitable gossip: Clarence W. Hess, long-time president of Miller Hess, had died in January 1953, and the word on the street was that he had been worth seven million dollars. Hess had given each of his grandchildren generous trust funds, which were to pay dividends until they reached the age of sixty. "Beady" told "Olive" that the children were going to buy the family's home "on the corner" of Eleventh and Main, because they did not want MCC to convert it to a "public institution"—as was the case with the Wolf home across the street.[81] The Wolf house was MCC's first headquarters.

Wherever in the world Orie happened to be—in June 1954, it was Africa—he paid close attention to the shoe business. He had Albert's occasional reports, but Orie wanted specific official numbers and reports from Abe Hallman, general manager, and Richard Ebersole, assistant treasurer. He was disappointed that they had not sent production and sales reports. He left no doubt about what he wanted to see: "essential figures" on Highland, the Monday morning weekly report, and "by cable next Monday, the essential production figures, and anything else especially pertinent covering this week."[82]

Explicitly yet diplomatically, Orie concluded: "I know that you, Abe, agree with me on the importance of good production figures . . . [and] would urge that you keep in daily contact . . . with those who are responsible for getting production." If the company was to boost its production over the previous year, it had to start now—"without fail." Further, "a brief, concise overview of the total six units [of] business" from Hallman "will be much appreciated."[83]

EMM EXPANSION: BUKIROBA TO VIETNAM

On September 15, 1935, a year after the first EMM mission base was established in Shirati, Tanganyika, fifteen new believers were baptized and six others received as members. Also that year, a second mission was started at Bukiroba, followed by more: Mugango in 1936, Bumangi in 1936, and Nyabasi in 1940. By 1953, there were thirty-nine missionaries in Tanganyika or at home on furlough. Church members numbered about 950 with about 600 more preparing for baptism.

When the East African revival swept through Mennonite missions and churches in 1942, it caused concern and anguish among EMM leaders at home. While missionaries and Africans spoke of confession and cleansing, EMM noted their disregard for traditional Lancaster symbols of nonconformity. EMM leaders on multiple deputations to Africa were unable to resolve the difficulties. Orie Miller, with characteristic wisdom, said he saw three options: send the missionaries home and start all over, trust them to work out their own policies, or take seriously the suggestions of the current missionaries. Since Orie put it that way, the third choice seemed the obvious answer.[84]

EMM opened new missions, often preceded by MCC programs, in Ethiopia in 1948, Honduras in 1950, Luxembourg in 1951, Italian Somaliland in 1953, France and Israel in 1953, Vietnam in 1957 (and Hong Kong in 1965).[85] In Orie's view, MCC's physical ministry prepared the way for the spiritual ministry of missions and church development. MCC often worked in partnership with other agencies and denominations.[86]

A Mennonite presence in Vietnam began in 1954 in response to the war's casualties of refugees and destruction. In 1950, the United States had started aiding the French colonial government then occupying Indochina (later Vietnam). That same year, Orie asked his brother Ernest, then a missionary in India, to assess needs for relief in Indochina. Ernest recommended a course of action, but MCC lacked the funds to act. Akron then tried to establish the self-funded Pax program in the Saigon area, but the Indochinese government refused to grant permission. A month after the 1954 Geneva Accords, which led to the division between the Democratic Republic of Vietnam (North Vietnam) and the independent State of Vietnam (South Vietnam), MCC sent Delbert Wiens, a volunteer serving at the Akron headquarters, to Saigon to meet Orie Miller. In the next eleven years, MCC volunteers provided medical and refugee care, and other services. Wiens stayed on, and as Orie recommended, two volunteers in Korea and one in Taiwan transferred to Vietnam. The relief unit went to work in partnership with other agencies. By 1956, MCC added a medical program under the direction of Dr. Willard and Grace Krabill. Krabill became the medical director of the Christian & Missionary Alliance (C&MA) leprosarium near Ban Me Thuot in the highlands northeast of Saigon.[87]

The needs were enormous; so were the obstacles. Political instability, conflicts with local mission agencies, and miscommunication between the Akron MCC office and workers in Vietnam, and between Akron and C&MA officials in New York made for an unimaginably complex situation. Things became even more complicated by EMM's determination to ignore the plans of the Mennonite Board of Missions and Charities in Indiana.

Both Orie and J. D. Graber, general secretary of MBMC, saw Vietnam as a potential mission field. In the spring 1955 EMM meeting, Orie introduced the idea of sending missionaries to Southeast Asia. Sumatra, an island in Indonesia, seemed the target of his thinking. When EMM approved a mission in Sumatra, Orie wrote to Graber, urging him to consider a mission in Vietnam. When it became clear that a mission in Sumatra was not possible, EMM turned its attention back to Vietnam. EMM moved quickly and one month later, January 1956, sent missionaries to Vietnam—without consulting the MBMC in Elkhart. Though Orie spoke of a possible partnership with MBMC, EMM forged ahead. Graber was disappointed, especially since MBMC represented the MC church as a whole, whereas EMM was a regional conference board. However, Graber and his board acquiesced to EMM's action.

Orie wrote to Graber saying he regretted the "chain of circumstances" that led to MBMC's withdrawal, but he was grateful for the Elkhart board's "gracious attitude." After EMM missionaries were on-site, MCC continued its more-than-temporary presence.[88] Despite evidence, Orie continued to put a positive spin on developments in Vietnam. Orie's optimism was unbounded and, in this case, unrealistic.

Back home, Orie was making plans for leadership succession at EMM. In 1953, he worked out an agreement with Paul N. Kraybill, teacher and hall manager at Lancaster Mennonite High School. In 1951, he had become editor of EMM's *Missionary Messenger*. Orie recommended Kraybill be appointed "Executive Committee Candidate Secretary," anticipating the time he would fill Orie's top administrative role. Kraybill was to manage routine administrative details at home and abroad, while Orie would continue to handle official correspondence with missionaries and the Israel Mission Committee, and anything to do with board policy. Orie would "growingly count" on Kraybill at the office in Intercourse, Pennsylvania, (before the move to Salunga) for research and information services.[89]

When Orie retired from office in 1958, EMM had forty long-term workers and 1,632 baptized members in East Africa. In 1960, the Lancaster Conference recognized the autonomy of the Tanganyika Mennonite Church, four months ahead of the transformation of Tanganyika, a colonial territory, into an independent nation. In 1964, Tanganyika was renamed Tanzania.

ORIE AT RETIREMENT

For Orie, 1958 was a year of relinquishment and transition. In January, at age sixty-five, he retired as executive secretary-treasurer of MCC, an office he had held since 1935. In March, he retired as secretary of EMM, a role he had also carried since 1935. For twenty-three years, Orie served the two institutions as executive administrator, simultaneously and continuously.

Among executive committee members of both agencies, it had been "generally understood" that at sixty-five, Orie would relinquish his offices.

Orie himself had advocated retirement at sixty-five. Harold Bender, MCC associate secretary, wanted more than a general understanding or an assumption—he wanted to make it a matter of record. At Bender's initiative, MCC's executive committee passed a resolution to that effect.

Orie's "retirement" needs definition. He was still on practically every committee or board "that counted." Both MCC and EMM gave Orie associate roles and honorary status for life. He took on a new role as president of Mennonite Indemnity, Inc. Late in the year, he began a four-month deputation tour—part of it with Eastern Mennonite College president John R. Mumaw—to Africa, Europe, India, Vietnam, Korea, and Japan. For the first time, he visited South Africa.[90] In addition to church offices and activities, Orie continued to have "real work" in the business world as a director and an officer of Miller, Hess & Company and its four corporate affiliates.

Opinions varied about how many offices Orie should have. The young critics in Europe, but also the younger generation in general, raised objections to the overlapping, interconnected matrix of offices Orie held—too great a concentration of power for anyone. There were "little revolts" within certain church boards, but in the view of Orie's successor at MCC, Bill Snyder, "Orie handled most of them well."[91]

As a CPS worker, Snyder had managed dairy testing, and then had led the Mennonite Aid Section with the programs in Paraguay. He played a major role in the migration of refugees to the colonies after World War II. Snyder became assistant executive secretary at MCC in 1950, then associate secretary in 1955 before being appointed as executive secretary in 1958. People were surprised when Snyder became Orie's successor. There was speculation that he would hold the office temporarily until Orie's youngest son, Bob (Robert Wolf) Miller, was ready to step in.[92] Orie overcame his earlier reservations about Snyder and groomed him for the office, always clarifying that only the executive committee could make the appointment.[93] Miller and Snyder had "a sort of fluid arrangement" based on mutual trust and respect, "not highly compartmentalized."

By the time of the transition, neither Miller nor Snyder had "any qualms" about working together. "Neither of us saw big problems ahead," remembered Snyder in interviews with Robert Kreider; "we talked frankly." Orie often stepped into Bill's office for conversation. On occasion, Orie would say, "Well, William, I think you are on the right track. I have seen you handle certain situations. You can say 'no' and unless you can say 'no' when it is necessary, you cannot be the executive secretary successfully."[94]

C. N. Hostetter, chair of the MCC executive committee, served in a pastoral role during the transition in leadership. Hostetter was the able and perceptive president of Messiah College, the Brethren in Christ institution in Grantham, Pennsylvania. Hostetter understood the potential hazards of such a change in office and helped both men adapt to their new roles. Snyder recalled Hostetter "hovering" a bit during the transition, but the chair understood human dynamics and organizational systems. Since Orie wanted to be busy, Snyder kept him occupied with projects and travel.

"When it came down to Orie respecting the lines of authority, I had no kick on that at all," said Snyder. He had seen problems with other retiring church executives, such as M. R. Zigler, who made things difficult for his successor by organizing competing agencies and projects. As for Orie, he "did not do anything of the kind. Orie kept it all very proper. I was very happy with the way Orie performed." It is remarkable that Orie could relinquish power and equally remarkable that Snyder could take on the executive role without considering Orie a threat. Snyder handled the transition with uncommon grace and humility.[95]

Naturally, there were differences of opinion. Orie could not, for example, see the wisdom of Snyder's focus on international voluntary service. "It did not appeal to him, but he said 'if you feel you should do that, and it is something of a witness and . . . is something Mennonites should do through MCC,'" he would not object.[96]

In another case, Snyder wanted to close the "obsolete" MCC vocational school in Korea. Orie had tried hard to get representatives of the MC and GC to establish a church there, but nobody wanted to do it. "Orie had a hard time changing his mind once he started something or had vision for a thing." His natural tenacity, strong sense of mission, and "expansionist" worldview overruled other more pragmatic factors. When a mission or vision had not been fulfilled, Orie could not conceive of closing a project. In the case of Korea, the executive board acted on Snyder's recommendation.[97]

The two also differed over personnel policies. Snyder wanted to remove "certain people" on staff "who had less capability than . . . their task required. I thought we could make some lateral changes. Orie was much more long-suffering." His personnel policy was rather simple: "You take what the Lord has given and be happy."[98]

Nor did Miller agree with Snyder's decentralization strategy. Snyder recalled a meeting of the Mennonite Mental Health Services at the Atlantic Hotel in Chicago when Elmer Ediger, director of the organization, and Orie "had tremendous differences" about the control of institutions under the MCC umbrella. "Elmer made his points forcefully about the need for decentralization and local control." Orie had set the "early vision" for mental health services and treatment centers. "He saw the thing through and helped raise the money."

Orie had also recruited a younger generation of leaders from CPS. Many of them later served on churchwide boards and committees. At the Chicago meeting, the issue had not been solved during the daylong session, so the meeting adjourned for the night. Snyder recalled, "Orie and I talked and it became increasingly clear that we had to give." Orie finally agreed. When the Mennonite Mental Health Services board reassembled the next morning, Orie said—as he had done on other similar occasions—"Now I have slept on this and it is all clear." Though he found this extremely difficult, Orie understood that it was time to trust the wisdom of a new generation.[99]

LEARNING FROM ORIE HOW TO LEAD

By example and instruction, Orie trained younger leaders. What did they learn from their mentor?

Orie "led by being ahead of everybody in the room," Edgar Stoesz remembers. He

was more prepared than others in the subject matter and he always had a plan. You know, I have always resented a bit this opinion that a lot of people have that Orie wrote the minutes before meetings. That's a cheap shot! Orie came to meetings prepared. He knew what he wanted out of that meeting, and more often than not, he got it. And he got it without dominating the air time. Rather, he got it by having something to put on the table. He did not dominate by the force of his personality, but by the force of his ideas.[100]

Orie was always several steps ahead of everyone else. Wilbert Shenk tells the story of Orie in India, visiting his brother.

Ernest came in to Nagpur from Yeotmal to meet Orie and he went out to the train station . . . and no Orie. And so Ernest knows Orie well enough to realize what Orie would do—go to the guesthouse. You don't stand around and wait. Ernest's first words to Orie were "You rascal you, you are always five or ten steps ahead of everyone else."[101]

Orie accomplished more than most because he was disciplined and focused. Wilbert Shenk, himself disciplined and organized, "never met anyone who was more disciplined than Orie Miller." Shenk learned from Orie to "keep your eye on the big questions; don't be distracted by the trivial." Edgar Stoesz recalled that Orie did not try to do everything. He did what he was asked to do or what he had determined needed to be done, and did not allow himself to be distracted. He followed a daily routine, going to bed at ten o'clock and getting up by seven. As one houseguest observed, "One can set his clock by Orie's strict habits." He was fastidious about his appearance. He got a haircut every week, drove to Lancaster to get his shoes shined, and his suits were neatly pressed. Under his gray plain coat he wore a black necktie tucked into his shirt. He simplified life, compensating for his color blindness by buying only black socks and white or off-white shirts.

Delegation was another key to Orie's success. In Shenk's words, "Delegation was his art!" He gave those to whom he delegated a great deal of freedom within a broad framework. Orie "had a fairly simple formula for getting things done: You see where you want to go, then you find the right people to take you there."[102]

Orie never lost sight of the church as central to the work of agencies. MCC and EMM were not invented to serve their own ends—they were servants of the church. Snyder outlined Orie's thought and attitude:

Now Orie did not hesitate to lead, to think new thoughts and take up new causes. But Orie was always conscious, and he got this across to me—that we had to have the churches with us. We were representing them, and so if we were *leading* them, we had to *interpret* to them. We had to get their assent to whatever we were doing. We could not go off, much as the American Friends Service Committee did, as an independent agency. We had to find both our representation on MCC and our life and meaning in the churches. That was his frame of reference; the way he approached every problem.[103]

Long-range planning was another key to Orie's effective leadership:

One of the frequent questions he would ask me was, "Well, what do we see
ahead for the next three years?" It was almost a reflex. He did not ask that
every day, but you knew when you took an idea to him, he wanted to look
at it in those terms—where it would be going.[104]

Fiscal responsibility was another administrative key. Again, Bill Snyder
recalled Orie saying,

"We have no authorization to borrow money in the MCC." I accepted that. I
suppose if the committee would take action tomorrow, we could and we did
borrow funds for certain short-term things in connection with building. But,
this was only for a very brief time. We have operated on a basis of not borrowing and that has been very good. That was the administrative technique
that he followed—face up to the need, get commitments, and then do what
you can with what you get.[105]

Wilbert Shenk said he "never saw anyone read financial statements
quicker than Orie." He had a good sense of what to look for and
what weight to put on those. "He was brilliant in his administrative
know-how."[106]

Recalling Orie's impact on missions, Jacobs reflected:

Orie understood the future. He understood what was going on and we were
ready to move with that. At EMM . . . we couldn't have done what we did
without Orie Miller. I mean it was just a constant presence and we had a sort
of a feeling that Orie could help us to solve the problem. . . . I realized that
even though he wasn't a trained missiologist . . . I knew that he was where I
was going. I just knew it and it's almost uncanny, but for my generation he
represented the way forward.

He was a visionary for missions. . . . So here was a man who was . . .
so many-sided that it astounded you. But that's what we wanted! We had
Harold Bender on the theological side; he was helpful. But when it came to
interacting with our world, that was Orie! That was Orie.[107]

On making decisions:

Orie was ready to make decisions. There were some things on which he might
postpone a decision, but usually he made decisions within the timeframe

that they had to be made. And, he did not have this debilitating thing of regrets, that is, once a decision was made . . . he [had few] second thoughts or regrets. He moved on. . . . That also got him into difficulty because at times, he moved ahead, made decisions, and then had to try to bring others along, those who were affected by those decisions. At times that was a bit difficult.[108]

Though he didn't always get it right, Orie could solve problems. A relief worker in Germany said, "It was amazing how in one hour he had the answer to a problem over which we had struggled for weeks."[109]

Orie's cryptic judgment during an EMM-Tanganyika conflict has emerged from multiple sources. When in 1960 the independent Tanganyika Mennonite Church was writing its constitution, EMM sent the conference discipline guidelines for inclusion. How could the daughter church say no to the mother church? Lancaster Conference standards were increasingly irrelevant in Africa. Orie's reported fix was, "Put it in a file and forget it."

Of the many examples of Orie's problem-solving ingenuity, perhaps none was more complex than working out a solution for an endowment at Eastern Mennonite College in 1957. President John R. Mumaw told Orie that the Southern Association of Colleges and Universities had denied the college's appeal for accreditation. The problem was EMC's lack of endowment that could guarantee an annual income of at least $15,000. Since Orie had given $25,000 to the college's Bible department, he proposed that his contribution be moved temporarily into the endowment fund. Discovering that no individual could be guarantor of annual income, Orie turned to Mennonite Mutual Aid.

He proposed to the MMA board in June 1957 that it become the guarantor for an annual income to EMC of $15,000. Should there be a shortfall, Orie would personally cover the amount needed through his contributions to the Mennonite Foundation. The MMA board agreed. As a result, the Southern Association in December 1959 approved the plan and granted accreditation. The class of 1960 was the first to graduate from EMC as an accredited college.[110]

Whether for EMC, MMA, EMM, or MCC, Orie worked from his home in Akron. In his final decade as executive secretary of MCC, Orie's vision for service and mission sent volunteers to "the ends of the earth." He kept global needs ever before the Brethren in Christ and Mennonites.

If his manner of delivery was not riveting, the content of his speeches was inspiring. He provided windows into worlds beyond North America. He kept MCC on task by "keeping the vision clear," as he often counseled others. He set the trajectory for his successors.

THE DEATH OF ELTA WOLF MILLER

On December 14, 1957, Elta saw Orie off at the Lancaster Pennsylvania Railroad Station on his way to attend the International Missionary Council at Accra, Ghana. She sent him off "as happily" as at any other time. Little did either of them know that Elta had only two more months to live. There was "no intimation of the health circumstances that became clear so soon afterward," Orie wrote to friends.[111] Her letters up to January 3, 1958, made little mention of an approaching health crisis. But a telegram, asking him to return home at once, changed everything.

The local physician, in the opinion of the family, misdiagnosed her illness, thinking she was a hypochondriac. When the Akron sons and daughters-in-law saw her declining health and the depression that came with it, they convinced her to get to the hospital. Orie reached Elta's bedside at the Graduate Hospital in Philadelphia on January 8. He found her gravely ill with a cancer-induced peritonitis, an inflammation of the entire abdominal cavity. Characteristically, Orie heard assurances in the doctors' reports. All were expecting full recovery.[112]

Elta, however, was ready to die—not to live. She was in great pain and very discouraged. "Why can't the doctors let me die?" she asked. Orie offered what he thought was an appropriate biblical text for their crisis: "For to me to live is Christ, and to die is gain" (KJV). The Philippians 1:21 text became the focus of their conversations, and Orie believed that it brought a measure of peace to them both. In the face of her reluctance, Orie urged her to "cooperate" with the attending doctors, since it was their job to restore her health. Elta seemed to improve steadily for about five weeks, until "daily chill-fever periods" indicated the continued presence of the cancer-induced infection.[113]

Susan Elta (Wolf) Miller died Friday, February 14, 1958, at age sixty-four. She and Orie had been married forty-two years. Neither Orie nor Elta had spoken of funeral plans, or of any possible implications of Elta's death for Orie.[114]

Amos S. Horst, family friend and bishop, conducted Elta's funeral services at the Ephrata church on Wednesday, February 19—delayed one day because of a weekend snowstorm that blanketed Akron and made travel hazardous or impossible. Three of Orie's colleagues assisted Horst: J. D. Graber, president of MBMC, the Elkhart mission board; H. Raymond Charles, chair of EMM; and Goshen College president Paul Mininger.[115]

These were Orie's colleagues, his choices. Would Elta have chosen others?

ELTA'S LEGACY

Elta—sensitive, generous, and financially independent—often bought gifts for family and friends as well as for people in need, and loved doing it. Many friends, relatives, employees and their families, visitors, and MCC workers tasted her excellent Pennsylvania Dutch fare around her bountiful table. Though she was refined, her meals were seasoned with warmth and congenial conversation. David Sauder recalled his parents' surprise when they were invited to a meal, because Great-Aunt Lizzie Sauder served the Millers as a housekeeper. The Sauders were impressed that Orie, known around the world, would take interest in their family, hardly on the same social level. David Sauder reflected that Orie and Elta "reached out to everybody; they were not status conscious."[116]

Returned mission and service workers sometimes found sanctuary in the Miller home. In 1952, EMM missionaries James and Marian Payne returned from Ethiopia to seek treatment for his debilitating headaches. During the week that James spent at the Ephrata hospital for neurological evaluation, Orie and Elta gave Marian "full use of their home." Fifty years later, Marian recalled with gratitude the Millers's "warm hospitality" during that time of crisis.[117]

Edgar Stoesz recalled her purchase of new furniture for the MCC chapel. When she noticed the benches in poor condition, she ordered and paid for new ones.

Elta's generous spirit did not translate to careful accounting. Orie told Wilbert Shenk that

> he used to try to get Elta to keep a checkbook, you know, because she's writing checks and buying things for the house and all that. But he said she would say, "Orie, I just can't make it come out!" And so then he would work

with her to get her checkbook back in order, and the same thing would happen the next month. It just wouldn't come out right. So he finally said to her, "Elta, you just write the checks."[118]

Elta was the "heart" of the family, daughter-in-law Jean Miller observed. "Nothing would make Elta happier than to go shopping with me and get me a new winter coat, or buy the kids toys. I remember after they had a dinner party, she would come with her basket with food for us. Or we'd be invited up there to eat and that was so nice."[119] She wrote warm, newsy letters to the children. Orie, on the other hand, sometimes wrote letters that ended with "Dictated but not read."

Tensions surfaced after Elta's death. "I thought that when she died things kind of fell apart in the family," Jean recalled.[120] Elta never put all of her assets under Orie's name, and so when she died, her estate had to be settled. She had her name on a lot of the properties that MCC was occupying. Those properties, at her death, were sold, and the estate was to be distributed to the children. According to some memories, some of the children refused their inheritance. Orie told Edgar Stoesz that son John, at Reba Place, "didn't want to be bothered with this wealth. . . . I don't know that it ever broke their relationship, but certainly there was tension in their relationship."[121]

John W. Miller recalled that his mother "always suffered" during Orie's absences. She was naturally anxious, but when Orie was gone, "she was sadder and more anxious." John and his siblings "all felt bad" about it. Given the amount of time Orie was traveling, this was no small matter. Elta suffered stoically and tried to manage "with a reasonable gladness, because she knew how much worth my father was to many people." The family appreciated how well Orie provided for Elta, for the family, and for the Wolfs. "He arranged a family vacation every year and he provided mother with a maid and nurse to help her care for her mother." He was a very good provider, but he "was not as attentive as he should have been to my mother's needs."[122]

Grandchildren treasured Elta's unconditional love. Tina Beach Bechtel (daughter of Lois) remembers that "the house on Main Street was a safe haven for me as a child." Grandmother "taught me how to love and be loved, and now as a grandmother myself, I think of those simple treasures she passed on."[123]

Elta's obituary described her as enthusiastic about supporting and promoting the work of the Willing Workers women's group, and as a regular Sunday school teacher since 1915.[124] Elta was buried among her Wolf and Hess relatives in the Wolf family cemetery on the outskirts of Akron. It was the site of the former Steinmetz German Baptist (Church of the Brethren) Meetinghouse, the church of the Wolf family.

SYMPATHY FROM AROUND THE WORLD

Orie received expressions of sympathy from around the world. If he had not always been attentive to Elta's needs, he certainly expressed tenderness to those who sent their sympathies. He wrote to Emmy and Eberhard Arnold, leaders of the Bruderhof "Hutterite" Colony in East Paraguay.[125] Perhaps with more optimism than reality, Orie said that "to the end her [Elta's] mind was clear and was in spirit relaxed, assured, and ready to go or stay." He was "deeply grateful" for the last weeks together with Elta, which were a "blessing and benediction" to them all. He was thankful for "understanding and praying friends," such as Emmy and Eberhard and the Primavera Colony, who had expressed by both telegram and letter "deep sympathy" for Orie's "great loss."[126]

To Arlene Sitler, former MCC secretary and relief worker, then working at the Children's Charity Hospital in Washington, DC, Orie wrote to thank her for "the thoughtful present" she had sent to Elta. Elta had commented several times about Sitler's visit to the hospital. He told Sitler about the weekend snowstorm that delayed Elta's funeral by a day. And finally, he said Elta "always appreciated your friendship and interest in her."[127]

His notes of thanks went beyond friends and colleagues. He wrote to thank Elizabeth Naugle, RN, at the Graduate Hospital in Philadelphia, for her "good services to Mrs. Miller." He asked Naugle to pass on his thanks, also, to Miss Heller, who "carried through the day shift from beginning to end even though her strength and physical resource was taxed to the limit." Other nurses were less visible, but Orie wanted Naugle to pass on to them the family's gratitude.[128]

Three days after Elta's death, Orie sent a note of appreciation to six voluntary service workers who had donated blood for Elta: Marie Hallman at the Waterloo MCC office; Melita Froese and Walter Rempel at Brook Lane Farm in Hagerstown, Maryland; Ellen Smucker at Prairie

View Hospital in Newton, Kansas; and Lucille Detweiler and John Berg at Akron headquarters. He sent a check as a personal donation to the business office "to thank the MCC family once again for all the help and kindness shown us through this time of sickness and bereavement."[129]

Orie asked the business office for all expenses related to Elta's illness and death, which included phone calls, telegrams, guest meals, lodging, and snow removal. Willis Detweiler, business manager, replied that MCC would not bill him for these services. "We feel as a token of appreciation for your services and as a note of sympathy with Elta's passing that we should absorb these expenses as MCC expense." With pencil, Orie scrawled on Detweiler's letter, "Send $100 thanks."[130]

Elta's death changed Orie, Don Jacobs recalled. The next time Orie visited Tanganyika, the two "chatted and it was as though we were alone on an island somewhere." This was more than an administrative visit. Orie was more reflective and was struggling with the concept of heaven and eternity, not as settled in his mind as it had been before Elta's death. He had learned to trust Don's counsel as a theological thinker and as an anthropologist.[131]

Early in 1959, Orie spent a week in Java, where Wilbert and Juanita Shenk were working with MCC. Wilbert recalled that Orie "was reflective, he was mellow; he didn't talk about his wife a great deal, but that colored everything because it was so fresh for him."[132]

When Elta died, son Bob, his wife Jean, and their family moved into his house. Orie "tried to make it very good because . . . he was always in command" wherever he was. He "had his little office right in the back room off the kitchen. We had a one-year-old boy at the time and he would creep back there, but, you know, Orie was so focused." He never noticed. He had his routine. Every night "at 10:00 he would come out of that little office, eat a banana, and go to bed." He was ready for breakfast with Bob and Jean at seven in the morning, but he ate the noon and evening meal at MCC. "That saved us," Jean remembered, "because that whole year we had burned toast." That was because Orie "manned the toaster." When the toast popped up, "down it went again until it got dark, because, I guess, he liked it that way." He paid someone to help because Jean and Bob had a young baby at that time, a toddler. "He was most considerate."[133]

Orie had acquaintances, colleagues, and friends on almost every continent. He had a few very close friends, such as Chris Graber and M. Robert Zigler, but none could fill the void caused by Elta's death. So Orie courted and in 1960 married Elta Myers Sensenig, namesake of Elta Wolf Miller. They moved into a new house across the street from the new MCC offices on Twelfth Street, Akron. It marked the end of one era and the beginning of another.

Chapter 11
Five-Year Plans and Words Fitly Spoken: 1960–1969

"The beginning of witness is taking off one's shoes and sitting eye-level with a conversation partner. If we wish to speak, we must first listen. If we wish to gain respect, we must first offer respect."

In order to understand the present, Orie said, one gained the best perspective by turning to the Scriptures. "You can understand our today's 1960 world in perspective much better by reading the Old Testament, as well as the New, than you can by just reading *Time*. The two Testaments tell us that God is sovereign and the world, which God loves, is a 'ripe harvest field.'" In a rambling speech during an overseas orientation session, July 17–20, 1963, Orie referred to the challenges of population growth, hunger, revolution, national independence movements, technological advances, economic imbalance, and the struggle for civil rights.[1]

The 1960s were indeed a time of revolution and rapid change. President John F. Kennedy captured the imagination of a new generation with his own youth and idealism, most famously expressed in his inaugural speech: "Ask not what your *country* can do for *you*; ask what *you* can do for your *country*" (emphasis added). The Peace Corps was the best programmatic expression of his mantra.

Young Mennonites mirrored the cultural revolution of the decade, visible at every turn. Urban pioneers—pastors, church planters, missionaries, and service workers with a heart for racial equality, urban renewal, and economic revitalization, and inspired by Dr. Martin Luther King Jr.—were among the first to participate in the civil rights movement. College and university students and other youth of draft age marched, chanted, and spoke out in protest against the Vietnam War. Some men of draft age, seeing registration as a cog in the wheel of the Pentagon's immoral war in Vietnam, refused to register. Various forms of protest increased as the U.S. government's "March of Folly" in Vietnam spread to Cambodia and Laos.

In a rather dramatic course of events at the 1969 MC General Conference in Turner, Oregon—where in 1937, MC delegates had adopted the landmark peace statement—youth advocating draft resistance were given a hearing. The venerable bishop John E. Lapp of the Franconia Conference, for one, reached across the "generation gap" to the long-haired, bearded draft resisters. Lapp saw them in common cause with the COs of World War I who refused to wear the uniform or perform military duties in military boot camps.

MISSION WORK AND INDEPENDENCE IN AFRICA

"The maturity of independent status of the Tanganyika Mennonite Church" was Orie's immediate response when *Gospel Herald* editors asked what in 1960 had been of "more than passing interest" in the life of the church. When EMM sent Elam Stauffer and Orie Miller to Africa in 1933 to find a mission field, they selected a region that contained "hardly any Christians." In twenty-six years, the witness begun at Shirati on the eastern shore of Lake Victoria in 1934 had developed into a "missionary-minded" church of 2,200 members.

Perhaps the first missionaries, Elizabeth and Elam Stauffer and Ruth and John Mosemann Jr., could have imagined such growth of the church, but they hardly could have believed its independent status. But that is what Orie predicted. In February 1952, while riding with three missionaries on the Shirati road, Orie pointed to Tanganyika's political independence within ten years. Dr. Merle Eshleman, with a decade of experience in the colony, immediately marshaled the usual arguments given by British colonialists against such a myth.[2]

African delegates and mission leaders at EMM headquarters, Salunga, 1961. EMM.

When, nine years and ten months later, Tanganyika did indeed win its political independence from Great Britain, J. Lester and Lois Eshleman, remembering the Shirati-road conversation, marveled, "Brother Miller is also among the prophets."[3] Tanganyika achieved its independence in 1961, became a republic in 1962, and joined Zanzibar in 1964 to become the United Republic of Tanzania.[4] Whether or not a prophet, Orie was attuned to world events through his daily reading of newspapers and his continuing global travel. Hershey Leaman, hospital administrator in Tanzania, Somalia, and Ethiopia, had an even higher opinion: "When Orie Miller spoke, it was . . . actually the voice of God. I mean, his forward thinking, his futuristic thinking, was something that really impressed me."[5]

Zedekia Marwa Kisare, ordained in 1967 as the first bishop of the Tanzania Mennonite Church, recalled the significance of a 1958 visit. Orie addressed "all of the church leaders and missionaries in the Komiti Kuu," proclaiming that the church should achieve independence ahead of the nation. It would be done, because it was "the right thing to do." From that moment, Kisare recalled, we "began to call ourselves the Tanganyika Mennonite Church."[6]

The point of greatest tension in the transition was the ownership and administration of institutions—educational, medical, and agricultural. The missionaries "were very opposed to having the African folk, the young African leaders run these institutions." Managing congregations was one thing, running "these technical and Americanized institutions" was yet something different. Medical administrator Hershey Leaman, also the youngest ordained missionary in Tanzania, recalled an earth-shattering moment in the verbal "tug-of-war" between missionaries and Tanzanians. Orie, distressed by the missionaries' "improper" attitudes and behavior during a meeting, tried to move the conversation toward understanding and resolution. At a moment when tension around the table reached its zenith and respect plummeted to its nadir, "just very suddenly, *very* suddenly, oh my! Orie sobbed, literally sobbed!"[7]

The shockwaves gave way to prolonged silence, as they had during the Amsterdam Seven confrontation of MCC in Basel, Switzerland. "And the reason," Leaman reflected, "was because of who Orie was. He was a church father. This very quiet, soft-spoken person . . . never spoke more than necessary, never, never." Once again, time stood still as frustration and disappointment with his people burst through his natural reserve. Others recall how Zedekia Kisare called the group to remember how humility, repentance, and confession led to reconciliation in the crisis caused by East Africa revivals of 1942. They should do the same now. They did, and as a result "partnership became real."

The implications of a transfer of power and property became apparent bit by bit. David W. Shenk, a teenager at the time, heard such questions as "Does that mean, we will probably need to walk because the Africans will take all the cars?" Orie's answer was, "That's right."[8]

The impasse in Tanzania was the antithesis of Orie's understanding of missiology as dialogue. The beginning of witness, he believed, was taking off one's shoes and sitting eye-level with a conversation partner. If one wishes to speak, one must first listen. If one wishes to gain respect, one must first offer respect. "You hold sacred the other person and his right to freedom. . . . There is nothing to be afraid of, except yourself and your fears."[9] Orie represented his generation's Protestant pattern of paternalistic missions and he embodied great authority, yet his personal approach was one of "love, care, and respect."[10] His paternalism did not mean imperialism or colonialism. He did not approach cultures as an anthropologist, with special interest in culture, food, and language; but when Orie came to visit, "he took time to meet with the church leadership and interact with them very graciously and wisely and insightfully." It was clear that Orie was "very highly respected by the Tanzanians."[11]

With good humor, they forgave him his lack of taste for local cuisine, as in the case of *ugali*, a thick cornmeal porridge, a staple in East Africa. "One of the jokes around was that Orie, when they would serve this common meal of *ugali*, would take one piece of *ugali*, and knead it, and knead it . . . until the meal was over, then he would finally eat his piece of *ugali*"—but only one![12]

David Climenhaga, acting general superintendent for the Brethren in Christ mission in Rhodesia, recalls a life-changing conversation with Orie in 1958. Orie visited the mission in southern Rhodesia to learn their attitudes toward the coming independence of the colony and the church. Climenhaga gathered together the Brethren in Christ executive committee composed of Rhodesian Christians and missionaries. "To the Rhodesians, the concept of an African indigenous church was incomprehensible, and to the missionaries, premature." David was impressed with Orie's "very low-key, but very persistent" manner. After asking a probing question, Orie waited patiently as the Rhodesians struggled to formulate their thoughts on an independent church. It was a new concept.[13]

Climenhaga observed that Mennonites did not refer to their ministry points as "mission stations," but simply as "stations"—emphasizing not the role of missionaries, but the work and the results: hospitals, leper clinics, schools, and churches.[14] A private conversation made an even greater impression on Climenhaga. The topic was South African apartheid, which had come up in the conversations with the Rhodesians. Climenhaga was not convinced that apartheid was "all bad," as Miller had implied. Climenhaga said he knew many Afrikaners who were quite fond of their African servants and treated them very well. Orie's immediate retort was, "Yes, well, I know people who are very fond of their dogs too." Orie's blunt, succinct response helped to shape the general superintendent's evolving views on apartheid.[15]

The remarkable story of building a mosque for Muslim students in a Somali school illustrates Orie's respect for the people and his sensitivity to their needs. EMM had entered Somalia in 1953. As an entrée to missions, Mennonites were permitted to build and operate such service institutions as medical, educational, agricultural, and literacy ministries. During the building of a secondary school, Somali authorities asked Mennonites to include a mosque for the students, since 96–97 percent of Somalis were Muslim. Hershey Leaman recalled Orie's reaction:

> "Well, yes, these people are Muslims. They've chosen to be Muslims. Why shouldn't they have a place of worship? Look, if we are interested in those people hearing . . . our witness, observing our lives, hearing how we approach God, then we also need to listen to them." And, would you believe it was approved by the EMM board?
>
> It seems unbelievable now! But, that is an example of Orie's missiology: you approach people respectfully . . . with care and love. If they don't have education, they *should* have education. If they don't have adequate health care, they *should* have adequate health care. And if they don't have a place of worship, they *should* have a place of worship.[16]

Another revealing aspect of Orie's missiology was his attitude toward the use of money. Missionaries were, of course, "extremely frugal." Orie was frugal too—once saying he had accounted for every penny spent since the age of sixteen—but that did not translate to the building of shoddy or temporary structures. "Mennonites build good buildings," he said, "so don't build buildings that you expect to fall down in ten years." In addition, good programs deserved strong financial backing. He once told Tanzania missionaries, "Don't be so afraid of the dollar."[17]

WHAT IS YOUR VISION?

The retention and retelling of Orie's words were sometimes striking. Later, as David Shenk traveled as international secretary for EMM, he often heard people say, whether in Indonesia, Europe, or Africa, "At this very spot Orie said this—." Shenk has his own story of a memorable encounter in Somalia:

> I was directing the school at Mogadishu and had just installed a diesel generator . . . so we had electric lights. I got this . . . electrical system working before Orie arrived. I was so thrilled! When Orie comes, we'll have electric lights, and he'll be so pleased to see . . . this kind of progress. And so after

having tea, we were walking out to the school, and I said, "Brother Orie, would you step aside here, I'd like to show you the generator I just installed." He kept walking and said, "Mennonites *always* get the generators installed. My question is what's the *vision* for the next five years?" I mean, that was a tremendously wise word of counsel to a young mid-twenties missionary.

That statement was transformative! It formed my administrative style. During my years in overseas and home missions, the directorship, or even local church pastoring, I would ask that question. It came to me from Orie. "What's the vision for the next five years?"[18]

Shenk's experience was not an anomaly. When Dr. Ivan Leaman was in charge of the hospital and clinic in Mogadishu, Somalia, Orie came to inspect the work. Leaman had also installed a generator and was eager to show it to Orie. Again, Orie had no interest at all in the generator: "No, I'm not interested in what you are doing right now; I want to know what your plan is for the next five years."[19]

Others also remembered Orie's queries. J. Elvin Martin, longtime pastor at Ephrata Mennonite Church, and Laverne Sensenig Martin recount a time when they invited visitors for Sunday dinner. Orie and Elta Myers Sensenig, Laverne's mother and now married to Orie, were among the guests. Elvin recalls that during the after-dinner conversation, "Orie looked at me and said, 'Elvin, what is your ten-year plan for the Ephrata Mennonite Church?' I didn't have a ten-*week* plan! So that was one of the most embarrassing moments of my life, I think."[20]

It seems Orie asked everyone for a plan, even his grandchildren. Ed and Jan Miller, sons of Albert and Esther, remember as boys that Orie would ask about their ten-year plans. If they didn't have one, and they usually didn't, Orie never pressed them. Ed was never put off by his grandfather's probing, remembering him as "energetic, interested, entertaining, bright-eyed, decisive, always ready to give advice, clear, a very clear sense of purpose." Albert's youngest son Jan recalls family reunions that were both "interesting and scary because we knew they were going to have a time where they would bring all the grandchildren in one by one and then Orie would say, 'Tell us, what are your plans for life?'"[21] Orie wrote sometime in the 1960s that time was moving too fast for ten-year plans, so he reduced the time to five years.[22]

David Shenk and Hershey Leaman recall Orie's mannerisms and conduct in EMM board meetings in Salunga. During an executive committee meeting, he would sometimes "hold up his finger" when he had something to say. When he spoke everyone paid attention. Even when partially debilitated by Parkinson's disease, "what he had to say had depth, and we would pay attention—sometimes it was just a word." Shenk remembers when Orie held up his finger to say, "The new word is *partnership*." Partnership replaced the earlier emphasis on the "local church" and became EMM's mantra "for years."[23]

In board meetings, Orie "seldom spoke." Hershey Leaman, hospital administrator in Tanzania, remembers the pattern during the years when H. Raymond Charles was EMM president, from 1956 to 1980. Often in executive committee meetings, when everyone had spoken, Charles would turn to Orie Miller and ask, "'Orie, could you help us on this one? Is there more to be said on this?' And he would ponder a little, and then he would make some succinct comments, and I'm telling you, they may not have always carried the day, but very often they did." In retrospect, Leaman mused about "why we allowed him to have that much power and concluded it was his quiet charisma. . . . When he spoke it was really like the voice of God in a group."[24]

A DIFFICULT LEADERSHIP TRANSITION AT EMM

Not everyone was in awe of Orie. Just as he passed the baton of MCC leadership to his "understudy," Bill Snyder, Orie relinquished the top office at EMM to Paul Kraybill. Orie had recruited Kraybill in 1953 to become assistant secretary, in effect a "candidate secretary," and nurtured him until the transition in 1958.[25] The MCC transition was smoother than that of EMM. Kraybill, a bit impatient, was ready for the reins before Orie handed them over.[26] After the swap of offices, Orie's expansionist worldview and independent action sometimes vexed Kraybill.

Orie also tested Kraybill. On one occasion when Orie and Paul Landis were returning from British Honduras, Orie showed Landis his recommendations for EMM. Surprised, Landis said, "Orie, I'm not sure that's going to work with Eastern Board." He said, "I don't think it will either, but I put that in there for Paul Kraybill. I want to see what Paul does with that." At the next EMM board meeting, Kraybill took exception to the recommendations but feared upsetting Orie. Orie listened, smiled, and said, "Paul, I'm so proud of you!"[27] Kraybill was not amused.

Occasional confidential memos to EMM board chair H. Raymond Charles reflected Kraybill's ongoing frustration with Orie. From Addis Ababa, Ethiopia, in 1960, Kraybill wrote that Orie was "not willing to face problems here." The mission was "quite disturbed" because Orie "refused to listen to the problem."[28] Kraybill complained that Orie had complicated EMM's Central American missions by inviting the Beachy Amish to British Honduras and was in conversation with the Holdeman Mennonites about a mission somewhere in the region. Kraybill was also unhappy with Orie's proposal that MCC workers be sent there as missionaries.[29] Orie helped to establish the Beachy Amish in El Salvador, the Conservative Mennonite Conference in Costa Rica, and the Brethren in Christ in Nicaragua. Orie was effective. Paul Landis observed that these leaders followed "Orie around like he was a prophet. Whatever Orie said, they did."[30]

Orie also insisted that both MCC and EMM send workers to Hong Kong, which they did in 1965. Kraybill wrote, "We are giving a great deal of respect and place to Orie which is certainly right . . . but on the other hand there are those who are concerned about the expansion of offices, staff, and budget." Another "particularly serious aspect" of the problem in Kraybill's mind was his observation that the executive committee had "surrendered to Orie its prerogatives" in regard to "strategy and planning." This left Kraybill in a vulnerable position when, for example, Orie, representing MCC, "rejected my proposal" and the committee said little. Kraybill wanted less interference and more deliberate and careful planning for any future expansion.[31]

Orie also "stubbed his toe" in the Middle East with a project called Nes Amim, remembers Edgar Stoesz. In 1960, Orie visited missionaries Roy and Florence Kreider and Paul and Bertha Swarr, Mennonite Board of Missions workers in Israel. The purpose of his visit was to help launch Sharon Tours, a Middle East version of Menno Travel Service that would organize pilgrimage tours to biblical sites. Paul Ruth, director of MTS in Amsterdam, had proposed the service and Paul Swarr became its manager.[32]

During that visit, Kreider introduced the vision of several messianic Jews to create an agricultural village on 260 acres of prime farmland in western Galilee. Jewish and Arab believers would work together in this community in a demonstration of God's reconciling work through Jesus. It would be a *nes amim*, a "sign to the nations" of the vision of Isaiah (11:10).[33]

Ecumenical national committees were formed in Holland, Germany, and the United States, with an international executive committee based in Zurich, Switzerland. Foreign investments would fund the program, and MCC and MBMC would help supply personnel. The opportunities were promising, but the eventual difficulties were greater. In order to win the approval of the Israeli government, one of the visionaries unilaterally promised to exclude Jewish Christians. The first manager could not be held accountable for the use of funds. There was also a crisis of leadership in Zurich that failed to set clear goals, policies, and strategies. National committees clashed with one another and with the Zurich office. Kreider, who was asked to stabilize the program, finally after two years recommended the withdrawal of the Swiss and American committees—leaving the project in the hands of the German and Dutch committees, which had been working at cross-purposes with each other.[34]

To Orie's great disappointment, Nes Amim became a "completely secular business-oriented enterprise." He invested personal money, but it never had broad support in the United States. Nor did Paul Kraybill and EMM embrace the vision. For Kraybill, it was another Orie idea that diverted funds from EMM. Orie had, indeed, been captured by the vision of a farm-based, multicultural Christian community, but he could not make the complex project work. Orie kept trying long after he should have given up, and finally his diagnosis of Parkinson's disease ended his involvement.[35] Rather than creating a reconciling "sign to the nations," the international committees themselves could not be reconciled.

ELTA MYERS SENSENIG

Of more than passing importance in Orie's personal life was his relationship with Elta Myers Sensenig, whom he married on January 9, 1960. He was sixty-seven; she was forty-nine. Elta's husband Isaac (Ike) had died as the result of an accidental fall from a roof. Donald Sensenig, who was four years old at the time of his father's death, recalls the special interest that Orie and Elta Wolf Miller took in their family, owing to the fact that his mother had been named after Elta Wolf Miller.

Laverne Sensenig Martin first learned of Orie's more-than-usual interest in her mother when Laverne happened across a letter from Orie in Elta's purse. The curious daughter read the letter, which revealed Orie's intentions. Laverne said nothing, nor did Elta. Elta at first refused Orie's overtures. "She was an only child, very bright, very capable, but unsure, I think, of her own abilities," was Donald's assessment. But she had provided capably for the family as a school-

Elta Myers Sensenig and Orie O. Miller, married January 9, 1960. John W. Miller.

teacher.[36] Laverne and her husband, J. Elvin Martin, agreed: "She had inferior feelings" and thought "she could never measure up to Orie Miller, so she refused" his overtures.[37]

When Orie's interest became a topic of conversation in the family, Elta's children, all adults, encouraged her to respond more positively. Orie, of course, was not easily deterred. "He kept contacting her until she said yes." The difference of almost nineteen years was not much of an issue. More significant was the difference in experience and worldview; he was a global traveler with an abundance of international friends, and she had not traveled, even to New York City—until their one-day honeymoon. The city was a convenient place for the honeymoon, since Orie had a committee meeting there the next day, most likely with the American Leprosy Mission or the Biblical Seminary in New York.[38]

Elta didn't care much for traveling, but Orie was pushy! Because he wanted her company, she traveled around the world several times. She believed it to be her role. Though it was not her inclination, she traveled bravely alone to meet him—in Africa or Indonesia, or wherever the destination. Her children were amazed how well Elta stepped up to Orie's expectations.[39] As for their age difference, Mahlon Hess spoke for many when he said, "Because of Orie, we accepted her and she made herself welcome."[40]

Of Orie's children, Lois had the most problems with the marriage. She and Elta were only five years apart in age and had played together as children. Furthermore, Elta's family "had farmed the lower farm for her Grandpa Wolf. And that didn't go down with her very well at all." Orie's other children were a bit younger, didn't know the history, and liked Elta a lot. Daughter-in-law Jean (Bob's wife), considered "Grandma Elta a real gem," but it "was not an easy marriage for her."[41]

DISCIPLINED WORK HABITS AND CONTINUED TRAVEL

Orie's expectations for himself, as well as others, continued to be high. As always, his work habits were disciplined and his calendar was full. Two weeks after his marriage to Elta Sensenig, Orie began a month-long deputation tour for EMM, MCC, and MEDA to Europe, Ethiopia, Somalia, Tanganyika, Northern Rhodesia, Belgian Congo, and Liberia. In June, he was on hand in Goshen to dedicate the new Goshen Biblical Seminary facilities, for which he and Elta Wolf Miller—"the former Elta, not the present Elta," as he sometimes put it—had each given $42,500.

In August, he and Elta Sensenig moved into a modest new brick, ranch-style house across the street from MCC headquarters on Twelfth Street in Akron. Also in 1960, Orie led in the formation of the Congo Protestant Relief Agency, became board chair for the American Leprosy Mission, and assisted in opening a hospital and clinic in Nhatrang, Vietnam. In November, he set off on a two-month tour of Europe, the Middle East, and Africa.

In Beirut, Lebanon, Orie held a series of planning meetings with Arnold Dietzel, director of Menno Travel Service. Three years after its founding, MTS "had grown to good self-support volume." Since Beirut was "a world travel crossroad and the main gateway to Holy Land travel," it was an ideal place for a travel agency. Orie dreamed with the workers about the future of the Hebron MCC orphanage, visited the refugee camp at Jericho, and stopped at the MCC home in Jerusalem. MCC had been doing relief work in Jordan for eleven years and the needs were "still desperate." Plans were in motion to open a relief station in Maian, a Bedouin area in southeast Jordan. In his diary, Orie noted, "One feels deeply that now we must enter more fully and deeply into Gospel communications." The next workers should be literate in Arabic in order "to teach and preach . . . to bring to harvest the seed planted."

When he received a copy of Orie's diary, EMM's Paul Kraybill took exception to Orie's plan to launch mission work under MCC in Jordan.

As usual, Kraybill prefaced his concerns about Orie with a word of appreciation: "I very much appreciate Orie's vision and concern but this is an example of a new kind of philosophy that should have more discussion."[42] Everywhere Orie traveled, he saw possibilities; his expansionist mode was irrepressible.

Expansion at MCC had less resistance. In 1961, for example, Orie supported the recommendation of Robert S. Kreider to form the Teachers Abroad Program (TAP) to supply much-needed educators in sub-Saharan Africa. As he had with Pax a decade earlier, Orie warmed quickly to the TAP program.

Orie had relinquished his roles as chief executive of MCC and EMM, but it seemed to have little effect on his schedule. He still attended executive committee meetings of both MCC and EMM as well as numerous other boards and committees. Typically, on his deputation tours he represented numerous agencies, and he divided the expenses—carefully, to the penny—to the appropriate organization. He wrote copious travel diaries, with copies sent to the appropriate agencies and to all family members, a practice he had begun with his first overseas trip to the Middle East in 1919. To the agencies he sent detailed reports and specific recommendations. As Orie's protégé, Edgar Stoesz recalled that no trip was complete until the diaries and reports had been written.

In 1961, he was in Congo for the fiftieth anniversary service of the inter-Mennonite Congo Inland Mission, later to become Africa Inter-Mennonite Mission (AIMM). In September, he was off on a deputation tour to France, Switzerland, Austria, Germany, the Netherlands, and Luxembourg. In December, Orie launched a three-month deputation tour to Africa with ports of entry in Accra, Ghana; Uyo, Nigeria; Leopoldville, Belgian Congo; Nairobi, Kenya; Addis Ababa, Ethiopia; Mogadiscio (Mogadishu), Somalia; and Musoma, Tanganyika. Elta joined Orie for more than a month of the tour. Not all the action was international. On December 13, Orie convened the first meeting of a planning committee for Landis Mennonite Homes in rural Lititz, Pennsylvania.

In his years of global excursions, Orie developed a few travel habits. He was typically the last one to board the plane, and the last to exit. Why stand in line when you can make good use of time by reading?[43] On board, he continued to read. In his briefcase, as many others have noted, Orie typically carried a world atlas, the Bible, the *Mennonite Yearbook*, the *New York Times,* the *Wall Street Journal,* and the *National Accounts Estimates of Main Aggregates* (or a similar resource). In addition, he carried several books, church papers such as *Gospel Herald, Mennonite Weekly Review, Christian Century,* and one of several mission papers. He also picked up newspapers at his destination points. When waiting, or if stranded, Orie never lacked for reading material. John Weber—Orie's friend, fellow member of the Ephrata church, business partner on several ventures, and MEDA partner—recalls Orie having in hand statistics for every country they visited. Good planning required such knowledge as population numbers, gross national product, and income.[44]

Orie also had mail forwarded to various hotels he frequented. Peter Dyck, longtime MCC worker, revered Orie but got irritated by his mentor's habit of sleeping in hotels rather than staying with the volunteers in more rustic quarters. It didn't make sense to Peter that someone so very cost-conscious would spend money for luxury. Finally, on one occasion, Peter and Orie were to meet up at the airport in Athens and then go to Macedonia to inspect the program. When leaving the airport, Peter asked, "Orie, why can't you stay where the rest of us stay?" And Orie simply said, "They know how to handle the mail." According to Peter's story, they "got out of the taxi, went into the hotel for Orie to get registered and checked in, . . . Orie stepped up to the desk, gave his name, and the clerk said, 'Oh, Mr. Miller.' He said as he reached under a desk behind the counter, 'Here's your mail.'" Orie smiled and Peter understood.[45]

In answer to the same question in Ethiopia, Orie said the hotel had air-conditioning. Was that not too much of a luxury? "Well," Orie explained, "in cold climates we need heaters so we can sleep well and work. Here where it's hot, we need air conditioners for the same reason."[46] Without a good night's rest, it would be difficult for Orie to do his work well the next day. It was a pragmatic matter. This was not a hard-and-fast rule; Orie sometimes stayed in EMM guest rooms or missionary homes.

While Orie was congenial, polite, and always a gentleman, he rarely made small talk with fellow passengers. Orie once told about a flight he took with his good friend Chris Graber to South America. By the time the plane landed, the gregarious Graber knew every passenger on board. Orie, on the other hand, had spent the entire flight in his seat alone, reading, writing, and thinking. When Orie related the story to Robert Kreider, he expressed both "admiration" and "reproof"—admiration for Graber, and reproof for his own lack of socializing.[47]

Orie was focused and rarely distracted—even by emergencies. John Weber recalled an incident in Managua, Nicaragua, to illustrate the point:

> I never knew Orie to worry about anything and I'll give you an example. We were traveling on one of our trips to Central America in the interest of MEDA. We boarded our plane in Managua, Nicaragua, to fly to Tegucigalpa, Honduras. As the plane was going down the runway, I think we might have been just airborne maybe 200–300 feet, flames started shooting out of the left engine . . . about 30–40 feet high. . . . As was his custom, Orie was reading the Bible. It was always the first thing he did after buckling his seat belt. So Orie was there reading his Bible with the plane on fire. I said, "Orie, this plane's on fire!" Orie looked up from reading his Bible, looked out the window, "Yes, well." He went back to reading his Bible.

When the plane landed safely and passengers were rushed off the burning plane, Orie was more concerned about his briefcase than about his own safety. Neither in this case nor in any other did Weber ever see Orie "rattled." In any emergency, he was quick to assess whether there was anything he could do. If not, he could ignore it.

If problems required manual labor, it was outside Orie's expertise. No one could remember a hammer or even a screwdriver in Orie's hands. The most iconic story of Orie's manual ineptitude—and lack of concern about it—occurred on a road in rural Lancaster County. Donald Sensenig, Elta's son, was driving on Route 322 between Hinkletown and Blue Ball, when he spotted a blue Buick parked by the side of the road. Since it was similar to the one his mother and Orie drove, Donald pulled off to check. Sure enough, it was Orie and Elta's Buick with a flat tire. "And mother was changing the tire, while Orie was sitting in the car reading!"[48] Elta, having been a widow with three children to raise, had learned by necessity how to manage such practical tasks. As for Orie, changing a tire was a distraction; it was not in his job description.

RATHER A FRIEND THAN A SON

Edgar Stoesz, who came to MCC near the end of Orie's era, had the greatest respect for his mentor. When speaking to the Miller family in 2008, Edgar said Orie "was the greatest man I ever knew."[49] He also said he wished to be Orie's friend, not his son. He knew how difficult it could be to live in Orie's shadow.

Albert, Orie and Elta's oldest son, had dutifully stepped into his father's shoes at Miller Hess in 1946. He also managed the Wolf farms Elta had inherited. When Orie was traveling abroad, he depended on Albert to keep him posted on shoe company matters, farm produce prices, family, and Akron community news. When the family decided to develop the Wolf farms, Albert managed the project.

But high expectations as Orie's son and the burdens he carried grew heavy. As Albert's son Ed Miller recalled, the Orie-Albert "relationship was rocky, difficult. . . . I always knew it was very hard for Dad to have been Orie's son." It didn't help that Albert's wife, Esther (Lehman) Miller, "idolized Orie" and thought he could do no wrong.[50]

Albert suffered from a genetic disposition to severe cyclical depression. It was during an episode of depression in the spring of 1961 that Albert confided in his brother John. In turn, John wrote a candid letter to Orie:

> Do not get back into the [shoe] business in a quiet way and see what you could do behind the scenes. . . . You should not do anything in the business without Albert knowing it. In fact, it would be my feeling, Dad, that you, especially at this point, should not try to do anything to help Albert. Either secretly or openly . . . do not try to help him. . . . It is not the help he needs.[51]

To leave this crisis entirely in God's hands meant that Orie had to resist his natural and almost overwhelming urge to intervene, to manage the crisis, and to solve the problem. Orie was a fixer. He was initiated in this role by his parents, and his apprenticeship in Beirut with Major Nichol in 1919–20 made Orie a master problem solver. But Albert's problem was one he could not solve.[52]

In May, Orie reported to John that Albert agreed to go to Reading Hospital for observation to get the help "Doctors Hess and Horst can give him." Albert had had "a full day of Sunday school and church work yesterday, but by evening was ready for this."[53] In July, Orie reported to John and Lois that Albert was home and sleeping well "without sedation." As for himself, Orie was delighting in his "work" and "deeply" appreciative of "the happy home life enabled us here."[54]

Orie and Albert's differences continued, though not on public display. They began moving in different spheres. Orie had a passion for business, but Albert did not. "Though Albert liked the business and did well in it, he didn't have a passion for it, so he left it." After the farm developments were finished, they no longer had common business interests that kept them engaged. At that point, Ed said, "I sense that Orie almost dismissed Albert from his life. That's a little harsh, and maybe to some extent, my Dad did the same thing. They certainly weren't close and they didn't share ideas or interests."[55]

Albert charted his own course, becoming a real estate broker, investing in the futures market, and working other jobs. Eventually, he gave away all his assets to avoid tax liability. He developed a conscience against paying war taxes. If it was wrong to participate in war, was it not inconsistent to finance the military industrial complex that conducted war? In this he was prophetic, leading the way to war tax resistance that later became more common. One can see Albert's conviction as a logical but unique version of Orie's lifelong peace advocacy.

ORIE MILLER AND HAROLD S. BENDER

"Our fathers were friends and colleagues in the work of the church, active in the church's reawakening."[56] Those words formed the prologue to Orie Miller's written tribute of Harold Bender after Bender died in September 1962. G. L. (George Lewis) Bender and D. D. (Daniel D.) Miller paved the way for Harold and Orie. Their standing and influence in the Mennonite Church gave their sons an entrée into the church and provided a protective "cover"—both decided advantages. Though Orie and Harold Bender ran their own race, their fathers gave them a jump start at the gate. Though they charted their own course, their fathers blazed the trail.

Both married into influential families. Elizabeth Horsch was the only daughter of the erudite German historian John Horsch, who introduced Bender to the scholarly world of Mennonite and Anabaptist history. Horsch's homeland gave Bender a natural link to European Mennonites. In marrying Elta Wolf, the only daughter of shoe manufacturer A. N. Wolf, Orie gained an entry in eastern Pennsylvania, where wealth and family counted. His marriage to Elta softened Lancaster County resistance to his status as an outsider and as a Goshen "liberal." The importance of familial links, by birth and by marriage, for both Bender and Miller can hardly be overestimated.

Orie identified Bender's gifts as proclamation and teaching. Bender's work in history and biblical studies "gave new, unparalleled, invaluable perspective and meaning to those in the Anabaptist heritage." Bender had given Mennonites and other heirs of Anabaptism a distinct identity and a usable history. After Bender's landmark *Anabaptist Vision*, given as an address in 1943 and published in 1944, Orie began using Anabaptism as the lens through which he viewed and promoted peace, service, and missions.[57] In his dual offices as executive of both MCC and EMM, Orie symbolized the union of peace and mission, word and deed, which he viewed as the genius of Anabaptism. In his spoken tribute to Bender at the memorial service on September 25, he said that during the time of their advocacy for peace since 1935, "the field . . . became the world, and Anabaptist biblical faith [became their] logic."[58] Orie added that Bender had pointed the way, but "it remained for others oft to supplement and implement as other gifts enabled."[59] Orie was thinking of additional work Bender had hoped to do, but also of his own role of implementing the ideas spawned by Bender's creative genius. He saw himself as "John Mark" ("without his lapses," he always said), the pragmatic administrator playing a supportive role to Bender as the "Apostle Paul."[60]

These roles also served as analogy for the occasional friction between the two. When Guy Hershberger sent Orie the proposed table of contents for the January 1964 Bender memorial issue of the *Mennonite Quarterly Review* and invited Orie's "critical evaluation," Orie immediately penciled his thoughts in the margins. Typically, Orie's jotted notes on letters received became main points in letters returned. In this case, Orie noted five points. Four of them became paragraphs in Orie's written tribute, but he wisely omitted the fifth: "Difficult as [the Apostle] Paul was."[61]

It would have been unusual had there been no conflicts between two such extraordinarily gifted leaders who worked together so closely for so long. Their personalities, gifts, and visions were, of course, dissimilar. Where Bender was outspoken and vigorous, Miller was reticent and controlled. In meetings, Bender spoke freely and forcefully; Miller listened long and spoke quietly. Bender exuded authority by force of personality; Miller spoke with quiet authority and dogged persistence. Bender was coercive; Miller was persuasive. Bender was impulsive; Miller was disciplined. Bender overreached; Miller calculated.

Bender was a master expositor and writer; Miller excelled in neither and readily acknowledged the fact. Bender was trained in history and theology; Miller appreciated both and deferred to Bender's expertise. Bender's office was organized chaos; Miller's desk was tidy and clean. Bender's tasks were ordered by urgency; Miller's, by methodical habit. Bender's income was sparse, and, as Al Keim, his biographer, noted, his spending was rarely within budget. Miller was wealthy, and counted dollars with the precision of an accountant.

Opposing visions caused the most substantial and enduring conflict. This difference was most apparent in MCC executive committee meetings during its post–World War II expansion. Chair C. N. Hostetter vented in his diary in 1954 that he was "annoyed" by the Bender-Miller "feud." Hostetter's conciliatory nature and his mediation skills enabled him to recognize the competing visions that sometimes interfered with the important work of the committee. Bender focused on Western Europe, the homeland of Anabaptism, and on European émigrés in South America. Postwar relief and reconstruction had been MCC's major focus since 1945. Bender believed MCC should continue to invest resources to help European Mennonites revitalize their congregations and reclaim their peace heritage, largely lost during the war. Bender's international travel had been largely restricted to Europe and South America, and his interactions were with Mennonites on both continents.

Orie's formative fifteen months in Beirut from 1919 to 1920 gave him a larger and more ecumenical worldview. His leadership in scouting and establishing a mission field in Africa for EMM in 1933 and 1934 had reinforced his global vision. Miller wanted to expand MCC's work beyond the preservation of traditional Mennonite communities. His vision for MCC, as for EMM, was to extend the Mennonite presence to the uttermost parts of the earth, as he often put it, in "total mission obedience."[62] MCC needed to be in Africa, Asia, and Latin America. On this issue, Miller's quiet, relentless persistence won the day. Bender preferred to keep MCC's activities within the MC household of faith.

They also differed on the role of Mennonite World Conference. Bender wanted MWC to have official status and authority to rule on matters of faith and practice. Miller believed such authority lay with congregations and conferences, and that MWC should be the means of fellowship and fraternal counsel.

MCC Chair Hostetter, ever the mediator, also addressed the personal issues. Hostetter's diary preserves a record of his conversation with Bender. "I . . . very frankly counselled [sic] him about his struggle for power with Orie Miller." Hostetter also reported to Bender the perceptions of "younger members of the committee," who shared Hostetter's interpretation of Bender's hostility toward Miller as a grab for power.[63]

Bender wrote to Hostetter two weeks later, saying there was "no feud between Orie Miller and myself," at least not on his part, nor would there be in the future. While it was true that the two were not as close as they had been—perhaps since Ernest Miller's removal from the president's office at Goshen College, and John W.'s expulsion from Goshen Biblical Seminary, it didn't mean they were hostile. Bender expected Hostetter to "correct" the opinions of the younger members of the committee, though it is not entirely clear how that could be effective, since their own observations had led to their conclusions. Inexplicably, Hostetter's diary reveals no information about his conversation with Orie Miller.[64]

When Edgar Stoesz began attending executive committee meetings in 1955, Hostetter told him that Orie and Harold "were like steel on steel. . . . They were correct, but they were not warm to each other." In Stoesz's retelling of the "feud," Orie came home from a trip to Europe and had

> a list of recommendations and he spun them out to the [MCC] executive committee on which Harold Bender served, and one after another Orie put them forward and Harold shot them down. And when the day was over, there was tension in the air and Orie's score was zero and Harold Bender had five or whatever. And so they came to the next meeting some months later and Orie had regrouped and he put forward basically the same material with the same result. . . . Hostetter said, "I made up my mind. If we come to the third meeting and it's the same, then I'm going to have to act as chairman." And so he came to the third meeting and sure enough, it was the same dynamic, Orie putting forward and Harold shooting down. That evening C. N. asked Harold to come to his room for a chat . . . and he said, "Harold, you are our number one scholar and your contribution to the church is second to none, but what's going on between you and Orie is not good. And this just has to change." Harold could hardly wait for him to finish speaking and he said, "But Orie's so wrong and somebody has to stand interference,

you know." He justified himself. The next morning, C. N. had a similar conversation with Orie: "Now, Orie, you are our number one Mennonite executive, but what's happening between you and Harold is not good." Orie accepted the admonition.[65]

When Bender was in treatment for cancer, Miller and Bender exchanged letters. The tone was collegial and warm. Miller hoped Bender could attend the 1962 MWC assembly in Kitchener, Ontario, and that God would enable Bender to finish projects he had started, so needed by the "church and the cause." Miller wrote that he had "deeply appreciated the friendship, and close church work relationship of these many years, and the bonds in Christ," for which he thanked God. His closing was a benediction: "May fullness, joy, and peace, and continued fruitfulness be your portion."[66]

In response, Bender wrote, "I was very happy to get your letter today with the assurance of prayers and concern." He was home from the hospital and was "in excellent shape" and was "gaining strength rapidly." Bender was receiving "daily cobalt treatment designed to destroy the tumor which was discovered on the pancreas." Referencing his working relationship with Miller, Bender too was "most grateful for the fellowship we have had over the years in the work of Christ and the church." He hoped by "God's grace that it . . . [could] continue for some time to come." Nevertheless, he was at peace whether he lived or died. He did expect to attend a part of the World Conference in Kitchener. Miller had signed his letter, "Sincerely, Orie O. Miller." Bender signed off, "Cordially, Harold S. Bender."[67]

At the September memorial service for Harold Bender, Miller recalled how in 1929, Bender had helped to manage the movement of Mennonites from the Soviet Union to Paraguay. Miller said he would "never forget" how Bender emerged as an articulate advocate of peace during the historic peace churches conference in Newton in the fall of 1935. Bender's succinct summary statement captured perfectly the sense of the conference. In 1937, Bender wrote the longer definitive MC statement on peace that was adopted in Turner, Oregon, and later used by others. That statement, Orie said, was "in large measure" still current.[68]

ORIE'S HUMILITY

Acknowledging his own contributions to the church was awkward for Orie. In 1962, J. Daniel Hess, then a journalism student at Syracuse University in New York, wrote a series of articles on Orie Miller for *Christian Living* magazine. He wrote that Miller's "gift left its mark on the church," and that Miller's words at age seventy were "like carefully prepared reports from a calculating machine." In similar fashion, "his life has been planned with deliberation."

That deliberation caused Hess some difficulty. After reading an early draft of the articles, Orie was "quite shocked at what I consented to, and of course agreed upon, and I hardly know how to respond. . . . I simply cannot release this material for publication." He thought it to be more an "exhibit than testimony." There was entirely too much reference to the word "Orie" and/or "Orie Miller." He was also surprised to see "the factual errors." He acknowledged that he was responsible for some of them."[69] Writer and subject met for another series of interviews. Drafts were exchanged until Orie was satisfied.

When Goshen artist Arthur Sprunger proposed making a "portrait sculpture," or bust, of Miller, Orie "hardly knew" what to say. Orie had heard that Sprunger had made a bust of "Friend Bender" and said he would "make special effort to see it." As for Sprunger's proposal, Orie responded, "In full appreciation of the invitation . . . and with encouragement too, to using your skill and gift creatively . . . I will appreciate your passing me for others."[70] Sprunger produced three busts of prominent Mennonites: Harold Bender, S. C. (Sanford Calvin) Yoder, and J. E. (John Ellsworth) Hartzler.[71]

The Mennonite Church commemorated Clayton Kratz, the young relief worker in South Russia who had been abducted by the Soviets, in the groundbreaking ceremony for a new dormitory at Goshen College on April 17, 1963. It was the second of a triad of dorms after Yoder Hall, named for Christian Z. Yoder, of Smithville, Ohio, and built in 1962. The Clayton Kratz Residence Hall for 132 men was funded by the Clayton Kratz Fellowship, an organization that promoted Kratz's spirit of sacrificial service among new generations of young Mennonites. Orie, the last North American to see Kratz before his disappearance in 1920, spoke on the "Life and Witness" of Kratz.[72] Three years later, in 1966, the Orie O. Miller Hall became the third in the cluster of dorms on the east side of campus. Its naming recognized Orie's long and dedicated service to Goshen College, his alma mater. Nowhere, it seems, did Orie mention this honor.

When Wilfred J. Unruh, executive secretary of the Board of Christian Service, asked Orie to spin out new ideas for the future, he said, "Brainstorms are probably not my lot anymore—and perhaps ought not be after three score and ten." Instead, Orie highlighted three current ministries that had barely begun. First, ministries such as MEDA were "bristling with challenge and opportunity." Subcommittees had recently been set up for Paraguay, Uruguay, and Congo, and Orie could "see no reason why MEDA should not expand into Argentina, India, and Japan." Second, MMA (Mennonite Mutual Aid), MII (Mennonite Indemnity, Inc.), and MCC had afforded "glimpses of frontier after frontier" still to occupy. Third, MMHS (Mennonite Mental Health Services), the bookstore in Addis Ababa, Ethiopia, and trading corporations in Belize and Honduras were examples of "capital structured with investment rather than charity funds." Further, 25 percent of EMM overseas missionaries would in ten years be "completely self-supporting."[73]

Paul E. Reed, editor of the Lancaster Conference *Youth Messenger*, asked Orie questions about his business career in preparation for a series of articles on Christian vocations. Orie reported on his work with Miller Hess, which in 1965 was employing nine hundred workers and daily shipped twelve thousand pairs of shoes for children and "growing girls." The company's goal was to maintain growth of 5–10 percent per year. This projected growth was the "norm for simplest, freest management—and for allowing flexibility to those engaged in responsibility for supplemental Church and community involvement." He said further that it was an "honorable business" that served "a basic human need." In addition, it had "built into it witness opportunity and challenge, and facets innumerable." Fifty years earlier, when Orie was preparing to enter the business, working in sales was on the edge of MC acceptability, not yet "honorable."[74]

Orie had once asked theologian J. C. Wenger whether there was such a thing as a patron saint for cobblers, makers of shoes. Wenger knew of none, but when a new dictionary of the Christian church was published in 1968, Wenger discovered that indeed there were two patron saints of cobblers and leatherworkers. He promptly reported to Orie by letter. They were named Crispin and Crispinian, who lived in Rome until Diocletian's crackdown on Christians. They fled to Saissons in Gaul where they made converts by day and shoes by night until they were tortured and beheaded, about AD 285. Wenger seemed to take this narrative at face value, though it is generally considered an "unreliable legend."[75]

When John Drescher, *Gospel Herald* editor, asked Orie to write a retrospective article on CPS in 1966, to mark the twenty-year anniversary of its end, Orie declined for two reasons. First, he was too involved in CPS to have an objective perspective, and second, because "I never could write well." Most of his written communication now consisted of dictating letters, he said.[76] When Ray Geigley asked for an article for *Youth Messenger* on "The Holy Spirit Speaking in the Twentieth Century," Orie wrote in return, "Really, my writing days (if they ever were worthwhile) are over. To do this well would take a combination of time, energy, prayer, and thought, which (although with a lessened schedule) I OUGHT not undertake."[77]

STILL IN EXPANSION MODE

As Orie's seventy-fifth birthday approached in 1965, Paul Kraybill passed on the "considerable concern" expressed by Earl Groff of the EMM executive committee that Orie's status be reviewed. Orie could still benefit EMM by consulting and advising, but he should not be so close as to be a detriment to "himself or the cause." Kraybill proposed four possible levels of membership and said the matter should be handled in an "unofficial meeting" of the executive committee.[78]

Throughout the 1960s, Orie made two or three overseas trips annually. In his letters and trip diaries, he did not hesitate to recommend program expansion, often suggesting places Paul Kraybill should visit. Nor did he hesitate to make changes on-site, whether or not it was his responsibility.

As a close friend to Paul Kraybill, Paul Landis "sweated with Kraybill so many times" after Orie "pulled one on him." Landis thought "Orie was sometimes wrong, . . . just a little too controlling."[79] In August 1968, Kraybill wrote yet one more confidential memo to EMM president H. Raymond Charles about his increasing concern about Orie. The issues included "pushing" Wilbert Lind, part-time pastor at Ephrata Mennonite Church, to increase his time in Haiti; therefore, he was "speaking of course, for both the Ephrata and Salunga [EMM]!" He was also

Orie (*left*) and Paul Kraybill, March 1967. EMM.

"pressing" Donald Sensenig not to return to the United States as planned for Evangelism Institutes. Kraybill was concerned about a confusing "pattern of direct relationship" with people directly responsible to him. A second concern was the diversion of Lancaster Conference funds for projects such as MEDA and Menno Housing, a low-income housing project in the City of Lancaster. This problem of leadership, Kraybill complained, was reaching a "crisis point."[80]

Kraybill had not yet received Orie's August 2 letter that added to Kraybill's concerns. In the letter, Orie asked EMM to take up the problem of establishing a mission in Korea. MCC was closing out its vocational school and Orie believed establishing a church there was imperative. Orie would "deeply appreciate" this being placed on EMM's agenda, "for which reason I have taken the liberty to send copies" to other members of the executive committee. "If in doing this you feel I have been too inconsiderate or too bold or senseless, please forgive."[81] Orie's proposal, Kraybill wrote, "would be less than realistic."[82]

Orie was still in expansion mode. He saw needs and possibilities everywhere and could hardly fathom withholding resources to meet obvious needs—internationally and locally. He said, "I've traveled around the world, I've never done anything locally." That changed when he became a participant in the establishment of Menno Housing and Tabor Community Services. Because of the need for low-income housing, local leaders in 1967 initiated Menno Housing to meet the need. Paul Leatherman, who had been a shoe salesman and director of Vietnam Christian Service, was asked to direct Menno Housing. Stockholders bought shares as investment, but it was primarily a ministry to the poor. As director, Leatherman bought, remodeled, and rented houses. "Buying thirteen houses for something like $89,000 . . . really put us on the map," he recalled. When he left the project, Menno Housing owned about twenty-eight homes.[83]

During his service with Menno Housing, Leatherman helped organize Tabor Community Services, an agency that was quite successful. As a nonprofit agency, it could receive government funding for Menno Housing. Tabor also offered financial counseling. Eventually, Menno Housing declined and closed, but Tabor Community Services continued.

Paul Leatherman was also involved in the formation of Menno Travel Service in 1947. While he was serving in the MCC unit in Puerto Rico, he was responsible for arranging the travel of volunteers to and from the island. First it was by passenger boat or freighter and then by air when American and United Airlines added Puerto Rico to their schedules. He discovered that as an agent he could save 5 percent for MCC. When Leatherman suggested organizing a travel agency, Orie's response was, "No, you can't do that because you are a VSer and you can't get involved in that." As Leatherman recalls it, Orie "went back home and started Menno Travel Service."

Leatherman reflected, "Orie was a big man in the church who I respected. . . . I was proud to know him and was glad to work with him. He got a lot done, but he didn't mind taking someone else's ideas and putting them to practice." He could also "manipulate people, move them around" to get things done. "He was genuinely interested in people" and cared about their welfare, but he "had a plan for the way it should happen, and it had to all go according to his plan."[84]

Not everything could be planned and orchestrated. The division of Lancaster Conference and the formation of the Eastern Pennsylvania Mennonite Church in 1968 was one such case. After a decade of growing differences among leaders of Lancaster Conference, some separated from the conference by "mutual agreement." Leaders of the new group had been unhappy about a general trend of Lancaster Conference toward change in practice and teaching. Among the issues were divorce and remarriage, use of radio and television, organized sports, and relaxed dress requirements.

During the time these differences were becoming more apparent, Orie received a jolt. At a joint meeting of the EMM board and the Board of Bishops, the conservative wing offered a motion requesting "our secretary to refrain from wearing a worldly long tie." Paul Landis remembered that Orie's "head just dropped, he put his hands on his head on the table and just sobbed, never defended himself, didn't say anything, he just sat there and sobbed." Landis was furious that a man he so loved and respected "could be treated like a naughty little boy." Orie had explained to Paul that his necktie was a symbol of business and of his membership in the broader Mennonite Church. "I wear this because it's a symbol, but I wear my plain suit because I want to be loyal to the Lancaster Conference."[85] Orie never wore his necktie again to meetings of the EMM board.

ORIE'S SEVENTY-FIFTH BIRTHDAY

Orie spent his seventy-fifth birthday at the Wailing Wall in Jerusalem. It was just after Israel repelled the Jordanians in the Six-Day War. Orie had a strong need "to see Israel in the aftermath of that war and see how this was going to change the geopolitical situation." As a result of the war, the Wailing Wall was opened to the public. In the company of Bill Snyder and Wilbert Shenk, Orie traveled to Jerusalem. Shenk recalled, "We were concerned about him because, here he was, seventy-five, and we had to walk quite a ways in the hot sun to get to that wall. But he was so determined; he *had* to get to that wall." Though the basis for his emotional attachment to Israel was not clear to Shenk or Snyder, on July 7, 1967, it was a historic place to mark his birthday.[86]

Despite the occasional difficulties, both EMM and MCC celebrated Orie's long years of service on his seventy-fifth birthday. He had now worked in associate roles for a decade. MCC sponsored a dinner in his honor after the annual meetings in Chicago on January 19–20, 1968. Colleagues and protégés recalled his effective service and wide influence. C. A. DeFehr of Winnipeg, Manitoba, an MCC member with roots in Russia, said, Orie's "name is engraved in the memory of our people in Russia, North and South America, and Europe" because he "personally

Orie's successor, Bill Snyder (*left*), recognizes Orie's long service to MCC, 1968. MCC.

came to Russia fifty years ago" to relieve their suffering.[87]

Robert Kreider, vice chair of MCC and secretary of the Mennonite World Conference executive committee, recalled Orie's counsel: When called to serve the church, the answer should be affirmative unless there was a valid reason for declining. "Scarcely a month goes by," he said, without remembering "what he said to me then." Chris Graber humorously called attention to Orie's habit of using "cryptic language" in his speech, but in writing letters approximating the linguistic complexity of the apostle Paul. Bill Snyder presented a certificate of appreciation recognizing Orie's "inspired leadership and devoted service to Christ and the churches of our constituency in a worldwide ministry."[88]

EMM honored Orie's forty-four years of service with a "fellowship dinner" at the Willow Valley Restaurant in Willow Street, Pennsylvania, on March 25, 1968. His various roles and years of service were recognized: *Missionary Messenger* editor, 1924–32; vice president, 1925–35; secretary, 1935–58; member of the executive committee (and associate secretary), 1958–68. The tribute given by Ira J. Buckwalter, long-serving treasurer, was especially fitting: "The greatest things in the world have been done by those who systematized their work and organized their time." Speaking of Orie's ability to see things that needed to be done, he said further, "At seventy-five he still has more visions than most of us can keep up with." His greatness was not because he "aspired" to it, but "because he has lived well the role of a servant."[89]

Elam Stauffer, who accompanied Orie to Africa in 1933, recalled Orie's counsel on board the SS *Bremen*: "We will be traveling together for many days; you will have to learn to put up with me." He also remembered Orie's response to the crisis caused by the directive of the home office to require Tanzanians to enforce Lancaster Conference discipline regarding plain-dress standards: "Now put the document in the file and get on with the job." When the East African revival broke out, causing dissension, Orie did not scold but "quietly read Moffatt's translation" of the love chapter, 1 Corinthians 13.[90]

True to form, Orie's speech, "Forty Years in Retrospect," was supplemented by "Prospect," a look into the future. He had learned early in life that further revelation of God's will comes by obedience to what is already known. He had learned to love and respect the "Mennonite Brotherhood as a living part of Christ's body, despite its failures and shortcomings." Describing himself as a "great reader," he had early determined to balance his reading regimen by reading the Bible through each year, which he had now done for forty years. Since it was impractical to carry commentaries, he habitually carried two translations of the Bible. The future would surely be marked by "wars and rumors of war," abounding sin, misuse of freedom, and waste of resources, but the reality of discipleship, the cross, freedom, and spiritual fruit would remain constant. Among the Scriptures he had "hid in his heart" and that he most often used were the words of Jesus: "Lift up your eyes, and look on the fields . . . ready to harvest [but] the laborers are few."[91]

Among the contributions to a bound book of memories was a note from a former missionary who recalled Orie's "disturbing" visits, knowing he was analyzing the work of the past five years and outlining his high expectations for the coming five years. Another referenced his writing style: "In your quiet walk with God you are like the Apostle John but your long sentences are like the Apostle Paul." Another missionary recalled a difficult crossing with a car on a pontoon. Orie's assessment: "I have never before been in such a place where my college education did so little good." The EMM staff gave Orie the gift of a wooden plate, turned on a lathe, using wood from "one of the old Salunga benches on which Orie often sat" for meetings.[92]

In 1969, Paul Erb wrote a biography, published by Herald Press, titled *Orie O. Miller: The Story of a Man and an Era.* Erb, *Gospel Herald* editor since 1944, was Orie's friend and colleague. When the biography was proposed, Orie was reluctant. Then he relented on the condition that it be published after his death. Was it not dangerous, Orie joked, to publish a biography of a living person? What if after publication the subject "robbed a bank" and spoiled the story? Eventually, Orie relented

Celebrating forty-four years at EMM (*from left*: Elta, Orie, Paul Kraybill). EMM.

and permitted publication after he reached age seventy-five. The biography had been proposed both by Bill Snyder at MCC and Paul Kraybill at EMM, and given enthusiastic support by Ben Cutrell, publisher at Mennonite Publishing House.

Erb and Miller signed the publishing contract on March 7, 1967. In case disagreements between author and subject reached an impasse, an arbitration committee was named: William T. Snyder, Paul N. Kraybill, and Ellrose D. Zook, publishing house managing editor.[93] As a friend of Miller, Erb acknowledged the book's lack of objectivity. Erb was well-acquainted with the era, having lived much of it himself. It would be, he said, an "instant" biography without the benefit of the perspective of distance and time. But it made the story of Orie's life and ministry accessible to readers. Perhaps most outstanding is the chapter on Orie's personal habits and his language use, sometimes cryptic and at other times complex.

Chapter 12
Accumulating Years: 1970–1977

"After about 85 years of age, there should be no excuse for anyone having an estate. . . . I believe that time spent accumulating wealth beyond the family's year-to-year needs also wastes time."

In 1970, Orie Miller turned seventy-eight. He had seven more years of life left, and the last five were complicated by Parkinson's disease. He remained active as long as he could, managing various family partnerships, developing the Wolf farms on the outskirts of Akron that had been inherited by Elta Wolf Miller, traveling for MEDA, vacationing in Jamaica, and attending MCC and EMM executive committee meetings—which, he told a friend in India, occupied twenty-seven days a year.

The volatility of the 1960s continued into the seventies. At Kent State University, National Guardsmen opened fire on students protesting the escalation of the Vietnam War into Cambodia. Four students died and nine were wounded. While students protested, Orie wept. The *New York Times* published the Pentagon Papers, "top secret" Defense Department documents revealing that four presidents had misled the public and Congress about the Vietnam War. The U.S. population passed 200 million, and *Roe v. Wade* legalized abortions. A Palestinian terrorist group, Black September, attacked Israeli athletes at the 1972 Olympic Games in Munich, Germany.

In Washington, DC, the Watergate scandal erupted. Congress held impeachment hearings against president Richard M. Nixon, causing him to resign. The United States pulled out of Vietnam; South Vietnam was defeated and joined North Vietnam to become the Socialist Republic of Vietnam, opening new service and mission possibilities. Haile Selassie, longtime emperor of Ethiopia and a friend to Mennonites, was deposed by the army. In 1977, the year of Orie's death, president Jimmy Carter pardoned ten thousand draft evaders, South African antiapartheid leader Stephen Biko was tortured to death, and there was a movement toward an international agreement regarding what would become a nuclear non-proliferation act.

PREDICTIONS AND REFLECTIONS

After the 1969 publication of Paul Erb's biography, *Orie O. Miller: The Story of a Man and an Era*, Erb and Miller received notes of congratulations, more stories, and questions. Having read of Orie's past, Mrs. Ralph Mumaw of Smithville, Ohio, wanted to know Orie's prediction for the future. Orie had just returned from an overseas trip where he observed "Brotherhood growth trends" in Asia, Africa, and Latin America. Based on the previous decade's growth, he projected the doubling of Mennonite and Brethren in Christ membership in a decade. By 1980, North American Mennonites and Brethren in Christ would become a minority in the worldwide Anabaptist church.[1]

North American trends were less clear. The church's "tie-up in politics and state and society" made a "pretense of prediction" more difficult. Orie hoped the United States could avoid additional "Vietnams," but was not optimistic. He hoped the North American church, which should enjoy relative affluence, would continue to share its resources around the globe. He was encouraged by the "scatteredness" of Mennonites and Brethren in Christ "throughout the world." In 1970, there were 700 MCC workers, averaging twenty-six and a half years of age, serving in thirty countries. In addition, an estimated 1,500 more were serving under various mission boards in fifty countries. This was a "tremendous" improvement over fifty years ago. Orie could see the worldwide ministries doubling around the world, with the "stronger Brotherhood churches overseas" becoming involved in ministry around the world.[2]

C. F. Yake, fellow officer of MBE and longtime editor of *Youth's Christian Companion,* wrote to congratulate Orie as the "Mennonite of the Century." Since Erb must have thought Yake's office was "too far" away to interview him for the book—both had offices in the same building—he was taking the liberty of recalling "shared experiences." Yake first met Orie at 111 North Cedar Street, Lititz, the home of Martha Eby, whom Yake married. It was a festive social occasion to honor Yake's twenty-eighth birthday. From that point on, they met socially with "the bunch," a Lancaster-based friendship group.[3]

Yake remembered the Young People's Institutes at Arbutus Park, 1936–43, planned by the Young People's Problems Committee, which Orie chaired, and their involvement in the 1944 purchase of Laurelville Camp in Mount Pleasant, Pennsylvania. "The fellowship during these years was an ennobling one," he recalled, "as we labored together in a conservative progressive program . . . for our young people." Finally, Yake recalled that Orie had nominated him for the office of secretary of MBE. Yake had felt God's "unusual guidance" while serving in this role from 1939 to 1949.[4]

Orie was shaken when on April 30, 1970, U.S. president Richard Nixon announced the invasion of Cambodia, an attempt to cut off North Vietnamese supply lines to troops in the south. After endless promises to de-escalate the war, the announcement shocked and angered many. Outraged students protested. At Kent State University, national guardsmen shot and killed four students, and wounded nine more.

Hershey Leaman recalled Orie's reaction the next day. When Orie arrived at the EMM executive committee meeting, "he could hardly function. He was . . . so very distraught!"[5] Orie had witnessed the terrible destruction of two world wars, the Korean War, and now the Vietnam War. Nixon's "highly militant" administration was wasting more resources in its destruction of still more of God's creation—people and their homelands. It was unthinkable. Yet, a year later the war spread to neighboring Laos.

FINANCIAL DECISIONS

Akron's population was growing, causing a housing shortage. Seeing an opportunity, Orie and his sons decided to develop two farms that were part of Elta Wolf Miller's estate. The farms, of sixty-seven and seventy-nine acres, respectively, were on the western outskirts of Akron, one up the hill from the railroad and one below the tracks. The farms had been part of a larger Wolf tract of thirteen hundred acres.[6] On December 31, 1958, the property was transferred to the five Miller children.[7]

A. N. Wolf had employed Walter Ridenour, a hardworking tobacco farmer, to manage both farms. Ridenour raised a variety of crops and livestock, but tobacco was his specialty and the best cash crop. When Elta inherited the farms, "tobacco was out," so Orie switched to chickens and potatoes. But what "tickled" Elta's cousin Arthur Wolf was that Orie didn't mind taking the Wolf inheritance that was built with tobacco. Raising tobacco was "always wrong," but Orie "took the tobacco money alright!"[8]

Now the Millers decided to sell nearly thirty-seven acres of the lower farm for $2,500 per acre to the Weber-Miller partnership, formed to create the new Westview development. This sale illustrated the dizzying array of debits and credits that characterized transactions in this era. The sale of lots was to provide payments of $200 a month to each of Orie and Elta's children. This left fifty acres of the upper farm for development, plus the farmhouse property. Against Orie's personal debt to the estate of $25,000, he was adding to Albert's and Lois's distribution accounts thirty-two shares of Miller Hess stock. He would credit the personal accounts of John, Bob, and Dan each in the amount of $5,120, to be charged against Orie's estate account.[9]

Orie had formed the Weber-Miller partnership with brothers John and Elvin Weber in 1969. The young Weber brothers were doing well in the construction business but had not yet developed a strong financial history. So Miller provided a line of credit at Fulton Bank in Akron. Orie turned the project over to the Webers and "didn't meddle," John Weber recalled. Orie had told them, "You've been successful in what you're doing; you pick up the ball and go."[10] The Webers built the Westview and Colonial Heights developments, with 125 houses in Westview and about 300 houses and apartments in Colonial Heights. Two street signs recall the previous owners of the land: Wolf Street in Westview, and Miller Street in Colonial Heights.[11]

Miller and the Webers signed no formal agreement to specify the division of profits. During the first year or two, Orie wanted to see the books. For the first few houses, Orie would say, "Give me $400 for my contribution." Beyond that "he never asked for any money as his part of the partnership." His mission was to get the farms developed. The Weber brothers learned Orie's economics philosophy: "It's okay to make money, but you don't want to die a rich man. That was Orie."[12] He had inherited that philosophy from his father, D. D. Miller.

A separate partnership was formed to develop Heritage Village Condominiums on Elta's farms, the region's first multifamily townhouses. Two structures contained ten apartment units, and were located on the southeast corner of Fulton Street and Rothsville Road. They were marketed as "a world of serene, gracious living." Albert Miller was the managing partner, with an office at 1115 Main Street, the home Orie and Elta built in 1936. Additional partners were the Weber brothers, Phares B. Rutt, Orie, and two of the children, Lois and Robert.[13]

THE DREAM OF THE PALM RIDGE RETREAT

Orie formed another partnership in 1971 to purchase a retreat far away from ordinary routines and Pennsylvania winters. But even so, he had bigger plans for Palm Ridge Retreat, the "beauty spot of Jamaica." Orie and J. Elvin Martin, Elta Sensenig Miller's son-in-law, explored the possibilities for the property, though Martin did not know what Orie had in mind. The Melba and Willard Heatwole family had lived on the property for twenty years as self-supporting missionaries and put the property up for sale when they decided to take their five children to better schools in Virginia. Orie dreamed of creating a Bible school and conference center for Caribbean and Central American pastors. Parkinson's disease, however, ended that dream and instead it became a vacation destination.[14]

On July 1, 1971, Miller and five partners took possession of Palm Ridge, located four miles east of Ocho Rios. The partnership consisted of the Weber brothers of Ephrata; J. Elvin Martin of Akron; Milo Shantz of St. Jacobs, Ontario; Glen Zeager of Elizabethtown; and Orie. The facilities accommodated eight couples, but the partners expanded the facilities for larger groups.[15] Orie told friends that the retreat was located about half a mile from "a good sized Mennonite Church," six miles from another Mennonite congregation and five miles from the airport, with daily service to major U.S. cities, including Philadelphia and New York.[16]

That first year, Orie and Elta planned to spend November and December, and then another three weeks in February at Palm Ridge. If they found the facilities agreeable, they would regularly make it their winter home. Elta's family spent the 1971 Christmas holidays at the retreat. Since Elta's two grandchildren had recently "accepted Christ" and joined the Ephrata congregation, Orie told a friend that he wanted to expose them to "other cultures, extreme poverty," and to the church in mission. All of this could be done "most inexpensively in time and money" in Jamaica.[17]

Orie's sister Alice Oesch was the first manager and housekeeper for Palm Ridge, from January until June 1972. Later, the partners arranged for a local manager to care for the property and provide transportation to and from the airports at Montego Bay or Kingston. In 1973, the manager was Mennonite deacon Eric Robinson. If visitors wanted the use of a vehicle, a Volkswagen van was available for eleven cents a mile, as Orie told his brother Samuel.[18] In January 1973, Orie extended the invitation to his siblings to come to Palm Ridge and freely invited others. For example, in a letter of sympathy to Ray Yoder of Kalona, Iowa, after the death of Yoder's wife, Katherine, Orie welcomed Yoder to come to Palm Ridge and stay as long as he wished.[19]

In a few years, talk of a communist government in Jamaica created uncertainty and devalued properties. The Palm Ridge partners, fearing greater losses, sold their shares to Milo Shantz at bargain prices. Not long after that, stability returned and land values soared. As he was known to do, Shantz profited from another good investment.[20]

THE MOVE TO LANDIS HOMES

Orie soon needed a retreat of a different kind. On April 1, 1972, Orie and Elta moved to a cottage at Landis Homes Retirement Community in rural Lititz, Pennsylvania. Somewhere on his around-the-world tour for MEDA in February and March 1969, Orie had a "slight stroke" that left him with a temporary speech impediment. In 1970, he returned from another eight-week, around-the-world MEDA mission feeling more tired than usual. Elta also noticed his "lips twitching" and urged him to see a doctor. Dr. William G. Ridgway of Akron thought it must have been another slight stroke and referred him to a specialist.

Dr. Arguire confirmed the diagnosis and "urged" hospitalization in order to prevent more serious strokes. After six days of observation at Lancaster General Hospital, Orie was released without restrictions[21]— except, as he told Menno Schrag of the *Mennonite Weekly Review*, he was to "remember your age and listen to your wife." He added, "Wife Elta smiles at this but I do try to listen, and am completely happy in life's relationship in Christ."[22] Elta did not smile, however, when Orie showed her plans for a cottage at Landis Homes and announced, "We are going here now and this spot right here is where we will live."[23]

In the summer of 1971, Orie's leg coordination, speech, and eyesight began to deteriorate. Dr. Arguire diagnosed the condition as Parkinson's disease. His failing eyesight was a different problem, due to "lens deficiency." The specialist developed a new medication formula and watched carefully for side effects. And Orie cancelled plans to travel to India.

At the end of 1971, he was holding his own "or a little better." He wrote his friend M. R. Zigler that he was "rapidly liquidating the responsibilities and things that hold me at one spot." As a postscript, Orie added Revelation 21:5, which refers to John the apostle's vision of God "making all things new." He concluded with a characteristic note of optimism: "Wonderful prospects ahead."[24]

By the spring of 1972, Orie had fewer responsibilities, but he still had a routine. As always, following a prescribed schedule simplified life and increased his efficiency. At 10:00 a.m., Elta took Orie to Akron where he spent the morning at Miller Hess. Albert took Orie to lunch where they discussed property development, and then Orie spent an hour at the MCC offices. At about 2:30 or 3:00 p.m., Elta picked him up and took him back to the cottage at Landis Homes. It was "a short working day, and just right for me."[25] In June, Orie gave up driving a car on doctor's orders and dutifully relinquished his operator's license to the Bureau of Motor Vehicles.[26]

Orie was still contributing to charitable causes, a lifelong practice, but his capacity to give had diminished. He was no longer able to give 30 percent of his income, which had been his practice. He wrote to those who were asking for money and explained that his financial resources were shrinking, so he could no longer contribute to all who asked. Ever hopeful, he retained fundraising letters until the end of the year, thinking there might be some money left that he could give. It is impossible to track all of Orie's financial contributions, given the multiple channels for giving. He offered to finance the education of numerous young persons with leadership potential, including Paul Landis and Richard Detweiler. Landis was unable to break free of responsibilities, but Detweiler accepted Orie's offer and eventually earned a doctorate.

In October and November of 1972, Orie had exchanges with John Howard Yoder about funding for a special project. John A. Lapp, Goshen College dean, had proposed a J. A. Schowalter Endowed Chair in Peace Studies at the Associated Mennonite Biblical Seminaries in Elkhart, Indiana. Yoder, from his seminary post, asked Miller about funding. Orie responded, saying the Schowalter Foundation did not have enough money available to fund the proposal, but he commented on Yoder's recent book, *The Original Revolution*, which Orie had read. The book "fits perfectly" the need for peace education among our "newer international brotherhood." More such resources would be useful, but "maybe on a bit lower intellectual level."[27]

Miller added that Yoder was among such "God-called folks" as John Horsch, Harold Bender, and Guy Hershberger. Other than Hershberger, they had not received financial support for "what they couldn't help doing." Hershberger received "gladly appropriated" funds for his writing on peace themes from the PPC. Miller wished for a church-sponsored prophet who could contribute to the cause of peace, as did Horsch and Bender. Miller was confident that Yoder was in the best position to judge the veracity of such speculation.[28]

Orie had not given up on his dream of establishing a school of missions. In 1969, he led in establishing the Mennonite Christian Leadership Foundation to help finance the training of missionaries. When Don Jacobs returned from Tanzania in 1973, Orie laid out his dream for a school of missions at New York Theological Seminary. He saw Jacobs as the ideal leader for this venture, and went so far as to rent space at the seminary. He believed the foundation could serve the dual function of financing the training of missionaries and "resuscitating" the struggling New York Theological Seminary, which he had served as a board member and board chair. The seminary, however, turned its efforts to toward urban ministries and Orie's dream died.[29]

Orie continued his long-established correspondence routine. MCC was still supplying a secretary to transcribe his Dictaphone tapes. At the end of 1973, Marge Ruth was assigned to Orie, replacing Janet Landis. Orie said that Marge Ruth "was very good," but she was having trouble understanding his Dictaphone tapes. In the 1960s, when stenographers had no longer been available, Urbane Peachey, MCC personnel director, encouraged Orie to switch to a Dictaphone, showing him how to use the machine. As Peachey recalled, Orie "really squirmed about that for a couple of weeks." Finally, with a typical, winsome, gracious smile, Orie reasoned, "Well, I'm not sure about the age, but I've learned how to fly in a jet airplane after sixty-five and so I guess I can learn how to use a Dictaphone." Peachey felt a sense of satisfaction in introducing "this highly esteemed figure" to new technology.[30]

Orie wrote to friends and former colleagues on such special occasions as a wedding anniversary or the death of a spouse. He sent condolences to S. C. Yoder after the death of "Sister (Emma Stutzman) Yoder" in 1972. The letter was heavily seasoned with biblical references.[31] Orie congratulated Henry A. and Ethel Fast for fifty years of marriage in 1973. As he often did in such letters, Orie reminisced about his forty-two years of marriage with "the former Elta." He remembered with appreciation Fast's work with Mennonite Mental Health Services and Voluntary Service. The success of those programs, Orie wrote, was due to "mostly you." When Elmer Ediger's wife died, Orie wrote, "We wish for you all the comfort spoken of in II Corinthians 1:3-4, John 14, John 11:25." In addition, "one especially precious" text was Revelation 21:5: "Behold, I make all things new." He said he and the new Elta were living at Landis Homes where everything was, indeed, new.[32]

Of all his correspondents, Orie wrote most often to M. Robert (Bob) Zigler, his Church of the Brethren counterpart on the NSBRO and CPS. Their correspondence was warm and collegial. Since that first association, their contacts had been "constant and frequent, and the personal friendship had steadily grown and deepened." During their work together, Orie recalled the "thrill of dreaming and praying together" as their own peace convictions grew stronger. That was when they first sensed that the "Field is the World" for peace education as well as for missions. When they met as families, their time was enriched because their spouses shared their "total discipleship concept." The loss of both their spouses had "ripened and deepened the friendship further." Orie looked forward to sharing more dreams and to their deepening friendship.[33]

Zigler recalled the time when "My dear Orie Miller" stopped to visit him in Vastervik, Sweden, after the death of Bob's wife, Amy. Zigler had been in "severe agony of body, mind, and soul," and Orie's visit "was like something from heaven, a gift of supreme meaning." The friendship forged in their collaboration through the years was "richer than anything I have ever read outside of Sacred Literature." Zigler wondered whether their successors, Bill Snyder at MCC and Harold Rowe at Brethren Service Commission, felt as close as he and Orie did. Probably not, he concluded, since Snyder and Rowe had not been "pushed as hard as we were."[34]

Zigler also recalled with pleasure Orie's "Biblical Remembrances" given at the May 25, 1968, dedication of the new M. R. Zigler Hall," in New Windsor, Maryland. The new Brethren Service Center named for Zigler was also to serve Church World Service, Lutheran World Service, and Inter-Church Medical Assistance.[35]

Paul Erb wrote early in 1975 to express his sympathies on the death of Orie's brother Ernest. When Ernest was in India, Orie's letters had been Ernest's lifeline to the North American Mennonite world. When Ernest returned to the United States, Orie "did him a real favor and the church too, as I now see it, when you brought him into the stream of church life as president of Goshen College." Erb commented on the recent MCC annual meeting in Winnipeg, the first such meeting Orie had missed. It was good to see, Erb said, "how well you laid the foundations" for the church's many ministries that were now continuing "in line with" and perhaps even "beyond your dreams." Orie may be physically limited, but his earlier work "still blesses our church, and through it, the world."[36]

"Yes," Orie wrote, he had given "Ernest his expenses at New York University and got him his degree." Orie went to Ernest's funeral in Elkhart even though "families on both sides objected." Erb wrote again, saying he was "not surprised" that Orie had assisted Ernest. It was an example of Orie's "kindness . . . to countless others." Erb could see that Orie, "as an inveterate reader," would find his poor eyesight a severe handicap.[37]

Not all of Orie's thinking was of past events. In a 1974 letter to nine-year-old Rochelle Zimmerman, Orie expressed a rare burst of warmth. Rochelle had reminded Orie the previous Sunday at the Ephrata church that they shared a birthday that day, July 7. "What a thrill!" Orie gushed. He was seventy-three years old when Rochelle was born in 1965. "Long after I am gone some young person may come to you and then you too will know how it feels to be remembered thus." Saying he hoped Rochelle had had a "happy day," he offered a blessing for her future. He hoped she would "develop further your gift and love of singing, and do much good

Orie and Elta attending the dedication of the Goodville facilities, May 11, 1974. Elvin and Laverne Martin.

and have much happiness, give to others through the use of your gift, and use the memory to make others happy too."[38] Orie often asked parents about their children and he typically recognized children, but his formal demeanor made him appear less approachable.

As long as he was able, Orie continued his lifelong practice of reading widely. Having read *My Search for an Anchor* by fellow Landis Homes resident Ira Franck, Orie responded: "I had less trouble finding my anchor than you did." While he expected to see in heaven "all kinds of folks" and knowing he might be surprised by "who is there and who is not," Orie had found his anchor "right in Mennonitism or Anabaptism." Then he quoted E. Stanley Jones, who had said "he expected to see in heaven about the same proportion of Methodists as of other folks." Orie figured the same would be true of Mennonites.[39]

With his eyesight failing, Orie depended on Elta and sons Albert and Bob to read to him, and began using cassette tapes after receiving a Weaver cassette player for his eighty-second birthday. Since technology was not his strength and cassettes were new to him, he told bishop Howard Witmer that he would have to "experiment a bit to get the most out of" the cassettes. He sent Witmer a list of cassettes he would like to borrow, and he wrote to J. Otis Yoder asking to rent tapes from Yoder's conservative *Heralds of Hope* radio station at Breezewood, Pennsylvania.[40]

In November 1974, Orie wrote to his family physician, William Ridgway. Marge Ruth, Orie's secretary, was concerned about his worsening Parkinson's disease and had photocopied one of his barely legible scrawlings as evidence of his deteriorating condition. Orie asked Ridgway whether he should give "sesame and sunflower seeds a trial." Ridgway's response: "Most likely [that remedy] appeared in something that Shakespeare wrote, going something like, 'Nothing is neither good nor bad, but thinking makes it so.'" He knew of no medical evidence for the effectiveness of such treatment, but there would be no harm in trying. "It certainly would be as effective as any medicine that I have used for you lately," he admitted.[41]

Typically, Orie's letters made reference to his physical condition. "I am not well," he wrote to Rev. Caleb D. Bella in Kotagiri, South India. He had Parkinson's disease, which was "Palsy in the Bible." It was "not yet curable but [was] controllable." He told Bella that as a "life member" of both MCC and EMM, he was "still busy." He reported that MCC had committed seven million dollars to the "food crisis" in Ethiopia and southern Sudan. He was also keeping in touch with the Mennonite Disaster Service project in Nicaragua after a recent earthquake. Orie enclosed a "good book" he had recently read: Marlin Jeschke's *Discipling the Brother: Congregational Discipline according to the Gospel*, published by Herald Press in 1972.[42]

In December 1974, Bob Miller wrote to his siblings with concerns about Orie's finances. Orie needed to build up a cash reserve for such things as car replacement, infirmary care at Landis Homes if needed, and higher medical costs. He also needed cash for the Heritage Estates project. Because of high development costs and slow lot sales, the partnership had almost no cash and a payment of $17,383 was due to the Elta Miller Estate Partnership. The other three partners had agreed to make personal payments of $4,590 toward the total. Orie would need to borrow that amount to make his share of the payment. In addition to cash reserves for personal items and healthcare, Orie should also build up a cash reserve for the further development of Heritage Estates.[43]

Parkinson's disease was taking a toll on Orie's ability to manage his personal finances, and his checks were increasingly illegible. Bob proposed that he and one or two siblings, along with Elta, handle the finances. They should also reduce Orie's charitable giving to 10 percent until cash reserves were built up. In addition, he could not afford to pay the $1,000 pledge to Mennonite Christian Leadership Foundation.[44]

Orie was losing vision, but he still had visions. He was now thinking of how to make use of people who were over eighty years of age, Orie reported to Atlee Beechy, MCC executive committee member. Orie asked for a copy of Beechy's February 24, 1975, letter, which he had lost in moving from the cottage to the infirmary at Landis Homes. In the letter, Beechy had affirmed Orie's life work and expressed his gratitude for Orie's ability to "place confidence in youthful and untried leadership" as himself.[45] Orie wanted a copy because it had been "unusual in the nice words it used and one doesn't get too many of those."[46]

Orie appreciated Beechy too. He had long admired Atlee's "Anabaptist peacemaking" nature and ways. When they needed a peacemaker for an MCC project, Orie would often say, "Get Atlee to do it." He added that the move to the infirmary with its "better care" and "stricter discipline" was good. Finally, with improbable optimism, he assured Beechy that he "was on the mend" and that he was sure he would see him again.[47]

While such affirmation was surely good to hear, it didn't mean Orie was resting on his laurels. He had a complaint: Mennonites still find people sixty-five to eighty years old useful in the church, but they "leave us out of planning, meetings, and kindred things." He wrote to George Lehman, Landis Homes director, to tell him they should form an "above 80s club." As Orie saw it, life could be divided into four parts: an era for learning, from ages one to twenty-five; an era to contribute one's gifts, from twenty-six to sixty-five; a period of reducing one's responsibilities, from sixty-six to eighty; and finally, those above eighty should be valued as consultants.[48] To Paul Erb, he said he would like to talk to him about an Anabaptist concept of making use of the gifts of those above eighty rather than following the "world's ideas on this."[49]

"THE GREAT DECLINE IN THE IMPERISHABLE ORIE MILLER"

During a March 1975 visit from Ira J. Buckwalter, EMM treasurer, Orie told him that he had been "too weak" to attend the recent executive committee meeting but was looking for the minutes. He thanked Buckwalter for visiting. He was grateful also for the visits of Norman Shenk, Nathan Hege, Mahlon Hess, and Raymond Charles. He assured Buckwalter that he was "improving," but would not be able to attend annual meetings. Landis Homes was a "wonderful institution," and the staff members were "the finest folks."[50]

That same month, Dr. William Ridgway wrote Orie a blunt letter of advice about the upcoming MCC executive committee meetings Orie wanted to attend: "We have always leveled with each other and have not ducked a straight question, and there is no reason to begin now, so here it is":

> Until now, I have advised that you be active . . . [for] we have agreed that it is better to wear out than rust out. My feelings are unchanged and yet, I am going to advise against your planning to attend the coming conference. You are less than totally aware of your effect on others. Your physical self has made such a change that those attending the conference would be appalled at the great decline in the imperishable Orie Miller. The impact would be such that there would be more anguish than you can imagine [and] . . . it would detract from the business at hand.[51]

Orie should, the doctor counseled, remain in his room at Landis Homes and be available for consultation with those at the conference by phone. Ridgway assured Orie that he could count on his counsel to be in his best interest and "in sympathy with all that Orie Miller stands for." Such counsel does not come easily, but he was doing so "in admiration of your accomplishments and intentions."[52]

Orie thought otherwise. On the same day, he wrote back, "It is well to do some consistent, practical, responsible trotting to assure running well!" As an MCC life member, he had attended meetings regularly and proposed going to the next meetings for short periods. He would be accompanied by Elta and Tom Wingert, a strong Amish orderly at the home. The doctor would be welcome to check with them at the end of the day and to give counsel about whether he should attend the next day's meetings.[53] The good doctor replied tersely, "Let's walk before we run."[54]

It was, indeed, difficult for others to see the formerly proper, poised, neatly dressed executive now confined to a wheelchair, drooling uncontrollably onto a towel tied around his neck. Paul Leatherman, for example, recalled Orie "already quite ill . . . not himself, but still sitting at these meetings and trying to participate in what was going on."[55]

Paul and Ann Gingrich found Orie's condition hard to take. "To see such a good, great man . . . suffer so much at the end," said Ann. "You can't imagine it!" Paul added. "Orie does not deserve that, God! There was something really wrong about that. . . . We'll have to talk to God about that sometime."[56] John Kraybill also reiterated Dr. Ridgway's advice: "Orie, you have to stop going to meetings. You are an embarrassment to people. They don't know what to say to you, because you drool . . . and can't talk."[57]

The family, however, learned to accept Orie's condition. Ed, Orie's grandson and attorney, visited Orie monthly to talk and to do business. They didn't discuss his physical limitations. "It was just something that we accepted," Ed recalled.[58] Orie did not seem to be self-conscious, nor did he expect pity from others. Like much of life, he took it in stride.

Though Orie had said he was entirely out of the Miller Hess shoe company, he still knew what was going on and was always at the table for the distribution of cash dividends, called, "cutting the melon."[59] He also weighed in on the issues when he thought it was necessary. To Ura Gingerich, a former Miller Hess partner, in May 1975, he admitted that the two had not seen "eye to eye on Miller Hess' first two or three problems," but still Orie appreciated Gingerich's "assurances . . . that making the three factories individuals rather than amalgamated" was good. He also appreciated knowing that Gingerich's business was "showing about 10% gain all around." The two had agreed on the value of Orie's "donated stock."

Orie believed "the biggest lack" in the company was in Abe Hallman and the board "not having found a way of working important decisions out together." He wondered why the three of them could not "get together and talk, something as you and I did yesterday?" Gingerich should attend the annual stockholders' meeting "prepared and ready with original ideas." Gingerich and Orie had "agreed that the business had too much debt."[60]

With the staff at Landis Homes, he could be both impatient and penitent. To Barbara Cooper, head nurse at Landis Homes, Orie reported that two nurses had just helped him in "relearning to walk." They had taken him right down the center of the corridor with the aid of a walker. "Since imbalance was one of the incurable factors of Parkinson's, I would think that a handrail" at each side of the hallway would be an improvement. He sent a copy to Dr. Ridgway.[61]

To Lillian Martin of the staff he wrote, "I want to obey all your rules, and yesterday after waiting a half hour after ringing the bell, and being on the chair Tom and I used in relearning to walk, I went to the station. . . .

This will not happen again." A postscript contained Orie's evaluation of healthcare professionals: sometimes doctors know the correct treatment—but apparently, not all the time.[62]

In June, he wrote to his optometrist, Dr. John M. Bowman, of Lancaster. Orie had new glasses as recommended, but his eyesight was getting worse. When Elta called to report Orie's unhappiness, Bowman said he should be content with the eyedrops; there was nothing better. Orie was not satisfied. He thought the nurses were giving him too many drops. "How many drops a day is the correct amount? What kind are they? What is prescribed? Shouldn't someone come occasionally and see whether the purpose is met?" While Bowman said Orie did not need to see him, Orie wrote, "Give me one more appointment for my mind's sake. Tell me what my trouble is."[63]

Then Orie wrote a pointed letter to Dr. Ridgway: "My sight and speech are terrible. The speech therapist was here and said 'no' she could not help, and referred to blowing, which you might have suggested. What was she talking about? Are you fully equipped with such?"[64] Ridgway responded, "The medicines we have for the treatment of Parkinsonism are not perfect. They . . . have side effects. We have arrived at the doseage [sic] that seems best for you and yet we realize that the effect is far from what you would like. I am unable to improve your speaking voice and am not concerned about your [loss of] weight."[65]

In June, Orie wrote to Tom Martin of the Landis Homes staff, "Today is a day when some words come through clear and plain. I can say 'yes' and 'no' which is why I don't try to talk in a conversation. I hear and listen well, but cannot read my own writing. I appreciate all you folks are trying to do for me. I hope you can teach me to walk again. I'd like to walk alone again, but perhaps cannot."[66] Orie's writing attempts were a trial to all. To help Marge Ruth, Elta rewrote all the words she could decipher. But Orie's scrawling became more and more illegible. Marge Ruth apologized to Lloyd Fisher, president of MEDA, in a December 9 letter, saying, "OOM had many more comments with this note, but I regret I could not read them." She had typed one sentence.[67]

Orie's attendance at MCC and EMM executive sessions were still an issue. In September 1975, Orie was trying to decide whether or not to attend the next MCC meetings. He asked the advice of MCC chair H. Ernest Bennett. "William [Snyder] always says 'Do just as you feel, attend part or all, as you feel able.'" Orie had been attending EMM sessions all along, and always clarified that for him it was just a "listening experience." Son Bob thought Orie should not attend the meeting, but Orie wanted Bennett to "write frankly how you feel." Orie said he always enjoyed the meetings, but "don't want to if not wanted."

Bennett wrote after the meetings, saying he had tried several times to call Orie. Chair Bennett said he was sure Orie would have enjoyed observing the committee wrestling with some "difficult agenda items." Bennett was ready to support Bob's counsel that the meetings were becoming too taxing for Orie.[68] Of course, Dr. Ridgway had given Orie straightforward counsel on attending public meetings, but Orie had chosen to disregard his advice.

Some were still seeking Orie's sage advice. Velma Eshleman, a missionary serving in Garissa, Kenya, asked what he thought of her marrying an African. Orie said Elta's youngest daughter had married Ted Hayes, who was "black" and a "Jesus Christian." They now had two children and were doing well in their marriage, so Orie could "see no reason for being against it." There will always be problems in marriages, he concluded, but "if real love operates," those problems can be resolved.[69]

Orie and Bob Zigler continued their correspondence as long as Orie could still write. After a trip abroad, Zigler was feeling discouraged because of his sense that the historic peace churches were "slowing down on their potential united strength." He felt a strong need to talk with Orie, for he had "never had a closer brother." He reminisced: "Out of the unknown we found each other and we added together our resources as we faced the always present state that wanted our sons and our resources." Little has changed: "How can we stop the next war?"[70]

Orie responded, saying, "God is also taking Mennonites through the wringer, but in different ways—money and budget-wise." Both MCC and EMM in 1972 had enough money, "perhaps too much." The crisis in Bangladesh and the results of Hurricane Agnes in the eastern United States "have opened hearts and pocketbooks."[71] To Milo Kauffman, who was revising his book on stewardship, Orie wrote, "I have noticed how many people seem to waste both Money and Time. Since Time wasted cannot be made up . . . that is even worse than mis-spending Money." And then, a word about estates: "After about 85 years of age, there should be no excuse for anyone having an estate to be . . . divided. Normally children are on their own. . . . I believe that time spent accumulating wealth beyond the family's year-to-year needs also wastes time."[72]

It had been a "hard trail from 1941 to the present," Bob Zigler wrote in May 1975. In their shared passion for peace while forging an alternative to military service on the National Service Board for Religious Objectors, Zigler could count on Orie's "wisdom as to what to do next." They had learned to delight in their parallel successes.[73] Orie's recent letter had revealed that he was still "very much alive and aware of this world." Orie "had an unusual skill in forecasting what to do next. You experimented in taking next steps, but there seemed to be a light . . . so you could penetrate the darkness called the unknown, and you had great faith in Christ as revealed by the people of your Church."[74]

Orie was now almost eighty-three and limited physically, but he had not stopped dreaming. He told Zigler about his "new thinking about aging," and Bob should not be surprised if a new book on the subject appeared soon. Then Orie returned to the war and the fall of Saigon. A Mennonite pastor and "one of the church's leading families got out" of Saigon before it fell. He thought that many were "a bit too concerned about spending money, and they don't want to be martyrs." Orie could count "only six martyrs" in his time, and he supposed there had been six hundred in the first decade of the Anabaptist movement.[75] A month earlier, he had written David Thomas, moderator of the Lancaster Mennonite Conference, to say that Mennonites were "too careless about spending money" and too careful about avoiding martyrdom. "In my day we would send all the folks we could [all over the world] to open fields for the gospel."[76]

In June 1975, Orie was counting his "handicaps and blessings." The work of promoting peace was now in the hands of another generation. He was heartened, because even his Episcopalian grandson, Larry Beach, when drafted, "found himself a CO, and the government went along." Orie was thinking about the new emphasis on justice in Mennonite and Brethren in Christ circles. To Zigler he wrote, "I am for justice too, but the greater is love." If the concern for justice became "too complicated for our young members," we should "leave vengeance to God."[77]

To Urbane Peachey, Orie reported a visit by Bill Snyder and Robert Kreider. "I threw out a general question: Do you get peace with justice? Bob answered emphatically, 'No,' which I believe too. The nonresistance of Paul and of Jesus and the Epistles is not the favored peace of the world today. I'm not sure what Sattler and Grebel taught and believed. Justice is not part of the spirit in Galatians 5:16. Peachey has had experience seeing how it works in the world's hot spots today. Let me know what you think about it."[78] Kreider remembers the visit too, as well as a second question: "How do you feel about women's liberation?" Orie did not comment on how Kreider answered the question.

By late summer of 1975, Orie told Zigler, "Just now I cannot see to read . . . and I have many bad dreams that seem real for several days afterward." He was most grateful, however, for his "good wife Elta." Again, Orie returned to the theme of justice. He was disappointed: "On peace I feel our younger generation has missed it. They tend to equate peace with justice, and the scriptures don't. 'Vengeance is mine, says the Lord, I will repay.' Nonresistance is a gift to the Christian only."[79]

To Harry A. Diener in Hutchinson, Kansas, Orie wrote a note of thanks for the copy of the [South Central] *Conference Messenger*, which featured Diener's sixty years as a minister. He told Diener that he could not speak above a whisper, and that the disease also affected swallowing and walking. He was confined to a wheelchair, but, he could still "hear, understand, and think." He would not be attending the MC general assembly in Eureka, Illinois, this year, the first such assembly he would miss since 1928. His final thought was about the hereafter. With Ernest Miller, Sanford Yoder, and others "gone on, we wouldn't find it difficult to join them."[80]

By January 1976, Orie's intake was limited to blended foods. His sight had left him, but with a touch of humor in his letter to Arlene Sitler, he described himself: "an almost sightless Secretary Emeritus is attempting to write blindly."[81]

Orie was still praying for overseas workers and missionaries. He had once chided missionaries in Ethiopia for limiting their prayers to their own needs. In February, Orie wrote to Jean Groff, saying, "We are praying for you in . . . Egypt, one of the hardest fields for mission there is." He recalled his first visit to Cairo in 1918 when he went to buy wheat for orphans in Beirut. Marge Ruth, who typed the letter, noted once again that "Orie had many other things to say, but they were not legible."[82]

One of the last times Don Jacobs visited Orie in his declining condition, Orie managed to say, "Don't forget Australia." He was still thinking of new frontiers. He had developed relationships with Mennonites there, and they talked of developing a camp as a gathering place. To honor Orie's wish, Jacobs and Lewis Strite, president of the Mennonite Christian Leadership Foundation, visited Australia on thee occasions. They attempted to foster relationship and to establish a mission, but all efforts failed. Another one of Orie's dreams died.

John W. Miller's last visit with his father is memorable. Orie asked John in writing what he was working on. John explained his latest writing project, a psychological study of Jesus, published as *Jesus at Thirty*. After he finished his long explanation, Orie scrawled, "Why are you answering questions nobody is asking?"[83]

DYING ACCORDING TO PLAN

Orie expected to live until age eighty-five. He had no plans beyond that age. By then, his assets were to be given away. Indeed, by the end, "he didn't have much left," said Ed Miller, Orie's grandson and legal counsel.

On a "blustery winter evening," on January 10, 1977, Orie passed from this world into the next. After spending most of his final days in a coma, he slipped away at six forty-five that evening. He was eighty-four, six months short of eighty-five. He even died according to plan!

On the evening of his death, Dan, Eunice, and Elta were among the family members around his bed. Dan held his father's hand. Having lost other means of communication, Orie could answer a question or signal his awareness of the conversation by squeezing Dan's hand. At some point, someone picked up the recent issue of the *Gospel Herald*, the MC periodical that Orie had followed since its founding in 1908, and began reading church news. When Orie heard something of interest, he pressed Dan's hand. It was during the reading of the *Gospel Herald* that Orie breathed his last. It seems fitting that his last conscious thoughts were of the church he had served and loved so deeply since his baptism in 1905.[84]

Dr. William G. Ridgway certified Orie's death at Landis Homes, noting that Parkinsonism, of five years' duration, had been the cause of death.

Five days later, on January 15, family, friends, and colleagues gathered at Ephrata Mennonite Church for a three-hour "Service of Thanksgiving." Wilbert Lind, Ephrata's pastor, led the service; Peter Dyck prayed; Don Jacobs gave the meditation; Paul Erb shared memories; Bill Snyder spoke of Orie's service with MCC; and Ira J. Buckwalter represented EMM. Peter Dyck also read letters and telegrams from friends around the world, recalling Orie's effective service and conveying condolences to the family. Others shared spontaneous memories. The final hymn, "Lift Your Glad Voices" sounded a joyous note of celebration for Orie's unusually productive life.

In Jacobs's meditation, he said,

> Brother Orie was a builder. Brother Orie finished many tabernacles. He built, the Lord glorified. There can be no higher human compliment, no higher human achievement. I have traveled recently to Africa, Central America, and Asia. I saw with my own eyes, the glory of the Lord has filled the tabernacle of Brother Orie's work. Orie points us not to himself or to the work he has done, but to the gracious, loving, Risen Lord. . . .

> Orie's work is finished. He labored faithfully to the end. May we, as a congregation of people, we who were touched by Orie's loving ministry . . . worship anew the Lord who has glorified not only the work of our brother, but in his own good providence has glorified the man.[85]

"Under his plain coat," the efficient, disciplined, and all-business Orie Miller had "a warm heart," said Peter Dyck. "Brother Orie was a humble giant of a man. He started enough programs to keep the rest of us occupied a lifetime carrying them out."[86]

Orie's protégé, Robert S. Kreider, wrote, "For me in my early twenties [Orie] symbolized a church that was seeking to be relevant, resourceful, and caring in a badly bruised world. He gave me and many others a new sense of worth. He helped us with our identity crisis, [and] he helped us to see our task worldwide." Further, Orie "brought secular savvy to the work of the church, missionary concerns to the relief program, and a salesman's persistency to the problems of meeting college budgets."[87]

The *Lancaster New Era* eulogized Orie Miller as a "contemporary Mennonite patriarch," former chair of the Miller Hess shoe company board of directors, a founder of MCC, and as secretary of both MCC and EMM. The obituary noted his relief work in the Middle East and in Russia, and rightly observed, "Until recent years, Miller was apt to show up any place in the world where people were in need."[88]

A *Gospel Herald* article characterized his death as a loss for the "entire Mennonite world." MCC associate secretary Edgar Stoesz said, "One dimension of his greatness was in relationship to institutions—his ability to create them, and equally, his ability to make them function within his expectations." Indeed, Paul Erb noted that Miller had served sixty-five church-related organizations, one for as long as forty-five years.[89]

During Orie's lifetime of eighty-four years, Anabaptist heirs in the United States had increased from 41,541 to 215,285; MC membership grew from 17,078 to 96,092; and GC membership increased from 5,670 to 35,673. At his death, Mennonites and Brethren in Christ worldwide numbered 613,600. Of that total, 313,300 were in North America, 96,100 were in Europe, 85,900 were in Africa, 74,300 were in Asia and the Pacific, and 44,300 lived in Central and South America and the Caribbean.[90] Mennonites in the Global South would soon outnumber those in Europe and North America. Orie did not live to see the day, but he saw it coming, and he rejoiced.

WILLS, ESTATES, AND A TRUST FUND

Orie's will of April 3, 1971, named Albert W. Miller and Fulton National Bank of Lancaster as coexecutors. Elta was to receive all their personal and household items, the 1965 Buick four-door Special valued at $150, and the continued support of a trust fund. To the five children, Orie bequeathed the remainder of the estate in equal shares. The remaining estate, mostly stocks, was appraised at $54,121. The majority of the stocks, valued at $45,000, were of Warren's Shoes, Inc. The liquidation of those stocks would require negotiation. Little was available for distribution.

The original value of Elta Wolf Miller's estate at her death in 1958 was $208,000. By 1976, the remaining taxable estate was $74,985.52. Much of it was tied up in various real estate partnerships: Weber-Miller, Westview, Heritage Estates, and Heritage Village. The Miller five were partners and shareholders. One or more of the siblings represented the family on the Miller Hess board of directors. Until 1970 Orie, and thereafter, Albert, Bob, and Jean, managed assets and investments, the Elta Wolf Miller estate, memberships in various development partnerships, stocks, and personal accounts. At death, Orie owed the Heritage Estates partnership $8,652.

As for support for the "second Elta," Orie had set up the Elta M. Miller Annuity Trust Fund in 1967. It was to provide for her as long as she remained a widow. The trust was opened with fifty-seven shares of Miller Hess stock, valued at $159.98 per share, plus a $1,000 note from MEDA for a total of $10,000.[91] The trust grew steadily and by December 1970, the total value exceeded $110,000. Any remaining funds after Elta's death were to be divided four ways: to EMM, MCC, MBE for Goshen College, and Eastern Mennonite College.

Orie had asked Norman Shenk to set up the charitable trust. Shenk had joined the EMM staff in 1955 as an assistant in the finance office and soon became treasurer of such multiple organizations as Menno Travel, Mennonite Indemnity, Inc., and EMM. Since Orie wanted to fund the trust with Miller Hess stock, he arranged for Shenk's appointment to the Miller Hess board of directors. Through the 1970s, the company was paying "a very nice dividend." Since EMM was one of the ultimate beneficiaries, dividends were paid to EMM. Norman Shenk kept his eyes on the funds. When Miller Hess filed for bankruptcy in 1984, the stocks and dividends evaporated.[92] Shenk "was very pleased," however, to have enough surpluses and dividends to support Elta as long as she lived. Elta died on December 3, 1988, at the age of seventy-seven.[93] But it was close—had she lived three more months, the trust would have been depleted.

Perceptions about how well Orie provided for Elta varied. Arthur Wolf, Elta Wolf Miller's cousin, mistakenly thought Orie hadn't even left enough money for his own burial. It was "low-down" not to give some money to the cemetery. Orie had been in the "Christianity business" and had given away all his money, so he had to be interred in his father-in-law's plot. When Arthur's brother Galen, the cemetery caretaker, talked to Elta Sensenig Miller about Orie's having left no money for the cemetery, Elta was quoted as saying, "Don't feel bad, I didn't get anything either."[94] Some others assumed the Miller Hess bankruptcy depleted all her funds, leaving her nothing.

Despite those perceptions, Elta Sensenig Miller, in addition to the trust fund, received full payment for a personal debenture note of $25,000 held by Miller Hess and paid at the point of bankruptcy in 1984.[95] As for the cemetery, Elta Wolf Miller had left $2,000 for the care of the Wolf and Miller graves, which paid annual interest to the cemetery association. In addition, a Wolf Cemetery cash statement for 1961 shows regular Miller Hess and Highland Shoe Company dividends were paid to the cemetery fund.

MCC purchased Orie and Elta's brick ranch-style house on Twelfth Street and some of its furnishings for $45,000. This helped pay back a longstanding $22,857 debt to Miller Hess. Orie had explained it this way: "A good many years ago . . . a few of us bought common stock on credit to bolster our Miller Hess financial statement." The partners had agreed that if any debt remained to an estate, it could be paid back with stock.[96] Orie also wanted to give each unmarried grandchild $500 in Miller Hess stock, as he had to each of the five children who married. This, Orie said, was following the example of Grandpa Wolf's gift of $1,000 to Lois when she married. The value of the stocks was short-lived.

MILLER HESS BANKRUPTCY

On December 21, 1984, Miller, Hess & Company filed under Chapter 11 of the Bankruptcy Law.[97] Bad debts of $272,387 had been accumulated by its four divisions—Hubler, Miller Hess, A. N. Wolf, and B. A. Corbin, and its four Pennsylvania stores in Akron, Lititz, Middletown, and Columbia.

What happened? A number of factors converged to spell the end of Miller Hess. "Orie and the whole team got old together. And the shoe lasts as well got old, and the shoe building and everything got old." One important factor was that Miller Hess did not change from manufacturing to marketing soon enough. In its later years, the managers founded the Highland Shoe Company, a wholly owned subsidiary marketing division, to promote and ship the finished product, purchased from foreign markets as well as from Miller Hess inventory, but it was too late. When foreign-made shoes flooded the market, Miller Hess could not compete. If the company had ended manufacturing earlier and marketed imported shoes, it could have stayed competitive.[98]

Orie had written to the family in March 1972, saying that the shoe business was not doing well. Abe Hallman reported the week before that it was the "first operation to break even" that season, with "considerable loss." Production at Miller Hess was down 50 percent, so it was not possible to predict midyear dividends.[99]

A second factor was a natural disaster. In June 1972, Tropical Storm Agnes hit the eastern seaboard, flooded the Middletown plant, and destroyed finished shoes valued at more than a million dollars. "This," said Norman Shenk, "was the beginning of the end."[100]

A third factor was the imprudent purchase of the B. A. Corbin Shoe factory, makers of Spalding Sport Shoes in Marlboro, Massachusetts. Miller Hess president Charles E. Sourber Jr., "hired from the outside," insisted on the deal at a time when Miller Hess was undercapitalized and required borrowing money at the very high interest rate of 18 percent. The company did not have the financial strength to get better rates. The deal "pulled us under," said Norman Shenk, who had voted against the acquisition.

Miller Hess first sold off Bachman Shoes, the children's shoe division in Middletown, to Ura Gingerich, who owned the Badorf Shoe Company.[101] After the company filed for bankruptcy, the other divisions were sold too.

FROM MILLER HESS TO TEN THOUSAND VILLAGES

The original Miller Hess factory on the corner of Main and Seventh Streets, Akron, was purchased by MCC for $251,000. It became the home of Ten Thousand Villages.[102]

The Ten Thousand Villages enterprise had originated with Edna Ruth Byler, who began the Overseas Needlepoint and Crafts Project, later called SELFHELP Crafts of the World. In 1946, she bought samples of crafts made in Puerto Rico and began selling them through her network of family and friends. In 1962, MCC took over operations and hired Byler as a half-time manager until 1969. Three managers followed: Joyce Bratton (Yoder), Jeannette Yoder, and Nick Dyck.[103]

In 1976, MCC asked Paul Leatherman to conduct a study of the projects in Central and South America, Asia, the Middle East, and Africa. He "was completely excited about" the potential he discovered. He often heard, "Paul, we don't need anything, except if you would buy what we are making and pay us a good price, we could take care of ourselves." This was a new way of helping people in need around the world. In 1977, Leatherman became the director of SELFHELP Crafts, a $300,000 business. Twelve years later, it had become a $5 million enterprise. Orie also saw the potential, telling an incredulous Edna Byler that SELFHELP Crafts "ought to be a million dollar business."

Leatherman sat on a committee of international organizations that incorporated in 1978 as International Free Trade Association, where the concept of free trade was coined and promoted.[104] Paul E. Myers was named CEO of SELFHELP in 1989, and in 1991, on its fiftieth anniversary, SELFHELP Crafts became Ten Thousand Villages.

It seems appropriate for Ten Thousand Villages to occupy the Miller Hess factory. Orie married Elta Wolf in 1915 and moved to Akron to join

Ten Thousand Villages office, Akron, Pennsylvania. John E. Sharp.

Miller, Hess & Company as a partner and salesman. This business provided a lifelong income and formed a solid base from which he launched worldwide programs of relief, service, and mission. Now the fruits of those endeavors have come back to the Miller Hess building in Akron through Ten Thousand Villages, one of the world's largest fair trade organizations. Handmade products from artisans in thirty-eight countries in Asia, Africa, Latin America, and the Middle East flow through the Miller Hess factory building to 319 retail outlets in the United States and Canada. These sales provide sustainable, fair trade incomes that improve the lives of tens of thousands of artisans around the world.

Surely this is a fitting tribute to Orie O. Miller, whose bread and butter was the shoe business and whose greatest passions were mission, service, and international peace.

Epilogue

Orie Miller's "greatness was not because he aspired to be a leader, but because he has lived well the role of a servant," said Ira J. Buckwalter in a tribute given at Orie's Eastern Mennonite Missions retirement dinner in 1958. Buckwalter, Orie's colleague and long-serving EMM treasurer, captured in a sentence the theme of Robert K. Greenleaf's popular books and lectures on servant leadership.

One who is a servant first and leader second will strive to meet the needs of others, and in the process, find that leadership roles are thrust upon him or her. The litmus test, Greenleaf suggests, is whether those being served grow toward maturity, whether they become "healthier, wiser, freer, more autonomous, more likely themselves to become servants," and whether the service benefits the "least of these."[1]

Orie was, indeed, a servant leader. He absorbed a sense of Christian service from his home, his church, and his college. With his conversion and baptism, he committed himself to a lifetime of service without knowing the manner of the service. The call to serve God and the church meant "everything," he said late in life. Nothing was more important.

While Orie assumed he would be called to pastoral ministry or evangelism, it was not to be. He once said that every time he turned around, he was given money to raise, count, and manage. At forty-three, and after struggling mightily, Orie recognized and accepted his gift for administration. This gift was expressed in a myriad of ministries. Orie's disciplined life, his commitment to follow the call of the church, and his quiet persuasion were a potent combination. When applied to opportunities around the world, these traits resulted in astounding productivity.

Yet his bearing was understated and quietly persuasive. He had ego strength but was not egotistical; self-aggrandizement was not in his nature.

He saw himself in a supporting role—as John Mark serving the apostle Paul, as Nehemiah assisting Ezra the prophet. An effective administrator works behind the scenes, Orie wrote, and "where the administrative gift tends to become noticeable and prominent anywhere, it's a pity, because it's not intended to be that."

His gift of administration was not foremost among the biblical listing of gifts but was nearly last, a point Orie made repeatedly. A person's gift "will make room for him," he said. That is, in exercising one's gift, more opportunities will become apparent. Orie's gifts were extraordinary, but his uncommon diligence and discipline magnified his gifts.

Orie's gifts "made room for him," but so did his family connections. D. D. Miller's reputation as a leader among MC Mennonites and Amish Mennonites paved the way for Orie. At Goshen College, Orie learned to know the primary leaders of the church and cultivated relationships with his peers, many of whom stepped into important positions of leadership in the Mennonite Church and the General Conference Mennonite Church. Orie's marriage to Elta Wolf, the only daughter of A. N. and Anna (Hess) Wolf, a family of means, gave Orie a passport into the Lancaster Mennonite Conference. Wealth and respectable family connections also gave Orie entrée to Lancaster County Mennonite culture, where such credentials mattered. These credentials softened the negative impact of his association with his alma mater, Goshen College, with its reputation among many easterners as liberal and dangerous. Orie's own disciplined work habits, his eagerness to serve the church, and his respect for leadership added to his credibility.

The convergence of Orie's abilities with the tremendous needs and opportunities of his era was a *kairos*, an opportune moment in history. Orie helped to move his people from rural isolation to global engagement and to weather the turbulent 1920s and '30s. He participated in the formation of MCC, and thanks to his influence it became the strongest and most effective international, inter-Mennonite agency in history, while situated in the center of Lancaster Conference, whose leaders feared such alliances. He helped to create and manage Civilian Public Service and the National Service Board for Religious Objectors, both a part of an unprecedented ecumenical response to World War II.

Orie brought business savvy to the church. His entrepreneurial success gave Orie added authority in the councils of the church. He knew how to manage institutions, to build budgets, to write constitutions and bylaws, to make a plan when others seemed unable to do so. He knew how to create and organize new organizations to meet needs. He knew how to mobilize the church to support relief and mission ministries, and to call and assign young volunteers to posts around the world. In doing so, he shaped lives and careers. Again and again, people whom I interviewed testified that "a call from Orie was a call from God."

Orie would surely take delight in the growth of the Mennonite and Brethren in Christ churches in Africa, Asia, and Latin America, a trend he noticed in 1970. He would appreciate the continued role of Mennonite World Conference in promoting fellowship and building understanding among the various expressions of the global church.

Since nothing was more important than a call to service, what of his family? The absent husband and father is the shadow in Orie's story. Time and time again, writing from afar, he promised to be a "better husband and father." Yet seldom did he alter his travel schedule for the sake of family. When he did, it was memorable. Protégés have remarked, "I would not have wanted him as a father," and "I wanted to be his friend, not his son." How could daughter and sons chart their own paths with a famous father? How could daughters-in-law live with husbands who struggled to live up to the expectations of their father?

Orie, of course, had a plan for each of his children. But as he told Edgar Stoesz, "One after another they kicked off the blankets."[2] Lois, feeling her father had abandoned her during her first five years of life, struck out on her own, marrying someone from outside the Mennonite community. "She was a rebel, you know. More like him, probably."[3]

After Lois married Ronald Beach, Orie and Elta adjusted to their Episcopalian son-in-law and to the daughter who charted her own path. Lois, Ronald, and family spent most of their time in New Jersey where Ronald worked with his father designing and building organs. Lois died of bone cancer on March 28, 1987, at age 70.[4]

Albert, married to Esther Lehman, was "very principled," as was Orie, but with different values. "He was not like Orie, who always had an answer and a clear sense of direction, and . . . wasn't afraid to tell people what to do," recalls Albert's son Ed Miller. Albert was "a lot more tolerant and not as interested in controlling the bigger picture." He had a theme, but not a ten-year plan. Despite their deep-seated differences, Orie retained Albert as executor of his estate.[5] At Albert's memorial service in late January 1996, the family displayed symbols characterizing Albert's life and values.[6] Prominent among them was a panel of IRS letters and levies, commemorating his war tax resistance.

Dan became a missionary, according to Orie's plan, but he struggled to live up to his father's expectations. Dan graduated from Goshen College and married Eunice Litwiller, daughter of missionary parents in Argentina. They became lifelong missionaries in Uruguay, Mexico, and Argentina where Dan also taught at the seminary. Dan became a courageous advocate for students during an era of political turbulence. More than once, he was arrested for his involvement. Dan died on February 23, 1993, at age 69. Eunice and the children remained in Argentina.[7]

John was to be a missionary doctor before being diverted by Harold Bender and Uncle Ernest, but his career as an academic was fine with Orie. John earned a ThD at the University of Basel, and taught at Goshen Biblical Seminary before helping to establish Reba Place in Evanston, Illinois. He is now Professor Emeritus of Religious Studies at Conrad Grebel University College, University of Waterloo. He has written numerous books; among them, *Proverbs* in the Believers Church Bible Commentary series, published in 2004. More recently, he wrote an autobiography. John and his wife Louise (Heatwole) live in Waterloo, Ontario.[8]

After graduating from Goshen College, Bob and his wife, Jean Carper, studied at the Biblical Seminary in New York, then went to Indonesia for three years before returning to Akron where Bob became the director of the MCC overseas department. Bob, a people person like his mother, traveled the world and loved it. While in Akron, he joined the board of Warren Shoes. He was, after all, as Jean put it, Orie's "golden boy," destined to follow his father's example. Unfortunately, Orie too often treated Bob as a boy.[9] They spent five years at Reba Place, and then Bob got into retirement home administration. From 1980 to 1995, he worked as the administrator of two large facilities, an American Baptist home in Detroit, Michigan, and Frederick Mennonite Community, near Pottstown, Pennsylvania. Bob was diagnosed with a stage 4 glioblastoma (brain tumor) in 1995, and died on June 17, 1996, at age 65.[10]

Reflecting on the life and witness of Orie Miller, the following themes and questions emerge:

What shaped his worldview and piety? The Bible and the *New York Times* or the *Wall Street Journal* shaped Orie's worldview; each illuminates the other, he often said. Few others of his generation held such a dual worldview. The *Times* and the *Journal* provided a window to the economy and to world events, often indicating new service and mission opportunities. Orie was also at home in the biblical world. He read through the Bible annually for more than fifty years and constructed his worldview in dialogue with the Bible. Biblical allusions and images seasoned his conversation and his letters. Almost anything was possible, he believed, because everything, even "the cattle upon a thousand hills," belong to God (Psalm 50:10). Orie was deeply spiritual, but without emotional overtones and without formulaic expressions of piety.

Two texts, more than any other, guided his life and ministry. Galatians 6:10 called him to care for his own people: "So then, whenever we have an opportunity, let us work for the good of all, and especially for those of the household of faith" (NRSV). Matthew 28:19-20 informed his ministry to those not yet in the faith: "Go ye therefore, and teach all nations, baptizing them in the name of the Father, and of the Son, and of the Holy Ghost: Teaching them to observe all things whatsoever I have commanded you." He believed God was actively using MCC, EMM, and other agencies to "make all things new," as described in Revelation 21:5.

The church as a community of nurture, faith, and worship. Orie did not live out his faith in isolation. For sixty-two years, he was a member of the Ephrata Mennonite Church, the local expression of God's international community. For most of those years, he taught a young men's Sunday school class, and he and Elta channeled much of their considerable charitable giving through the congregation. Orie's vision of the church as God's redemptive community never wavered. The church was the human embodiment of Jesus and the primary expression of God's kingdom on earth. Missions, service projects, and peace advocacy were expressions of the church and the means through which God extended the global heavenly kingdom on earth. The church was the means of his calling and therefore the source of his authority. Orie found honor in the church's call, even when his peers did not, and even when church leaders lacked his more wide-ranging vision. He accepted the correction of Lancaster Conference leaders because they represented the church to which he was accountable. Until the end, he was confident that when called upon to meet a need anywhere in the world, the church would supply the volunteers and the funding. It was, after all, the church's work, not that of any agency or board.

What were the sources of his ecumenical impulses? One could point to his father's advocacy of the merger of Mennonite and Amish Mennonite conferences, the classical education he received at "old" Goshen, and the extracurricular activities and conferences of the YMCA. Surely, the greatest source of Orie's ecumenical impulse was his fifteen months of service with the NER in Beirut in 1919–20. As commanding officer and quartermaster of the Beirut City District, Orie interacted with Christians and Muslims. He observed the work and piety of Presbyterian missionaries and the faculty of the American University of Beirut. Most significant of all was his mentor and boss, Major James H. Nichol, of the Red Cross and the NER. Orie cited Nichol as one of the three most influential mentors in his life—along with his father, D. D. Miller, and his father-in-law, A. N. Wolf. Under Nichol, Orie honed his administrative gift, becoming more adept at leading, supervising, and delegating.

During Orie's mission to organize relief efforts to Russia, he negotiated with American and Russian military commanders, NER and Red Cross leaders, and Turkish officials in Constantinople and merchants in Cairo. He rode American Navy destroyers across the Black Sea, he related to the wife of General Wrangel, commander of Russian military forces. While some of Orie's elders and peers feared the erosion of identity as a cost of ecumenical partnerships, Orie saw the strength of cooperation and retained his denominational identity. Denominational differences, he said, should not be minimized, but commonalities should be maximized.

A prophetic word? Orie was an institution builder, having had a hand in organizing most things Mennonite from the founding of MCC in 1920 to the Mennonite Christian Leadership Foundation in 1969. What counsel might he give now in an era of diminishing denominational loyalty, shrinking budgets, and mature bureaucracies?

Perhaps he would offer three litmus tests: Does the institution serve the church? Is it fulfilling its mission? Does it bring people together? He founded no institution to serve itself. When an institution no longer serves the church, what is the basis for its continued existence? When it no longer fulfills the mission for which it was created, what is its purpose? Orie believed that effective ministries would unite rather than divide people, as does, for example, the expanding nature and mission of Mennonite World Conference. He might also point to his Amish heritage to remind us to strengthen relationships with Old Order Anabaptist groups, who share common roots and core commitments with Mennonites.

He would approve of the consistent witness to government as represented by the MCC offices in Washington and Ottawa. The shrinking membership of Mennonite Church USA and the expanding budgets of its institutions would call for reflection. And Orie would surely ask who is calling younger generations into mission and service.

Orie would counter efforts to separate evangelism and peace, mission and service. The genius of the Anabaptist vision, he believed, was the unity of word and deed. Neither should be compromised nor sacrificed for the sake of the other. He saw no seam to suggest a rending of the whole cloth. Orie modeled this well by serving as chief executive officer of both MCC and EMM simultaneously for twenty-three years.

As he was troubled by the wars of his day, from World War I to the Vietnam War, Miller would have been distressed by the Gulf Wars, the invasion of Iraq, and the war in Afghanistan. He would grieve at the resultant divide between Christians and Muslims. He would call us to maximize our similarities without minimizing our differences. He would say, as he did in Somalia, that Muslims deserve good healthcare, education, and a place to worship. Would he still advocate the building of a mosque for Muslim students in a school taught by Mennonites? Rather than fearing a weakening of faith because of such contact, he would think of it as an opportunity for witness. More than an opportunity, he would say it is an imperative, a "total-mission" obligation, a great commission "ought." All the world is, after all, a field for mission and service.

Orie Miller, extraordinary servant leader, continues to speak to our time and place.

Appendix A

Orie O. Miller, MCC Fiftieth Anniversary Speech, 1970

This speech is classic Orie. True to form, he combines cryptic expressions, inventive word forms, linguistic complexity, and interminably long sentences. (He was an English major in college!) Nevertheless, Orie gives voice to that which after seventy-eight years is still closest to his heart: the church's witness of mission, service, and peace. After a rambling review of Mennonite history and a string of biblical texts, Orie characteristically projects the church's ministries into the future. God's worldwide fellowship, employing a myriad of agencies, will still be engaged in "making all things new"—fifty and seventy years later.

"THE MENNONITE CENTRAL COMMITTEE, GOD'S MIRACLE AMONG US: THE MEANING OF THE PAST FIFTY YEARS"

"'Eager to maintain (or *endeavoring to keep* as in the King James Version) the unity of the spirit in the bond of peace' (Ephesians 4:3) is one of the more apt scriptural words characterizing the church fathers of our older generation. The 46 ½ percent membership growth of the 1904 to 1918 period, the structuring of boards of publication, education, and mission and Mennonite conferences since 1890, the fruit of Sunday school begun even earlier, the more general use of English in the Mennonite Church beginning with the turn of the century, making possible the influence of Moody, J. F. Funk, and J. S. Coffman, making 'all things seem new' again (Rev. 21:4), probably accounted at least in part for this scriptural 'eagerness.' By

1920, after President Wilson's 'war to end war' and the wider world having become visible, from this beginning obedience in Dhamtari in India, Pehuajo in Argentina, war sufferers' housing rebuilding in France and the Russian Mennonite deputation visits among us in the United States in 1920 another scriptural word, 'As we have therefore opportunity let us do good unto all men, especially unto them who are of the household of faith' (Galatians 6:10) seemed particularly applicable and easily led to beginning the MCC and this wider brotherhood structuring.

"The American Friends Service Committee, founded in 1917 and preceding the MCC by several years, had taught us much about consensus and non-polarization, and respect for differences in decision making— and so one notes all MCC actions of the first twenty years 'unanimously' passed (in good Mennonite parlance) and the steady moving towards Holy Spirit-led-togetherness. By 1941 and the particular preparation of the six years preceding in our nonresistance and peace position understanding, one found this togetherness possible from grass roots to leadership and youth to old age. Romans 12:21: 'Be not overcome of evil, but overcome evil with good'. and Matthew 5:38-41: 'Ye have heard that it hath been said, An eye for an eye, and a tooth for a tooth, but I say unto you, that ye resist not evil, but whosoever shall smite thee on thy right cheek, turn to him the other also. And if any man will sue thee at the law, and take away thy coat, let him have thy cloak also. And *whosoever* shall *compel* thee to go a *mile*, go with him *twain*.' Both were particularly, speaking to us all, across the North American brotherhood plus the Brethren in Christ Church via Civilian Public Service, Voluntary Service, War Sufferers' Relief, and with world vision pull and tug. The MCC in mission implication was sensed by then, although not yet ripely spoken, as was the case also in the fathers' designation of "missions and charities" as a two-sided entity.

"And so this Anabaptist scripturally-unique vision could begin to flower as at no other time in the brotherhood's historical background heretofore. This vision of so much promise in 1525 to 1540, Swiss Brethren days, which through and after dire persecution, reemerged in part in Pietism, and similarly in Holland eventually in Liberalism, and flowering for a time in Moravian Brotherhood communities, then into legalism, now in its 'freedom' setting, promised and promises much. The MCC's accepted scriptural priority of prayerful, Christian-committed workers, then, contributed varied gifts and things in the name of Christ and the needed administration, not only simplified the Treasure-Controller function but prepared for the merging with mission and world brotherhood partnership in gospel outreach obedience. Even before this ripeness, the MCC here and there has taken and still takes a 'John the Baptist' forerunner role, and then phases out—or a John Mark to Paul role without John Mark's lapse.

"A few additional observations: First, the service, or gift, or labeled contribution, 'In the Name of Christ' clarified immeasurably worker standards and motivation, the resource relationship, and deed perspective and dimension, and enabled testimony opportunity, despite language, cultural and other barriers. Second, as also in Jesus' striking feeding miracle, the concern for 'fragments' and 'crumbs' and that nothing be wasted, finds similar symbolization in baskets labeled VS, TAP, PAX, MTS, MEDA, GMCC, MMHS, MDS, MII, Eirene, SEA, Km. 81 and Asuncion Center, Paraguay, Starenstrasse 41, Basel, Cottagegasse, Vienna, Austria, and others aborning."[1]

"And so from this perspective in time, may there continue being, rather than becoming—mobility rather than arrival—a new Galatians 6:10 world brotherhood perspective, in unique testimony to 'Brother' in Christ and to 'Brother' partner in continuing outreach—obedience to our Lord's commission to every man. May affluence be shared via Heaven's bank account. May the 'eagerness' characterizing 1919–20 characterize 1970 as well—to those reflecting similarly as we here do in 2020 and 2070. And may similar love of Word and sensitiveness to Holy Spirit breakthrough and leading, and in seeing 'all things made new' continue likewise."

Appendix B
List of Acronyms and Abbreviations

ACRS	Anabaptist Center for Religion and Society
AFSC	American Friends (Quaker) Service Committee
AIMM	Africa Inter-Mennonite Mission
ALERT	All Africa Leprosy, Tuberculosis and Rehabilitation Training
ALM	American Leprosy Mission
AM	Amish Mennonite
AMBS	Associated Mennonite Biblical/Anabaptist Mennonite Biblical Seminary
AMRC	American Mennonite Relief Commission
ARA	American Relief Administration
ASW	Alternative Service Work (Canada)
BIC	Brethren in Christ
BSC	Brethren Service Committee
CCHPC	Continuation Committee of Historic Peace Churches
CMBC	Canadian Mennonite Board of Colonization
CMRC	Canadian Mennonite Relief Committee
CO	conscientious objector
CPS	Civilian Public Service (United States)
CRALOG	Council of Relief Agencies Licensed for Operation in Germany
EMBMC	Eastern Mennonite Board of Missions and Charities

EMC	Eastern Mennonite College
EMHS	Eastern Mennonite High School
EMM	Eastern Mennonite Missions
FBI	Federal Bureau of Investigation
FCC	Federal Council of Churches
FOR	Fellowship of Reconciliation
GBS	Goshen Biblical Seminary
GC	General Conference
HPC	historic peace churches
MB	Mennonite Brethren
MBE	Mennonite Board of Education
MBM	Mennonite Board of Missions
MBMC	Mennonite Board of Missions and Charities
MBS	Mennonite Biblical Seminary
MC	"old" Mennonite Church
MCC	Mennonite Central Committee
MCC Canada	Mennonite Central Committee Canada
MCLF	Mennonite Christian Leadership Foundation
MCPC	Mennonite Central Peace Committee
MEDA	Mennonite Economic Development Associates
MII	Mennonite Indemnity, Inc.
MMA	Mennonite Mutual Aid Association
MMHS	Mennonite Mental Health Services
MPH	Mennonite Publishing House
MRCWS	Mennonite Relief Commission for War Sufferers
MTS	Menno Travel Service
MWC	Mennonite World Conference
NATO	North Atlantic Treaty Organization
NER	Near East Relief
NCRCO	National Council for Religious Conscientious Objectors
NSBRO	National Service Board for Religious Objectors
PPC	Peace Problems Committee
TAP	Teachers Abroad Program
VS	Voluntary Service
WCC	World Council of Churches

YMCA   Young Men's Christian Association
YPCA   Young People's Christian Association

Notes

AUTHOR'S PREFACE

1. Kreider, introduction to Erb, *Orie O. Miller*.
2. Juhnke, *Vision, Doctrine, War*, 284–85.

CHAPTER 1

1. Clarke, *Sixty Years with the Bible*, 169. All epigraphs of chapters are quotations from Orie O. Miller.
2. Ibid., 247.
3. Orie O. Miller (hereafter OOM), interviewed by Paul Erb, 18 September 1962, transcript, 9–10. f. 7, b. 12, Paul Erb Papers, 1909–67.
4. John W. Miller, interviewed by author, 15 May 2010.
5. Town of Shipshewana website, http://www.shipshewana.org/history.php; "History of the Potawatomie Trail of Death," http://www.potawatomi-tda.org/ptodhist.htm.
6. Shari Spiker and Charles Speicher, "Spikers and Speichers in America," ancestry .com, RootsWeb, http://freepages.genealogy.rootsweb.ancestry.com/~whozrdadi/ Spiker_Speicher/ps40_265.htm.
7. "Family Roots of Elaine K. Hooley," genealogy.com, http://www.genealogy.com/ genealogy/users/h/o/o/Elaine-K-Hooley/index.html.
8. E. E. Miller, *Daniel D. Miller*.
9. Ibid., 12.
10. Umble, unpublished thesis on Mennonite preaching, ch.14, f. 14, b. 1, D. D. Miller Papers.
11. "GC and MC Membership Statistics in the United States of America, 1860–2003," Mennonite Church USA Historical Committee, http://www.mcusa-archives.org/ resources/membership.html.
12. For more on Mennonite "quickening" and institution building, see Schlabach, *Gospel vs. Gospel*, and Juhnke, *Vision, Doctrine, War*.
13. OOM to Guy F. Hershberger, manuscript of tribute to Harold S. Bender, 1 August 1963, f. 2, b. 77, OOM Papers.
14. OOM, interviewed by Paul Erb, transcript, 1. Paul Erb Papers.
15. Born 1885 and died at age one. MennObits, *Herald of Truth*, 15 March 1885, http://www.mcusa-archives.org/MennObits/1885/mar1885.html. The birth record will confirm it, but it is almost certain that Orie was named "Ora." On one occasion, Trueman addressed his brother in a letter as "Dear Ora." In the 1902–3 East Brick School souvenir school record, his name appears as Orus O.

16.   Ohio bishop O. N. Johns, born 1889. MennObits, *Gospel Herald (GH)*, 20 May
      1985, http://www.mcusa-archives.org/MennObits/75/may1975.html
17.   E. E. Miller, *A Biographical Sketch*, 16.
18.   Erb, *Orie O. Miller*, 30.
19.   Erb interview notes, b. 9, Paul Erb Papers.
20.   OOM, interviewed by Paul Erb, 18 September 1962, transcript, 6–7, f. 7, b. 12,
      Paul Erb Papers.
21.   Erb, *Orie O. Miller*, 35.
22.   Ibid., 41.
23.   OOM, interviewed by Paul Erb, notes, "Family" section of index cards, b. 9, Paul
      Erb Papers.
24.   E. E. Miller, *A Biographical Sketch*, 12, 22–23.
25.   Rachel Kreider, interviewed by author, 8 August 2012.
26.   Ibid.
27.   Rachel Nafziger Hartzler conversation, 29 December 2010.
28.   E. E. Miller, *A Biographical Sketch*, 44.
29.   Umble, "Mennonite Preaching," ch. 16, f. 14, b. 1, D. D. Miller Papers.
30.   OOM, Paul Erb transcript, 6, 8, f. 7, b. 12, Paul Erb Papers.
31.   Ibid., 3–4.
32.   Ibid., 2.
33.   F. 6, b. 31, OOM Papers.

CHAPTER 2

1.   OOM, interviewed by Paul Erb, 18 September 1962, transcript, 2–3. f. 7, b. 12,
      Paul Erb Papers.
2.   Ibid.
3.   As told to Jill Miller, *Goshen College Record*, 27 October 1967, 1.
4.   Umble, "Mennonite Preaching, 1864–1944," 40, 48, 277, f. 14, b. 1, Roy Umble
      Papers, 1932–85.
5.   Goshen College, *Maple Leaf*, 1914–15, 67.
6.   OOM, Paul Erb, 18 September 1962, transcript, 3. Paul Erb Papers.
7.   Bender, "Young People's Bible Meeting," 1959, *Global Anabaptist Mennonite
      Encyclopedia Online (GAMEO)*.
8.   Wenger, *The Mennonites in Indiana and Michigan*, 202.
9.   David Sauder, interviewed by author, 7 July 2011.
10.   Erb, *The Story of a Man*, 47; to Elta, 15 October 1914, f. 1. b. 22, OOM Papers.
11.   "Albert N. Wolf," Obituary, *GH* 32 (27 April 1939): 96; MennObits, www.mcusa
      -archives.org/MennObits/39/apr39.html.
12.   Anna's brothers A. L. (Abraham Lincoln) and Amos Hess were founders of the city
      of Hesston in south central Kansas, in 1886. A. L. was also one of the founders of
      Hesston College, the second Mennonite Church college, established in 1909. Anna
      also had two sisters: Lizzie, who married T. M. (Tillman Mahlon) Erb, the primary
      founder of Hesston College and its long-serving business manager; and Maria,
      who married M. M. (Moses Musser) Weaver, formerly of the Weaverland Valley in
      Pennsylvania. Sharp, *A School on the Prairie*, 71–72.
13.   Goshen College, *Maple Leaf*, 1914, n.p.
14.   Anna Wolf to Elta Wolf, 13 May 1913, f.1, b. 22, OOM Papers.
15.   Anna Wolf to Elta Wolf, series of letters 28 February–25 June 1913, f. 1, b. 22,
      OOM Papers.

16. The company's official name eventually became Miller, Hess & Company, but was often written as Miller Hess and sometimes, Miller-Hess. For convenience, I will generally use the short, unhyphenated form.

17. To OOM, 23 July 1913, f. 1, b. 22, OOM Papers.

18. To OOM, 25 June 1913, f. 1, b. 22, OOM Papers.

19. To Elta Wolf, 6 July 1913, f. 1, b. 22, OOM Papers.

20. Ibid.

21. Ibid.

22. To Elta Wolf, 10 August 1913, f. 1, b. 22, OOM Papers.

23. To OOM, 17 September 1913, f. 1, b. 22, OOM Papers. Though few wear it today, the prayer veil, or covering, was worn by MC women in obedience to Paul's teaching in 1 Corinthians 11 that women should pray or prophesy with head covered. Related plain groups such as the Church of the Brethren, Brethren in Christ, Amish, Hutterites, and Old Colony Mennonites also have followed this custom, though the style may differ.

24. To Elta, 7 January 1914, f. 2, b. 22, OOM Papers.

25. Ibid.

26. To Elta, 13 January 1914, f. 2, b. 22, OOM Papers.

27. To OOM, 18 June 1914, f. 2, b. 22, OOM Papers.

28. To Elta, 30 July 1914, f. 2, b. 22, OOM Papers.

29. To Elta, 22 June 1914, f. 2, b. 22, OOM Papers.

30. To OOM, 18 June 1914, f. 2, b. 22, OOM Papers.

31. To Elta, 29 June 1914, f. 2, b. 22, OOM Papers.

32. *Goshen College: A Pictorial History*, 1894–1994, 54–55.

33. Miller, *Culture for Service*, 54, 86.

34. To Elta, 17 September 1914, f. 3, b. 22, OOM Papers.

35. To Elta, 22 October 1914, f. 3, b. 22, OOM Papers.

36. To Elta, 25 January 1915, f. 1, b. 23, OOM Papers.

37. To Elta, 31 January 1915, f. 1, b. 23, OOM Papers.

38. To Elta, 14 February 1915, f. 1, b. 23, OOM Papers.

39. To Elta, 4 March 1915, f. 1, b. 23, OOM Papers.

40. To OOM, 13 March 1915, f. 2, b. 23, OOM Papers.

41. To Elta, 16 March 1915, f. 2, b. 23, OOM Papers.

42. A. N. Wolf to OOM, 18 March 1915, f. 2, b. 23, OOM Papers.

43. To Elta, 18 March 1915, f. 2, b. 23, OOM Papers.

44. To Elta, 25 March 1915, OOM Papers.

45. To OOM, 29 March 1915, OOM Papers.

46. To Elta, 1 April 1915, OOM Papers.

47. To Elta, 7 May 1915, OOM Papers.

48. To Elta, 1 July 1915, OOM Papers.

49. To Elta, 26 July 1915, OOM Papers.

50. To OOM, 12 July 1915, f. 2, b. 23, OOM Papers.

51. Loewen and Nolt, *Seeking Places of Peace*, 82.

52. Ibid., 106.

CHAPTER 3

1. Akron Borough, *Comprehensive Plan*, 13.

2. Lowry, "Tobacco in Amish Country," *Cigar Aficionado*, 1 March 1997.

3. Acton, "Tobacco Rebound Fruitful for Farmers," *Pittsburgh Tribune Review*, 16 February 2009.

4. Ruth, *The Earth Is the Lord's*, 658–59.
5. Acton, "Tobacco Rebound Fruitful for Farmers."
6. Smith, *Mennonites in Illinois*, 180. C. F. Derstine (1891–1967) served the Roanoke Mennonite Church, Eureka, Ill., from 1915 to 1924. He was ordained bishop in 1921.
7. John W. Miller, interviewed by author, 15 May 2010.
8. Wanner, *Akron, Pennsylvania Centennial 1895–1995*, n.p.
9. Akron Borough, *Comprehensive Plan*, 3.
10. Ibid., 99–105.
11. Ibid., 9.
12. Kissinger, *The Buggies Still Run*, 96–97.
13. Cited in Erb, *Orie O. Miller*, 48.
14. To Elta, 7 July 1915, f. 1, b. 23, OOM Papers.
15. Operations began on the third floor and basement of Elias Wolf's warehouse on Front Street, across the tracks from the Akron depot. They produced one hundred pairs of shoes daily during the first two years. In 1902, production moved uptown to a new two-story brick building at the intersection of Main and Seventh Streets, which they purchased in 1911 for $6,000. Production there increased to five hundred pairs of shoes per day. (Ebersole, "A Sketch of the Shoe Industry in Akron, Pa.," *Akron, Pennsylvania Centennial 1895–1995*, n.p.)
16. Peter Miller, a business leader and burgess, had hosted the first borough council meeting in his office. Simon P. Hess was A. N. Wolf's brother-in-law, having married Sara Wolf. The Wolfs lived at the end of Orie and Elta's block at Main and Eleventh Streets. ("Simon P. Hess," Obituary, *GH* 25 (18 August 1932): 432; MennObits.
17. The Conlins knew how to make shoes, having learned from their immigrant father, who had learned the trade in Ireland. They also provided some early capital. When the other partners learned the trade, the Conlins sold their shares in the company and discontinued their partnership. The Conlins left behind a landmark: a stately brick home at 1216 Main Street, a replica of the family home in Camden, N.J. (Marcy Conlin, email message to author, 28 February 2012.)
18. Brubaker lived in Akron and was a member of Metzler's Mennonite Church. ("Elizabeth N. Brubaker," Obituary, *GH* 25 (10 November 1932): 703–4, MennObits.
19. Klein, *Lancaster County*, 679.
20. Ibid., *The Borough of Akron*.
21. Ibid.
22. To Fellow Classmates, 18 April 1916, f. 2, b. 32, OOM Papers.
23. Loewen and Nolt, *Seeking Places of Peace*, 222–48.
24. To Dear Classmates, 9 October 1916, f. 2, b. 32, OOM Papers.
25. Beyer, *Bringing in the Sheaves*, 11–12.
26. Ibid., 29–30.
27. Nellie Miller to Cleo Mann, 19 August 1921, David Mann manuscript, "From Prairie Street Mennonite Church to Beirut, Syria, unpub. The letter is not included in the published version, *Letters from Syria 1921–1923: A Response to the Armenian Tragedy*. Transcribed and edited by David Mann, undated.
28. Ray and Ruth Brunk Horst, interviewed by author, 31 December 2010.
29. Ibid.
30. Minutes, Board of Bishops, 12 April 1914, Lancaster Mennonite Historical Society, Lancaster, Pa.

31. Ruth, *The Earth Is the Lord's*, 869.
32. *GH* 7 (9 July 1914): 233.
33. Hartzler, *Mennonites in the World War*, 56.
34. Ibid., 61–65.
35. Address in Support of the League of Nations, Pueblo, CO, 25 September 1919. Primary Documents, First World War.com www.firstworldwar.com/source/wilson speech_league.htm.
36. OOM to Elta, n.d., "Misc. Undated Family Correspondence," f. 1, b. 31, OOM Papers.
37. Juhnke, *Vision, Doctrine, War*, 227.
38. Minutes, Board of Bishops, 18 July 1918.
39. OOM, interviewed by Paul Erb, 6 March 1967, notes, b. 10, Paul Erb Papers.
40. Ruth, *The Earth Is the Lord's*, 869.
41. Lawrence, *Lady Chatterly's Lover*, 65.
42. Menno Simons, "Why I Do Not Cease Teaching and Writing," 1539, in Simons, *Complete Writings of Menno Simons*, 307.
43. Hershberger, "Historical Background to the Formation of the Mennonite Central Committee," *Mennonite Quarterly Review* (*MQR*) 44 (July 1970): 233; Goldfield et al., *The American Journey*, 652.
44. OOM, interviewed by Paul Erb, 18 September 1962, transcript, 12–13, b. 12, Paul Erb Papers.

CHAPTER 4

1. OOM diary, 25 January 1919. f. 3a, b. 31, OOM Papers.
2. Hershberger, "Mennonite Relief Commission for War Sufferers (Mennonite Church)," 1957, *GAMEO*.
3. The organization, originally named the American Committee for Armenian and Syrian Relief, was renamed the American Committee for Relief in the Near East (ACRNE) in 1918, and renamed once again as Near East Relief (NER) in 1919. The organization, still active, is now known as the Near East Foundation.
4. Audited report, 30 June 1919, f. 23, b. 71, OOM Papers.
5. To OOM, 29 January 1919, f. 1, b. 24, OOM Papers.
6. Hershberger and Beechy, "Relief Work," 1989, *GAMEO*. In the next two years, the MCRWS sent thirteen more men and two women to Syria and Turkey.
7. To OOM, 29 January 1919, f. 1, b. 24, OOM Papers.
8. During the winter of 1917–18, Nichol had addressed more than seven hundred audiences on a speaking tour in the United States, according to *The Auburn* (N.Y.) *Citizen*. Herbert Hoover recognized Nichol for his good work in promoting food conservation during the war. "Man from Syria to Speak Monday Night at Forum," *The Auburn Citizen*, Auburn, N.Y., Saturday, 2 February 1918.
9. To Elta, 24 February 1919, f. 1, b. 24, OOM Papers.
10. William Stoltzfus stayed in Syria, serving as Presbyterian missionary, teacher, and principal. From 1937 to 1958, he became president of the American Junior College for Women. From the time of his return to the United States in 1958 until his death in 1965, Stoltzfus served as secretary for college relations for Beirut College. "Stoltzfus, William A. (William Alfred) (1891–1964) Papers, 1920–1963," Presbyterian Historical Society, http://www.history.pcusa.org/collections/findingaids/fa.cfm?record_id=166.
11. Hershberger and Beechy, "Relief Work."

12. To Elta, 24 February 1919, f. 1, b. 24, OOM Papers.
13. To OOM, 28 February 1919, f. 1, b. 24, OOM Papers.
14. To Elta, 11 March 1919, f. 1, b. 24, OOM Papers.
15. Ibid.
16. To OOM, 16 March 1919, f. 1, b. 24, OOM Papers.
17. Diary, 16 March 1919, b. 31, OOM Papers.
18. Diary, 20–21 March 1919, b. 31, OOM Papers.
19. Ibid.
20. To Elta, 18 March 1919, f. 1, b. 24, OOM Papers.
21. To OOM from Chicago, 24 March 1919, f. 1, b. 24, OOM Papers.
22. To Elta, 15 March 1919, f. 1, b. 24, OOM Papers.
23. Ibid.
24. OOM to Ernest E. Miller, 6 April, 1919, f. 1, b. 24, OOM Papers.
25. OOM to secretaries of the MRCWS and MBMC, 9 April 1919, f. 1, b. 24, OOM Papers.
26. OOM to Aaron Loucks, 9 April 1919, f. 1, b. 24, OOM Papers.
27. To OOM, 6 April 1919, f. 1, b. 24, OOM Papers.
28. To Elta, 15 April 1919, f. 1, b. 24, OOM Papers.
29. To Elta, 20 April 1919, f. 1, b. 24, OOM Papers.
30. "Administrative History, United Presbyterian Church in the U.S.A. Syria Mission," *Presbyterian Historical Society*, Philadelphia, Pa., http://www.history.pcusa.org/collections/findingaids/fa.cfm?record_id=115.
31. To Elta, 27 April 1919, f. 1, b. 24, OOM Papers.
32. To OOM, 21 April 1919, f. 1, b. 24, OOM Papers.
33. Ibid.
34. Ibid.
35. To Elta, 2 June 1919, f. 1, b. 24, OOM Papers.
36. "Paris Peace Conference, 1919," *New World Encyclopedia*, http://www.newworld encyclopedia.org/entry/Paris_Peace_Conference%2C_1919.
37. To Elta, 25 May 1919, f. 1, b. 24, OOM Papers.
38. Diary, 4 May 1919, f. 3a, b. 31, OOM Papers.
39. To Elta, 25 May 1919, f. 1, b. 24, OOM Papers.
40. Ibid.
41. To Elta, 2 June 1919, f. 1, b. 24, OOM Papers.
42. To Elta, 7 June 1919, f. 1, b. 24, OOM Papers.
43. To OOM, 24 June 1919, f. 1, b. 24, OOM Papers.
44. To Elta, 6 July 1919, f. 2, b. 24, OOM Papers.
45. A. N. Wolf to OOM, 9 July 1919, f. 2, b. 24, OOM Papers.
46. To Elta, 6 September 1919, f. 2, b. 24, OOM Papers.
47. To Elta, 20 July 1919, f. 2, b. 24, OOM Papers.
48. To Elta, 1 September 1919, f. 2, b. 24, OOM Papers.
49. To OOM, 2 August 1919, f. 2, b. 24, OOM Papers.
50. To Elta, 1 September 1919, f. 2, b. 24, OOM Papers.
51. To OOM, 6 October 1919, f. 2, b. 24, OOM Papers.
52. Ibid.
53. To Elta, 30 November 1919, f. 2, b. 24, OOM Papers.
54. To OOM, 7 December 1919, f. 2, b. 24, OOM Papers.
55. OOM to Elta, n.d., "Misc. Undated Family Correspondence," f. 1, b. 31, OOM Papers.
56. To Elta, 3 January 1920, f. 1, b. 25, OOM Papers.

57. To Elta, 25 January 1920, f. 1, b. 25, OOM Papers.
58. Hershberger and Beechy, "Relief Work."
59. To Elta, 25 January 1920, f. 1, b. 25, OOM Papers.
60. Ibid.
61. To Elta, 1 April 1920, f. 1, b. 25, OOM Papers.
62. Erb, *The Story of a Man and an Era*, 270–76.
63. Ibid., 82.
64. To Elta, 11 March 1934, f. 2, b. 26, Family Correspondence, January 1930–34, OOM Papers.
65. To Elta, 30 November 1919, f. 2, b. 24, OOM Papers.

CHAPTER 5

1. C. W. Fowle to Barclay Acheson, Near East Relief, New York, N.Y., 26 April 1923; Fowle to OOM, Akron, Pa., 26 April 1923; Nellie Miller to Cleo Mann, Elkhart, Ind., 3 June 1923; Cleo Mann to Nellie Miller, Beirut, Syria, 11 June 1923; David W. Mann, a series of conversations, 2009–12. The letters are in a forthcoming book by David W. Mann, *Letters from Syria.*
2. To D. H. Bender, quoted in Erb, *Orie O. Miller*, 140.
3. Toews, *Lost Fatherland*, 21.
4. Krahn, "Molotschna Mennonite Settlement," 1956, *GAMEO.*
5. Goerz, trans., Reimer and Toews, *The Molotschna Settlement*, 213.
6. Goerz, Molotschna, 236–37.
7. Neufelt, "'We are aware of our contradictions': Russlaender Mennonite Narratives of Loss and the Reconstruction of Peoplehood, 1914–1923," 139.
8. Toews, "An Historical Reflection for Narrator and Four Voices."
9. OOM to Ernest Miller, 7 July 1920, f. 3, b. 33, OOM Papers.
10. OOM quotes Clarence Hess in his letter to Elta, 8 July 1920, f. 1, b. 25, OOM Papers.
11. Ibid.
12. Hiebert, *Feeding the Hungry*; Hershberger and Beechy, "Relief Work."
13. Hiebert, *Feeding*, 36.
14. Ibid., 44.
15. Loucks, "Report of Members of the Relief Commission," 814.
16. *GH* 13 (24 June 1920): 253; Hershberger, "Historical Background," 240.
17. Hiebert, *Feeding*, 51–53.
18. Hershberger, "Historical Background," 224.
19. Juhnke, "Turning Points," 237.
20. The reported numbers vary. Juhnke makes the point that some may have attended as spectators.
21. Loucks, "Russian Relief Work," *GH* 13 (5 August 1920): 363.
22. Juhnke, "Turning Points," 75.
23. Kauffman, "Unity," *GH* 13 (22 July 1920): 321; See also Juhnke, "Turning Points."
24. Loucks, "Russian Relief Work," *GH* 13 (5 August 1920): 363.
25. Ibid.
26. *The Elkhart Truth*, 28 July 1920; Toews, 1995.
27. Smucker, Relief Notes, *GH* 13 (8 July 1920): 300.
28. Committees invited were: Mennonite Relief Committee for War Sufferers, Old Mennonites, Levi Mumaw, Scottdale, Pa.; Emergency Relief Committee of the

General Conference, John Lichti, Deer Creek, Okla.; Emergency Relief Committee of the Mennonites of North America, D. E. Harder, Hillsboro, Kans.; Relief Commission of the Central Conference of Illinois Mennonites, Val. Strubhar, Washington, Ill.; Mennonite Brethren Church of North America, P. C. Hiebert, Hillsboro, Kans.; and Krimmer Mennonite Brethren Church of North America, D. M. Hofer, Chicago, Ill.

29. Hiebert, *Feeding*, 52–53; Dyck, 14–19.
30. Erb, *Orie O. Miller*, 143.
31. "Relief Notes," *GH* 13 (29 July 1920): 349.
32. OOM, Interviewed by Paul Erb, 18 September 1962, transcript, 20, f. 7, b. 12, Paul Erb Papers.
33. Ibid.
34. Lapp, MCC blog after a New Wineskins discussion, MCC website, http://Newwineskins.mcc.org, 2011. Lapp was executive secretary of MCC, 1985–96.
35. Kreider, email to author, 14 November 2012.
36. Diary, 2 September 1920, f. 3c, b. 31, OOM Papers, 1913–76.
37. OOM, "Farewell Message," *GH* 13 (9 September 1920): 477.
38. "GC and MC Membership Statistics in the United States of America, 1860–2003," Mennonite Church USA Historical Committee, http://www.mcusa–archives.org/resources/membership.html.
39. Epp, *Mennonites in Canada*, 304.
40. To OOM, 5 September 1920, f. 2, b. 25, OOM Papers.
41. To Elta, 26 September 1920, f. 2, b. 25, OOM Papers.
42. OOM, Interviewed by Paul Erb, 18 September 1962, transcript 15, f. 7, b. 12, Paul Erb Papers.
43. A. N. Wolf to Orie, Elta, and Lois, 21 August 1920, f. 2, b. 25, OOM Papers.
44. To OOM, 12 September 1920, f. 2, b. 25, OOM Papers.
45. Full identities of officials were gleaned from *New York Times* articles archives.
46. To Elta, 6 October 1920, f. 2, b. 25, OOM Papers.
47. Tuchman, *The Guns of August*, 79.
48. Toews, *Czars*, 110.
49. Nazarova, "Crisis in Mennonite Colonies of the Russian Soviet Federal Socialistic Republic and Ukrainian Soviet Socialistic Republic in 1917–1921 and Reactions of Western Fellow Believers," 4.
50. Nazarova, Table 1, 3.
51. Toews, *Czars*, 85.
52. Ukraine has embraced Nestor Makhno (1888–1934) as a liberator who fought to eliminate the *kulaks*. He was born in Guly-Apoli/Huliaipole in the region of Zaporozhye. There is a room dedicated to his memory in a Zaporozhye city museum. It features, ironically, a Mennonite carriage with a machine gun mounted on the back.
53. Nazarova, 9.
54. The grain seeded in 1921–22 dropped by as much as 83 percent. Wheat production, the primary staple, was in 1921 only 4 percent of that harvested in 1915. Nazarova, 7.
55. Toews, *Czars*, 113.
56. Janzen to the *"Mennonitischen Hilfsaktionen im In und Auslande"* (Batum, 20 October 1922). Quoted by John B. Toews, *Czars*, 122.
57. Diary, 6 October 1920, f. 3c, b. 31, OOM Papers. The mission was supported by various North American Mennonite committees.

58. To Elta, 8 October 1920, f. 2, b. 25, OOM Papers.

59. To OOM, 8–18 October 1920, f. 2, b. 25, OOM Papers.

60. Minutes, Lancaster Mennonite Conference Board of Bishops, 30 September 1920. Lancaster Mennonite Historical Society, Lancaster, Pa.

61. Diary, 10 October 1920; Hiebert, *Feeding*, 94.

62. Diary, 10 October 1920, f. 3c, b. 31, OOM Papers.

63. Hege and Neff, "Melitopol (Zaporizhie [*sic*] Oblast, Ukraine)," *GAMEO*.

64. Diary; Hiebert, *Feeding*, 94–95.

65. Diary, 13 October 1920; Hiebert, *Feeding*, 95. Manuscript, "The First Essay into Russia and the Subsequent Work in Constantinople," in the Ed Miller Private Collection, 5.

66. Diary, 15 October 1920, f. 3c., b. 31, OOM Papers.

67. Hiebert, *Feeding*, 95.

68. Ibid.

69. Diary, 16 October 1920, f. 3c, b. 31, OOM Papers.

70. Orie sometimes read this psalm with protégés, as he did with Paul Landis in Honduras in 1962. They had traveled together from Belize to Honduras, and on the following morning they were to part; Landis would remain in Honduras and Miller would go on to Bolivia to assist in the resettlement of Old Colony Mennonites. That night Orie turned to Psalm 91, saying, "Now, just like you and I are going to separate tomorrow, Clayton Kratz and I separated the next day." With Landis in the hotel room, Orie read the psalm audibly and led in prayer. Paul G. Landis, interview.

71. Diary, 16 October 1920, f. 3c, b. 31, OOM Papers; Hiebert, *Feeding*, 96.

72. King, "In the Footsteps of Clayton Kratz," in John E. Sharp, *Gathering at the Hearth*, 212.

73. Ibid.

74. Ibid.

75. Wilbur K. Thomas to OOM, 25 May, 1925; Charles V. Vickery to V. E. Reiff, 30 March 1925; William S. Dodd to V. E. Reiff, 1 April 1925; G. A. Peters to OOM, received 23 May 1925, all in the Ed Miller Private Collection.

76. In 1989, Branch Valley Productions produced a DVD, *Clayton Kratz: Can We Depend on You?* But still, Kratz's story continues to intrigue new generations. In 2000, eighty years after his abduction, four Goshen College students and graduates followed Kratz's trail to South Russia in an attempt to understand his sacrifice as well as to uncover new details of his disappearance. Though they unearthed nothing new, their journey is told on a DVD produced by Sidney King, *Shroud for a Journey: The Clayton Kratz Story*. The biography is Geraldine Gross Harder's *When Apples Are Ripe: The Clayton Kratz Story*, published by Herald Press in 1972.

77. OOM to Eli Stoltzfus, 1927, as quoted by Paul Erb, *Orie O. Miller*, 148.

78. OOM to David Thomas, 8 April 1975, f. 45, b. 77, OOM Papers.

79. Ibid.

80. To Elta, 23 October 1920, f. 2, b. 25, OOM Papers.

81. "American Supplies Looted in Near East," *New York Times*, 14 September 1920. *New York Times* Archive, www.nytimes.com.

82. To Elta, 31 October 1920, f. 2, b. 25, OOM Papers.

83. Toews, *Lost Fatherland*, 52.

84. Simkin, "The Russian Civil War," Primary Sources, Spartacus Educational, http://www.spartacus.schoolnet.co.uk/RUScivilwar.htm.

85. To Elta, 23 October 1920, f. 2, b. 25, OOM Papers.
86. Diary, 17 November 1920, f. 3c, b. 25, OOM Papers.
87. James Huebert, memo to author, 7 February 2012; Jacob Huebert, tape-recorded memories, made available to the author by James Huebert.
88. To Elta, 19 November 1920, f. 2, b. 25, OOM Papers.
89. To Levi Mumaw, Scottdale, Pa., received 29 November 1920, f. 2, b. 31, OOM Papers.
90. P. C. Hiebert to Mumaw, 21 November 1920, P. C. Hiebert Collection, MCUSA Archives—North Newton, Kan.
91. To Elta, 28 November 1920, f. 2, b. 25, OOM Papers.
92. Hiebert, *Feeding*, 96.
93. To Elta, 12 December 1920, f. 2, b. 25, OOM Papers.
94. Diary, 16 December 1920, f. 3c, b. 31, OOM Papers.
95. Ibid.
96. To Elta, 13 February 1921, f. 2, b. 25, OOM Papers.
97. *Feeding the Hungry*, 109.
98. To Elta, 13 February 1921, f. 2, b. 25, OOM Papers.
99. *Mennonitisches Hilfswerk, Christenpflicht.*
100. Diary, 20 February 1921, f. 3c, b. 31, OOM Papers.
101. Diary, 23 February 1921, OOM Papers
102. Kreider and Goossen, *Hungry, Thirsty, a Stranger*, 32–36.
103. Hiebert, *Feeding*, 214–15.
104. Benjamin Janz, quoted by Maxwell Kratz, in the foreword to Hiebert, *Feeding*.

CHAPTER 6

1. Toews and Bender, "Fundamentalism," 1989, *GAMEO*.
2. Brunk, *History of Mennonites in Virginia*, 501.
3. "Christian Fundamentals," Loewen, *One Lord, One Church, One Hope, and One God*, 1985, 71.
4. Neff, Wenger, Bender, and Loewen. "Confessions, Doctrinal," *GAMEO*.
5. Loewen, *Confessions*.
6. 2 Timothy 3:16 (KJV).
7. Sharp, "Balancing Power: Our Journey with Authority and Autonomy," 2000.
8. Bender, "Introduction," to Wenger, *The Mennonites in Indiana and Michigan*, 1961, 42–43.
9. OOM to D. D. Miller, 25 July 1921, f. 4, b. 34, OOM Papers.
10. OOM to D. D. Miller, 27 March 1923, f. 1, b. 40, OOM Papers.
11. Susan F. Miller, *Culture for Service*, 337, n. 72.
12. Minutes, Mennonite Board of Education, 18 June 1923, b. 1, Mennonite Board Of Education Records, V-1-8. Mennonite Church USA Archives—Goshen. Goshen, Ind.
13. OOM, interviewed by Paul Erb, 18 Sept. 1962, Transcript, 19–20, f. 7, b. 12, Paul Erb Papers, 1909–67. HM1-230. Mennonite Church USA Archives—Goshen.
14. Ibid.
15. Ibid.
16. Minutes, Lancaster Mennonite Conference Board of Bishops, 2 October 1930, LMHS.
17. Minutes, Special Meeting, MBE, 26 April 1923, V-1-8 b. 1. Mennonite Church USA Archives—Goshen.
18. Kreider, *My Early Years*, 127.

19. Minutes, MBE, 18 June 1923, b. 1, MBE Records.
20. Ibid, Minutes, 21 December 1923.
21. To Frank Smucker, 8 June 1923, b. 9, Paul Erb Papers.
22. To Vernon Smucker, 23 June 1923, b. 9, Paul Erb Papers.
23. From Vernon Smucker, 26 June 1923, b. 9, Paul Erb Papers.
24. To Elta, 18 November 1923, f. 3, b. 25, OOM Papers.
25. S. C. Yoder, "Plans for Reorganization of Goshen College," 1923, f. 8, b. 64, OOM Papers.
26. S. C. Yoder to Noah Oyer, 14 February 1924, Dean's Files, Noah Oyer Collection, MCA-G. For context, see Sharp, *A School on the Prairie*, 165, 170.
27. S. C. Yoder to OOM, n.d., f. 3, b. 2, S. C. Yoder Papers, 1917–74. HM 1-162. Mennonite Church USA Archives—Goshen.
28. OOM, interviewed by Paul Erb, 6 March 1967, notes, b.10, Paul Erb Papers.
29. Miller and Witmer to Alumni, 9 August 1924, f. 6, b. 14, OOM Papers.
30. Annual Reports, 1922–25, EMBMC.
31. To A. N. and Anna Wolf, 6 November 1920, f. 5, b. 33, OOM Papers.
32. J. S. Shoemaker to OOM, 20 January 1920, f. 5, b. 33, OOM Papers.
33. Hiebert, *Feeding*, 65.
34. OOM, "Report on Russian Refugee Immigration," 1921, f. 9, b. 62, OOM Papers.
35. Erb, *Orie O. Miller*, 150–51.
36. OOM, "Report," *Missionary Messenger* (*MM*).
37. Ibid.
38. Levi Mumaw to P. C. Hiebert, 20 October 1921, MLA.MS 37, P. C. Hiebert Collection, MCUSA Archives—North Newton, Kans.
39. James Huebert, memo to author, 7 February 2012; Jacob Huebert, tape-recorded memories, made available to the author by James Huebert.
40. Erb, *Orie O. Miller*, 150.
41. Toews, *Czars*, 123.
42. Itemized in pencil on United States Hotel, Boston, Mass., letterhead, f. 7, b. 64, OOM Papers.
43. Quoted material in this and the following paragraphs from OOM to Elta, series of letters, 4 March 1924 through 4 September 1927, f. 3, b. 25, and f. 1, b. 26, OOM Papers.
44. OOM, interviewed by Paul Erb, 18 September 1962, transcript, 19, f. 7, b. 12, Paul Erb Papers.
45. John Mellinger, handwritten note, miscellaneous files, EMM archives, Salunga, Pa.
46. Beyer, *Bringing in the Sheaves*, 143–44; Erb, *Orie O. Miller*, 21, identifies Landis as the one chosen instead of Orie.
47. OOM, interviewed by Paul Erb, 18 September 1962, transcript, 16, 58–59, f. 7, b. 12, Paul Erb Papers.
48. Schlabach, *War, Peace, and Social Conscience*, 42.
49. Ibid., 25–26.
50. Editorial, *MM*, II, no. 8 (15 November 1925): 1.
51. *MM* 2 (15 December 1925): 1.
52. "Our Peace Message," *GH* 19 (7 October 1926): 595–98.
53. Ibid.
54. Ibid.
55. Bender, "Peace Problems Committee (Mennonite Church)," 1959, *GAMEO*.
56. Hershberger, interviewed by Leonard Gross, 3 December 1986, published in the *Mennonite Historical Bulletin* 48 (January 1987): 5.

57. Ruth, *The Earth Is the Lord's.*
58. Kraus, ed., *Evangelicalism and Anabaptism,* 11.
59. Hostetler editorial, *Christian Monitor* (26 February 1926): 68–69, in response to Mosemann, "The Modern Peace Movement," *GH* 27 (28 January 1926): 898.
60. Ruth, *The Earth Is the Lord's,* 907.
61. Mosemann to Miller, 16 August 1926, f. 1, b. 9, Peace Problems Committee, 1917–71, I-3-5; OOM, 1925–65, I-3-5-3, Correspondence 1926.
62. OOM to Moseman, 30 September 1927, f. 1, b. 9, Mennonite Church Peace Problems Committee Records.
63. Mosemann to OOM, 27 December 1926, f. 1, b. 9, MC PCC Records.
64. OOM to Richard Wood, Philadelphia, Pa., 29 December 1926, f. 6, b. 26, PPC Correspondence.
65. OOM to Richard Wood, 29 December 1926, f. 1, b. 26, MC PPC Records.
66. Wood to OOM, 7 January 1927, f. 2, b. 9, MC PPC Records.
67. Ibid., 98.
68. Mosemann to OOM, 30 December 1927, f. 3, b. 9, PPC Records.
69. OOM to Frey, 25 October 1927, f. 3, b. 9, PPC Records.
70. Mosemann to John Horsch, 11 Oct. 1927, f. 3, b. 9, PPC Records.
71. Juhnke, *Vision, Doctrine, War,* 283.
72. OOM to Mosemann, 30 January 1928, quoted by Juhnke in *Vision, Doctrine, War,* 283–84.
73. To Elta, 30 April 30 1928, f. 1, b. 26, OOM Papers.
74. To Elta, 3 January 1929, f. 1, b. 26, OOM Papers.
75. Snyder, interviewed by Robert S. Kreider, 15 February 1982, Transcript p. 8. Snyder was quoting John Snyder at OOM's memorial service.
76. Hiebert to "Our Brethren and Contributing Constituency," P. C. Hiebert Papers, 27.36.263, MCUSA Archives—North Newton, Kans.
77. OOM to Hiebert, 26 February 1924, P. C. Hiebert Papers, 37.27.269.
78. Minutes, Preliminary Meeting of the American Mennonite Relief Commission, 30 December 1924, f. 3, b. 1, Mennonite Central Committee Minutes (MCC), 1920–95. IX-5-1. Mennonite Church USA Archives—Goshen. Goshen, Ind.; Hiebert, *Feeding,* 422–27.
79. Minutes, MCC executive committee, Philadelphia, Pa., 1 August 1925, b. 1, MCC Minutes.
80. Hiebert, "Report of the Sub-Committee on Policies to the MCC," f. 52, b. 8, MS. 37, P. C. Hiebert Collection, MC USA Archives—North Newton, Kans.
81. Ibid., 329–30.

CHAPTER 7

1. OOM to Elta, 8 October 1930, f. 2, b. 26, Family Correspondence, Jan. 1930–34, OOM Papers.
2. Bentley et al., *Traditions & Encounters,* 608–9.
3. Ibid.
4. OOM to Elta, 30 April, 1930–13 April, 1931, f. 1, b. 26, Family Correspondence, January 1930–34, OOM Papers.
5. OOM, *MM,* I, no. 1 (15 April 1924): 1.
6. Editorial, *MM* II (15 January 1926): 1.
7. Editorial, *MM* III (15 April 1926): 2–3.
8. *MM* III (15 May 1926): 1.

9. *MM* III (15 January 1927) through *MM* IV (15 September 1927).

10. OOM, "The Present Mennonite Migration," *MQR* I (April 1927): 11.

11. *MM*, III (15 May 1926): 1.

12. Harder, *David Toews Was Here*, 176.

13. *MM* VI (15 December 1929): 10–11.

14. Duerksen, *Lest You Forget the Stories*, 2009, 65; Dyck, Kreider, and Lapp, *From the Files of MCC: The Mennonite Central Committee Story*, vol. 1. "Documents," 40.

15. *MM* VI (15 December 1929): 10–11.

16. Ibid.

17. At a special meeting of MCC at Elkhart, Ind., 25 January 1930, Orie Miller and two others were appointed to bring a recommendation the same day. The nineteen persons present unanimously affirmed the study committee's recommendation that MCC be given the task of moving one hundred families then in Germany to Paraguay. Also, *From the Files*, C. J. Dyck et al., 40–42.

18. Redekop, *Strangers Become Neighbors*, 94. For a review of the debate in the Paraguay Congress leading to the privileges, see Edgar Stoesz, *Like a Mustard Seed*, 31–32.

19. Stoesz, to tour group to Paraguay, March 2012.

20. Ibid., C. J. Dyck et al., 42–43.

21. Redekop, *Strangers*, 100; Stoesz, *Mustard Seed*, 50–52, reports numbers similar to Redekop: 1,945 plus 373 from Amur via Harbin.

22. Duerksen, *Lest You Forget*, 65.

23. *MM* VI (15 December 1929): 10–11.

24. *MM* VII (25 January 1931) 14–15; (3 May 1931): 10–11.

25. Redekop, *Strangers*, 100; Stoesz, *Mustard Seed*, 52.

26. *MM* VIII (26 July 1932): 3.

27. *MM* III (23 Aug 1931): 3.

28. Duerksen, *Lest You Forget*, 86–92.

29. Stoesz, *Mustard Seed*, 56.

30. To Elta, 17 September 1931, f. 2, b. 26, Family Correspondence, Jan. 1930–34, OOM Papers.

31. Diary, 16 September 1931, 1, Aug–Sept. 1931, f. 3e, b. 31, 1–3, OOM Papers.

32. Ibid., 3–4.

33. Edgar Stoesz as told to the author in March 2012, and summarized in his book, *Like a Mustard Seed*, 134. The Fernheimers had used cooperatives in Russia, and in a meeting with T. K. Hershey on February 24–25, 1931, before Orie arrived, the idea of cooperatives had been discussed. See C. J. Dyck et al., 48.

34. Diary, 29 September 1931.

35. Ibid.

36. Ibid.

37. Ibid.

38. *MM* VIII (29 November 1931): 2

39. *MM* VIII (29 November 1931): 2–4.

40. *MM* VIII (17 January 1932): 1.

41. Enclosed in the letter to Elta, 31 March 1932, f. 2, b. 26, Family Correspondence, Jan. 1930–34, OOM Papers.

42. Minutes, Local Board, 2 October 1933, RG I -1-A Early Papers, b. 1, Hesston College Archives; Sharp, *A School on the Prairie*, 204–5.

43. Yoder to OOM, 28 July 1932 f. 1, b. 58, H. S. Bender papers. Quoted by Al Keim, *Harold S. Bender*, 228.

44. Wilbert Shenk interview.

45. OOM to Bender, 8 March 1932, f. 1, b. 57, Bender papers; Al Keim, *Harold S. Bender*, 229.

46. Ibid., 230.

47. OOM to H. S. Bender in Baden, Germany, 24 June 1935, f. 2, b. 1, Correspondence, January–July 1935, OOM Papers.

48. For more, see Ruth, *The Earth Is the Lord's*, 878–79.

49. Ibid., 879, 868.

50. *MM* IV (24 October 1928): 15.

51. *MM* V (22 March 1929): 10.

52. *MM* VII (27 July 1930): 1.

53. *MM* VII (26 October 1930): 1.

54. Ibid.

55. Landis, "God Uses Men," *MM* XXXV (August 1958): 3–4.

56. *MM* VIII (3 May 1931): 7–8.

57. *MM* X (23 April 1933): 2.

58. *MM* X (22 October 1933): 3.

59. *MM* X (17 December 1933): 4.

60. Ibid., 12.

61. Mcleish, "The World Dominion Movement: Its Ideals and Activities," *International Review of Mission*, 23, 215.

62. Elam W. Stauffer, interviewed by Charles Bauman and Maynard Kurtz, May 1971, Transcript, 4, Archive files, Eastern Mennonite Missions, Salunga, Pa.

63. Ibid.

64. To Clarence, Ray, Milo, Walter, et al., 24 December 1933, f. 2, b. 26, Family Correspondence, January 1930–34, OOM Papers.

65. To Elta, 23 December 1933, f. 2, b. 26, OOM Papers.

66. Elam W. Stauffer to OOM, 20 March 1968, "Miller, Orie O," 1967–68, EMM Archives, Salunga, Pa.

67. To Elta, 23 December 1933, f. 2, b. 26, Family Correspondence, Jan. 1930–34, OOM Papers.

68. Stauffer, "Orie O. Miller's Vision for Mission," Tribute, 25 October 1977, OOM folder in Nathan Hege, *MM* editorial file, EMM archives, Salunga, Pa.

69. Lewin, "The Old Man of Olduvai Gorge," *Smithsonian* (October 2002), http://www.smithsonianmag.com/history-archaeology/olduvai.html. Louis and Mary Leakey made their most famous discovery of *Zinjanthropus boisei* in 1959. They had begun their significant archeological work in 1931. They were excavating the Olduvia Gorge (now spelled Oldupai) site in the Great Rift Valley some 250 miles east of Shirati. In 1974, paleoanthropologists Donald Johanson and Tom Gray, while digging in Hadar, Ethiopia, found remains of the still-older "Lucy" calculated to be 3.2 million years old. Hadar is in the northern extension of the Great Rift Valley. See Ann Gibbons, "The Human Family's Earliest Ancestors," Smithsonian (March 2010), http://www.smithsonianmag.com/science-nature/The-Human-Familys-Earliest-Ancestors.html.

70. Bentley et al., *Traditions & Encounters*, 293–95.

71. Ibid., vol. II, 568–69, 627.

72. To Elta, 12 January 1933. The year is surely mistaken; it is 1934, f. 2, b. 26, Family Correspondence, Jan. 1930–34, OOM Papers.

73. Elam W. Stauffer to OOM, 20 March 1968, "Miller, Orie O," 1967–68, EMM Archives, Salunga, Pa.

74. *MM* X (18 March 1934): 3–5.

75. OOM, *MM* X (18 March 1934); Elam Stauffer, interviewed by Charles Bauman and Maynard Kurtz, May 1971, transcript, 4, Archive files, Eastern Mennonite Missions, Salunga, Pa.

76. Ibid., Stauffer.

77. *MM* X (18 March 1934): 3–5; Elam Stauffer, interviewed by Charles Bauman and Maynard Kurtz, May 1971, transcript, 5, Archive files, Eastern Mennonite Missions, Salunga, Pa.

78. Stauffer, "Orie O. Miller's Vision for Mission," OOM folder in Nathan Hege, *MM* editorial file, EMM archives, Salunga, Pa.

79. To Elta, 11 February 1934, f. 2, b. 26, Family Correspondence, Jan. 1930–34, OOM Papers.

80. Shirati Mission Chronology, EMM Archives, Salunga, Pa.

81. Elam W. Stauffer, interviewed by Charles Bauman and Maynard Kurtz, May 1971, transcript, 7, Archive files, Eastern Mennonite Missions, Salunga, Pa.

82. *MM* XI (8 July 1934): 4; "Panorama: 50 Years in Mission," *MM* XLI (December 1964): 15.

83. J. N. Kaufman to OOM, telegram, 11 January 1934, f. 2, b. 26, Family Correspondence, January 1930–34, OOM Papers.

84. Ruth B. Miller to OOM, 12 December 1933, f. 2, b. 26, Family Correspondence, January 1930–34, OOM Papers.

85. OOM Individual Tax Returns for 1932 and 1933, Ed Miller Private Collection.

86. Elta to OOM, 23 January 1934, f. 2, b. 26, Family Correspondence, Jan. 1930–34, OOM Papers.

87. Ruth, *The Earth*, 931.

88. Elta to OOM, 28 January 1934, f. 2, b. 26, Family Correspondence, Jan. 1930–34, OOM Papers.

89. A. N. Wolf to OOM, 28 January 1934, f. 2, b. 26, Family Correspondence, Jan. 1930–34, OOM Papers.

90. Elta to OOM, 1 February 1934, f. 2, b. 26, Family Correspondence, Jan. 1930–34, OOM Papers.

91. Lois to OOM, 8 February 1934, f. 2, b. 26, Family Correspondence, Jan. 1930–34, OOM Papers.

92. Ruth, *The Earth*, 926.

93. "Mennonite Farewell," *Time* magazine (5 March 1934): 5, f. 2, b. 26, OOM Papers.

94. Ibid.

95. Elta to OOM, 28 February 1934, f. 2, b. 26, Family Correspondence, Jan. 1930–34, OOM Papers.

96. OOM to Elta, 28 February 1934, f. 2, b. 26, Family Correspondence, Jan. 1930–34, OOM Papers.

97. Elta to OOM, 5 March 1934, sent to Baden, Germany, f. 2, b. 26, Family Correspondence, Jan. 1930–34, OOM Papers.

98. OOM to Elta, 21 March 1934, from Bombay, f. 2, b. 26, Family Correspondence, Jan. 1930–34, OOM Papers.

99. Elam W. Stauffer, interviewed by Charles Bauman and Maynard Kurtz, May 1971, transcript, 17, Archive files, Eastern Mennonite Missions, Salunga, Pa.

100. Shirati Mission Chronology, EMM Archives, Salunga, Pa.

101. Sue Herr Burkholder, interviewed by author, 29 May 2011.

102. OOM to Elta, 17 September 1935, f. 1, b. 27, Family Correspondence, Jan. 1935–39, OOM Papers.

103. OOM, interviewed by Paul Erb, 6 March 1967, notes, p. 26, b. 10, HM1-230, Paul Erb Papers.

104. OOM, "The Historic Peace Church[es] Fellowship," n.d., f. 3, b. 7, Family Correspondence, January 1935–39, OOM Papers.

105. In late 1966, Orie sold the 1125 Main Street home to Paul and Marjorie Ruth, saying in a letter, "In this house I was married in 1915 and in it all our children were born—it being our home for the first 20 years of our married life, so with it are our best wishes that it may continue a happy place for your family and home life." OOM to Paul Ruth, 22 November 1966, Ed Miller Private Collection.

106. The old house was worth $8,000, while the new house and lot were valued at $19,000. Statement of Assets, 15 December 1936, f. 18, b. 72, O.O. Miller financial statements, 1930–1943, OOM Papers.

107. S. C. Yoder to OOM, 12 January 1939, f. 3, b. 2, Family Correspondence, Jan. 1935–39, OOM Papers.

108. D. A. Yoder to OOM, 30 May 1938, f. 1, b. 2, Family Correspondence, Jan. 1935–39, OOM Papers.

109. S. C. Yoder to OOM, 16 January 1939, f. 3, b. 2, OOM Papers; Orie was the chair of an administrative committee appointed by MBE to oversee the presidential transition. Since another on-campus administrative committee is under discussion and to avoid confusion I will refer to Orie's committee as an oversight committee.

110. Kauffman to OOM, 15 April 1939, f. 3, b. 2, Family Correspondence, Jan. 1935–39, OOM Papers.

111. OOM to Daniel Kauffman, 17 April 1939, Family Correspondence, Jan. 1935–39, OOM Papers.

112. Graber to OOM, 14 April 1939, f. 3, b. 2, Family Correspondence, Jan. 1935–39, OOM Papers.

113. OOM to Graber, 17 April 1939, f. 3, b. 2, Family Correspondence, Jan. 1935–39, OOM Papers.

114. OOM to Graber, 6 July 1939, f. 4, b. 2, Family Correspondence, Jan. 1935–39, OOM Papers.

115. Graber to OOM, 18 July 1939, f. 4, b. 2, Family Correspondence, Jan. 1935–39, OOM Papers.

116. Graber to OOM, n. d., f. 10, b. 4, Family Correspondence, Jan. 1935–39, OOM Papers.

117. Lois to "dear Folks," 29 January 1936, Family Correspondence, Jan. 1935–39, OOM Papers.

118. Lois to "dear Folks," 9 February 1936, Family Correspondence, Jan. 1935–39, OOM Papers.

119. Lois to OOM and Elta, 9 February 1936–9 January 1937, Family Correspondence, Jan. 1925–39, OOM Papers.

120. "Articles of Agreement," 30 September 1937, f. 7, b. 1; Ibid.

121. John W. Miller, interviewed by author, 15–16 May 2010; Tina Bechtel and Larry Beach correspondence with author, 28 and 29 November 2012. Larry Miller Beach was born in Nutley, 28 October 1938. During the war they moved to Washington, D.C., where Christine (Tina) Lois Beach was born 14 February 1943. In 1945, they moved to Montclair, N.J., where Lawrence Miller Beach was born 24 September 1947. After living in Buckingham, Conn., they moved to Doylestown, Pa.

122. "Nettie Miller" Obituary, *GH* 30 (3 February 1938): 958–59, MennObits, www
      .mcusa-archives.org/MennObits/38/feb38.html.
123. "Wolf, Albert N." Obituary, *GH* 32 (27 April 1939): 96, MennObits, www.mcusa
      -archives.org/MennObits/39/apr39.html.
124. Real estate consisted of his home, the "Shirker" lot, Front Street property, a ware-
      house, and two farms worth $13,100 and $17,500. His stocks and bonds were
      valued at $46,300. Aberdeen-Angus steers, poultry, equipment, and a Packard
      car rounded out the estate. A. N. Wolf estate papers including his will dated 16
      January 1934, Ed Miller Private Collection.
125. OOM Balance Sheet, 1 January 1940, Ed Miller Private Collection.

CHAPTER 8

1. Bentley et al., *Traditions & Encounters*, 639–41.
2. Ibid., 641.
3. Tindall and Shi, *America: A Narrative History*, 1156–57.
4. Juhnke and Hunter, *Missing Peace*, 207–10.
5. Tindall and Shi, *America: A Narrative History*, 1194–96.
6. "U.S. Military Spending, 1945–91." The Center for Defense Information reports
    annual U.S. military spending during the Cold War of $298.5 billion annually and
    a total cost of $13.1 trillion (in 1996 dollars), http://academic.brooklyn.cuny.edu/
    history/johnson/milspend.htm; *Traditions & Encounters*, 652–54.
7. Memo from the Continuation Committee, R. W. Balderston, Ray Keim, and OOM
    to "Friends of Peace Everywhere," [1936].
8. Minutes, Conference of Historic Peace Churches, Newton, Kans., 31 October–1
    November 1935, PPC 1917–71, I-3-5 HPC 1925–40, b. 24, f. 3.
9. Ibid.
10. Ibid.; "Christian Patriotism, a Statement Outlined by Representatives of Brethren,
    Friends, Mennonites, Assembled at Newton, Kansas, Oct. 31–Nov. 2, 1935."
11. Ibid., Minutes.
12. Ibid., Memo, Continuation Committee.
13. Handwritten notes in correspondence files, Correspondence, H. S. Bender, 1962–
    67, b. 77, f. 2, OOM Papers; Miller, "Faith of My Father . . . Living Still?" *GH* 71
    (16 May 1978): 389–90.
14. Paul G. Landis, interview by author, 3 March 2011.
15. Minutes, PPC, Goshen, Ind., 4 January 1936, PPC Minutes, 1925–44, I-3-5-3,
    Minutes & Reports, b. 7–8.
16. Quoted in Erb, *The Story of a Man and an Era*, 262.
17. Minutes, Joint Committee of Historic Peace Churches, 18 February 1936.
18. Minutes, Continuation Committee of Historic Peace Churches, Chicago, Ill., 16
    May 1936.
19. Minutes, Sub-Committee on Literature of the Historic Peace Churches, 18
    September 1936.
20. Quoted in Erb, *Orie O. Miller*, 213.
21. Minutes, PPC, 14 April and 14 June 1937, Minutes, Reports, b. 7–8.
22. Minutes, PPC, 14 June 1937.
23. Mennonite Church, "Statement of Our Position on Peace, War and Military
    Service," 1937)," 1937, *GAMEO*; Keim, *Bender*, 274–75.
24. "Our Position on Peace, War, and Military Service," adopted by MC General
    Conference, August 1937.

25. Keim, *Bender*, 274.
26. French, *We Won't Murder*, 128, quoted in Hershberger, *The Mennonite Church in the Second World War*, 3.
27. Gingerich, *Service for Peace*, 19–20; Schlabach, *War, Peace, and Social Conscience*, 92.
28. "Plan of Action for Mennonites in Case of War," Mennonite Central Peace Committee (MCPC), 30 September 1939, World War II Documents, I-3-5-7, PPC Collection, 1917–71, f. 1 b. 36.
29. Ibid.
30. Minutes, MCPC, March 1939.
31. Keim, *Bender*, 277.
32. Unruh, *In the Name of Christ*, 213. The delegates on 12 February 1937 were Alvin J. Coate and Rufus M. Jones, Quakers; Paul H. Bowman and Rufus Bowman of the Brethren; and representing Mennonites were C. L. Graber and Andrew J. Neuenschwander as per Schlabach, *War, Peace, and Social Conscience*, 91.
33. Minutes, Continuation Committee, Goshen, Ind., 17 September 1939.
34. Ibid.
35. Keim, *Harold S. Bender*, 285–86.
36. Minutes, Continuation Committee, Chicago, Ill., 17 February 1940.
37. Keim and Stoltzfus, *Politics of Conscience*, 80–81.
38. Minutes, executive committee, MCPC, Goshen, Ind., 9 June 1940.
39. OOM, interviewed by Paul Erb, 18 September 1962, transcript, 42. HM1-230, Paul Erb Papers.
40. Ferhenbach, T. R. *F.D.R.'s Undeclared War, 1937–1941*, Robertson Library, 33.
41. Ibid., 193.
42. Ibid., 118.
43. Keim, *The CPS Story*, 17.
44. Ibid., 78–79.
45. Ferhenbach, *F.D.R.'s Undeclared War*, 88; Keim, *The CPS Story*, 18–19.
46. Joseph N. Weaver, interviewed by Grant M. Stoltzfus, 25 May 1972, transcript, 7, II-MS-29 B1 F8, Transcripts of Interviews OOM et al., EMU Archives.
47. Ibid., 8.
48. M. R. Zigler interview, 8.
49. OOM, undated article on historic peace churches. In 1974, OOM sent the article to Donald Durnbaugh as requested for inclusion in a book on Brethren Service. Miller wrote, "I do not remember quite when I wrote the paper, nor at whose request, but in rereading same, it states my convictions now precisely." 22 July 1974, f. 3, b. 77, OOM Papers.
50. Ferhenbach, *F.D.R.'s Undeclared War*, 78–89.
51. Marmion, *Selective Service*, 9.
52. Minutes, executive committee, MCPC, Newton, Kans., 14 September 1940.
53. Hershberger, *The Mennonite Church in the Second World War*, 15–16.
54. Minutes, Annual Meeting of the MCPC, Chicago, Ill., 4–5 October 1940.
55. Ibid.
56. Ibid.
57. M. R. Zigler, interviewed by Grant M. Stoltzfus, 9 October 1968, transcript, 5.
58. Ibid.
59. Minutes, NCRCO, Washington, D.C., 22 October 1940.
60. Ibid.
61. Marmion, *Selective Service*, 10.

62. M. R. Zigler, 6.

63. Ferhenbach, *F.D.R.'s Undeclared War*, 89; Marmion, *Selective Service*, 10.

64. Bush, *Two Kingdoms, Two Loyalties*, 72–73.

65. Joseph N. Weaver, interviewed by Grant M. Stoltzfus, 25 May 1972, transcript, 11, 14, II-MS-29 f. 8, b. 1, Transcripts of Interviews OOM et al., EMU Archives.

66. "Report of a Meeting Related to the Civilian Public Service Program," 17 March 1942, transcript, 35, II-B-55, E. G. Gehman Collection, f. 3, b. 5, EMU Archives.

67. General Lewis B. Hershey, interviewed by Grant M. Stoltzfus, 8 November 1968, transcript, 18, II-MS-29 f. 8, b. 1, Transcripts of Interviews OOM et al., EMU Archives.

68. Keim, *CPS Story*, 34.

69. Colonel Louis Kosch, interviewed by Grant M. Stoltzfus, 8 November 1968, transcript, 16–17, II-MS-29 f. 8, b. 1, Transcripts of Interviews OOM et al., EMU Archives.

70. Hershberger, *Mennonite Church in the Second World War*, 19.

71. Ibid.; John D. Unruh, *In the Name of Christ*, 234–35.

72. OOM to H. A. Fast, 13 November 1940, MCC Correspondence, IX-6-3, f. 27, b. 2.

73. Unruh, *In the Name of Christ*, 236–37.

74. Keim, *CPS Story*, 31.

75. OOM, Record of Conversations, 31.

76. Keim, *CPS Story*, 29.

77. Ibid.

78. Kosch, interview, 4.

79. Keim, *CPS Story*, 32.

80. Weaver, interview, 12.

81. Kosch, interview, 4.

82. Weaver, interview, 12.

83. Keim, *CPS Story*, 33, 40.

84. Sanford Shetler to E. G. Gehman, 2 May 1942, Ernest G. Gehman Collection, f. 4, b. 5, II-MS-55, CPS General Correspondence, EMU Archives.

85. Toews, *Mennonites in American Society*, 153–54.

86. "Report of a Meeting Related to the Civilian Public Service Program," 17 March 1942, II-B-55, E. G. Gehman Collection, f. 3, b. 5, EMU Archives.

87. Robert S. Kreider, interviewed by author, 3 February 2010; and later personal conversations.

88. Ruth Krady Lehman, "Orie O. Miller as I Remember Him," letter to author, 22 September 2011.

89. E. G. Gehman to Sanford Shetler, 2 May 1942, Gehman Collection.

90. Gehman to Shetler, 14 January 1946, Gehman Collection.

91. Gehman to C. Z. Martin, 18 May 1942, Gehman Collection.

92. Sanford G. Shetler to E. G. Gehman, 12 May 1942, f. 4, b. 5, II-MS-55, CPS General Correspondence, Ernest G. Gehman Collection, EMU Archives.

93. Ibid.

94. George R. Brunk to E. G. Gehman, 29 May 1942, Gehman Collection.

95. George R. Brunk to E. G. Gehman, 8 June, 1942, Gehman Collection.

96. Sanford Shetler to E. G. Gehman, 11 June 1942, Gehman Collection.

97. E. G. Gehman to John L. Horst, 8 August 1942, Gehman Collection.

98. Ibid.

99. Smith to E. G. Gehman, CPS, f. 5, b. 5, II-MS-55, Mont. H. Smith Correspondence, Gehman Collection.

100. Ibid., 9 July 1941.
101. Smith to War Department, 21 December 1941, Mont. H. Smith Correspondence, f. 5, b. 5, II-MS-55. Gehman Collection, CPS, EMU Archives.
102. Smith to Ernest Gehman, 4 May 1942, f. 5, b. 5, CPS, Mont. H. Smith Correspondence, Gehman Collection.
103. Ibid.
104. Ibid.
105. Gehman to Smith, 18 May 1942, B5, F5, CPS, Mont. H. Smith correspondence, Gehman Collection.
106. Harold S. Bender to John R. Mumaw, 21 May 1942; Mumaw to PPC, Bender as chmn., 28 May 1942; Mont. H. Smith to Bishop John L. Stauffer, 26 May; 1942, f. 1, b. 17, Hist. Mss. I-3-5.3, OOM PPC papers, AMC. Ibid., HSB to JRM, 13 June 1942, f. 9, b. 26.
107. J. Edgar Hoover to Ernest Gehman, 6 August 1941, CPS General Correspondence, Gehman Collection.
108. Toews, *Mennonites in American Society*, 182–83.

CHAPTER 9

1. John Miller to "Dear Mom," 10 February 1947, f. 1, b. 29, Family Correspondence, Jan.–Dec. 1947.
2. "Plain People," *Time* (10 February 1947): 60–61.
3. Albert Miller to Elta Miller, 27 April 1942.
4. Albert to Elta, 27 April 1942.
5. Albert to Elta, 3 May 1942.
6. Albert to Elta, 9 September 1942.
7. OOM to Elta, 4 October 1942
8. Albert to Elta, 21 October 1942.
9. Daniel Miller to Elta, March 17, 1943.
10. Albert to Orie and Elta, 2 December 1943.
11. Toews, *Mennonites in American Society*, 173–74.
12. Raymond Schlichting, interviewed by author, 7 January 2010.
13. Wilbert Shenk, interview.
14. Sider, *Messenger of Grace*, 160–61.
15. Ibid., 163–70.
16. Ibid.
17. Robert S. Kreider, *My Early Years*, 282–83.
18. Kreider, *Early Years*, 303.
19. Kreider, interviewed by author, 3 February 2010.
20. Schlichting, interview.
21. Ibid., 317.
22. Ibid., 319–20.
23. Ibid., 328.
24. Ibid., 355.
25. The amendment was sponsored by Joseph Starnes of Alabama, "CPS Camp 101," *The Civilian Public Service Story: Living Peace in a Time of War*, http://civilian publicservice.org/camps/101.
26. Ibid., 351.
27. Epp [Esther Epp-Tiessen], "The Origins of Mennonite Central Committee (Canada)," 131–32.

28. Ibid., 137–38.
29. Ibid., 140–45.
30. Ibid., 148.
31. Ibid., 187–89, 206.
32. Kreider, *Early Years*, 314.
33. Keim, *CPS Story*, 59.
34. Joseph Shapiro, "WWII Pacifists Exposed Mental Ward Horrors," *All Things Considered*, National Public Radio (30 December 2009), http://www.npr.org/templates/story/story.php?storyId=122017757.
35. Keim, *CPS Story*, 59.
36. Cited in Shapiro, "WWII Pacificists."
37. Ibid.
38. Kreider, *Early Years*, 382.
39. Ibid., 393.
40. Neufeld, "The Mennonite Mental Health Story," *MQR* 56 (January 1982): 18.
41. Boldt, ed., "Wiebe, Henry Peter (1898–1980)," May 2007, *GAMEO*.
42. Fast and Jost, "Mennonite Health Facilities and Services," 1987, *GAMEO*.
43. Raber, *Eyewitness to Prairie View History*.
44. Neufeld, 21–23.
45. Kreider interview.
46. Neufeld, "Mental Health Story," 24–28.
47. Ediger, "Influences on the Origin and Development of Mennonite Mental Health Centers," *MQR* 56 (January 1982): 46.
48. Ray Schlichting, interviewed by author, 7 January 2010; Kreider, *Early Years*, 381.
49. Schlichting interview.
50. Erb, *Orie O. Miller*, 248.
51. Ibid.
52. Schlabach, *War, Peace, and Social Conscience*, 277. This was how Hershberger recalled the occasion at the Miller home.
53. Schlabach, 266.
54. Schlabach, 269–70.
55. Kauffman, ed., *Doctrines of the Bible*, 534–38.
56. The Inter-Board Committee, a type of coordinating committee, was made up of the executive secretaries of other boards and committees.
57. Schlabach, 280.
58. OOM to MMA committee, 8 September 1944, b. 17, f. 4, HM1-171, G. F. Hershberger Papers.
59. Erb to OOM, 22 March 1945, f. 1, b. 1, XII-8-1, MMA Board of Directors correspondence, MCUSA Archives—Goshen, IN.
60. OOM to Erb, and Erb to OOM, 21 May 1945, f. 1, b. 1, XII-8-1, MMA Board of Directors correspondence, MCUSA Archives—Goshen, IN.
61. Schlabach, 284.
62. Dan Miller to Elta, 9 March 1944, Family Correspondence, f. 2, b. 28.
63. Dan to Elta, 17 September 1944 .
64. Dan to OOM and Elta, 11 September 1944.
65. Dan to Elta, undated, but context suggests 1944.
66. Dan to Elta, 8 January 1945.
67. John to Elta, 30 July 1945.
68. John to Elta, 1 October 1945.
69. John to Elta, 27 January 1947.

70. Cal Redekop, interviewed by author, 7 March 2010, Harrisonburg, Va.

71. Ibid.

72. Paul Peachey, interviewed by author, 8 March 2010, Harrisonburg, Va. (Peachey died 18 August 2012.)

73. Freda Pellman Redekop, interviewed by author, 7 March 2010, Harrisonburg, Va. (Freda died 8 August 2011.)

74. Freda (Pellman) and Cal Redekop, interview.

75. R. S. Kreider, *My Early Years*, 409.

76. Ibid., 415.

77. Ibid., 417–18.

78. Robert S. Kreider, interviewed by author, 3 February 2010.

79. Kreider, *Early Years*, 425–26.

80. Ibid., 426.

81. Kreider, interviewed by author, 3 February 2010.

82. Raymond C. Schlichting, interviewed by author, 15 March 2011.

83. William T. Snyder, interviewed by Robert S. Kreider, 1 March 1982, transcript, 147.

84. Ibid., 451–52.

85. Kreider, interview, 3 February 2010.

86. Schlichting, interview.

87. Dyck, *Up from the Rubble*, 183.

88. Ibid., 184.

89. Ibid., 206.

90. Paul G. Landis, interviewed by author, 11 March 2011.

91. "In Memorium, Orie O. Miller," *American Leprosy Mission Bulletin* (Spring 1977): 2.

92. Ibid.

93. Peter Wiebe, interviewed by author, 20 February 2012.

94. John A. Lapp, communication with the author, 16 June 2011.

95. *Proceedings of the Fourth Mennonite World Conference, 3–10 Aug. 1948* (Akron, Pa: MCC, 1950), 36–37.

96. OOM and Harold S. Bender, "A Brief Account of the Third Mennonite World Conference Held at Amsterdam, Elspeet and Witmarsum, Netherlands, June 29 to July 3, 1936," *MQR* XI (Jan. 1937): 5. Other American Mennonites were P. C. Hiebert, representing the American MB constituency; P. R. Schroeder, president of the GC Mennonite Church; and historian C. Henry Smith from Bluffton College, Ohio. Canadian representatives were David Toews, moderator of the Conference of Mennonites in Canada; C. F. Klassen of the Canadian MB Conference; and Heinrich H. Hamm of Altona, Man. (H. H. Hamm identified by Alf Redekop, Mennonite Heritage Centre, Winnipeg, Man.)

97. Ibid., 9.

98. Ibid.

99. Editorial, *GH*, XXIX (24 September 1936): 557; Quoted in Lapp and van Straten, "Mennonite World Conference 1925–2000: From Euro-American Conference to Worldwide Communion," *MQR* Online (2003), http://www.goshen.edu/mqr/pastissues/jan03lapp.html#Ref39.

100. Mosemann Sr., "The Proposed Fourth Mennonite World Conference," *GH* (24 September 1936): 637.

101. Keim, *Bender*, 398–99.

102. *Proceedings*, viii, xi.

103. *Proceedings*, xi.
104. William T. Snyder, interviewed by Robert S. Kreider, 15 February 1982, transcript, 28.
105. Schlichting, interviewed by author, 15 March 2011.
106. Snyder, interviewed by Kreider, 15 February 1982, transcript, 28.
107. Ibid.
108. Lapp and van Straten, "Mennonite World Conference 1925–2000: From Euro-American Conference to Worldwide Communion," *MQR* (2003), http://www .goshen.edu/mqr/pastissues/jan03lapp.html#Ref39.
109. Cattepoel, "The Mennonites of Germany, 1936–1948, and the Present Outlook," *Proceedings*, 14; also quoted by Lapp and van Straten.
110. Fast, "Closing Conference Message," *Proceedings*, 320.
111. "Editorial," *GH* XLI (24 August 1948): 779; quoted by Lapp and van Straten. The photo is in *Proceedings*, Plate III.
112. Ira S. Johns to E. G. Gehman, 3 July 1941, CPS general correspondence.
113. Sanford Shetler to E. G. Gehman, 9 February 1943, CPS general correspondence.

CHAPTER 10

1. Calvin W. Redekop, interviewed by author, 7 March 2010.
2. Redekop, *The Pax Story*, 41.
3. Redekop, interview.
4. Redekop, interview.
5. Redekop, *Pax Story*, 47.
6. Redekop, interview.
7. Ibid.
8. Redekop, *Pax Story*, 33.
9. Ibid., 71.
10. Clair Brenneman, "My Pax Experience: Building a Road across the Chaco," Pax-MCC, http://www.paxmcc.com/stories.html.
11. Willard E. Roth, ed., "*Youth's Christian Companion* 43 (16 September 1962): 12–13.
12. Freda (Pellman) and Cal Redekop, interview.
13. Ibid.
14. John W. Miller, interviewed by author, 15 May 2010.
15. John W. Miller to Elta and OOM, 21 January 1951.
16. Ibid.
17. "727 Reba Place," (1 June 1958), Evanston, Ill., f. 6, b. 74, OOM Papers.
18. Miller, "Report of Conversations between Reba Place Fellowship and Harold Bender and Paul Mininger," 9 December 1959, "Correspondence, 1954–1966," f. 6, b. 74, OOM Papers.
19. Ibid.
20. J. W. Miller, interview.
21. Minutes, Joint Church Building Committee, 27 November 1950, f. 2, b. 14, OOM Papers.
22. Ernest Miller to OOM, 14 November 1951, f. 4, b. 14, OOM Papers.
23. OOM to Ernest Miller, 20 November 1951, f. 4, b. 14, OOM Papers.
24. Nelson E. Kauffman to OOM, 26 September 1950, f. 2, b. 14, OOM Papers.
25. Notes, 1952, f. 2, b. 17, OOM Papers.
26. Harold S. Bender to OOM, 14 January 1952, f. 2, b. 17, OOM Papers.

27. Kauffman to OOM, 14 January 1952, f. 2, b. 17, OOM Papers.
28. Kauffman to Ernest Miller, 22 February and 30 January 1952; received on 25 February 1952, f. 2, b. 17, OOM Papers.
29. Ruth Miller to OOM, 5 March 1952, f. 2, b. 17, OOM Papers.
30. Jacob C. Meyer to OOM, 2 November 1952, f. 3, b. 17, OOM Papers.
31. Handwritten note, 31 May 1953, f. 1, b. 17, OOM Papers.
32. Lois Winey to OOM, 28 June 1953, f. 5, b. 17, OOM Papers.
33. Bender to OOM, 3 October 1953, f. 2, b. 17, OOM Papers.
34. Acting dean Karl Massanari to MBE executive committee, 25 July 1953, f. 1, b. 17, OOM Papers.
35. OOM to professor Samuel Yoder, 31 July 1953, f. 1, b. 17, OOM Papers.
36. Carl Kreider to OOM, 22 June 1953, f. 1, b. 17, OOM Papers.
37. Ibid.
38. Memo of understanding between MBE and Ernest E. Miller, 9 April 1954, f. 1, b. 17, OOM Papers.
39. Nelson Kauffman to Ernest Miller, 29 March 1954, f. 1, b. 17, OOM Papers.
40. Memo of understanding between MBE and Ernest E. Miller, 9 April 1954, f. 1., b. 17, OOM Papers.
41. Keim, *Bender*, 422.
42. "History of Anabaptist Mennonite Biblical Seminary," http://www.ambs.edu/about/History.cfm.
43. Donald R. Jacobs, interviewed by author, 28 June 2011; Ray and Ruth Brunk Horst, interviewed by author, 31 December 2010.
44. John W. Miller to Orie and Elta, 27 May 1952, f. 3, b. 30, OOM Papers.
45. Redekop, interview.
46. Keim, *Bender*, 451.
47. The two other renewal movements singled are evangelicalism and Old Order spirituality, a careful preservation of communal witness and discipline. Loewen and Nolt, *Seeking Places of Peace*, 154–58.
48. Paul Peachey, interviewed by author, 3 August 2010.
49. Cal Redekop, interviewed by author, 7 March 2010.
50. Peachey, interview.
51. Minutes, MCC executive committee, Basel Switzerland, 7 August 1952, Exec. Com. Minutes, Aug–Dec. 1952, IX-5-1.
52. Peachey, interview.
53. Redekop, interview.
54. Redekop, "MCC Worker Concerns," 6 August 1952. Attached to Minutes, IX-5-1.
55. Horst, "Some Remarks Regarding the Mennonite Central Committee," 5 August 1952. Attached to Minutes, IX-5-1.
56. Peachey, "To the MCC Executive Committee," 6 August 1952. Attached to Minutes, IX-5-1.
57. Horst, "Some Remarks."
58. Redekop, "MCC Worker Concerns."
59. Ibid.
60. Minutes, executive committee, IX-5-1.
61. Erb, *Orie O. Miller*, 258.
62. Albert J. Meyer, interviewed by author, 31 December 2010.
63. Ibid.
64. Ibid.
65. Ibid.

66. Susan Sommer, Lehman's daughter, to author during a meeting of the MC USA Constituency Leaders Council, Hartland Presbyterian Retreat Center, 25 October 2001.
67. In addition to Orie Miller, attending the meeting were Ed. J. Peters (Wasco, Calif.), Erie J. Sauder (Archbold, Ohio), Edward G. Snyder (Preston, Ont.), Ivan Miller (Corry, Pa.), Howard Yoder (Wooster, Ohio), C. A. DeFehr (Winnipeg, Man.), and Henry Martens (Reedley, Calif.). Peters was elected chair; Snyder, vice chair; and Sauder, secretary.
68. Fretz, *The MEDA Experiment*, 14–19.
69. Kroeker, ed., "Orie Miller: One Way to Grow" (sidebar), *The Marketplace* 33 (November/December 2003): 18.
70. Ibid., 20–21; "MEDA Timeline, 1953–2000." http://www.meda.org/a-short-history.
71. Frances (Bontrager) and Lawrence Greaser, interviewed by author, 1 June 2011.
72. Ibid.
73. John Hostetler, interviewed by author, 10 March 2011; Urbane Peachey, interview, 20 June 2011.
74. Jacobs, *What a Life! A Memoir*, 155.
75. Paul M. and Ann Keener Gingrich, interviewed by author, 8 June 2011; Paul and Ann Gingrich, *Memories, 1929–2010*, ed. Bob Gingrich (unpublished, December 2010), 60.
76. Gingrich, interview.
77. Ibid.
78. Albert to OOM.
79. Daniel and Eunice Miller to "Mother and Dad," 31 October 1952, f. 3, b. 30, OOM Papers.
80. Ibid.
81. Albert to "Mother and Dad," not dated, but appears to be February 1953, f. 4, b. 30, OOM Papers.
82. OOM to Abe Hallman and Richard Ebersole, 10 June 1954, f. 9, b. 73, OOM Papers.
83. Ibid.
84. Leatherman, "At the Savior's Feet," in A. Grace Wenger, *A People in Mission*, 56.
85. Garber, "Eastern Mennonite Missions (Lancaster Mennonite Conference)," 1955, *GAMEO*, http://www.gameo.org/encyclopedia/contents/E238780.html.
86. Beechy, "Peacemaking in Vietnam," in Lapp, *Peacemakers in a Broken World*, 54.
87. Martin, "Mennonite Entry into Vietnam; the First One Hundred Days," 1–4.
88. Martin, "Mennonite Entry into Vietnam," 3–12.
89. OOM to Paul N. Kraybill, 12 August 1953. Orie O. Miller files, 1945–54, EMM Archives, Salunga, Pa.
90. 19 November 1958–24 March 1959.
91. Snyder, interviewed by Robert S. Kreider, 10 March 1982, transcript, 207.
92. Edgar Stoesz, interview.
93. Snyder, interviewed by Robert S. Kreider, 10 March 1982, 207.
94. Ibid., 207–8.
95. Ibid.
96. Snyder, interviewed by Robert S. Kreider, 208.
97. Ibid., 210–12.
98. Ibid., 212.
99. Ibid., 213–14.
100. Edgar Stoesz, interview.

101. Wilbert Shenk, interviewed by author, 29 December 2010.
102. Ibid.
103. Bill Snyder, interview, 218.
104. Ibid.
105. Ibid.
106. Wilbert Shenk, interview.
107. Donald R. Jacobs, interview.
108. Ibid.
109. J. Paul Sauder, handwritten note, miscellaneous files, EMM Archives, Salunga, Pa.
110. Catherine R. Mumaw, email, 15 August 2011; Proposed Statement of Agreement, 18 June 1957; Minutes, MMA Board of Directors, 16 October 1957; President John R. Mumaw to OOM, 29 October 1957.
111. OOM to Mr. and Mrs. Eberhard C. H. Arnold, 7 March 1958, Primavera, Alto, Paraguay, f. 19, b. 74, OOM Papers.
112. Ibid.
113. OOM to Mr. and Mrs. M. R. Zigler, 7 March 1958, f. 19, b. 74, OOM Papers
114. Erb, *Orie O. Miller*, 62–63.
115. Obituary, *GH* 51 (11 March 1958): 238, 239, MennObits, http://www.mcusa -archives.org/MennObits/58/mar1958.html. The obituary dates her burial on 20 February, four days before her death.
116. David Sauder, interviewed by author, 2 July 2011.
117. James and Marian Payne, communication with author, 15 January 2011.
118. Wilbert Shenk, interview.
119. Jean Carper Miller, interviewed by author, 11 March 2011.
120. Ibid.
121. Edgar Stoesz, interviewed by author, 9 March 2010.
122. John W. Miller, interviewed by author, 15 May 2010.
123. Tina Bechtel, correspondence to author, 4 May 2012.
124. Ibid.
125. The Bruderhof members had been expelled from Germany by Hitler's Gestapo in 1937, and resettled in 1941 by MCC at Primavera, Alto, East Paraguay. Barth, *No Lasting Home*, xvi.
126. OOM to Mr. and Mrs. Eberhard C.H. Arnold, 7 March 1958, Primavera, Alto, Paraguay, f. 19, b. 74, OOM Papers.
127. OOM to Arlene Sitler, 20 February 1958, f. 19, b. 74, OOM Papers.
128. OOM to Elizabeth Naugle, R.N., Graduate Hospital, Philadelphia, Pa., 20 February 1958, f. 19, b. 74, OOM Papers.
129. OOM to Willis Detweiler, MCC Business Office, Akron, Pa., 27 February 1958, f. 19, b. 74, OOM Papers.
130. Willis Detweiler to OOM, 24 February 1958, f. 19, b. 74, OOM Papers.
131. Donald R. Jacobs, interviewed by author, 28 June 2011.
132. Wilbert Shenk, interview.
133. Jean Carper Miller, interview.

CHAPTER 11
1. OOM, "Our World—Our Church—Our Mission," Overseas Missionary Orientation, 17–20 July 1963, Salunga, Pa., f. 43, b. 77, OOM Papers.
2. Hershey Leaman, interviewed by author, 2 July 2011.

3. Lois and J. Lester Eshleman, letters presented to Orie Miller on the occasion of his seventy-fifth birthday and in honor of forty-four years of service to EMM, scrapbook, Ed Miller Private Collection.
4. Tanzania is used from here forward, rather than Tanganyika.
5. Leaman, interview.
6. Ibid.
7. Ibid.
8. David W. Shenk, interviewed by author, 21 June 2011.
9. OOM, interviewed by Paul Erb, 1967.
10. Leaman, interview.
11. David Shenk, interview.
12. Ibid.
13. David Climenhaga, interviewed by author, 20 September 2011.
14. Ibid.
15. Ibid.
16. Leaman, interview.
17. David Shenk, interview.
18. Ibid.
19. Donald Sensenig, interviewed by author, 8 March 2011.
20. J. Elvin and Laverne (Sensenig) Martin, interview by author, 9 March 2011.
21. Jan Miller, interviewed by author, 11 March 2011.
22. Ed Miller, interviewed by author, 10 March 2011.
23. David Shenk, interview.
24. Leaman interview.
25. OOM to Paul N. Kraybill, "Tentative Working Arrangement," 12 August 1953, "Miller, Orie O., 1945–1954" folder, EMM Archives, Salunga, Pa.
26. John Kraybill, interviewed by author, 18 June 2011.
27. Paul G. Landis, interview.
28. Paul N. Kraybill to H. Raymond Charles and Ira J. Buckwalter, "Confidential Memo," 20 August 1960, "Deputation and Admin trips, Europe, Africa, July–Sept '60" file, EMM Archives, Salunga, Pa.
29. Kraybill to H. Raymond Charles and Ira J. Buckwalter, 3 December 1962, EMBMC executive committee, 1950–68 file, EMM Archives, Salunga, Pa.
30. Paul G. Landis, interview.
31. Ibid.
32. Edgar Stoesz, interview; Roy Kreider, *Land of Revelation*, 135.
33. Kreider, Interview with William T. Snyder, transcript, 136–37.
34. Ibid., 137–38; 156–57.
35. Wilbert Shenk, interview; and Edgar Stoesz, interview.
36. Donald Sensenig, interview.
37. J. Elvin and Laverne Martin, interview.
38. Ibid.
39. Martin and Sensenig, interviews.
40. Mahlon Hess, interview by author, 21 June 2011.
41. Jean Carper Miller, interview by author, 11 March 2011.
42. OOM, Diary, 23 November 1960–18 January 1961, EMM Archives, Salunga, Pa.
43. Leaman, interview, and others.
44. John L. Weber, interviewed by author, 9 March 2011.
45. Wilbert Shenk, interviewed by author, 31 December 2010.
46. Ibid.

47. Robert S. Kreider, communication with author, 1 August 2011.

48. Donald Sensenig interview.

49. Edgar Stoesz, interviewed by author, 10 March.

50. Ed Miller, interviewed by author, 10 March 2011.

51. John W. Miller to OOM, 28 March 1961, Family Correspondence, f. 6, b. 74, OOM Papers.

52. Ibid.

53. OOM to John W. Miller, 22 May 1961, Family Correspondence, f. 6, b. 74, OOM Papers.

54. OOM to John W. Miller and Lois Miller Beach, 10 July 1961, Family Correspondence, f. 6, b. 74, OOM Papers.

55. Ed Miller, interview.

56. OOM, "H.S. Bender, Life and Work, Appreciation," manuscript sent to Guy F. Hershberger for January 1964 *MQR*, 8 August 1963, Correspondence "A" – 1961–1974, f. 2, b. 77, OOM Papers.

57. Ibid.

58. OOM, spoken tribute given at Bender's memorial service, 25 September 1962, Correspondence "A" – 1961–74, f. 2, b. 77, OOM Papers.

59. Ibid.

60. Table of contents, January *MQR*, attached to GFH letter, 8 August 1963, Correspondence, Bender H. S., 1962–67, f. 2, b. 77, OOM Papers.

61. Ibid.

62. A common phrase Miller used to describe the call of the Mennonite Church to fulfill the great commission, as in a letter to R. H. Edwin Espy, general secretary, National Council of Christian Churches in Christ, 9 June 1965, f. 10, b. 77, OOM Papers.

63. Sider, *Messenger of Grace*, 172–73.

64. Ibid.

65. Edgar Stoesz, interview.

66. OOM to Bender, 14 July 1962, Correspondence, "Bender H. S.," 1962–67, f. 2, b. 77, OOM Papers.

67. HSB to OOM, 18 July 1962, Correspondence, "Bender H. S.," 1962–67, f. 2, b. 77, OOM Papers.

68. OOM spoken tribute, 25 September 1962, Correspondence, "A," 1961–74, f. 2, b. 77, OOM Papers.

69. OOM to J. Daniel Hess, 15 June 1962, Correspondence, "Hess, Daniel," 1962, 1963, f. 18, b. 77, OOM Papers.

70. OOM to Arthur Sprunger, 16 July 1963, Correspondence, "Bi – By," 1961–76, f. 4, b. 77, OOM Papers.

71. Bender's bust is in the Mennonite Historical Library at Goshen College; Yoder's is in the MC USA Archives–Goshen; and Hartzler's bust is with his book collection at Anabaptist Mennonite Biblical Seminary, Elkhart, Ind.

72. Program, Groundbreaking Ceremony, Clayton Kratz Residence Hall, 17 April 1963, Correspondence, "Clayton Kratz Fellowship," 1962–68, f. 24, b. 77, OOM Papers.

73. Wilfred J. Unruh, executive director of the Christian Board of Service of the General Conference Mennonite Church and director of Voluntary Service, to OOM, 5 February 1964, Correspondence, "U–V, 1961–73," f. 46, b. 77, OOM Papers.

74. OOM to Paul E. Reed, editor, *Youth Messenger*, 6 July 1965, Correspondence, "Y,"1963–75, f. 51, b. 77, OOM Papers.

75. J. C. Wenger to OOM, 15 February 1968, Correspondence, "Wed–Wz," 1961–75, f. 49, b. 77; "Sts. Crispian & Crispinian," *Catholic Online*, catholic.org, http://www.catholic.org/saints/saint.php?saint_id=113.

76. Drescher, editor, *GH*, to OOM, 14 February 1966, Correspondence, "D," 1961–75, f. 9, b. 77, OOM Papers.

77. OOM to Ray M. Geigley, editor, *Youth Messenger* 20 October 1969, EMM Archives, Salunga, Pa.

78. Kraybill to H. Raymond Charles, Confidential Memo, 29 May 1967, EMM Archives, Salunga, Pa.

79. Paul G. Landis, interviewed by author, 11 March 2011.

80. Kraybill to H. Raymond Charles, Confidential & Personal Memo, 4 August 1968, EMM Archives, Salunga, Pa.

81. OOM to Paul N. Kraybill, 2 August 1968, EMM Archives, Salunga, Pa.

82. Kraybill to OOM, 9 September 1968, EMM Archives, Salunga, Pa.

83. Paul Leatherman, interviewed by author, 9 March 2011.

84. Paul Leatherman, interview.

85. Paul G. Landis, interview.

86. Wilbert Shenk, interview with author, 28 December 2010.

87. "Orie Miller Honored at Annual Meeting," MCC News Service, Akron, Pa., 26 January 1968, EMM Archives, Salunga, Pa.

88. Ibid.

89. Hess, "The Young Man Who Came East," *MM* (June 1968): 18.

90. Ibid., 19.

91. Ibid.

92. Ibid.

93. "An Agreement," contract with EMM, MCC, MPH, Paul Erb, and OOM, 7 March 1967, Correspondence, "Erb, Paul," 1960–75, f. 11, b. 77, OOM Papers.

CHAPTER 12

1. OOM to Mrs. Ralph Mumaw, 19 March 1970, "M," 1963–75, f. 51, b. 77, OOM Papers.

2. Ibid.

3. C. F. Yake to OOM, n.d., 1969, Correspondence, "Y," 1963–75, b. 77, f. 51, OOM Papers.

4. Ibid.

5. Leamon, interview.

6. A. N. Wolf purchased the "lower farm" of seventy-nine acres for $13,870 in 1918, Arthur Wolf, interviewed by author, 30 June 2011.

7. OOM to Albert W. Miller, Memo, 8 June 1970; Ed Miller, interview.

8. Ibid.

9. OOM to Willis Detweiler, treasurer, MCC, 18 December 1970, Correspondence, "D," 1961–75, f. 9, b. 77, OOM Papers.

10. John L. Weber, interviewed by author, 9 March 2011.

11. Ibid.

12. Ibid.

13. "Heritage Village Condominium Declaration," 23 March 1972, Ed Miller Private Collection.

14. J. Elvin and Laverne (Sensenig) Martin, interviewed by author, 9 March 2011.
15. Edgar Stoesz, communication with author, 9 December 2011.
16. OOM to Aden Yoder, Christian Fellowship Mission, Sarasota, Fla., 12 October 1971, Correspondence "C," 1960–75, f. 8, b. 77, OOM Papers.
17. OOM to Matthew Zachariah Family, Calgary, Alta., 10 December 1971, Correspondence "Z," 1968–74, f. 52, b. 77, OOM Papers.
18. OOM to Samuel Miller, 5 February 1973, Correspondence, "Mi," 1961–74, f. 30, b. 77, OOM Papers.
19. OOM to Ray Yoder, 10 September 1973, f. 51, b. 77, OOM Papers.
20. J. Elvin Martin, interview.
21. OOM to J. Paul Sauder, Tampa, Fla., 17 April 1969, Correspondence, "S," f. 39, b. 77, OOM Papers.
22. OOM to Menno Schrag, 14 July 1969, Correspondence, "Ha," 1961–76, f. 17, b. 77, OOM Papers.
23. Laverne (Sensenig) Martin, interview.
24. OOM to M. R. Zigler, 20 December 1971, Correspondence, "Z," 1968–74, f. 82, b. 77, OOM Papers.
25. Ibid., 24 April 1972, OOM Papers.
26. OOM to the Pennsylvania Department of Transportation Bureau of Motor Vehicles, Harrisburg, Pa., 13 June 1972, f. 45, b. 77, OOM Papers.
27. OOM to John Howard Yoder, associate director, IMS, 8 November 1972, Correspondence, "Y," 1963–75, f. 51, b. 77, OOM Papers.
28. Ibid. For more on the troubled legacy of John Howard Yoder, see the January 2015 issue of MQR focused on sexual abuse, discipline, healing, and forgiveness.
29. Donald R. Jacobs, interview.
30. OOM, interviewed by Urbane Peachey, 20 June 2011.
31. OOM to S. C. Yoder, 14 November 1972, Correspondence, "Y," 1963–75, f. 51, b. 77, OOM Papers.
32. OOM to Elmer Ediger and family, 14 June 1974, Correspondence, "E," 1963–75, f. 10, 77, OOM Papers.
33. OOM to M. R. Zigler, 30 April 1959, Correspondence, "Z," 1968–74, b. 77, f. 82, OOM Papers.
34. M. R. Zigler to OOM, 18 May 1960.
35. M. R. Zigler to OOM, 1968.
36. Paul Erb to OOM, 20 January 1975, Correspondence, "Erb, Paul," 1960–75, OOM Papers.
37. OOM to Paul Erb, 28 January 1975; Paul Erb to OOM, 4 February 1975, Correspondence, "Erb, Paul," 1960–75, b. 77, f. 11, OOM Papers.
38. OOM to Rochelle Zimmerman, c/o Leon Zimmerman, Rte. 2, Ephrata, Pa., 9 July 1974, Correspondence, "Z," 1968–74, f. 82, b. 77, OOM Papers.
39. OOM to Ira Franck, 26 August 1974, Correspondence, "F," 1961–75, f. 12, b. 77, OOM Papers.
40. OOM to J. Otis Yoder, Quarryville, Pa., 8 July 1974; OOM to H. Howard Witmer, Salunga, Pa., 18 July 1974, Correspondence, "Y," 1963–75, f. 51, b. 77, OOM Papers.
41. William G. Ridgway, Md., to OOM, 30 November 1974.
42. OOM to Rev. Caleb D. Bella, Kotagiri, South India, 19 December 1974, Correspondence, "Ba–Be," 1961–75, b. 77, f. 3, OOM Papers.
43. Robert Miller, to family, 28 December 1974, Ed M.
44. Ibid.

45. Atlee Beechy to OOM, 24 February 1975, Correspondence, "Ba–Be," 1961–75, b. 77, f. 3, OOM Papers.

46. OOM to Atlee Beechy, 17 March 1975.

47. Ibid.

48. OOM to George Lehman, 16 April 1975, Correspondence, "L,"1961–76, OOM Papers.

49. OOM to Paul Erb, 18 August 1975, Correspondence, "Erb, Paul," 1960–75, b. 77, f. 11, OOM Papers.

50. OOM to Ira J. Buckwalter, 11 March 1975, 77/4.

51. Ridgway, to OOM, 17 March 1975, Correspondence, "Ridgeway, William G.," 1974–76, f. 38, b. 77, OOM Papers.

52. Ibid.

53. OOM to Ridgway, 17 March 1975.

54. Ridgway to OOM, [1]7 March 1975.

55. Paul Leatherman, interviewed by author, 9 March 2011.

56. Paul and Ann Gingrich, interviewed by author, 8 June 2011.

57. John N. Kraybill, interviewed by author, 18 June 2011.

58. Ed Miller, interviewed by author, 10 March 2011.

59. Edgar Stoesz, interviewed by author, 9 March 2010.

60. OOM to Ura Gingerich, Akron, Pa., 2 May 1975, Correspondence "F," 1961–75, b. 77, f. 12, OOM Papers.

61. OOM to Barbara Cooper, 22 April 1975, f. 8, b. 77.

62. OOM to Lillian Martin, 14 May 1975, f. 27, b. 77.

63. OOM to Dr. John N. Bowman, 30 June 1975, f. 4, b. 77.

64. OOM to Ridgway, 22 July 1975, f. 38, b. 77.

65. Ridgway to OOM, n.d., but is a response to Orie's July 22 letter.

66. OOM to Tom Martin, 17 June 1975, f. 77, b. 27.

67. OOM to Lloyd Fisher, MEDA, 9 December 1975, f. 12, b. 77.

68. OOM to H. Ernest Bennett, 16 September 1975; Bennett to OOM, 10 October 1975, Correspondence, "Ba–Be," 1961–75, f. 3, b. 77, OOM Papers.

69. OOM to Velma Eshleman, Garissa, Kenya, 29 December 1975, Correspondence, "Erb, Paul, 1960–75," f. 11, b. 77, OOM Papers.

70. M. R. Zigler to OOM, 21 July 1972, Correspondence, "Zigler, M. R., 1958–75," f. 54, b. 77, OOM Papers.

71. OOM to M. R. Zigler, 19 July 1972.

72. OOM to Milo Kauffman, 24 February 1974, f. 23, b. 77.

73. Zigler to OOM, 9 May 1975.

74. Ibid., 23 May 1975.

75. OOM to Zigler, 16 May 1975.

76. OOM to David N. Thomas, 8 April 1975, f. 45, b. 77.

77. OOM to Zigler, 3 June 1975.

78. OOM to Urbane Peachey, 6 August 1975, f. 24, b. 77.

79. OOM to Zigler, 24 August 1975.

80. OOM to Harry Diener, 22 July 1975, f. 9, b. 77.

81. OOM to Arlene Sitler, 7 January 1976, f. 40, b. 77.

82. OOM to Jean Groff, 24 February 1976, f. 15, b. 77.

83. John W. Miller, interview.

84. Paul Erb, letter to Elta Miller, 11 February 1977.

85. Donald R. Jacobs, funeral tribute, EMM files, 1977.

86. Dyck, funeral tribute, recording, private collection of J. Elvin and Laverne (Sensenig) Martin.
87. Kreider, "In Appreciation of Orie Miller," 24 January 1977, manuscript submitted to the *Canadian Mennonite Reporter.*
88. "Orie O. Miller, Mennonite Leader was 84," the *Lancaster New Era* (Tuesday, 11 January 1977): 3.
89. "In Tribute to Orie O. Miller," *GH* XXV (25 January 1977): 83.
90. "GC and MC Membership Statistics in the United States of America, 1860–2003," and "Worldwide Mennonite Statistics, 1978–2003," Mennonite Church USA Historical Committee, http://www.mcusa-archives.org/resources/membership.html.
91. Ira J. Buckwalter, EMM treasurer, to OOM, 20 December 1968, Ed Miller Private Collection.
92. Norman Shenk, interviewed by author, 11 March 2011.
93. "Miller, Elta M. Myers Sensenig" Obituary, *GH* LXXXI (27 December 1988): 904; MennObits, http://www.mcusa-archives.org/MennObits/88/dec1988.html.
94. Arthur Wolf, interviewed by author.
95. Check #4821, Miller, Hess & Co. to Elta M. Miller.
96. OOM to Albert Miller, 1 December 1970, Ed Miller.
97. Case No. 84-04408T, Bankruptcy Court, Eastern District of Pennsylvania, copies in Ed Miller Papers.
98. Edgar Stoesz interview; Norman Shenk, interviewed by author, 11 March 2011; Paul Leatherman, interviewed by author, 9 March 2011.
99. OOM to Lois, Albert, Daniel, John, and Robert, 27 March 1972, Edward L. Miller Private Collection.
100. Leatherman, Shenk, Stoesz, interviews.
101. Paul Leatherman, interview.
102. Purchase Agreement, Ed Miller Private Collection.
103. Paul Leatherman, interviewed by author, 9 March 2011; Ten Thousand Villages, http://www.tenthousandvillages.com/about-history/.
104. Ibid.

EPILOGUE
1. Greenleaf, *Servant Leadership*, 13–14.
2. Edgar Stoesz, interviewed by author, 9 March 2010.
3. Jean Carper, interview.
4. Lois and Ronald's children are Larry and Tina.
5. Ed Miller, interview.
6. Albert and Esther's children are Ed, Jill, Connie, and Jan.
7. Dan and Eunice's children are Gregory, Marisa, and Kent.
8. John and Louise's children are Christopher and Jeanette.
9. Jean Carper Miller, interviewed by author, 11 June 2011.
10. Robert and Jean's children are Jennifer, Jeff, John, and Jim.

APPENDIX A
1. GMCC—Goodville Mutual Casualty Company; MII—Mennonite Indemnity, Inc.; Eirene—European Mennonite alternate service program for COs. The street addresses in Basel, Switzerland, and Vienna, Austria refer to MCC centers.

A Note about Sources

Among the rich sources at the MC USA Archives–Goshen, Indiana, are the eighty boxes of Orie Miller's personal collection, a source used throughout this project. Of most significance are the correspondence files, particularly family letters between Orie and Elta Wolf Miller, and between parents and children, contained in boxes 22–31 and personal data files in box 79. For Orie's service in Beirut (1919–20) and Russia (1920) his diaries are significant.

Also important were the letters of Orie and friends and colleagues, along with the papers of Paul Erb, D. D. Miller, Ernest E. Miller, Harold S. Bender, Guy F. Hershberger, Paul Mininger, and Sanford C. Yoder.

Other useful and relevant sources were the organizational records of the following agencies and committees: Mennonite Central Committee (MCC), Mennonite Board of Education (MBE), Mennonite Church Peace Problems Committee (PPC), Goshen College, Goshen Biblical Seminary, Mennonite Mutual Aid, Inc. (MMA), and Mennonite Economic and Development Associates (MEDA).

Also essential were the archival collections at: the Mennonite Heritage Centre Archives, Winnipeg, MB; Eastern Mennonite University Archives, Harrisonburg, VA; Eastern Mennonite Missions files, Salunga, PA; Lancaster Mennonite Historical Society, Lancaster, PA; Fernheim Colony Archives, Filadelfia, Paraguay; Mennonite Library and Archives/ MC USA Archives–North Newton, KS; Mennonite Heritage Center, Harleysville, PA.

The most significant online sources were the *Global Anabaptist Encyclopedia Online (GAMEO)* and MennObits, the collected obituaries on the MC USA Historical Committee website.

Personal sources of information, central to the project, are the following:

FAMILY:

Larry Beach

Tina Bechtel

Elvin and Laverne Martin

Edward L. Miller

Jan Miller

Jean Miller

John W. and Louise Miller

Donald Sensenig

OTHERS:

Bertha Beachy

Herman Bontrager

J. R. and Sue Burkholder

John Driver

Richard Ebersole

Paul and Ann Gingrich

Lawrence and Frances Greaser

Leonard Gross

Gertrude Habegger

Doreen Harms

Nathan Hege

Howard Hershberger

Mahlon Hess

Amos Hoover

Kenneth Hoover

Ray & Ruth Horst

James C. Juhnke

Robert S. Kreider

Albert J. Meyer

Blanche Mohler

Paul Peachey

Urbane Peachey

Cal and Freda Redekop

John L. Ruth

Paul and Marge Ruth

David Sauder

Theron Schlabach

Raymond Schlichting

Ken Sensenig Jr.

David W. Shenk

Norman Shenk

Wilbert Shenk

Frank and Erika Shirk

Sue Shirk

Alice Snyder

Edgar Stoesz

John Weber

Chester Wenger

Howard Witmer

Arthur Wolf

Bibliography

ARCHIVAL SOURCES

A. N. Wolf Papers	A. N. Wolf Estate papers, private collection of Ed Miller, Akron, Pennsylvania
D. D. Miller Papers	D. D. Miller Papers, HM1-427SC. Mennonite Church USA Archives–Goshen, Goshen, Indiana
Gehman Papers	E. G. Gehman Collection, II-B-55. EMU Archives, Harrisonburg, Virginia
Hiebert Papers	P. C. Hiebert Collection, 37.27.269. MC USA Archives–North Newton, Kansas
OOM Papers	Orie O. Miller Papers, 1913–76. HMI-45. MC USA Archives–Goshen
Paul Erb Papers	Paul Erb Papers, 1909–67. HMI-230. Mennonite Church USA Archives–Goshen
Roy Umble Papers	Roy Umble Papers, 1932–85. HM1-176. MC USA Archives–Goshen
Stoltzfus Papers	Grant M. Stoltzfus Collection, II-MS-29. EMU Archives, Harrisonburg, Virginia
Miscellaneous Papers	Eastern Mennonite Missions Archives, Salunga, Pennsylvania
Miscellaneous Images	Mennonite Central Committee Photo Archive, Akron, Pennsylvania

SECONDARY SOURCES

Acton, Robert. "Tobacco Rebound Fruitful for Farmers," *Pittsburgh Tribune Review*, 16 February 2009. TribLive.com online edition. http://www.pittsburghlive.com/x/pittsburghtrib/news/cityregion/s_611873.html.

"Administrative History, United Presbyterian Church in the U.S.A. Syria Mission." *Presbyterian Historical Society*, Philadelphia, Pa. http://www.history.pcusa.org/collections/findingaids/fa.cfm?record_id=115.

Akron Borough Planning Commission. *Comprehensive Plan of the Borough of Akron*. Akron, PA: Borough of Akron, 1963.

Bender, Harold S. "Peace Problems Committee (Mennonite Church)." *Global Anabaptist Mennonite Encyclopedia Online*. 1959. http://www.gameo.org/encyclopedia/contents/P4273.html.

Bentley, Jerry H., et al. *Traditions & Encounters: A Brief Global History*. Vol. 2. New York: McGraw-Hill, 2010.

Beyer, Karen Groff. *Bringing in the Sheaves: A History of the Ephrata Mennonite Church*. Ephrata, PA: Ephrata Mennonite Church, 2009.

Boldt, Ed. "Wiebe, Henry Peter (1898–1980)." *Global Anabaptist Mennonite Encyclopedia Online*. May 2007. http://www.gameo.org/encyclopedia/contents/W54305.html.

Boyle, Beth Ellen, and Interreligious Service Board for Conscientious Objectors National, eds. *Words of Conscience: Religious Statements on Conscientious Objection*. Washington, DC: National Interreligious Service Board for Conscientious Objectors, 1983.

Brunk, Harry Anthony. *History of Mennonites in Virginia, 1900–1960*. Vol. 2. Verona, VA: McClure Printing Co., Inc.

Brunk, J. E. *Dear Alice: The Tribulations and Adventures of J. E. Brunk, A Mennonite Relief Worker in Turkey in 1920–1921 as Depicted in Letters to His Wife*. Ivan Brunk, ed. Goshen, IN: Historical Committee of the Mennonite Church, 1978.

Bush, Perry. *Two Kingdoms, Two Loyalties: Mennonite Pacifism in Modern America*. Baltimore: Johns Hopkins University Press, 1998.

Clarke, William Newton. *Sixty Years with the Bible: A Record of Experience*. New York: Charles Scribner's Sons, 1909.

Congress, United States. *Congress Looks at the Conscientious Objector*. Washington, DC: National Service Board for Religious Objectors, 1943.

Cottrell, Robert C. *Smokejumpers of the Civilian Public Service in World War II: Conscientious Objectors as Firefighters for the National Forest Service.* Jefferson, NC: McFarland & Co., 2006.

Duerksen, Heinrich. *Lest You Forget the Stories: Life Recollections.* Filadelfia, Paraguay: 2009.

Dyck, C. J., Robert S. Kreider, and John A. Lapp. *From the Files of MCC: The Mennonite Central Committee Story.* Vol. 1, Documents. Scottdale, PA: Herald Press, 1980.

Dyck, Cornelius J., Robert S. Kreider, and John A. Lapp. *The Mennonite Central Committee Story: Documents.* Scottdale, PA: Herald Press, 1980.

Dyck, Peter and Elfrieda. *Up From the Rubble.* Scottdale, PA: Herald Press, 1991.

Eastern Mennonite Board of Missions and Charities. *Missionary Messenger.* Scottdale, PA: Lancaster Mennonite Conference, 1964.

Epp, Esther Ruth [Esther Epp-Tiessen]. "The Origins of Mennonite Central Committee (Canada)." Master of Arts thesis, University of Manitoba, 1980.

———. *J. J. Thiessen: A Leader for His Time.* Winnipeg, MB: CMBC Publications, 2001.

Epp, Frank H. *Mennonites in Canada, 1786–1920: The History of a Separate People.* Scottdale, PA: Herald Press, 1974.

———. *Mennonite Exodus: The Rescue and Resettlement of the Russian Mennonites since the Communist Revolution.* Altona, MB: D. W. Friesen and Sons, 1962.

Erb, Paul. *Orie O. Miller: The Story of a Man and an Era.* Scottdale, PA: Herald Press, 1969.

"GC and MC Membership Statistics in the United States of America, 1860–2003." Mennonite Church USA Historical Committee. http://www.mcusa-archives.org/resources/membership.html.

Gingerich, Hugh F., and Rachel W. Kreider. *Amish and Amish Mennonite Genealogies.* Gordonville, PA: Pequea Publishers, 1986.

Gingerich, Melvin. *Service for Peace: A History of Mennonite Civilian Public Service.* Akron, PA: Mennonite Central Committee, 1949.

Gingrich, Paul and Ann (Keener). *Memories, 1929–Present.* Unpublished, 2010.

Goldfield, David, et al. *The American Journey: A History of the United States*. Vol. 2. Upper Saddle River, NJ: Pearson Education, Inc., 2004.

Greenleaf, Robert K. *Servant Leadership: A Journey into the Nature of Legitimate Power and Greatness*. Mahwah, NJ: Paulist Press, 2002.

Harder, Helmut. *David Toews Was Here, 1870–1947*. Winnipeg, MB: CMBC Publications, 2002.

Hartzler, J. S. *Mennonites in the World War*. Scottdale, PA: Herald Press, 1921.

Hershberger, Guy F. "Historical Background to the Formation of the Mennonite Central Committee," *Mennonite Quarterly Review* 44 (July 1970): 213–44.

———. *The Mennonite Church in the Second World War*. Scottdale, PA: Herald Press, 1951.

———. *The Way of the Cross in Human Relations*. Scottdale, PA: Herald Press, 1958.

———. *War, Peace, and Nonresistance*. Scottdale, PA: Herald Press, 1969.

Hess, J. Daniel. "And God Has Appointed Administrators." *Christian Living* (March 1963): 7–9, 40.

Hess, Mahlon M. *The Pilgrimage of Faith of Tanzania Mennonite Church, 1934–83*. Musoma, Tanzania: The Church; Salunga, ca. 1985.

Hiebert, Peter Cornelius. *Feeding the Hungry; Russia Famine, 1919–1925; American Mennonite Relief Operations under the Auspices of Mennonite Central Committee [by] P. C. Hiebert [and] Orie O. Miller*. Scottdale, PA: Mennonite Central Committee, 1929.

Horst, Rebecca Bontrager. *Goshen College: A Pictorial History, 1894–1994*. Goshen, IN: Goshen College, 1994.

Jacobs, Donald R. *What a Life! A Memoir*. Intercourse, PA: Good Books, 2012.

Juhnke, James C. "Turning Points, Broken Ice, and Glaubensgenossen: What Happened at Prairie Street on July 27–28, 1920?" In *A Table of Sharing: Mennonite Central Committee and Expanding Networks of Mennonite Identity*, edited by Alain Epp Weaver, 66–83. Telford, PA: Cascadia Publishing House, 2011.

———. *Vision, Doctrine, War: Mennonite Identity and Organization in America, 1890–1930*. Scottdale, PA: Herald Press, 1989.

Juhnke, James C., and Carol Hunter. *The Missing Peace: The Search for Nonviolent Alternatives in United States History*. Kitchener, ON: Pandora Press, 2001.

Keim, Albert N. *The CPS Story: An Illustrated History of Civilian Public Service*. Intercourse, PA: Good Books, 1990.

———. *Harold S. Bender, 1897–1962*. Scottdale, PA: Herald Press, 1998.

Keim, Albert N., and Grant M. Stoltzfus. *The Politics of Conscience: The Historic Peace Churches and America at War, 1917–1955*. Scottdale, PA: Herald Press, 1988.

Kisare, Z. Marwa. *Kisare, a Mennonite of Kiseru: An Autobiography as Told to Joseph C. Shenk*. Salunga, PA: Eastern Mennonite Board of Missions and Charities, 1984.

Kissinger, Warren S. *The Buggies Still Run*. Elgin, IL: Brethren Press, 1982.

Klassen, Herbert. *Ambassador to His People: C. F. Klassen and the Russian Mennonite Refugees*. Winnipeg, MB; Hillsboro, KS: Kindred Press, 1990.

Klein, H. M. J., ed. *Lancaster County, Pennsylvania: A History*. Vol. 2. New York/Chicago: Lewis Historical Publishing Co.

Kraus, Norman C., ed. *Evangelicalism and Anabaptism*. Scottdale, PA: Herald Press, 1979.

Kraybill, Nicholas A. *General Lewis B. Hershey and Conscientious Objection during World War II*. Columbia: University of Missouri Press, 2011.

Kraybill, Paul N., ed. *Called to Be Sent: Essays in Honor of the Fiftieth Anniversary of the Founding of the Eastern Mennonite Board of Missions and Charities, 1914–1964*. Scottdale, PA: Herald Press, 1964.

Kreider, Robert S. *Looking Back into the Future*. North Newton, KS: Bethel College, 1998.

———. *My Early Years: An Autobiography*. Kitchener, ON: Pandora Press, 2002.

———. Oral History Project on William T. Snyder's experience with Mennonite Central Committee from 1943–1982.

Kreider, Robert S., and Rachel Waltner Goossen. *Hungry, Thirsty, a Stranger: The MCC Experience*. Scottdale, PA: Herald Press, 1988.

Kreider, Roy H. *Land of Revelation: A Reconciling Presence in Israel.* Scottdale, PA: Herald Press, 2004.

Lapp, John A., ed. *Peacemakers in a Broken World.* Scottdale, PA: Herald Press, 1969.

Lapp, John A. *The Mennonite Church in India, 1897–1962.* Scottdale, PA: Herald Press, 1972.

Lapp, John A., and C. Arnold Snyder, eds. *Anabaptist Songs in African Hearts: Africa.* Global Mennonite History Series. Intercourse, PA: Good Books, 2006.

Lawrence, D. H. *Lady Chatterly's Lover.* New York: Bantam Classic re-issue, 2007.

Lederach, Paul M. *On the Road to Goodville, 1926–2001: The Story of Goodville Mutual Casualty Company through Seventy-five Years.* New Holland, PA: Goodville Mutual Casualty Company, 2002.

Loewen, Howard John. *One Lord, One Church, One Hope, and One God: Mennonite Confessions of Faith in North America.* Elkhart, IN: Institute of Mennonite Studies, 1985.

Loewen, Royden, and Steven M. Nolt. *Seeking Places of Peace: North America.* Global Mennonite History Series, edited by John A. Lapp and C. Arnold Snyder. Intercourse, PA: Good Books, 2012.

Lowry, Tom. "Tobacco in Amish Country." *Cigar Aficionado.* 1 March 1997. http://www.cigaraficionado.com/webfeatures/show/id/Tobacco-In-Amish-Country_7556/p/1.

Mann, David W. "From Prairie Street Mennonite Church to Beiruit, Syria." Unpublished manuscript, n.d.

———, ed. *Letters from Syria: A Response to the Armenian Tragedy, Including Stories, Travel, and Reports by Nellie Miller Mann.* Self-published, n.d.

Marmion, Harry A. *Selective Service: Conflict and Compromise,* Hoboken, NJ: John Wiley & Sons, 1968.

Marr, M. Lucille. *The Transforming Power of a Century: Mennonite Central Committee and Its Evolution in Ontario.* Kitchener, ON: Pandora Press, 2003.

Martin, Luke, "Mennonite Entry into Vietnam: The First One Hundred Days." Unpublished manuscript, 2013.

Mennonite Central Committee. *Handbook of the Mennonite Central Committee.* Akron, PA: The Committee, 1950.

———. *Twenty-Five Years, the Story of the M.C.C., 1920–1945*. Akron, PA.: Mennonite Central Committee, 1946.

Miller, Ernest E. *Daniel D. Miller: A Biographical Sketch by One of His Sons*. Self-published, 1957.

Miller, John W. *An Epiphany of Sorts: Reflections on a Lifelong Ideological Journey*. Waterloo, ON: Blenheim Bible, 2013.

Miller, Susan Fisher. *Culture for Service*. Goshen, IN: Goshen College, 1994.

Miller, Keith Graber. *Wise as Serpents, Innocent as Doves: American Mennonites Engage Washington*. Knoxville: University of Tennessee Press, 1996.

Mouw, Richard J., and Eric O. Jacobsen, eds. *Traditions in Leadership: How Faith Traditions Shape the Way We Lead*. Pasadena, CA: The Depree Leadership Center, 2006.

Muste, Abraham John. *Not by Might: Christianity: The Way to Human Decency, and Of Holy Disobedience*. New York: Garland Pub., 1971.

National Service Board for Religious Objectors. *The Reporter*. [Washington] "National Service Board for Religious Objectors" [n.d.].

———. *They Serve without Weapons*. Washington, DC: 1944.

Nazarova, Tatyana Pavlovna. "Crisis in Mennonite Colonies of the Russian Soviet Federal Socialistic Republic and Ukrainian Soviet Socialistic Republic in 1917–1921 and Reactions of Western Fellow Believers." Unpublished paper.

Neufeld, Vernon. "The Mennonite Mental Health Story," *Mennonite Quarterly Review* 56 (January 1982).

Neufelt, Reina C. "'We Are Aware of Our Contradictions': Russlaender Mennonite Narratives of Loss and the Reconstruction of Peoplehood, 1914–1923." *Journal of Mennonite Studies* 27 (2009): 129–54.

Pannabecker, Samuel Floyd. *Ventures of Faith: The Story of Mennonite Biblical Seminary*. Elkhart, IN: Mennonite Biblical Seminary, 1975.

"Paris Peace Conference, 1919." *New World Encyclopedia*. http://www.newworldencyclopedia.org/entry/Paris_Peace_Conference,_1919.

Prieb, Wesley J. *Peter C. Hiebert: He Gave Them Bread*. Hillsboro, KS: Center for Mennonite Brethren Studies, 1990.

Raber, Merrill F. *Eyewitness to Prairie View History 1954–1984*. DVD, 2010.

Redekop, Calvin. *The Pax Story: Service in the Name of Christ, 1951–1976*. Telford, PA: Pandora Press U.S., 2001.

———. *Strangers Become Neighbors*. Scottdale, PA: Herald Press, 1980.

Reist, Arthur L. *Tobacco Lore in Lancaster County*. State College, PA: Science Press, 1974.

Roark, James L., et al. *The American Promise: A Compact History*, vol. 2, 3rd ed. Boston: Bedford/St. Martins, 2007.

Rohrer, Peter Lester. *The Story of the Lancaster County Conference Mennonites in Civilian Public Service, with Directory [by] Peter Lester Rohrer and Mary E. Rohrer*. Lancaster, PA, 1946.

Ruth, John Landis. *The Earth Is the Lord's: A Narrative History of the Lancaster Mennonite Conference*. Scottdale, PA: Herald Press, 2001.

Schlabach, Theron F. *Gospel versus Gospel: Mission and the Mennonite Church, 1863–1944*. Scottdale, PA: Herald Press, 1980.

——— *War, Peace, and Social Conscience: Guy F. Hershberger and Mennonite Ethics*. Scottdale, PA: Herald Press, 2009.

Shapiro, Joseph, "WWII Pacifists Exposed Mental Health Horrors," *All Things Considered*, National Public Radio, 30 December 2009. http://www.npr.org/templates/story/story.php?storyId=122017757.

Sharp, John E. "Balancing Power: Our Journey with Authority and Autonomy." Address presented to Indiana-Michigan Mennonite Conference Ministers Special Session, Waterford Mennonite Church, Goshen, IN, 21–22 June 2000.

———, ed. *Gathering at the Hearth: Stories Mennonites Tell*. Scottdale, PA: Herald Press, 2001.

———. *A School on the Prairie: A Centennial History of Hesston College, 1909–2009*. Telford, PA: Cascadia, 2009.

Sider, E. Morris. *Messenger of Grace: A Biography of C. N. Hostetter, Jr.* Nappanee, IN: Evangel Press, 1982.

Simons, Menno. *Complete Writings of Menno Simons*. Scottdale, PA: Herald Press, 1956.

Smith, Willard. *Mennonites in Illinois*. Scottdale, PA: Herald Press, 1983.

Snyder, C. Arnold. *Anabaptist History and Theology: An Introduction*. Kitchener, ON: Pandora Press, 1995.

Stoesz, Edgar. *Contagious Compassion: Celebrating 100 Years of American Leprosy Missions*. Franklin, TN: Providence House Publishers, 2006.

————. *Like a Mustard Seed*. Scottdale, PA: Herald Press, 2008.

————. "Reflections on the Life of Orie O. Miller." Miller reunion speech, 23 June 2008.

Tindall, George Brown, and David E. Shi. *America: A Narrative History*. 8th ed. London: W. W. Norton & Company, 1984.

Toews, John B. *Czars, Soviets, and Mennonites*. Newton, KS: Faith and Life Press, 1982.

————. *Lost Fatherland: The Story of the Mennonite Emigration from Soviet Russia, 1921–1927*. Scottdale, PA: Herald Press, 1967.

Toews, Paul. "An Historical Reflection for Narrator and Four Voices," MCC Seventy-Fifth Anniversary Service in the Former Mennonite Church in Chortitza, September 1995. Home page of the Mennonite Heritage Cruise. http://home.ica.net/~walterunger/mcc.htm.

————. *Mennonites in American Society, 1930–1970: Modernity and the Persistence of Religious Community*. Scottdale, PA: Herald Press, 1996.

Toews, Paul, and Harold S. Bender. "Fundamentalism." *Global Anabaptist Mennonite Encyclopedia Online*, 1989. http://www.gameo .org/encyclopedia/contents/F85ME.html.

Tuchman, Barbara. *The Guns of August*. New York: Bantam Books, 1980.

Umble, Roy. "Mennonite Preaching, 1864–1944." PhD thesis, Northwestern University, 1949.

Unruh, John David. *In the Name of Christ: A History of the Mennonite Central Committee and Its Service, 1920–1951*. Scottdale, PA: Herald Press, 1952.

Wanner, Richard, ed. *Akron, Pennsylvania Centennial 1895–1995*. Akron, PA: Borough of Akron, 1995.

Weaver, Alain Epp. *A Table of Sharing: Mennonite Central Committee and the Expanding Network of Mennonite Identity*. Telford, PA: Cascadia Publishing House, 2011.

Wenger, A. Grace. *A People in Mission: 1894–1994*. Salunga, PA: EMM, 1994.

Wenger, John Christian. *The Mennonites in Indiana and Michigan*. Scottdale, PA: Herald Press, 1961.

Wilson, Roger C. *Relief and Reconstruction; Notes on Principles Involved in Quaker Relief Service*. Wallingford, PA: Pendle Hill, 1943.

Yoder, Edward. *Pilgrimage of a Mind: The Journal of Edward Yoder, 1931–1945*. Wadsworth, OH: Ida Yoder and Irwin, PA: V. E. Yoder, 1985.

Zahn, Gordon C. *A Descriptive Study of the Social Backgrounds of Conscientious Objectors in Civilian Public Service during World War II*. Washington, DC: Catholic University of America Press, 1953.

Index

Author

John Sharp teaches history and
Bible at Hesston (Kansas) College.
He is the author of *A School on
the Prairie: A Centennial History
of Hesston College, 1909–2009*
and editor of *Gathering at the
Hearth: Stories Mennonites Tell.*
Sharp is the former director of the
Mennonite Church USA Historical
Committee and Archives, a former
pastor, and a graduate of Hesston
College, Goshen (Indiana) College,
and Anabaptist Mennonite Biblical
Seminary, Elkhart, Indiana. A
member of Hesston Mennonite
Church, he and his wife, Michele
Miller Sharp, are the parents of
three adult children.

CPSIA information can be obtained at www.ICGtesting.com
Printed in the USA
BVOW04s1638061015

421176BV00009B/33/P

9 780836 199338